SECOND EDITION

# MEDIAMAKING

KNADJIAN   aida88@yorku.ca

SECOND EDITION

# MEDIAMAKING

## MASS MEDIA IN A
## POPULAR CULTURE

LAWRENCE GROSSBERG
UNIVERSITY OF NORTH CAROLINA, CHAPEL HILL

ELLEN WARTELLA
UNIVERSITY OF CALIFORNIA, RIVERSIDE

D. CHARLES WHITNEY
UNIVERSITY OF CALIFORNIA, RIVERSIDE

J. MACGREGOR WISE
ARIZONA STATE UNIVERSITY WEST

SAGE Publications
Thousand Oaks ▪ London ▪ New Delhi

*For information:*

Sage Publications, Inc.
2455 Teller Road
Thousand Oaks, California 91320
E-mail: order@sagepub.com

Sage Publications Ltd.
1 Oliver's Yard
55 City Road
London EC1Y 1SP
United Kingdom

Sage Publications India Pvt. Ltd.
B-42, Panchsheel Enclave
Post Box 4109
New Delhi 110 017  India

Printed in the United States of America.

*Library of Congress Cataloging-in-Publication Data*

Mediamaking : mass media in a popular culture / Lawrence Grossberg . . . [et al.].— 2nd ed.
    p. cm.
Includes bibliographical references and index.
ISBN 0-7619-2543-0 (cloth) — ISBN 0-7619-2544-9 (pbk.)
    1.  Mass media and culture. 2.  Mass media—Social aspects.
I. Grossberg, Lawrence.
P94.6.M4265 2006
302.23—dc22                                2005009850


This book is printed on acid-free paper.

06   07   08   09   10   10  9  8  7  6  5  4  3  2  1

| Acquiring Editor: | Margaret H. Seawell |
| Editorial Assistant: | Sarah Quesenberry |
| Project Editor: | Claudia A. Hoffman |
| Typesetter: | C&M Digitals (P) Ltd. |
| Indexer: | Jean Casalegno |
| Cover Designer: | Michelle Kenny |

# Brief Contents

# Detailed Contents

# Preface to the Second Edition

The project of *MediaMaking*, when it first began, was to mark and celebrate media studies coming into its own as a field and to map the diversity of the field and its history. It was in many ways the work of a generation of scholars who helped to establish this field (see the Preface to the First Edition, which follows this one). For the second edition, we seek to build on the framework of the first, but also incorporate the ways that the shifting media landscape transforms not just the examples we use but the ways that media can be conceptualized and studied. In this edition, we have introduced a fourth author. Since the original *MediaMaking* was shaped by the biographies of its authors, a brief account of the fourth author will establish the rationale for some of the changes to the second edition.

The first three authors place themselves within the baby boom generation (the "television generation") as well as within the generation of media scholars who came into the field in the 1970s when issues of politics, culture, and education challenged the field (as well as society). The fourth author was born in the mid-1960s and missed the baby-boom bubble. Not only this, he grew up in Southeast Asia and the Middle East, and so encountered mass media (let alone American mass media) only sporadically in his early years. He entered graduate school in the late 1980s when the Internet was a growing presence on college campuses, cable and satellite television had eroded the dominance of the broadcast television networks, and postmodernism and cultural studies had been challenging the dominant paradigms of media studies for well over a decade. He was a student at the University of Illinois at the time *MediaMaking* was being conceived and its early drafts written. His voice, added to those of the original authors, has brought about three thematic changes to the book: considerations of the globalization of media, the rise of cyberculture, and media alternative to that of the dominant corporate institutions.

First, global media are not something adjunct to national media; they cannot be considered as a separate case, simply accorded their own chapter as a special instance. The global is a dimension of media and has to be considered throughout. In many ways, this book is about mediamaking in a North American context, and the theories of media that arise out of and address that context. But what we try to recognize throughout the book are the ways that this context connects up with other contexts in other places to generate different theories. For example, we consider how different institutions and ways of thought influence meaning making, media institutions, and the nature of a public. We still retain a chapter on global media at the end to draw these threads together.

Second, the Internet has challenged not only the structures of the media but also how the media are studied. The Internet tends to be more interactive than traditional media and is scattered in ways that make its study difficult. In addition, Internet texts are produced in homes and offices as well as in newsrooms and on soundstages. But rather than considering it as a new medium (like television, radio, newspapers, or CDs), the Internet is more part of the context of contemporary media studies as well as being one of its objects. It is a part of everyday life for many, and cuts across, adds to, and combines aspects of other media.

Third, the focus of the first edition, like that of much media scholarship, was on media as institutions (that is, *media* often becomes shorthand to mean *mass media*). Audience studies sought to add a new dimension to that analysis, but left the media corporations as a prime source of media texts (though these texts could be interpreted in many ways by the audience, who made their own meaning). But, in many ways, most of us make media texts ourselves. To twist a phrase from Raymond Williams (1989), mediamaking is ordinary. Personal cameras have been around since the Brownie and are now embedded in cell phones, Super-8 films have been capturing moments of everyday life for decades, and so on. The audience and distribution of these media texts are fairly limited (consisting of moments of personal nostalgia, the boredom of guests, or the embarrassment of offspring). New technologies have enhanced our ability to make media: hours of videotape that few will ever see, digital movies, and so forth. Occasionally, these examples of personal media production do get a wider distribution (the digital camera images from the Abu Ghraib prison, the Zapruder film, the Rodney King video, home videos picked and broadcast as America's "funniest," or basement/garage recordings that get released), but they rely on the media industries for that wider distribution. What is different today with the new media is that the means of distribution, not just production, have entered into many homes: the Internet. Original songs, videos, images, art, can now be distributed worldwide, and even gain a following. Moreover, the extraordinary cases such as Abu Ghraib illustrate the key point that the Internet is making global public life ever more transparent.

There is a long history of what is called the alternative media movement; of small-scale media, cable-access television, local radio stations (pirate stations reaching only a few blocks, for example), newspapers, fanzines printed by mimeograph machines, and alternative networks of distribution (for example, Paper Tiger video, Indymedia, MoveOn.org's email lists, and personal mailing lists). Especially since the rise of the Internet, the abilities of so-called DIY (do-it-yourself) media have expanded. In addition, the quality of DIY media can begin to match that of the big organizations. Mediamaking is a movement. Media production as well as reception can be local and personal.

However, just because something is produced alternatively does not mean that it is antagonistic to dominant cultural institutions, or even politically progressive. In fact, for the most part, DIY media are influenced by the format and style (what we call the *cultural form*) of mainstream media; people act, film scenes, and edit stories much like the other actors, directors, and editors that we have watched, read, and learned from have done.

This does not mean that this is a book about alternative media; rather, we introduce this theme to broaden the possibilities that we see with mediamaking; that is, to state that the way it is, is not necessarily the way it has to be. The subtitle of the book remains the same: *Mass Media in a Popular Culture*, and the mass media remain the focus of its pages because, for better or worse, most of the media messages we encounter daily are mass produced by large media institutions. As we wrote in the first edition, the media make society just as the society makes media; but we wish to add here that media and society are made in many locations, in many institutions, and by many people.

We have retained the overall structure of the first edition, dividing the book into four major sections: Placing the Media (in which we cover the context, history, organizations, and economics of the mass media), Making Sense of the Media (in which we cover issues of meaning and ideology), The Power of Media (in which we cover issues of identity, consumers, and media effects on behavior), and Media and Public Life (in which we cover issues of politics, the public, and globalization). For this edition, we have combined the chapters on media effects on behavior and debates over media effects and also the chapters on media and the public and normative theories of the media. The final chapter, Media Globalization, has been completely rewritten for this edition.

The authors wish to thank a number of reviewers who have provided us with constructive and detailed feedback on the first edition and our first draft of this edition. These include Claudette Guzan Artwick, Washington and Lee University; Majorie Fish, St. Cloud State University; Fred Fejes, Florida Atlantic University; Radhika Gajjala, Bowling Green State University; Gary Thompson, Saginaw Valley State University; Janet M. Cramer, University of New Mexico; and Chris Russill, Penn State University. Their insights and suggestions have been most welcome and we hope that we have addressed many of their concerns. We especially would like to thank Margaret Seawell at Sage Publications for championing (and urging and prodding) a second edition of this book. Thanks also to Jennel MacDonald for hunting down new stats for the second edition and acting as an interlocutor for the revisions as they proceeded. And Greg would like to thank deg farrelly, Gil Rodman, Raka Shome, and Greg Seigworth.

# Preface to the First Edition

Communication is perhaps the most human of all human activities. Humans have been seeking new media through which to extend the possibilities of communications—their ability to transcend time and space—since the invention of writing, paper, and much later, the printing press. While communication is one of the oldest objects of study in human societies, the formal study of communication is relatively young. Concerns about the new electronic media have motivated both public debate and scholarly research since the introduction of the telegraph and the telephone. However, it is only since the 1920s that a unified body of knowledge has begun to take shape, and only since the 1950s that a formal discipline has existed. This body of knowledge, the discipline of mass communication (sometimes called media studies), attempts to understand the significance, not only of particular communications media, but of the general processes of media communication in contemporary society. The need for such a broad-based approach to the study of mass communication can in part be understood as a response to the changes that have taken place in society during the twentieth century and especially since the end of the Second World War. These changes are commonly described as the transformation of culture into a media culture. No place in the world can escape entirely the power of contemporary media, although different places (and populations) experience that power in different ways and to different degrees.

The expansion (and subsequent legitimization) of the field of communication has been fueled and supported by that postwar generation, the "baby boomers," which is often characterized and defined by its relationship to the media and to the popular culture which was distributed through the media. In fact, all three of the authors of this book are baby boomers. We are part of "the television generation," and each of us remembers when the first television set was brought into his or her home; we ranged in age from 1 year to 10 years old. This generational identity has influenced the way we have written this textbook in at least three ways.

First, we are part of the first generation to grow up on an entirely commercially defined but domestically located (and hence, family oriented) system of mass media. But we are also part of "the rock and roll generation," a generation of kids bound together in a common identity as youth, an identity that was defined less by shared experience than by a shared popular culture, which we claimed as our own despite the fact that it was commercially produced. We are part of the first generation that has lived its whole life immersed in media culture. We are part of the first generation for whom the media (along with education) were dominant institutions of culture. In addition, we were all in university during the late 1960s, when questions of the relationship between culture, especially media and education, became part of the agenda of a movement that challenged the directions of society. The counterculture of the 1960s, built upon and alongside the civil rights movement, was the first national (and even international) political struggle that understood the significance of the media and popular culture and incorporated them into its analyses and strategies. Thus, one of the unique features of this book is that we refuse to separate the study of mass media from popular culture.

Second, we were all in graduate school, either in journalism or communications, in the early 1970s. As strange as it may sound, we were part of the first generation of scholars studying communications that actually saw itself as *communication* scholars. Like any discipline, the study of mass communication was defined not only in terms of its object of study but also in terms of its perspectives, theories, and frameworks. Originally, these were drawn from a number of other fields, including literature, psychology, and sociology; but over time, these borrowings were modified to meet the demands of studying the media. And by the 1970s, the field could claim to have its own theories and models, which were, in turn, being taken up and used by other disciplines. No longer simply psychologists, or sociologists, or literary critics who were studying the media, communication scholars were defining their work both in relation to and independently of those other disciplines, so that the discipline of mass communication could no longer simply be reduced to them. As a generation, we argued that whereas the study of the mass media had to be interdisciplinary, it had to declare its own independence and that it was already more unified than people had assumed.

We do not mean to deny that the field of mass communication was, and to some extent still is, divided and even fragmented. From the very beginning of the discipline, the study of mass media drew upon both scientific and humanistic theories and research. These two versions of scholarship have very different notions of explanation, evidence, and progress. At the same time, the field is divided between those attempting to make the processes of communication more efficient and effective and those committed to criticizing the forms and practices of the media in contemporary society. A number of fundamentally different languages are used by communication theorists: languages of measurement, experimentation, experience, and aesthetics; languages of description, explanation, evaluation and criticism. But this is no different from most disciplines that talk about human social and cultural life. Communication scholars have begun to address the relationship between these languages, to debate the kinds of knowledge about communication that each produces, and even to bring them together. While the organization of disciplines and knowledge in the U.S. educational system discourages such efforts, it is becoming more important to draw the lines between science and interpretation, between description and criticism. We firmly believe that our understanding of media and media power can only be adequately described if we constantly work to bring the multiple languages and perspectives on communication to bear on the media and popular culture. Furthermore, we believe that over the past century, a sophisticated body of knowledge about the media and media culture has been developing, a body of knowledge that transcends the diverse languages, traditions, and theories upon which it has been built.

Sometimes this is not always obvious. After all, there are still significant disagreements about some of the most basic questions concerning the media and their effects. Sometimes it seems that the emergence of every new generation of communication technologies (magazines, film, radio, television, videogames, computers) leads us to ask the same questions over again: What is this new medium? What kinds of messages is it offering? Who is using the medium? How are they using it? What are its effects? What is its power? That these questions are constantly being re-asked should not be taken as evidence that we do not have the ability to begin to answer them. The fact is that new technologies appearing in new contexts in new historical situations demands that we re-ask the questions of media power, that we refine our knowledge and reassess our theories. But in fact, we know a great deal about the answers to some of these questions, and we know a great deal more about the complexities that make other questions so difficult to answer. There are questions that are still be explored, and there are new questions constantly emerging.

Hence, in this textbook, we propose to pay rigorous and explicit attention to the accumulating and burgeoning research on the media, at the same time that we draw attention to and examples from a wide range of modern media. This represents a sharp break from the approach taken by most introductory textbooks in the field. Most texts approach the field of mass communication as anything but a unity; instead, they begin by dividing the field into the various media of communication and treat each independently of both other media and of the broader processes of communication and culture. Typically, textbooks in the field are organized around isolated discussions of the different media: newspapers, magazines, radio, television, film, and so on. Moreover, because they cannot cover all of the significant ground simply by considering specific media, they are forced to introduce some topics that describe forms of popular culture (music, comic books) rather than actual media. We reject this framework in order to present a sense of the interrelations, not only among the media themselves, but between the development of a media culture and the broader social context within which the media are always located. Thus, this book is likely to appear much more theoretically and analytically oriented than the typical descriptively and empirically based approach of most textbooks in the area. We take this perspective because we believe that a broadly based and theoretically grounded understanding of the nature of media communication processes is an absolutely necessary part of any real understanding of contemporary life. And only with such an understanding will people be able to confront the rapidly changing and largely unpredictable future role of the media and popular culture in society.

Third, like so many members of the baby boom generation, we have continued our relationship to the media and to popular culture as fans, and in our case, as scholars. Although our tastes differ, and the role that popular culture plays in our lives differs as well, none of us would voluntarily renounce the place of the media and popular culture in our lives. Hence, we assume that there is a certain kind of media literacy, developed outside the classroom, that people bring with them to a class on mass communication. People have experience, knowledge, even expertise about the media from their own lives, from their use of the media. We hope to draw on those experiences and relate them to the theoretical and critical understandings of scholars of the media.

We assume that contemporary students are reasonably media literate, and not merely in the sense that they know what they like and where to find it. Rather, we assume that they have a very real and sophisticated "tacit" knowledge of the media, which enables them to use media in very specific and concrete ways to satisfy some of their needs and desires in the context of their lives. On the other hand, this does not mean that they are entirely in control of the media or its effects or that they have an explicit awareness of how the media are working or even of what they are doing when they use it in particular ways. This is important because it defines the pedagogical intention of this book: We do not think that the media are some evil powerful force against which we need to inoculate our students. Nor do we think that the function of a better understanding of the media is to educate our students' palate, to wean them off of the culture they like and, with our new critical tools in hand, to lead them to the higher pleasures of more legitimate cultural tastes. Rather, our goal is much simpler and much more complex.

We recognize that different people are drawn to the study of mass media for many different reasons: The media occupy a central space and a great deal of time in all of our lives; they are interesting, attractive, exciting. Some people hope to work in the media industries—as creators, artists and producers, advertisers, or journalists. Many people suspect that the media have significant power, if not over their lives then over the lives of others, or perhaps over society more generally. For whatever reasons, all of these motivations challenge us to know more about the media and how they are made and to know what we know in structured, systematic ways.

We want to share with students the knowledge and thoughts that scholars have developed about the relationships among media, culture, and society so that they will have a better understanding of how the world is shaped by human actions and decisions. What they choose to do with this knowledge, whether they will work to change that world, and whether those changes will be for their own advantage, for better or for worse, we cannot control. But it is always better to have more knowledge, more understanding, about the nature of human life and society, especially when, as today, we confront so uncertain a future.

Putting all of this together, we can say that the basic assumption of this book is that the media can only be understood in relation to their context, a context that is simultaneously institutional, economic, social, cultural, and historical. We have called this book *MediaMaking* because our basic assumption is that the media are actively helping to produce the context in which they exist, even as they are themselves the product of that context. In fact, in the contemporary world, it is becoming increasingly difficult, if not impossible, to separate the two parts of what is more and more a single process: The media make the world even as the world makes the media. Descriptions of the media, and discussions of the meaning, impact, and effects of media cannot be separated from a broader discussion of culture, history, and changing relations of power. It is not merely a matter of adding the context in all of its dimensions and complexity, or of treating the context as a secondary question, an afterthought, a footnote or even a separate chapter. We will treat communication and its context as intimately interwoven. We cannot study communication apart from the other institutions in the society, or from the other dimensions of social life. The media are part of the economy, the history, the social relations of power, and the forms of identity, meaning, and experience of contemporary life; each is shaping and defining the others. Thus, this is a text about contemporary culture and society as much as it is a text about contemporary media. Although the book is designed primarily for courses in mass communications and media studies, we hope it may be of interest in courses focusing on such issues in other departments as well, including cultural studies, American studies, American literature and history, and sociology.

In this book, we attempt to explore the variety of ways in which mediamaking is involved in our social lives. We explore the different relationships between the media and the systems of social value and social differences that organize power in contemporary society. We examine how the media are produced and consumed and what they produce in turn. Thus, we have chosen to organize this book on the basis of the most important dimensions of this mutual process of making. [ . . . ]

Ironically, even a book such as this cannot escape the very issues that it raises, for it too is part of the very media culture that it purports to describe and interpret. Two examples should suffice. First, writing a text in media and popular culture poses at least one problem that other disciplines do not face. Given the time lag between writing and publication, almost any example of its objects of study that might be offered is so ephemeral and transitory that it is likely to be not only outdated but forgotten by the time the book is actually read. Textbooks on literature can use the classics; textbooks in sociology can use typical interactions or structures. But the media do not lend themselves to such appeals. Hence, unlike other media textbooks, we shall not use lots of extended examples, leaving it to readers to insert their own examples. Second, our negotiations with various publishers exemplified many of the arguments we will make, especially in Chapter 4: Publishers, like other media corporations, are driven to maximize their profit. Because the easiest way to do this is to increase the size of the audience, many publishers wanted us to decide what to include in this book on the basis of its difficulty (on the assumption that the more difficult the book, the smaller the audience). But the importance of mediamaking in the contemporary world and the possibility, if not inevitability, that it will matter even more in the future, seems to compel all of us, scholars, communicators, and consumers alike, to think about the enduring questions of mediamaking and the kind of world that is being made with the best and most rigorous concepts and tools that we have available.

This book was begun when the authors were colleagues at the University of Illinois at Urbana-Champaign. We want to acknowledge the influence and contributions of our colleagues and students, in particular James W. Carey, and through him, his teachers, Jay Jensen and Ted Peterson, both of whom have recently passed away. We also want to thank the Program in Cultural Values and Ethics for providing us with a semester free from teaching to begin work on this book. In many ways, this book reflects the singular culture surrounding the study of communication at the University of Illinois in the 1980s. That culture allowed three scholars with very different perspectives and commitments to come together as friends and interlocutors. The result, we hope, demonstrates the worth of reading and thinking beyond one's own necessarily narrow education.

# PART I

# Placing the Media

# Media in Context | 1

Human beings have always lived in a world of communication, but we live in a world of *media* communication, where we can travel great distances and across centuries, all in the comfort of our own living rooms. We can "see" what is happening across the globe or out in space or even in unfamiliar neighborhoods of our own cities. We can recreate the Civil War or picture life after a nuclear holocaust. We can vicariously experience enormous suffering and great joy. And we can hear the sounds of other cultures and sense how different peoples experience the world. We may discover that others in the world live very differently from us. We can learn that not everyone lives in the world of media communication and that not everyone who *does* lives in the same way.

The media have become an inseparable part of people's lives, of their sense of who they are and of their sense of history. The media provide an ever larger part of the imagery and soundtrack of people's memories. Some of our most powerful, most intensely emotional, and most important moments are intricately bound up with the media: the 1963 Kennedy assassination and funeral, urban riots from 1965 to the present, the Watergate hearings in 1973 and 1974, the 1986 Challenger disaster, the Persian Gulf War of 1991, the 1995 O. J. Simpson trial and bombing in Oklahoma City, Princess Diana's funeral in 1997, the Columbine High School shootings in 1999, the Millennium celebrations, the terrorist attacks of September 11, 2001, and the second Iraq War of 2003.

From a less subjective point of view, the media seem to dominate and demand more and more of people's attention. For the media seem increasingly to have become the news. More and more political issues and debates revolve around the media themselves: There have been numerous cover stories about rap music and violence, about pornography (in cyberspace and on television), about the role of the media in elections, about staging the news, about new telecommunications laws and deregulation, and about new technologies.

If we live in a world of media, it is still important to remember that we do not live in a media world. The media bring the world to us and help to shape that world, but there is still a reality outside of the media. It is becoming harder all the time to tell the real world from the media world, but it is essential to know the difference if diverse peoples and nations are to live together in peace. This book is about the ways in which the world and the media make each other, about *mediamaking*.

Whereas the world has a kind of durability and reality that resists the media's ability to remake it, the media have a kind of ephemeral quality that make them hard to hold on to. Most stories are fleeting and short lived, and they go out of date all too quickly. But some stories live on in popular memory. Nevertheless, we must choose examples if we are to study this relationship between the world and the media. The terrorist attacks of September 11, 2001, provide a recent illustration of the complexity and the power of the media in contemporary life as well as of many of the problems the contemporary media pose.

In the early morning hours of September 11, 2001, groups of hijackers took control of four different planes, two departing from Boston heading to Los Angeles, one from Newark going to San Francisco, and one from Washington's Dulles Airport en route to Los Angeles. At 8:45 a.m., American Airlines flight 11 slammed into the north tower of the World Trade Center (WTC) in New York City. Alerted that there had been some sort of collision involving a plane and the WTC, many television stations trained their cameras on the burning building. When United Airlines flight 175 hit the south tower of the WTC at 9:06 a.m., the collision was carried live on national TV.

A third flight, American Airlines flight 77, was flown into the side of the Pentagon building in Washington, D.C., at 9:40 a.m. Aboard the fourth flight, United Airlines flight 93, the hijackers instructed the passengers to call their loved ones from their cell phones or the airplane phones in the seats in order to say goodbye. With these calls, the passengers were made aware of the fate of the other hijacked planes and realized what was happening to them. A group of passengers decided to fight back against the hijackers. At 10:37 a.m., the plane hit the ground in a rural area outside of Shanksville, Pennsylvania, and all were killed.

Not only were these events an unprecedented tragedy, and a tragedy covered extensively by the media, but also several of the key events occurred on live television: the second plane hitting the WTC and the subsequent collapse of both towers. The major networks broadcast uninterrupted coverage, commercial free, for three days. Television, as it had during past crises, was the primary source of news, images, and information about these events for the majority of the U.S. population (J. Carey, 2002). In addition to this, the media coverage that day revealed the extent to which the mass media have globalized. Live broadcasts from Cable News Network (CNN) went to all the CNN outlets worldwide. Local media outlets from Brazil to Singapore would show a live feed from CNN rather than their own news, especially in the hours soon after the events took place. Live images from U.S. broadcasters were taped and rebroadcast on television globally. Besides the simple fact of this being a cataclysmic event, the WTC employed citizens from a great number of different countries.

But the events of September 11 were also a time when a new medium—the World Wide Web—came into its own as a disseminator of news and information. Initial reports described the Internet as a failure during the crisis because news Web sites were quickly overwhelmed and users found their Internet connections unreasonably slow as networks were overloaded (Rappaport, 2002). But the Internet quickly recovered, and by afternoon the Web established itself as a significant source of news and information. An estimated 40% of Internet households visited Web sites dedicated to news (up from 12% prior to the attacks). Media researcher Paul Rappaport (2002) draws this conclusion:

> The Internet emerged from September 11 as a mainstream channel for obtaining news. The events of September 11 empowered users to become active participants in the organization, collection and dissemination of news. It appears that these efforts were long lasting. After September 11, a larger percentage of Internet households continued to rely on Internet news sites when compared to pre-September 11 levels. (p. 256)

5

One and a half years later, when the United States went to war with Iraq, the Pew Internet and American Life poll showed that "77% of online Americans turned to the Internet in connection with the war" (Rainie, Fox, & Fallows, 2003, p. 2).

After the events of September 11, the Internet also became a site of alternative news, of information not provided by the established news outlets. Individuals' personal narratives about their experiences that day (including personal photographs and video) were posted to a myriad of Web sites, and innumerable discussion sites appeared where debate over the events, the responsibility for them, and appropriate courses of action raged. The Internet also provided opportunity for a number of alternative theories as to the nature of the attacks to be posed and discussed.

And the Internet was put to more personal uses during the crisis, when e-mails and instant messages were used to contact loved ones in New York and Washington, D.C., once the phone lines became overloaded. The Web also became a site of personal memorials for the victims of the attacks, and acted as a place for counseling and solace for the survivors.

There are a number of ways in which the events of September 11 can be used to springboard a discussion of the mass media today. These have been just a few. Others include the representation of Muslims and those of Middle Eastern descent in the media, the question of civil liberties in the wake of the passage of the Patriot Act, the effect of the WTC images on the audience, and so on. We will return to the example of September 11 throughout the book as different perspectives on the mass media are presented.

The event becomes entwined with the media representations of the event. Though this was an event witnessed first-hand by possibly millions of New Yorkers, for the rest of the country and the world the event is inseparable from its images. Everyone knows that there is a difference between the media coverage and the actual events, we know that thousands of people lost their lives that morning, yet there is no way to imagine or comprehend the attack except through media images. As time has passed, it has become even more difficult to separate the events from the media's images; even people who were there have had to negotiate with the representations and images that have bombarded them ever since.

The example of the events of September 11 illustrate what we mean by saying that human beings live in a world of media but not in a media world. Communication has always been a crucial aspect of human life, but in the second half of the twentieth century, especially in the Western industrial democracies, the media have become so intertwined with every aspect of our reality that the line between the two, media and reality, has become blurred and even porous. To try to isolate the media from other parts of our lives—as if we could talk about media *and* politics, media *and* culture, media *and* society, media *and* economics, or media *and* audiences—even for the purpose of study is an oversimplification. For the media are already implicated in these other realms: The media are already involved in making them what they are, even as these other realms are involved in shaping the media.

Consequently, this book is based on a different model of the place and power of the media in contemporary life: the model of *mediamaking*. This term is intentionally ambiguous. It implies that the media are *themselves being made* while they are simultaneously *making something else*. Above all, it suggests that we must see the media and all of the relationships that the media are involved in as active relationships, producing the world at the same time that the world is producing the media. This means that the media *cannot* be studied apart from the active relationships in which they are always involved: We cannot study the media apart from the context of their economic, political, historical, and cultural relationships. Studying the media is not an additive process, as if we can first understand the media and then add their effects on politics and economics. But at the same time, we cannot study some real political or economic events and then hope to understand the role of the media in representing them. To repeat ourselves, the media are constantly being made by the very same relationships that they themselves are making. If this sounds circular and somewhat confusing, think about the relationships in your own life. Virtually by definition, relationships are matters of reciprocal influence.

*Making* is the primary activity of media: making money, making everyday life, making meaning, making identities, making reality, making behavior, making history. And it is in these various activities of making that the media themselves are made, that we can speak of the media as making media. *Making*, then, points to the fact that the world of human life is a world of *practices*. Practices are the various forms of human activity that transform some aspect of human reality. Practices are activities that change the world, such as political practices, economic practices, intellectual practices, social practices, sexual practices, and so on. We must always be aware of the complexity of the media in relation to human practices as we attempt to understand the contributions that the media make, both positive and negative, to the very form and substance of contemporary social existence.

In this chapter, we will discuss the dimensions of the concept of media and its relation to the idea of mediation. Then, we will present the two dominant models of communication that have influenced the study of media. What each model presents is a way of analyzing the media that uncovers media's power to effect or control.

## MEDIA AND MEDIATION

### Defining and Distinguishing the Media

Everyone is familiar with the term *media;* people see it and use it all the time. But what do they mean? Many people use the term *media* to refer to television, yet the term cannot be limited in this way, although television is certainly one of the most important media of our times. (Note also that *medium* is singular and *media,* plural: *television is a medium; the media are . . . .*) Some people assume that the media are simply technologies that can be described in terms of the hardware of production, transmission, and reception. Although technology is obviously crucial to contemporary communications media, they cannot be understood simply as hardware, as if they existed independently of the concepts people have of them, the uses people make of them, and the social relations that produce them and that are organized around them every day.

Let's begin by outlining how the media can be described and differentiated. There are many ways of categorizing media, precisely because they are complex and multidimensional structures or formations.

We can categorize the media according to the geography or type of social relationships they are designed to construct or used to support: *Interpersonal media* are primarily used for point-to-point, person-to-person, communication; *mass media* are primarily used for communication from a single point to a large number of points, or from a single source to an audience that includes many people. Whereas interpersonal media usually give the communicator a good deal of control over the audience, mass media allow the communicator little power to select and little likelihood of knowing much about the audience. Whereas interpersonal media enable the sending and receiving of messages from both ends, mass media tend to separate the sender and receiver. Interpersonal media include the telephone and the telegraph. Mass media include newspapers, magazines, books, radio, broadcast, satellite and cable television, film, records, and tapes. There is a third category, *network media,* which can be used as either interpersonal or mass media; even more important, they can also be used to create a new geography of social relations, connecting many points to many points, all of which can be both senders and receivers. Examples of network media are teleconferencing, the postal service, fax, e-mail, the World Wide Web, and new hybrid cellular telephones connected to the Internet. These categories are not mutually exclusive. For example, we often think of the telephone as an interpersonal medium, but at the turn of the last century, it was also used as a mass medium, broadcasting news and even opera performances into the home.

We can categorize the media according to a number of different *modalities.* One modality is the channel used in communicating: print (books), electronic (television), chemical (film). Another modality is the sense experience on which particular media operate: visual (books), aural (radio), tactile (Braille), mixed (television). Economic modalities are important, as well: directly purchased media (books, records, magazines, and tapes), media that can be delivered to an audience without direct cost (network television or radio), media that charge for general access (cable television, Internet providers), and media that charge for the right to view specific content (pay television, films).

We can categorize media by the *institutions* that produce and disseminate them. For example, we distinguish network television from local independent television stations from cable systems. We also distinguish between media produced by corporations (like television networks and film studios), those produced independently (known as *grassroots* or *alternative* media), and those produced for personal use (like home videos). We can distinguish different *technological manifestations,* especially of what appears to be the same communication technology: Think of the difference between a family television, the large television in a sports bar, and the Diamond Vision screen behind the stage at a concert arena. But there are also different *uses* of a technology: The same television set can be used to watch broadcast or cable television (in other words, receive a TV signal), to watch a prerecorded videotape or digital video disc (DVD), to play a videogame, or to surf the Internet (with WebTV and its counterparts).

We can also distinguish different forms of *media content*, which often cut across the media technologies themselves, as when we talk about entertainment or fictional programming, news or journalistic content, and advertising content. We can make finer distinctions among these, as when we separate soap operas from situation comedy shows from Westerns and action adventure fare, all located within the category of television entertainment.

Two other distinctions are worth making in the effort to locate and define a useful concept of communications media. First, we can distinguish communications media from other kinds of *information technologies* that are also involved in processes of communication. These include patents, copyrights, photocopying, and non-Internet computer programs. Second, we can distinguish media from culture. In fact, one of the most common misuses of the term *media* equates it with popular culture. People tend to confuse television as a medium of communication with the entertainment content that defines the vast bulk of its programming. Since the beginning of the twentieth century, the new technologies of communication have quickly evolved into the major sources of popular culture, and most of the major forms of popular culture are not only distributed by but have often emerged in one or more of the mass media.

This confusion and conflation has resulted in a persistent and common form of criticism of the media: that each new media technology threatens other, more traditional, forms of popular culture. (See Box 1.1, "Sousa on the Menace of the Phonograph.")

---

**BOX 1.1**

**Sousa on the Menace of the Phonograph**

Every new media technology is greeted with alarmist rhetoric. Often, the most extravagant and dire consequences are predicted as the inevitable result of the introduction of the technology. In the early part of the twentieth century, the phonograph was widely disseminated, and the recorded music industry grew rapidly. Here is what John Philip Sousa (1906), perhaps the greatest American composer of marching songs

---

(including "Stars and Stripes Forever"), said about the consequences of the phonograph's popularity:

Sweeping across the country with the speed of a transient fashion in slang or Panama hats, political war cries or popular novels, now comes the mechanical device to sing for us a song or play for us a piano, in substitute for human skill, intelligence and the soul. Only by harking back to the day of the roller skate or the bicycle craze, when sports of admitted utility ran to extravagance and virtual madness, can we find a parallel to the way in which these ingenious instruments have invaded every community in the land. And if we turn from this comparison in pure mechanics to another which may fairly claim a similar proportion of music in its soul, we may observe the English sparrow, which, introduced and welcomed in all innocence, lost no time in multiplying itself to the dignity of a pest, to the destruction of numberless native song birds, and the invariable regret of those who did not stop to think in time. On a matter upon which I feel so deeply, and which I consider so far-reaching, I am quite willing to be reckoned an alarmist, admittedly swayed in part by personal interest, as well as by the impending harm to American musical art. I foresee a marked deterioration in American music and musical taste, an interruption in the musical development of the country, and a host of other injuries to music in its artistic manifestations, by virtue—or rather by vice—of the multiplication of the various music-reproducing machines. . . . When a mother can turn on the phonograph with the same ease that she applied to the electric light, will she croon her baby to slumber with sweet lullabies, or will the infant be put to sleep by machinery? Children are naturally imitative, and if, in their infancy, they hear only phonographs, will they not sing, if they sing at all, in imitation and finally become simply human phonographs—without soul or expression? Congregational singing will suffer also, which, though crude at times, at least improves the respiration of many a weary sinner and softens the voices of those who live amid tumult and noise. The host of mechanical reproducing machines, in their mad desire to supply music for all occasions, are offering to supplant the illustrator in the classroom, the dance orchestra, the home and public singers and players, and so on. Evidently they believe no field too large for their incursions, no claim too extravagant. But the further they can justify these claims, the more noxious the whole system becomes.

Likewise, even fans of a new form of popular culture, especially when it is made available through new media, often themselves assume that the new form is inferior to the older forms it is replacing. Criticism of new forms of popular culture may turn into criticism of the media that carry them. Parents fret that electronic games keep their children away from better activities, such as reading or exercising. It is true that the media have become the primary space for new forms of leisure activities and popular culture. The twentieth century saw a transformation in older forms of culture as well as a redefinition of leisure and leisure activities. (See Box 1.2, "Leisure in 'Middletown.'")

---

**BOX 1.2**

**Leisure in "Middletown"**

One of the classic studies of American social life is Robert and Helen Lynd's (1929) *Middletown,* the study of an American small town in the 1920s. The Lynds examined the changes that modernity brought to Middletown between the 1890s and 1920s, looking at such activities as making a living, making a home, training the young, using leisure, and engaging in religious practices and community activities.

Of particular interest to us is their examination of how the automobile and movies—both new technologies in the early 1920s—changed how Americans spent their leisure. The automobile was important for spreading the idea of vacation when families could travel relatively cheaply away from home. Moreover, and for the first time, ordinary Americans could go for a ride on any day of the week. Thus the automobile helped make "leisure time enjoyment a regularly expected part of every day and week rather than an occasional event" (p. 260):

> Like the automobile, the motion picture is more to Middletown than simply a new way of doing an old thing; it has added new dimensions to the city's leisure. To be sure, the spectacle-watching habit was strong upon Middletown in the [1890s]. Whenever they had a chance people turned out to a "show," but chances were relatively fewer. Fourteen times during January, 1890, for instance, the Opera House was opened for performances ranging from Uncle Tom's Cabin to The Black Crook, before the paper announced that "there will not be any more attractions at the Opera House for nearly two weeks." . . . Today nine motion picture theaters operate from 1 to 11 p.m. seven days a week summer and winter; . . . twenty-two different programs with a total of over 300 performances are available to Middletown every week in the year. . . . About two and three-fourths times the city's entire population attended the nine motion picture theaters during the month of July, 1923, the "valley" month of the year, and four and one-half times the total population in the "peak" month of December. (p. 263)

---

Understanding the media requires acknowledging and accounting for the complexity of the media. Every medium comprises and is shaped by technologies, social relationships (institutions), and cultural forms. Each of these ways of thinking about the media is important, for each contributes something unique to how we understand the media and their relationship to society and social reality. These three aspects of the media are central to our discussions throughout the book.

### Technologies

When we think about media, the first thing that comes to mind is the various technologies of communication. *Technology is the physical means of producing, reproducing, and distributing goods, services, materials, and cultural products.* In the case of communication, technology includes the physical media and techniques, the technical practices and machinery, by which we communicate. Communication technologies are expanding and proliferating at an increasingly rapid rate. It wasn't until 1954 that television was in the majority of American households; by 1960, seven of eight families had TV sets. Stereos were nonexistent. There were no cassette tapes, no videos, no cable television, no satellites, no personal computers or personal data assistants, no video games, no cellular phones. Today, even as we write, new technologies are being announced all the time. We anxiously await the arrival of wearable computers, the continued miniaturization of devices, and, someday, teleportation devices. Imagine how our understanding of an event like the attacks of September 11, 2001, might change if the cellular telephones with the capability to capture and send digital still images and video that are now widely available had been commonplace then. What new images, perspectives, and stories could have been told?

### Institutions

Technologies are not an independent part of society. Technologies are often created within, shaped by, and controlled by institutions involved in their production and use. *An institution is any large-scale entity, embodying a range of social relationships and social functions, created by humans to perform an essential function for a society.* An institution, then, is a specific social organization where particular decisions are made and can be carried out. For example, organized religion, the military, the school system, and the government or state can be seen as institutions. Their functions and relative power vary over time. The institution of contemporary mass media comprises industries (such as the television industry) and organizations (such as the National Broadcasting Company [NBC]) that use professionals—people who are trained in and paid for specific skills to produce and distribute media products to a market or audience. In addition, other organizations, such as government regulatory agencies and universities, may also play a role in the complex institutional existence of the media.

More specifically, the relationship between communication technologies and institutions has varied over time as well: In Western Europe through the Middle Ages, the Roman Catholic church controlled the technologies of writing and manuscript production. Only the church was allowed to teach writing, and only the church had the resources to control the labor (of monks and priests) necessary for the arduous reproduction of manuscripts. Because of this, the church was able to control what was written and, hence, disseminated. When Johannes Gutenberg, with the backing of his banker, Johann Fust, coupled the printing press with movable type (individual letters of type that could be moved around and reused) in the fifteenth century, he challenged the power of one institution, the church. But the printing press was created within and became part of other institutions—medieval institutions such as guilds and later modern commercial institutions such as banks and mass media industries. And these, in their turn, controlled how the technology was used and what sorts of things could be written, printed, and distributed.

We could also discuss the long history of government regulation of communication and its technologies, from the licensing of printing presses to the licensing of broadcast stations today. Communication technologies are also developed within specific institutions. For example, there was great corporate interest in the development of radio and television in the United States, and great government interest in the development of those same technologies as a public service in the United Kingdom. Governments and corporate institutions also develop and decide the standards and norms for a technology: on what frequencies a broadcast technology can transmit, or how many scan lines will be in a television screen.

## Cultural Forms

Many organizations in contemporary American society produce and distribute things; often, these items are meant to be sold and purchased to make a profit for their owners. Media organizations are no exception (although in some cases and in some other societies, media products are distributed freely). Yet media organizations produce something less tangible than the typical products of business. Rather than producing things (cars, toasters, coffee mugs), media organizations produce cultural *forms;* that is, formats, structures, ways of telling stories. By cultural form, *we mean how the products of media technologies and organizations are structured; how their languages and meanings are structured into codes* (see Chapter 5). For example, a typical product of television is the half-hour situation comedy or sitcom, such as an episode of *Will and Grace.* The cultural form of that product is how it tells its stories, a consistent plot structure, ways of presenting and resolving issues, or other genre conventions. It can also be a consistent look or image (a living room with a couch) or use of language (short, one-line quips rather than long, elaborate discourse). Though the idea of cultural form has much in common with the idea of genre, they are not the same thing. A newspaper is a particular cultural form, but it is not in and of itself a genre (though there are genres of newspapers). In many cases, especially when they are first introduced, new media technologies simply borrow cultural forms from older technologies. Early films look a lot like theatrical plays, early television copies the serial form of much radio programming, and so on. Cultural forms are an essential part of how the media make meaning. And cultural forms can be structured and influenced by institutions. For example, the fact that commercials appear every 10–15 minutes on American television, as opposed to every hour—or not at all—in other systems, is a decision of the broadcast companies and occasionally is federally regulated. Cultural forms are also structured and influenced by technologies. For example, you can display a more complex and detailed image on a large cinema screen, but that complexity and detail gets lost on the much smaller screen of a television.

What holds the three aspects of media—technology, institutions, and cultural forms—together, and what provides the unity of the concept of media, is the idea of *mediation,* to which we now turn.

## Mediation

The meaning of the complex term *mediation* has changed over the centuries, but there are consistent themes to these meanings. Rather than giving one definition of mediation, we will give you four of them, because there are four different ways that the term gets used, and all of them are relevant to the study of communication.

According to *Webster's New World Dictionary, Third Collegiate Edition,* a medium is "something intermediate . . . a middle state . . . an intervening thing through which a force acts or an effect is produced." A very old and commonsensical sense of the term is "to occupy a middle position or intermediary," as in interceding between adversaries in an attempt to reconcile a dispute. We still talk about mediating labor disputes between business and workers. Similarly, in Christian doctrine, mediation describes the role of Christ interceding between God and humans. So, the first definition of mediation is *interceding or coming between.*

A second sense of mediation contrasts the mediated with the immediate or the real: for example, when we contrast the media world with the real world, or when we think that there is a difference between objective knowledge and that which has been mediated through the interests of some party. This sense implies that *that which has been mediated has been biased or shaped by the mediator* and can be contrasted with immediate, objective information.

The third sense of mediation is a more modern sense that combines these two meanings. *Mediation is the space between the individual subject and reality.* That space is a space of experience, interpretation, and meaning. In other words, this definition of mediation implies that our notion of reality is always shaped by these things (experience, interpretation, and meaning), which come between one's self and reality.

Finally, there is a fourth sense of the term mediation that refers to a formal relationship that connects previously unconnected activities or people: for example, the relationship between the producer and the consumer of some message. In this sense, mediation refers to *how messages are transmitted from one person to another.*

The notion of communication is complex because it embodies all four of these senses of the term *mediation:* reconciliation or intercession, the difference between reality and an image or interpretation of reality, the space of interpretation between the subject and reality, and the connection that creates the circuit of the communication of meaning. This complexity helps to explain the apparently contradictory effects of communication in society, but it also helps us understand why it is so difficult to arrive at a singular understanding of the process of communication. These different notions of mediation underlie the dominant models through which communication usually has been theorized.

## TWO MODELS OF COMMUNICATION

Any attempt to describe, explain, and understand the media must presuppose something about the nature of the process of communication, for it is assumed that this process defines the essential function or nature of the media. This task is made more difficult because communication is something that we take for granted all of the time. Yet the things that are most familiar are frequently the most difficult to notice, to say nothing of appreciate and comprehend, for we "know" them so comfortably and tacitly. The word *communication* comes from the Latin term for *common*. The question is, *What is it that is made or held in common through the process of communication?*

Communication is not only taken for granted in our society; it is often seen as a magical solution for many if not all of our problems. Some people assert that undesirable situations can be significantly improved through more effective communication. People write books claiming the key to success is better communication skills. People may act as if all of our problems were merely "problems of communication" and not real differences of opinion and values, skill and desire, resources and power. But improved communication may not be enough to relieve the racial tension in our society or, for that matter, to end a war. It may not even be enough to guarantee success in a career, a relationship, or life.

There are two different answers to the question of what constitutes the commonality implicit in communication. These have given rise to two fundamentally different perspectives on the process and practice of communication. The first perspective is grounded in the idea of *transportation,* in which some *thing*—a message or meaning—is transported from one place or person to another. Based on the image of transportation, scholars have developed a transmission model of communication. This model relies more on the fourth definition of

17

mediation discussed above, the circuit of communication and meaning. The second perspective depends on the idea of the *production of a common culture* through which the concept of communication is closely tied to notions of community and communion. Communication, like communion, is a process by which a particular community is bound together. This common culture surrounds everyone and everything in its commonality; it is the groundwork upon which both community and every specific act of communication are built. Based on the assumption that a common culture is the basic context of communication, scholars have developed a cultural model of communication. These two models have played a central role in the development of the discipline of communication studies.

## The Transmission Model

Modernization is closely tied not only to industrialization, but also to the development of new technologies that facilitated the movement of goods, people, and information. In the eighteenth century, modernization was crucially dependent on the development of modes of transportation, such as all-weather roads and canals. In the nineteenth century, modernization included the advent of the railroad, the telegraph, the elevator, and the telephone.

Among the earliest attempts to develop a theory of communication in the twentieth century, the most successful reproduced the commonsense assumption that communication looks exactly like transportation; that is, that *communication is the process of moving messages from a sender through a medium to a receiver.* The analogy to transportation is straightforward. In transportation, something—wheat, for example—is moved from a source to a receiver by a certain agency or medium—for example, a train. In communication, a message—a certain sentence or meaning, for example—is moved from a source to a receiver by a certain agency or medium—for example, a linguistic code carried through a telephone. In fact, as media scholar James W. Carey (1989) puts it, "In the nineteenth century . . . the movement of goods or people and the movement of information were seen as essentially identical processes and both were described by the common noun 'communication'" (p. 15). By the time the discipline of communication had been established in American universities in the early twentieth century, this transmission model had become the dominant model among communication theorists. Here is a typical diagram of this view of communication:

Source → Message → Receiver

The transmission model of communication is based on the inter-personal context, in which the major concern is the fidelity of communicating—that is, the accuracy with which the message is transported from one person to another in a linear trajectory—although the model may allow for feedback loops. This model assumes that all communication operates like interpersonal communication. At its simplest level, whether you are talking on the telephone or watching television, your first concern as a receiver of communication is whether what you are receiving is actually the same as (i.e., reproduces) the message that has been sent. The model implies that the major challenge of the process of communication is to successfully transmit the content of a message as if from the mind of one person to that of another—the exact thought and meaning in the mind of the sender is what can, should, and will be placed in the mind of the receiver. This sharing of meaning is called *understanding* or *intersubjectivity*.

The transmission model was the basis of Harold Lasswell's (1948) famous description of the study of mass communication. Lasswell, who wrote about mass media in the first half of the twentieth century, described the study of communication as a series of questions: *Who / says What / to Whom / through what Channel / and with what Effect?* Indeed, almost all of the scientific research in the field of mass communication is built upon this model. Drawing upon research methodologies in sociology, psychology, and social psychology, researchers have studied each of Lasswell's questions. Researchers have studied the "who" in studies of communicators—the people and organizations that produce media messages and control what gets transmitted. They have studied the "what" in systematic analyses of media content. And they have studied the "to whom" and "with what effect" in the voluminous research on the effects of media on audiences (see Chapter 10).

For example, the school shootings at Columbine High School in 1999 renewed debates about the effects of violence in the media on youth. For the most part, these debates relied on the transmission model of communication. They argue about *who* (the source—Marilyn Manson or the makers of video games) says *what* (the message of the

19

songs or the violence represented in the games) through what *channel* (compact discs [CDs] and videogames) to *whom* (the receiver—impressionable youth) to what *effect* (the murder of 13 people and the deaths of the two shooters). This model assumes that these effects are relatively direct between source and receiver, and so people search for the source or sources of the violent behavior. We can also see this model at work in discussions of propaganda and even education (where it describes a particular model of lecturing: teacher → information → student).

## The Cultural Model

The transmission model is the more prevalent model of communication in society today. The cultural model is less well known, so we will spend more time outlining it. The cultural model of communication draws a very close connection between the processes of social communication and the production of a common culture. The notion of culture is one of the most complex yet powerful concepts in modern thinking. Raymond Williams, a British literary critic and communication theorist, has traced the changing meanings of this term.

According to Williams (1958), the oldest use of the term *culture* already combined two different senses: On the one hand, culture involved notions of honor and worship; on the other hand, it described the agricultural process of cultivation, "the tending of natural growth." By the nineteenth century, these two meanings were extended to human development, and culture came to take on new meanings. Now the term described the process of "cultivating" particular abilities, sensibilities, and habits in human society (such as when we think of a "cultured person"). It described a particular form of human association and existence (for example, in notions of "folk culture" and "images of the organic or natural community"). Increasingly, the notion of culture was used to describe a particular set of highly valued activities and the "creative practices" that produce them—culture as the set of artistic and intellectual activities and products. For example, one of the most famous definitions of culture was offered by the nineteenth-century English literary critic and state education bureaucrat Matthew Arnold (1869/1960): "The best that has been thought and said." Finally, in its most recent form, culture becomes synonymous with the whole way of life of a society or people; thus we might talk about the culture of the Middle East or of Iraqis or of African Americans or even of the dominant American culture.

Williams suggests that even as this last anthropological notion of culture becomes prevalent in contemporary language, the earlier meanings of culture remain active in our commonsense uses of the term. He explains that the reason culture became such an ambiguous and important term in our modern lexicon may have been that it offered a way of both describing and judging the changes that have radically altered the nature of social life since the seventeenth century. These changes, commonly referred to under the general term of *modernization* or *progress,* were so sweeping that they challenged any attempt to describe them or to judge them. The theory of culture is based on the attempt to describe the pervasive changes captured in notions of modernization and, at the same time, to identify some criterion against which these changes could be measured.

Williams notes,

> Culture was not a response to the new methods of production, the new Industry alone. It was concerned, beyond these, with the new kinds of personal and social relationships: again, both as a recognition of practical separation and as an emphasis of alternatives. (p. xvi)

In his words, "The idea of culture is a general reaction to a general and major change in the condition of our common life. Its basic element is its effort at total qualitative assessment" (p. 295).

Williams makes an important addition to this history of the concept of culture. He argues that what connects the notions of a whole way of life and a privileged set of activities is a set of processes that can properly be called cultural and that are, above all else, ordinary. These processes are ordinary in the sense that they are routinely performed by everyone in their daily lives; they are the processes of language and meaning production, of sense making and interpretation, of communication. It is above all the ordinariness of communication that defines culture as art and that unites the various elements of a whole way of life. For Williams, the dilemma of modern life is not that there is a struggle between the creative (art) and the uncreative (popular culture), but that there is no way for the vast majority of the population to enter into more public and social processes of communication. To transform the culture of the society according to every individual's experience requires that people be able to use language and the media of communication to both speak within and transcend the already existing common or shared culture. This process is what Williams calls "the long revolution."

Individuals continually attempt to give meaning to their experiences. Interpretations are usually provided for them by the shared languages (verbal, literary, visual) of their culture. But people have to constantly struggle to find ways to interpret experiences that appear to have no place within the existing culture. They create such interpretations, Williams suggests, through their attempts to communicate their experience. Thus communication is a constant process of balancing the possibilities of the culture (social languages, shared experiences, and meanings) with the needs of individuality. If culture remained totally within the already constructed social language, everyone would understand everything, but there could be nothing new in the world. If culture were limited to the innovative realm of the individual, then shared understanding would be impossible. Culture as communication is the process of producing new shared meaning out of the interaction of historically given shared meanings and individually created meanings.

At the same time, for Williams, culture is the set of activities in which this process of producing new shared meanings is carried in the various forms of art and media communication. Making the leap from culture as art and literature to culture as film and television is a simple one. Today's media have certainly augmented older forms of art and have become the dominant means by which culture is created and shared.

*The cultural model of communication sees communication as the construction of a shared space or map of meaning within which people coexist.* Rather than a linear model, which first isolates the message and then sends it from one place or person to another, the cultural model emphasizes the fact that people already exist within a world of shared meaning that they take for granted. Without this common reality, communication would be impossible, and, in fact, the vast majority of our communication merely serves to ritualistically reproduce that system of shared meanings within which we live.

A number of writers have followed media scholar James W. Carey's (1989) ritual view of communication and suggested that one can look at media presentations as "rituals" to illustrate the ways in which the media function as a cultural forum. When we think of rituals, we think of ceremonies and religious events—a graduation, the swearing in of naturalized citizens, a wedding, a Holy Communion. Rituals are formal but emotional public events, endlessly repeated, with special meanings for their present participants and equally important meanings for the wider society that has established them. A ritual serves to remind the society's members of cornerstone beliefs for that society. The ritual's repetition serves as a marker, both of the importance of those beliefs and of their durability. A cultural model of communication extends this notion of ritual to encompass all of the repetitive practices of communication, such as saying grace before dinner, answering the phone, or greeting a friend.

This system of shared meaning represents the world for us; it gives us a common picture of reality. This concept is often described as *ideology*. But *picture* is perhaps not the most accurate description of this process, for we live within these pictures of reality. *Map* may be a better term, although even that is too abstract and distant from the way in which, in this model, communication defines and determines our experience of the world. But communication as culture can never be limited to ritual, to the reaffirmation of what a community shares, for it must also allow for and even institutionalize the possibility of creativity, growth, and change.

In fact, the cultural model of communication lies within a broader set of theories of the social construction of reality. Such theories start out with the observation that human beings lack the instinctual relationship to reality that enables other species of animals to make sense of and respond to the world. Culture is for humans the compensatory medium of information without which we would be condemned to live in a chaotic reality. Without culture, reality would be available to us only as what William James called a "booming buzzing confusion"; with culture, reality becomes ordered and manageable. Culture exists, then, in a kind of space of mediation, the space between humans as incomplete animals and reality, the space of communication as the production of meaning. This is the third definition of mediation, from our earlier discussion. Human experience is defined in part by the contribution of the specific human culture that binds together a particular community or society. Human beings live in a meaningful world, which they have produced through their own culture. Culture is the medium in which human beings externalize (objectify) and internalize (subjectify) their meaningful experiences of the world. (Chapter 5 will consider these issues in greater detail.)

23

## Contrasting the Two Models

Consider the relation of the media to the attacks of September 11, 2001, again. Using a transmission model, the analyst understands news coverage primarily in terms of the information that is sent from the media to the audience, or from the government to the media to the audience. Researchers might study the relationships between the various organizations involved in producing various messages: They might look at how the messages are constructed and what correlations there are between features of the message and the audience's response to them; they might try to figure out how audience members process the messages, and what individual audience members do with them. But the transmission model cannot deal with the enormous amount of misinformation and redundancy in the coverage, or with the relationship between news and entertainment.

Using a cultural model, an analyst would ask very different questions and offer very different descriptions of those events. The analyst might begin by pointing out that the language and images (in other words, the cultural forms) used in the news are already understood by the audience; thus the attacks can be incorporated into already existing frames of reference. Some audience members reported that watching the coverage, even live as it happened, was like watching a movie. The live photos of actual events matched the cultural form of the disaster picture and seemed to follow the codes of contemporary special-effects sequences in popular film. Cultural forms give the audience a way of understanding these events—in this case, it was a way of understanding that was at odds with the seriousness of the events (this was not a film; thousands of people lost their lives). Two communication researchers have even argued that the cultural form of the media coverage itself (constant, uninterrupted television coverage; repetition of key images or videotape; the continual speculation as to who was responsible) was sufficiently similar to other media events of this type as to constitute a particular genre, the *disaster marathon*. This cultural form itself, they argue, greatly enhanced the effectiveness of the terrorists' goal; in other words, the form of the coverage enhanced the terrorists' message (Blondheim & Liebes, 2002).

Similarly, an analyst using the cultural model might offer a different account of people constantly viewing the war coverage on television. Rather than assuming that people are seeking information about the attack, we might assume that television viewing in this crisis serves to create and reinforce our sense that we are part of a community that is sharing this highly emotional and dramatic event (as evidenced by the great increase in the display of flags and other patriotic signs soon after the events). More viewers watched the news in groups than usual (J. Carey, 2002). This is indeed a *media event*, through which we ritualistically share the experience of being part of the American community. In this ritual watching of television, we find a way of coping with the anxieties and fears of a people at war. In this regard, we can compare this event to other instances of national grieving or celebration in front of the television set, as when the Challenger space shuttle exploded after liftoff in 1986, when O. J. Simpson was tried for murder in 1995, or when the Millennium was celebrated.

A cultural model of communication might also begin by recognizing the enormous power of language, culture, and rituals, focusing its attention on the ways in which the coverage reaffirms the shared systems of meaning and values that define American culture. In this light, we can view the presentation of Osama bin Laden as an evil threat not only to peace but to the fundamental values of liberty, justice, and the American way. The coverage of the war on terror continuously reaffirms our own sense of our moral and technological superiority.

The model would also recognize that the very language used to describe the events of September 11, 2001, structures both our interpretation of those events and the possible responses to that event. For example, the events were labeled as an *attack*, which is an act of war, and the United States' response was made within that framework: A war on terrorism was launched, al-Qaida prisoners were considered prisoners of war and treated according to the rules of war. Conceivably, these events could have been labeled as *crimes* (theft, kidnapping, and mass murder) and the perpetrators *criminals* (rather than *militants* or *soldiers*). Our response to crimes involves a quite different procedure and different laws than war does.

Cultural reaffirmation is a constant element of our relationship to the media. In light of the cultural view, we can understand most of popular culture in terms of its constant affirmation and reproduction of already taken-for-granted meanings and values in American society: the importance of the family, belief in the power of the individual, the value of competition.

25

There are a number of ways to distinguish between the two models. Many people assume that research carried on under the auspices of the transmission model is always quantitative, based on statistic analyses applied to data gathered through either experimental or survey research methods, whereas research within the cultural model is predominantly qualitative, based on either the researcher interacting with the people he or she is studying in natural settings (ethnography) or the interpretation of texts. However, this distinction is by no means absolute, and there can be qualitative work within a transmission model and quantitative work within a cultural model. The sociologist Edward Shils once made a similar distinction by suggesting that the transmission model had lots of answers, but the questions were usually so specific as to be uninteresting, whereas the cultural model had lots of interesting and important questions, but they were so difficult that no answers were possible. Underlining Shils's distinction is the fact that the transmission model develops by generating and accumulating specific answers from specific case studies, whereas research within the cultural model develops more as the result of theoretical argument. Rather than accumulating and averaging across specific results, cultural research develops increasingly sophisticated concepts to deal with its growing recognition of the complexity of the processes of media communication. In this book, we are concerned less with the specific findings of research than with the conceptual and theoretical tools that enable scholars and critics to understand the media in all their complexity.

The two models also have different relationships and responses to the idea of context. As we have already said, it is impossible to separate communication from its context, to isolate its forms and effects from its relations with other forms and institutions of practices. Researchers committed to the transmission model nevertheless make a choice to isolate specific aspects of the media and also to isolate the media from the various elements of the context. By focusing on particular relationships between elements of the media and other similarly isolated aspects of the context of social reality, such as a particular political campaign or a particular economic trend or aspect of the audience's identity or response, researchers hope to address very important questions about the influence or effect of the media on local events and circumstances, such as the effect of certain kinds of war reporting on public opinion about the war. Choosing the transmission model allows

that pornography is responsible for its users' violent behavior toward women. If that is the case, pornography can be said to determine attitudes and even behaviors toward women.

Another sense of determination follows from the more contextual vision of social life that we have advocated here. In this view, *the relationship of any practice to its effects cannot be isolated and identified, because it depends on the entire context.* What a specific practice or set of practices can do is limit and shape the outcomes; we then say the effects are *overdetermined.* Consider some examples: In this view, pornography cannot be isolated from a wider range of other media representations that portray women as objects to be used by men (think, for example, of many ads in such popular magazines as *Maxim* or *Vogue*). But the effects of even this broad range of media portrayals cannot be identified outside of the context of social relationships and other aspects of our culture that help to define, shape, and limit the construction of sexual identities and differences. These social relationships not only qualify the impact of pornography, they also help to explain its production: It is not surprising that pornography is a major product of a sexist society. That is why we can speak of the overdetermination of pornography's effects.

Let's consider again the relationship of education and economic success. How is this relationship overdetermined? Consider that access to education is itself dependent on many other factors, including social class, race, gender, and family income. Furthermore, the very meaning of education is constantly being challenged and rethought. Some ask whether life experience should earn credit in school or college; others debate whether the point of college is vocational training or general intellectual advancement. Similarly, current discussions around the question of multicultural curricula in colleges raise a number of crucial questions: Does becoming well educated mean learning about European-derived culture only, or should students be exposed to the broad range of cultures, ethnicities, and histories in the world? To the extent that education level is related to a whole host of other social factors in one's life that mediate its relationship to income level, that relationship is overdetermined.

## Power as Control: Consensus and Conflict

There is a second meaning of the notion of power: *control* over people and resources. In this sense, power can be understood as producing, and then operating through or exploiting, social differences in the world. To begin to understand how media have power, we need a theory of how social differences are produced and of their importance in society. Some theories of society, commonly referred to as *consensus models*, emphasize the unity and harmony within society and the ability of different peoples to get along together. Typically, Americans think of their nation as a "melting pot" in which different groups come together in a common identity: We are all Americans.

One of the most influential examples of a consensus model of society in media theory is the work of John Dewey, the eminent philosopher, educational theorist, and communication critic of the first half of the twentieth century. Dewey (1925) offered a sophisticated cultural model of communication based on the idea that communication is the process through which different groups in the society come to understand and accept each other despite their differences. Communication is the means through which a nation forges a common identity, a common purpose, and a common resolve.

Dewey felt that the new media of communications were not meeting the challenge presented by the complex problems facing America at the turn of the twentieth century: vast immigration from eastern and southern Europe, shifts of population from rural to urban areas, and increasing economic interdependence among the different regions of the country. These historical changes in American life meant that different groups in the society were unable to understand each other and to act together toward a common goal. Dewey thought the mass media of the day (including newspapers, magazines, films, and later radio) were failing to fulfill their essential purpose of creating a common language that would result in a sense of national community with which people could understand each other and which would enable people to act together. This enormous faith in the power of communication and its ability to create new forms of unity out of the chaos produced by historical change explains Dewey's belief that "of all things communication is the most wonderful" (1939, p. 385). Although Dewey was writing in the second and third decades of the twentieth century, his argument has a modern parallel: Throughout the 1990s the Internet was often seen as providing an opportunity to bring people together and to bring back a dimension of community that was seen to be missing in American life.

However, other theories of society, commonly referred to as *conflict models*, emphasize the conflicts and inequalities within social life and the difficulties different groups have in living together. These critical theories of society emphasize the fact that the various resources of a society are unequally distributed according to various structures of social difference. Every society has resources that are highly valued: force, money, meanings, morals, identities, political position, emotions, pleasures, and so on. Some of these are more highly valued than others. Each of them enables those who possess and can use the valued item to have certain powers or capacities to make a difference (the first sense of power described earlier) in the world. The case of money is quite clear: Money can produce more money—when you know how to use it—and it can enable its possessor to purchase many other things as well. But as the old Beatles' song goes, "Money can't buy me love." On the other hand, we might not think of emotions as a resource of value until we think about the way in which people use emotion to control other people or the fact that people need emotional bonds to remain healthy. By the same token, the power to influence meanings—a topic we explore in detail in Chapter 6—is the power to define questions or the power to define what others view as important and how they think about them. It is the power to define what others take as common sense. This is power, indeed.

These resources are not equally distributed across all members of the society. Different groups have more or less access to resources and a differing ability to use them. Moreover, such groups are not randomly defined; the distribution of resources is organized hierarchically according to systems of social differences. Every society identifies a variety of features that differentiate groups, but only some features are considered relevant to the distribution of resources. For example, in American society, we certainly distinguish blond-haired, blue-eyed people from brown-haired, brown-eyed people. However, no one justifies segregation in schools according to such differences. On the other hand, we do organize the distribution of resources differentially by social class, race, ethnicity, nationality, gender, sexual identity, age, and differential abilities. And this is what critical scholars mean by *a system of social differences*.

For example, feminism is a theory of society that emphasizes the unequal distribution of resources by gender and sexuality: It describes a society that subordinates women and privileges men, and it labels this society as patriarchal. Although almost every society in human history has been patriarchal, feminism argues that it is important to identify the particular forms of inequality that characterize contemporary society. Women, for instance, tend to make less money than men and often they are expected to work in the home, without pay; women tend to be subject to verbal and physical violence by men; women tend to have less access to political power (in the United States, there has never been a woman elected president or vice president); women are often viewed and represented solely as sexual objects; and women are thought of in our society as being more emotional and less rational than men. You might think of many other ways in which women are subordinated to men in our society. Feminism is a theory of society that attempts to identify and challenge the subordination of women in these systems of difference. A feminist theory of communication examines the ways in which media communication contributes to these relations of inequality between men and women.

Other conflict theories of society look at the subordination of racial and ethnic groups relative to the White majority; of the working class relative to the wealthier elites; of children and the aged relative to young and middle-aged adults; of homosexuals relative to heterosexuals; of various religious minorities relative to the Protestant majority of America; and of the physically handicapped relative to the physically able.

In recent years, many of these subordinate groups in society have challenged their subordination—including their portrayals in and access to the mass media. Increasingly, questions of culture and media communication have been central in such struggles. These struggles are transforming the political and cultural life of the United States and the rest of the world. And they have had a profound impact on the study of media, for they have placed questions of power as control at the center of the discipline.

It is difficult to choose between consensus and conflict models of society. Media theorists who favor a conflict model of society generally view the more consensus-oriented alternative as defending the status quo, the current way of life and all of its inequalities. On the other hand, media theorists who stress the consensus model of society tend to defend their vision by appealing to the liberal faith that society is continuously progressing and that the lives of all people within society will improve in the future as they have in the past. Moreover, they argue that conflict theorists give too much importance to the problems of power and overlook progress and harmony in human life.

In this book, we use both models of society—the consensus and conflict models—because we believe both theories of society describe important aspects of the media's role in making American society and people's lives. As we have said, the media do play an important part in making the structured inequalities of different groups in the society. But, although we recognize that the media contribute to these relations of subordination, we also believe that the media have positive and beneficial effects in society. And we believe, like Dewey, that media help to make us a community. Many contemporary struggles have been addressed by the media in a variety of ways. Media have a vital role to play in transforming society and in producing a more equitable social structure.

Somewhere between the pessimism of the conflict model and the optimism of the consensus model, we have to find the space for an appreciation of both the positive and negative sides of the media's role in American society. To become a critic of media is to walk a thin line between these two alternatives. The danger of pessimism is that you begin to think that people are so vulnerable to the media's messages that every exposure to entertainment subordinates them further. However, the danger of optimism is to ignore the ways in which real people suffer as a consequence of the power of the media.

One final note: There is no correlation between social theories and communication models. Or, to put it differently, there is no necessary relation between one's view of society and the model of communication one supports. Scholars who use a cultural model can hold to either a critical or a consensual model of society, as can those who use a transmission model. The questions facing communication scholars are too complex to reduce the field of possibilities before we have even begun.

## SUGGESTED READING

Carey, J. W. (1989). *Communication as culture: Essays on media and society*. Boston: Unwin Hyman.

# Narratives of Media History | 2

To understand how the media operate today, we need a better understanding of how communication media have shaped and influenced human existence. Will the Internet fundamentally alter culture and society in the twenty-first century? Would we be able to tell if it did? We are, after all, sometimes quite blind to slow and gradual change around us: As Marshall McLuhan is reported to have quipped, "We don't know who discovered water, but it certainly wasn't the fish." (Actually, the line's probably from one of his promoters, Howard Luck Gossage). When we speculate about the future, we must ground such speculations and our understanding of contemporary media by considering the history of the relationship between communication and society. We believe that history is a useful guide to understanding the present and the future. In this chapter, we consider some of the narratives of media history.

Typically, media history is presented as a series of technological inventions, a story about great people and organizations, and an analysis of particular events shaped by communication technologies. For example, such histories focus on Johannes Gutenberg's invention of the moveable type printing press in the 1450s, Samuel Morse's invention of a workable electric telegraph in 1844, Alexander Graham Bell's invention of the telephone in 1876, and so on.

However, there is another way of thinking about the history of the media, which emphasizes the role of communication in shaping human existence. History is a retelling of the past, an attempt to explain how something that occurred in the past affects who or what people and society are now. But the story of the past can be told in many different ways. The French historian Fernand Braudel (1972) offers a set of categories for viewing the scope of historical events. First, there is the shortest unit of historical time, the *event*. An event is a thing like a war, a decree, a meeting, or the introduction of television. As pointed out above, most typical histories of media simply list a series of such events, each event focused on a technological development. Second, there is the level of the *conjuncture,* which describes short periods of time, usually measured in decades. Conjunctures comprise many events. For example, we speak of America in the postwar years and of the Roaring Twenties. Third, there is the level of *historical eras,* a period that can be viewed as a whole, usually less than a century, such as the Industrial Age, the Nuclear Age, or the Enlightenment. Finally, there are *historical epochs* representing major and significant trans-formations of human life that often cross national boundaries and that encompass events, conjunctures, and eras. Braudel refers to these as the *longue duree* or the long term, a temporal unit that encompasses centuries: for example, the Middle Ages and the Modern Period.

The three different historical narratives that we will consider here offer accounts of the role of communication and culture in human history. The first narrative theorizes the transformation from orality to writing to print to electronic communication. It is a grand narrative on the epochal scale, examining the impact of changes in the modes and technologies of communication across the *longue duree.* It asks, *To what extent has the history of communications fundamentally shaped the directions of human endeavor and social life?* The second historical narrative, on theories of the masses, is conjunctural in Braudel's sense and focuses on communication, culture, and social relationships in modern life. The third narrative describes a different transformation in the *longue duree,* the transformation from modernity to postmodernity. In this narrative, communication is seen as a part of a broader cultural transformation in history.

## FROM ORAL TO ELECTRONIC CULTURE

The first of the narratives is the longest of the *longue duree* histories of media, from oral culture to electronic culture. But we should emphasize that although this can be seen as a narrative of historical periods (like geological epochs), it is actually a narrative of different cultures and there is much overlap between these cultures. In fact, different media cultures can be operating more or less simultaneously within a single society in a particular period.

In an oral culture, all interaction takes place in face-to-face situations. It is a preliterate society that has no shared form of fixing or writing messages. A writing culture is a literate society in which a shared system of inscription, or writing, exists so that communication can take place outside of face-to-face situations, across time and space. A print culture is an expansion of a writing culture by means of the printing press, but it also encompasses the consequent social and cultural changes that result from the proliferation of printed matter. In an electronic culture, communication can transcend time and space without physically moving the same object from one place to another. A variety of writers have described the general differences among oral, writing, print, and electronic cultures, including Walter Ong (1982), Eric Havelock (1982), Harold Innis (1950, 1951), Marshall McLuhan (1964; McLuhan & Fiore, 1967), and Elizabeth Eisenstein (1978).

## Oral Culture

It is difficult to reconstruct what it was like to live in a purely oral culture. Scholars of oral culture have had to base their understandings of this epoch on the anthropological study of nonliterate peoples (for example, Walter Ong has looked at oral culture in Yugoslavia) and on the epic poetry of Homeric Greece (in the work of Eric Havelock).

Perhaps more than any other scholar, Walter Ong (1982) has characterized oral culture. First, Ong insists that there is a *different sense of time* in an oral culture. Because it has no records, its memory cannot be a recorded one; its history can only reside in the present moment, in the telling of its story. There is no way to go back and check the record to see if it differs from contemporary views of an event. There are no aids to recall the "facts" or even what other people have said in previous tellings. Ong says that "the past is indeed present but it is present in the speech and social institutions of the people, not in the more abstract forms in which modern history deals." Therefore, it is more likely that both myth and facts are intertwined in an oral culture's memory of its past, much like people's family histories: For many who desire to rediscover their family history, all they have is what has been passed from generation to generation orally, and, not surprisingly, such stories are often conflicting and full of gaps that have to be filled in imaginatively.

Second, Ong argues that the *psychology* of oral cultures uses a different kind of memory system. Memory is not verbatim repetition; memory is thematic and formulaic. For instance, research shows that upon hearing a lengthy epic song just once, Yugoslav singers can repeat hundreds of lines, but no single singer, and no two singers, will ever sing the song in precisely the same way. Every singing is a different version of the epic. Yet the general story varies little from telling to telling, although the specific words that are used in the telling do differ. Hearing a new song, epic singers break it down and memorize the themes of the song. They then verbalize it in the formulas they have in their own stock of epic stories. Different epic singers become known for different phrases and ways of telling stories. The epic singers use certain aids to recall particular songs, such as strong visual imagery and mnemonic devices.

Third, in oral cultures, *performance* is more important than author-ship, according to Ong. Every time a work is performed, it is reshaped by the performer and provides a new model for future performances. The notion of composition as fixing the form and sense of a message in an original act of creation does not exist in oral cultures. Instead, those with the best memories and those elders who have become the repository of knowledge are likely to be the most respected members of the culture. There are no authors in an oral culture; there are only performances.

Oral cultures are likely to be relatively homogeneous with respect to their knowledge and social norms. A relatively small number of people are likely to possess and control the knowledge of and stories about the culture, as well as their distribution. Power is concentrated in these few people.

At the same time, oral culture tends to be very public and shared across generations. Education or learning involves a lot of demon-stration and participation on the part of the student and less attention to abstract principles and logics. Hence the world of children is less segregated from the world of adults. Children absorb the knowledge they will need during public rituals and public discussions. Notions of privacy and individuality are less important than a commitment to the social whole.

Social relations and social norms have to be more rigorously policed in face-to-face situations because there can be no recourse to some fixed text of rules or standards of conduct. It is the same with the very meaning of words and stories; meanings are always defined for the particular performance rather than in universal terms (i.e., there can be no dictionary).

For Ong (1982), oral culture represents a more personal and socially involved form of communication and consequently form of life. People rely on one another and operate collectively for the social good. At the same time, oral culture is rigid and extremely hierarchical, intolerant of differences and disagreements, and harsh on those who challenge or deviate from the social norm. Oral culture is resistant to radical change, though it does incrementally change over time as stories pass from generation to generation.

## Writing Culture

The consequences of written forms of communication are quite extensive. The Canadian economist and communication historian Harold Innis (1950, 1951), for example, describes how written communication allowed societies to persevere through time by creating durable texts which could be handed down and referred to. This allowed for the control of knowledge by central hierarchies (such as a priesthood). But the invention of more transportable media, such as papyrus, allowed for centralized control to expand over a wider area. (See Box 2.1, "The Bias of Communication.") Writing changes the relationship between a communicator and the person with whom he or she is communicating. Audiences now can be remote in time and space, and the communicator can guarantee that the message received is identical with the one sent, without having to rely on the memory of a messenger. This means that a communicator can reach a much wider and disparate audience. To the extent that society was no longer dependent upon face-to-face communication, societies could expand their boundaries to encompass vast spaces and diverse populations. This was, as Innis (1950) argues, the beginning of empire.

---

**BOX 2.1**

**The Bias of Communication**

The following is from Innis (1951):

> A medium of communication has an important influence on the dissemination of knowledge over space and over time and it becomes necessary to study its characteristics in order to appraise its influence in its cultural setting. According to its characteristics it may be better suited to the dissemination of knowledge over time than over space, particularly if the medium is heavy and durable and not suited to transportation, or to the dissemination of knowledge over space than over time, particularly if the medium is light and easily transported. The relative emphasis on time or space will imply a bias of significance to the culture in which it is imbedded.
>
> Immediately we venture on this inquiry we are compelled to recognize the bias of the period in which we work. An interest in the bias of other civilizations may in itself suggest a bias of our own. Our knowledge of other civilizations depends in large part on the character of the media used by each civilization in so far as it is capable of being preserved or of being made accessible by discovery as in the case of the results of archaeological expeditions. Writing on clay and on stone has been preserved more effectively than that on papyrus. Since durable commodities emphasize time and continuity, studies of civilization such as Toynbee's tend to have a bias toward religion and to show a neglect of problems of space, notably administration and law. The bias of modern civilization incidental to the newspaper and the radio will presume a perspective in consideration of civilizations dominated by other media. We can do little more than urge that we must be continually alert to the implications of this bias and perhaps hope that consideration of the implications of other media to various civilizations may enable us to see more clearly the bias of our own. In any case we may become a little more humble as to the characteristics of our civilization. We can perhaps assume that the use of a medium of communication over a long period will to some extent determine the character of knowledge to be communicated and suggest that its pervasive influence will eventually create a civilization in which life and flexibility will become exceedingly difficult to maintain and that the advantages of a new medium will become such as to lead to the emergence of a new civilization. (pp. 33–34)

---

The creation of the phonetic alphabet changed things even more. Walter Ong (1982) argues that the creation of the Greek alphabet (about 720 BCE) changed how the Greeks thought and handled knowledge.

It was now possible both to think abstractly and to create canonical texts, texts that could be used to measure the truth of any specific performance of a story. Writing allows the creators of a story to ensure that it is recorded just as they intend it to be. Thus the function of memory changes from thematic and visual memory to verbatim memory. In fact, Plato argued against writing precisely because it would change the nature of memory and perhaps make people lazy since they would not have to rely on memory as much. At the same time, the existence of writing meant that memory itself could be judged or held accountable to something else (the text or the written word). This is the advent of writing culture.

According to the Canadian media theorist Marshall McLuhan (1964), "It can be argued then, that the phonetic alphabet, alone, is the technology that has been the means of creating 'civilized man' [sic]— the separate individuals equal before a written code of law" (p. 86). In oral cultures, the community is the basic unit of social existence. Individuals within such a community are defined by their place in the ongoing performance of social life. In a writing culture, fixed, written, and permanent rules or codes of law develop. Individuals can appeal to and be held accountable to such codes. At this point, the individual emerges as a unique entity separate from the community. When we can say "Joe says" or "Mary told me," then authorship has created individuality.

The separation of the individual from the community, from society, entails a different conception of space and time. In an oral culture, neither space nor time has much meaning apart from the particular place in which the community lives and the particular moment in time that defines the community's sense of the present. Writing allows for an understanding of both space and time as continua that encompass other groups of people, other places, and other times.

Those who possess the skill of writing and reading, those who are literate, are also powerful. Writing enables knowledge to be hoarded, because knowledge no longer requires public performance. Knowledge is stored in private places out of public sight, and the ability to read and to write the texts of knowledge is itself of value and therefore not widely available. This allows for the development of rigid hierarchies and of formal institutions of power, such as the Church and the state.

## Print Culture

But the revolution that McLuhan grounds in writing was only completed—and at the same time, transformed—with the invention of the printing press and movable type. The ability to mechanically reproduce a text freed writing from its reliance on an elite group of individuals (such as monks in the Middle Ages), and it guaranteed that each copy of the text would be literally identical to every other copy.

A number of consequences follow the invention of the printing press. It took control of writing out of the hands of the Church and the scribes assigned to copying ancient texts. With printing came the possibility of spending time to create new knowledge, new texts, and new interpretations of old texts. Increasingly, this search for knowledge, this ability to compare a variety of texts, to seek out new ideas and interpretations, could not be entirely controlled by any one institution, especially the Church. Thus printing was instrumental in the development of a secular society and a body of writing about nonreligious life. Secular writers challenged the authority of the Church on religious and nonreligious matters in favor of individual conscience. The historian Elizabeth Eisenstein (1978) has persuasively argued that printing and the book were instrumental in the establishment of democracy in the upper middle classes of early modern Europe.

Walter Ong (1982) suggests that with writing, things were not just given but could now be questioned abstractly. Even more, because writing allows backward scanning, one can revise a text, going back and eliminating errors and inconsistencies. Although one can't take back a word once it is uttered, one can look over a text and change written words to ensure the meaning intended. Therefore, Ong argues, with writing comes a mindset that likes exactitude and precision, even in speech. This obsession with precision and exactitude gives rise to dictionaries embodying the desire to legislate the correct use of language.

Printing further reinforced the sense of individuality and privacy. Books, according to Ong, allowed for communication in private, reading by oneself, rather than in public settings. It also created a sense of the private ownership of words. Writing also separates the knower or speaker from what is known, therefore making possible introspection. "Opening the psyche as never before, not only to the external, objective world, [is] quite distinct from itself but also to the interior self against whom the objective world is set," Ong wrote (p. 14). With printing, sight rather than hearing begins to dominate consciousness.

Printing enabled the emergence of the newspaper and novel. Although these forms of communication cannot be explained solely on the basis of the technology of printing (many other economic, social, and historical developments contributed to their emergence), it is fair to say that they could not have come into existence without the invention of printing technology. The merger of the printing press and movable type made texts cheaper, because it cost far less to make a second copy of a text than to write and produce the first copy. Affordable reading material helped to spread literacy.

Raymond Williams (1965) has pointed out the ironic consequences of this spread of literacy in the seventeenth through nineteenth centuries. For example, the working class was taught to read so that they could read the Bible as well as manuals for the new industrial machinery, but it was difficult to control what a literate audience consumed. Workers often read political tracts and newspapers, which contributed to the growing political gap between the classes of workers and capitalists of the Industrial Revolution. This helped create new political forms of organization and power, such as political parties and democratic governments.

Historian Robert Darnton (1995a, 1995b) found in an exhaustive survey of clandestine literature published in the conjuncture leading up to the French Revolution that such literature fell into two major categories—radical antistate and antichurch works, to be sure, but about *half* was pornography. Official suppression of both categories led to increasing resentment among the literate classes, and censoring the latter, Darnton argues, was as important in fomenting revolution as the former.

Marshall McLuhan (1964) makes another claim for the impact of printing technology: Printing altered the very structure of human consciousness and thought. According to McLuhan, the physical relationship between the reader's eyes and the text comes to define a linear mode of thinking. Just as eyes move across the page, line after line, in a rigorous and necessary way, so too does one begin to think in a similarly rigorous, linear fashion, one idea logically connected to the next.

The result of such linear modes of thought is a different conception of time and space. It is in the age of printing that European powers explored and colonized the world, spreading their culture, their politics, and their religions across the globe. Time becomes a linear vector moving toward an indefinite future defined as progress. The belief in progress reinforced the drive for knowledge and discovery that printing had opened up. What followed was the age of scientific discovery.

## Electronic Culture

When we think about electronic media, we are likely to think about radio, television, movies, and computers. But to understand these developments, we need to go back to the emergence of the telegraph in the nineteenth century. The telegraph had at least two important consequences: It reorganized people's perception of space and time, and it allowed for new kinds of organizational control. The telegraph enabled the almost instantaneous transmission of messages across space, and it fostered a rational organization of time. The need to coordinate the measurement of time around the globe gave rise to the establishment of standard time zones and the fixing of Greenwich Mean Time as the norm defining the correct time at any place in the world.

According to James W. Carey (1989),

> The simplest and most important point about the telegraph is that it marked the decisive separation of "transportation" and "communication." Until the telegraph, these words were synonymous. The telegraph ended that identity and allowed symbols to move independently of geography and independently of and faster than transport.... The great theoretical significance of the technology lay not merely in the separation but also in the use of the telegraph as both a model of and a mechanism for control of the physical movement of things, specifically for the railroad. That is the fundamental discovery: not only can information move independently of and faster than physical entities, but it can also be a simulation of and control mechanism for what has been left behind. (pp. 213, 215)

The telegraph merely began a process that has continued to this day at an ever-increasing rate. Whatever one's opinions about the shape of the modern world, it is fair to say that the new electronic means of communication have revolutionized not only how people communicate, but how they live as well. If written media centralized and made knowledge hierarchical, and then the printing press began a process of dispersion and democratization of knowledge, then the electronic media have drastically accelerated both of these trends.

If printing enabled the transmission of messages across time, their ability to cross space was still severely limited. Although a ruler could now send a message to the far reaches of his or her empire and be fairly certain of the accuracy of the transmission, the process relied on the physical transportation of the written message. Even books that could be sent around the world, creating a single audience for an identical text, required the physical movement of the book as an object. But with the advent of electronic means of communication, instantaneous transportation of messages around the globe became a reality. A new form of empire, expanded across space, becomes possible, according to Innis (1950).

When information is beamed through the airwaves or through wires and cable, it becomes far more difficult to regulate and control access to it; many commentators have noted that the dissolution of the Warsaw Pact and the breakup of the Soviet Union were accelerated by the porosity of their borders to democratic messages from the West made available through the electronic media.

Furthermore, if print individualized and privatized what had been an essentially public oral culture, the effects of the electronic media have been both to reinforce the sense of individuality and privacy and to create new forms of what McLuhan (1964) has called the "global village."

Like books, the electronic media have become, over time, personal, mobile, and private. People no longer have to sit in large theater palaces or even in living rooms to watch movies or television programs; miniaturization allows them to carry music and television and computer networks in the palms of their hands. Furthermore, like books, the electronic media have developed in two directions simultaneously: They have created larger audiences for particular messages (the Bible and network television), and they have created highly selective audience segments organized around particular tastes, from philosophical books to the Home Shopping Network to thousands of Web sites on the Internet.

Thus, as J. W. Carey (1989) argues, the electronic media have radically transformed our awareness and conception of both time and space. Space now can be measured in temporal terms: by the time it takes to transmit a fax, a television image, a computer file. Space no longer appears to be an obstacle in the organization of social, political, and economic relationships.

Time, too, has changed in people's understanding. The invention of computers has speeded up this process, leading to the introduction of almost infinitely small divisions. Can anyone imagine how short a nanosecond is? Time has become increasingly fractured and discontinuous. Printing challenged the stability and continuity of oral culture and created a commitment to change and progress; time in print culture was understood as continual, linking the past with the present. The electronic media seem to create real gaps between generations, and the time span of generational differences seems to get smaller and smaller even as the gaps become more and more pronounced.

There is a significant debate about the consequences of electronic communication for the exercise of control and power in the modern world. Some have suggested that the result of these technologies is the centralization of information and power; others argue that a countervailing tendency of the electronic media is to disperse and decentralize the control of information and power. The proliferation of regional television production centers (for example, Brazil and Mexico are major production centers for Portuguese and Spanish programming) and film production centers (such as Hong Kong and India) are examples of the diffusion or decentralization of power. Yet there has also been a reconcentration of power. The concentration of global film and television companies in a handful of corporations is a countervailing force to regional film and television production centers.

It is clear that with the electronic media, for the first time in history, the vast majority of the world's population can now participate in the dominant cultural forms and practices. There is some debate about whether the electronic media require literacy, whether the new media have introduced new forms of literacy, or whether they are creating an illiterate population. However, as Walter Benjamin (1969) argued in the 1930s, the incorporation of the masses into the cultural arena as both consumers and potential producers of cultural products is a revolution. The effects of this are not well understood.

Some observers of the contemporary world have argued that the electronic media are transforming basic modes of awareness and thinking. If oral cultures are largely aural, emphasizing hearing and sound, and if print cultures are largely visual, emphasizing sight and the ability to read, then the new electronic cultures are multisensorial, requiring a constant monitoring and coordinating of a wide range of sensory experience and information. Moreover, although it is difficult to know how to describe the formal properties of today's electronic media products, one thing is clear: They are rarely linear in their logic

45

and narrative form. The linear conventions of both time and space are constantly violated and played with, and the traditional logic of rationality seems irrelevant. And the impact of these technologies on the evolution of human existence is not at all clear. We are simply too close to the historical emergence of these technologies.

## Criticisms of Technological Determinism

Before we move on to the second narrative, we need to address an assumption that underlies some versions of the previous one: technological determinism. These grand narratives that lead from oral to electronic culture offer important insights about the role of communication in human culture, but they can be criticized as examples of theories of technological determinism. Technological determinism is the belief that technology is the principal, if not only, cause of historical change. Whether theories of technological determinism are optimistic or pessimistic about the present and the future, they assume that history is guaranteed in advance. Their proponents assume that the future is the result of the necessary and inevitable unfolding of the consequences of the past and present. Such theorists fail to adequately consider the ways in which people make history. When talking about the context of media power, one needs to recognize that the context is not stable and fixed; it is in fact constantly changing over and through time. Any discussion of media power must take history into account, both in the sense that the media themselves change through history and in the sense that the media's place and power in society are constantly changing.

It is perhaps easiest to identify technological determinism in the writings of Marshall McLuhan (1964; McLuhan & Fiore, 1967), who assumed that people's normal use of technology necessarily modifies their consciousness. McLuhan argued that the forms of communication technology (oral, print, electronic) available to people at a particular historical moment determine the ways in which they can perceive reality and the logics they use to understand it. To McLuhan, the content of the media, the actual messages, are irrelevant. This is the meaning of his aphorism, "The medium is the message."

McLuhan's theory clearly assumes that technology determines everything else in history and, moreover, that communication technology is the crucial invention for humankind. McLuhan's is only one version of the common view that places the burden of historical change on

46

the shoulders of communication technology. It is important to realize that on a smaller scale, many people make a similar assumption when they think about and often criticize "what television has done to society" or "how computers are changing the nature of work, social relations, and ways of thinking."

In his book *Television: Technology and Cultural Form,* Raymond Williams (1975/1992) offers a general critique of technological determinism. Williams argues that all of the versions of determinism assume that technological invention is accidental and that it is the result of "an internal process of research and development" (p. 7); but, he argues, these assumptions are both false. Communications technologies have always been sought in the context of solving particular social needs. These needs were often military and political, not economic and cultural. For instance, radio communication was first used by the Navy for ship-to-shore communication, and only later was it exploited for commercial purposes. Thus Williams argues that we need to restore human motivation and intention into our understanding of how technologies are created and their role in history. Technologies are used in direct response to perceived social needs and problems. They are not merely symptoms but are intentional attempts at solutions. In this way, Williams attempts to recognize the complexity of the relationships among media, their contexts, and the production of history. (See Box 2.2, "A Social History of Television as a Technology.")

---

**BOX 2.2**

**A Social History of Television as a Technology**

The following is from Williams (1975/1992):

> The invention of television was no single event or series of events. It depended on a complex of inventions and developments in electricity, telegraphy, photography, and motion pictures and radio. It can be said to have separated out as a specific technological objective in the period 1875–1890, and then, after a lag, to have developed as a specific technological enterprise from 1920 through to the first public television systems of the 1930s. Yet in each of these stages it depended for parts of its realization on inventions made with other ends primarily in view.

*(Continued)*

---

(Continued)

Until the early nineteenth century, investigations of electricity, which had long been known as a phenomenon, were primarily philosophical: investigations of a puzzling natural effect. The technology associated with these investigations was mainly directed towards isolation and concentration of the effect, for its clearer study. Towards the end of the eighteenth century there began to be applications, characteristically in relation to other known natural effects (lightning conductors). But there is then a key transitional period in a cluster of inventions between 1800 and 1831, ranging from Volta's battery to Faraday's demonstration of electro-magnetic induction, leading quickly to the production of generators. This can be properly traced as a scientific history, but it is significant that the key period of advance coincides with an important stage of the development of industrial production. The advantages of electric power were closely related to new industrial needs: for mobility and transfer in the location of power sources, and for flexible and rapid controllable conversion. The steam engine had been well suited to textiles, and its industries had been based on local siting. A more extensive development, both physically and in the complexity of multiple-part processes, such as engineering, could be attempted with other power sources but could only be fully realized with electricity. There was a very complex interaction between new needs and new inventions, at the level of primary production, of new applied industries (plating) and of new social needs which were themselves related to industrial development (city and house lighting). From 1830 to large-scale generation in the 1880s there was this continuing complex of need and invention and application.

In telegraphy the development was simpler. The transmission of messages by beacons and similar primary devices had been long established. In the development of navigation and naval warfare the flag-system had been standardized in the course of the sixteenth and seventeenth centuries. During the Napoleonic wars there was a marked development of land telegraphy, by semaphore stations, and some of this survived into peacetime. Electrical telegraphy had been suggested as a technical system as early as 1753, and was actually demonstrated in several places in the early nineteenth century. An English inventor in 1816 was told that the Admiralty was not interested. It is interesting that it was the development of the railways, themselves a response to the development of an industrial system and the related growth of cities, which clarified the need for improved telegraphy. A complex of technical possibilities was brought to a working system from 1837 onwards. The development of international trade and transport brought rapid extensions of the system, including the transatlantic cable in the 1850s and the 1860s. A general system of electric telegraphy had been established by the 1870s, and in the same decade the telephone system began to be developed, in this case as a new and intended invention.

In photography, the idea of light-writing had been suggested by (among others) Wedgwood and Davy in 1802, and the *camera obscura* had already been developed. It was not the projection but the fixing of images which at first awaited technical solution, and from 1816 (Niepce) and through to 1839 (Daguerre) this was worked on, together with the improvement of camera devices. Professional and then amateur photography spread rapidly, and reproduction and then transmission, in the developing newspaper press, were achieved. By the 1880s the idea of a 'photographed reality'—still more for record than for observation—was familiar.

The idea of moving pictures had been similarly developing. The magic lantern (slide projection) had been known from the seventeenth century, and had acquired simple motion (one slide over another) by 1736. From at latest 1826 there was a development of mechanical motion-picture devices, such as the wheel-of-life, and these came to be linked with the magic lantern. The effect of persistence in human vision—that is to say, our capacity to hold the 'memory' of an image through an interval to the next image, thus allowing the possibility of a sequence built from rapidly succeeding units—had been known since classical times. Series of cameras photographing stages of a sequence were followed (Marey, 1882) by multiple-shot cameras. Friese-Greene and Edison worked on techniques for filming and projection, and celluloid was substituted for paper reels. By the 1890s the first public motion-picture shows were being given in France, America and England.

Television, as an idea, was involved in many of these developments. It is difficult to separate it, in its earliest stages, from photo-telegraphy. Bain proposed a device for transmitting pictures by electric wires in 1842; Bakewell in 1847 showed the copying telegraph; Caselli in 1862 transmitted pictures by wire over a considerable distance. In 1873, while working at a terminal of the Atlantic telegraph cable, May observed the light-sensitive properties of selenium (which had been isolated by Berzelius in 1817 and was in use for resistors). In a host of ways, following an already defined need, the means of transmitting still pictures and moving pictures were actively sought and to a considerable extent discovered. The list is long even when selective: Carey's electric eye in 1875; Nipkow's scanning system in 1884; Elster and Geitel's photoelectric cells in 1890; Braun's cathode-ray tube in 1897; Rosing's cathode-ray receiver in 1907; Campbell Swinton's electronic camera proposal in 1911. Through this whole period two facts are evident: that a system of television was foreseen, and its means were being actively sought; but also that, by comparison with electrical generation and electrical telegraphy and telephony, there was very little social investment to bring the scattered work together. It is true that there were technical blocks before 1914—the thermionic valve and the multi-stage amplifier can be seen to have been needed and were not yet invented. But the critical difference between the various spheres of applied technology can be stated in terms of a social dimension: the new systems of production and of business or transport communication were already organized, at an economic level; the new

*(Continued)*

(Continued)

systems of social communication were not. Thus when motion pictures were developed, their application was characteristically in the margin of established social forms—the sideshows—until their success was capitalized in a version of an established form, the motion-picture *theatre.*

The development of radio, in its significant scientific and technical stages between 1885 and 1911, was at first conceived, within already effective social systems, as an advanced form of telegraphy. Its application as a significantly new social form belongs to the immediate post-war period, in a changed social situation. It is significant that the hiatus in technical television development then also ended. In 1923 Zworykin introduced the electronic television camera tube. Through the early 1920s Baird and Jenkins, separately and competitively, were working on systems using mechanical scanning. From 1925 the rate of progress was qualitatively changed, through important technical advances but also with the example of sound broadcasting systems as a model. The Bell System in 1927 demonstrated wire transmission through a radio link, and the pre-history of the form can be seen to be ending. There was great rivalry between systems—especially those of mechanical and electronic scanning—and there is still great controversy about contributions and priorities. But this is characteristic of the phase in which the development of a technology moves into the stage of a new social form.

What is interesting throughout is that in a number of complex and related fields, these systems of mobility and transfer in production and communication, whether in mechanical and electric transport, or in telegraphy, photography, motion pictures, radio and television, were at once incentives and responses within a phase of general social transformation. Though some of the crucial scientific and technical discoveries were made by isolated and unsupported individuals, there was a crucial community of selected emphasis and intention, in a society characterized at its most general levels by a mobility and extension of the scale of organization: forms of growth which brought with them immediate and longer-term problems of operative communication. In many different countries, and in apparently unconnected ways, such needs were at once isolated and technically defined. It is especially a characteristic of the communications systems that *all were foreseen— not in utopian but in technical ways—before the crucial components of the developed systems had been discovered and refined.* In no way is this a history of communications systems creating a new society or new social conditions. The decisive and earlier transformation of industrial production, and its new social forms, which had grown out of a long history of capital accumulation and working technical improvements, created new needs but also new possibilities, and the communications systems, down to television, were their intrinsic outcome. (pp. 8–13)

Technological determinism also ignores the active role of people (and social institutions) in making their own lives. It assumes that the use of a technology is prescribed by its own structure, rather than understanding that any technology can be used in any number of different ways and can be restructured according to the demands that different uses may impose. Depending on how people use them, technologies can have very different effects, not only on individuals but on society and history as well. That is, nothing essential to a technology determines its impact on its users. This is not to say that you can do *anything* with a technology. The shape and nature of a technology do not determine, but they can place limits—technological effects are therefore *overdetermined*.

## THEORIES OF THE MASSES

A conjunctural narrative stresses the sociological nature and impact of the media in history. The most influential of these theories focuses on the changing nature of social relationships and cultural products: a theory of mass society and mass culture. There are at least two versions of this theory. One starts with social relationships and moves to culture. The other starts with cultural products and moves to society.

### From Social Relationship to Culture

In the late nineteenth and early twentieth centuries, the emergence and development of the discipline of sociology was largely defined by the *theory of mass society*. Mass society theory held that as a result of various social changes, including industrialization, both the nature of social life and the form of social interaction were fundamentally altered for the worse. The Industrial Revolution had prompted a transformation from a rural, agrarian society in which people knew each other intimately and personally (in German, the *Gemeinschaft*) to an urban, mechanical society in which people did not know their own neighbors except in terms of their professional function (the *Gesellschaft*).

The social importance of the transformation is that, in the *Gesellschaft*, rather than being bound to one another by tradition and custom, mutual regard, and understanding, people now constitute a society *only* by formal, contractual relations. Think about the current popularity of marital and educational contracts. Social relationships are thus anonymous, alienated, and disconnected. The individual in the mass society is isolated and vulnerable to manipulation and coercion. He or she is denied the reinforcing support of primary groups, organized around family, church, work, and community.

The individual becomes part of a mass—undifferentiated, unsupported, and easy prey for authoritarian appeals. Such theories of mass society view culture as having become little more than a tool for manipulating the masses, for providing an artificial sense of security and belongingness, for appealing to people's irrational and lowest desires.

## From Culture to Society

The theory of mass society reappeared in a slightly different form after World War II in the United States, when a wide range of social and cultural critics attempted to define the unique aspects of postwar American society and to differentiate it from the totalitarian societies that had emerged in Germany under Hitler's Nazism and in the Soviet Union under Stalin's communism. Identifying these two societies as mass societies, critics then had to address the question of whether mass culture inevitably produces a totalitarian mass society, because both Hitler and Stalin made important use of the media to create and maintain their power. But because the United States also has a mass culture, could there also be a totalitarian regime here? What is the relationship between a mass culture and a democratic society?

By far, the most popular response to these questions defined American society as fundamentally liberal: Critics argued that the diversity of American culture and the plurality of audiences for a range of cultural products guaranteed America's ability to resist the manipulation of authoritarian appeals. During the 1950s and 1960s, critics attempted to draw distinctions between different sorts of cultural products and between the different audiences to which these products appealed. These distinctions—high culture, mass culture, popular culture, folk culture, middlebrow culture—continue to play an important role in contemporary attitudes about media products. Critics also argued that different audiences responded differently, based on their own cultural background and resources, to the same media messages.

Such distinctions embody particular judgments about forms of culture and their legitimacy. To call something *mass* or *low* culture is to deny it value or prestige; for many years, it was enough to guarantee that such cultural products would not be the subject of serious critical scrutiny. Yet it is important to try to define these terms, as they have been and still continue to be used in public and critical debates.

People often assume that *high culture,* or what we commonly call art, is both spiritually and formally (or aesthetically) more developed than other forms of culture, such as mass, popular, or folk culture. High culture is produced by specially trained professionals and/or uniquely inspired creative individuals. This is the art that is collected, that sells for ever-higher prices, that appears in museums and is performed in concert halls. Within music and the visual arts, high art is defined by very particular formal rules; it is largely the art of the European, White, male, upper and middle classes since the birth of capitalism. It embodies specific values (individuality, the world as a set of objects to be possessed, etc.) that these classes fought to establish. These art forms themselves were often seen as quite revolutionary in their own time and were frequently suppressed and roundly criticized by the cultural elites of the day. Many of these forms, from the waltz to the novel, and many artists we now associate with Arnold's (1869/1960) "best that has been thought and said," from Shakespeare to Beethoven, were initially considered "too popular" or "too radical" and thus denied legitimacy. Yet, over time, as these classes and their values have come to dominate our lives, the art too has come to define the norm of legitimate cultural expression.

*Folk culture* refers to those cultural products and forms that can be traced to a particular community or socially identifiable group. Folk culture is assumed to be an expression of the experiences of this group. Folk artists are not professionals; usually, they are not distinguishable from the rest of the population, and the interaction that occurs between artist and audience is informal, because both artist and audience share a common life. Thus bluegrass has always been seen as folk music, with its roots in Appalachian culture. On the other hand, country music is more problematic, for it is too commercial and too dispersed to be easily seen as folk music. Similarly, for most of the twentieth century, blues was seen as a form of folk music, always traced to its roots in the African American population. On the other hand, rap music, although it certainly started within a certain Black community, would

53

likely not be considered folk music. There are many critics who would defend both high and folk art against what they consider to be mass or popular arts, both because of their broad popularity and their commercial base.

We might take *popular culture* to be that culture which, regardless of where or by whom it is produced, speaks to a large public audience that cannot be simply described by a single social variable, such as class or gender or age. That is, popular culture does not assume anything about the artist. The artist can be formally trained, a professional, or an amateur with little or no formal knowledge of the aesthetic forms he or she is using. Many rock musicians—the late Frank Zappa is one example—have extensive classical conservatory training, whereas others have never learned to read sheet music. The artist may or may not be part of any community. It is irrelevant in the end. Moreover, the audience for popular art is itself diverse and complicated. It is not a community with a shared common set of experiences. It is simply some portion of what might be called "the people." The people are not a class or a gender or a race or anything else; they are made up of different classes, races, genders, ages, and regions.

In some sense, popular culture sees itself in opposition to high art, although it often shares many of the same values. Popular culture is often seen by its fans (perhaps mistakenly, given the economics of popular culture) as working from the bottom up, or as coming from the people and their interests. An enormous amount of exchange takes place between these two bodies of cultural work, popular and high. Pop art makes high culture out of popular icons: In the 1960s, Roy Lichtenstein made art out of comic strips; Andy Warhol made it of Campbell's soup cans. And numerous rock groups have attempted to appropriate techniques of classical music to produce what has come to be called "art rock" (for example, Genesis).

Finally, there is *mass art*. Is mass art something different from popular culture? Many critics will still argue that a distinction needs to be drawn between the two. Popular culture, it is assumed, somehow speaks to people's experience or perhaps, as John Fiske (1989) argues, at least allows people the freedom to interpret the text to fit into their experiences.[1] Mass culture, on the other hand, is assumed to be purely and entirely commercially motivated; it is assumed to come from the top down, given to the people whether they like it or not. It is manipulative, attempting to force its audience to interpret its texts according to the interests of those who have produced it for the masses. This is why critics of mass culture fear that it will inevitably lead to authoritarian political regimes.

Yet it is difficult to sustain these distinctions. Just about all of popular culture (and even folk culture) is commercially produced. And experience has taught us that it is difficult to predict the ways in which cultural products can be interpreted by various segments of the population. Making distinctions between cultural products and giving them different degrees and kinds of legitimacy is itself an expression of political and economic power (Bourdieu, 1984). This conjunctural narrative of media history emphasizes how these ideas of mass and elite culture have developed and changed over a period of decades. Pursuing this narrative further allows the examination of how media and media products were understood at these times and aids reflections on contemporary understandings of media products.

But it is important as well to consider such ideas within the framework of a longer historical time span, from modernity to postmodernity, where we look at, for example, how notions of both elite and mass culture are part of a formation of modernity.

## FROM MODERNITY TO POSTMODERNITY

There is a third grand narrative about the role of communication and culture in history: the description of the passage from modernity to postmodernity. This passage takes place over the course of centuries, making this a narrative of the *longue duree.*

### The Modern

There is vast disagreement over just when the modern era begins— and ends. Some critics mark the beginning of the modern with the end of the Renaissance period in the sixteenth century. Others locate the beginning of the modern with the advent of Enlightenment philosophy in the eighteenth century. Still others distinguish between the Enlightenment and the modern, dating the latter from the mid- or late nineteenth century.

Discussions of the modern are quite dense and difficult, for they entail the relationship among three different concepts or domains:

modernization, modernism, and modernity. In its simplest terms, these can be understood respectively as the historical processes, cultural practices, and social experience of change.

*Modernization* describes the broad spectrum of interrelated historical forces that radically changed the world since the beginning of the Industrial Revolution, capitalism, and colonialism in Europe and America. Thus modernization is more than simply a question of industrialization, of the changing modes and relations of production. It includes as well new economic relations of distribution and consumption and new commodity markets. It includes new technologies and scientific developments, some of which contributed to changes in the patterns of social migration both within countries (urbanization) and across nations (diasporas). And it includes political (democratization, the modern nation-state, imperialism) and cultural events (public education and museums), as well as changes in the relations between them. For instance, Antonio Gramsci (1971) argued that, with modernization, ideological consensus, rather than force, began to play a central role in the legitimation of power. And Michel Foucault (1977) argued that modernization brought new forms of power—normalization, disciplinarity, governmentality, and biopolitics—through which governments increasingly attempted to regulate the population by making people the object of knowledge and producing subjects who were responsible for policing themselves according to the norms of power.

*Modernism* refers to the cultural forms, discourses, practices, and relations—both elite and popular, both commercial and folk—with which people attempted to make sense of, represent, judge, rail against, surrender to, intervene into, navigate through, or escape from the new worlds of modernization. These cultural practices and products were themselves shaped by the new forms of leisure and communications technology put into place by processes of modernization. That is, modernism usually refers to the cultural developments that began in the sixteenth and seventeenth centuries. And yet modernism is more often used to refer to cultural developments of the late nineteenth century, which fully expressed in a variety of ways the pressures and consequences of modernization. It indexes all of the developments in art, beginning with the emergence of Impressionism and ending with Abstract Expressionism (Picasso, Gauguin, Duchamps, Renoir, Kandinsky, Klee, Georgia O'Keefe). It included developments in literature, from the Bloomsbury group of writers in England such as Virginia

56

Woolf to self-conscious forms of writing offered by Gertrude Stein, T. S. Eliot, Luigi Pirandello, Samuel Beckett, and James Joyce. It includes as well the architectural innovations of Louis Sullivan, Frank Lloyd Wright, and Mies van der Rohe. Modernism also has to include the new forms of mass media and popular culture—the dime novel, the Hollywood film, jazz, and the radio soap opera.

*Modernity* refers to the changing structure and nature of the lived social realities to which modernism and modernization responded and which were themselves shaped by both modernism and modernization. This is obviously an ambiguous and difficult concept to specify. It attempts to describe what it felt like to live in the new modern world, a world that attempted to break away from the customs, norms, and traditions of earlier generations. According to philosopher Marshall Berman (1982),

> To be modern is to find ourselves in an environment that promises us adventure, power, joy, growth, transformation of ourselves and the world—and, at the same time, that threatens to destroy everything we have, everything we know, everything we are. (p. 15)

As Karl Marx and Friedrich Engels (1967) put it, in modernity, "All that is solid melts into air" (p. 83). Marx was suggesting that modernity is the experience of constant change, flux, or transformation; the search for the new; the turning away from tradition. Modernity is not just the fact of the development and change, but the yearning for change. Modernity involves the recognition that change cannot be stopped and that if one stops to rest, the world will pass you by or you will be swept away by these changes.

Many different intellectual traditions of the twentieth century can be seen as responding to the perceived historical rupture that was signaled in different forms in a vision of the modern. The modern in every instance always implies this rupture, an alienation from some past that served critics both as a measure of the change and a norm against which to judge the changes. Sometimes, that past was defined by an image of community, of face-to-face communication, of pure art unsullied by the media and commercial interests, of traditional forms of value, rationality, and social relations. Think about how common it is for people who argue about the past to harken back to an idyllic time when "things were better," when life was simpler, when people were happier. Thus the modern is defined on the one hand by the relations between modernization, modernity, and modernism. But, on the other hand, it is also defined by its opposition to the old, to tradition, to the past.

## The Postmodern

Recently, some cultural and media critics have argued that another rupture in history has taken place sometime since the end of World War II, probably since the 1970s. Such critics argue that we are now living in a postmodern age.

Capitalism has changed. Transnational corporations, accountable to no nation-state or political ideology, have created not only global markets for goods and services but also global networks of production. New computer technologies have been applied to every stage of the economic process (such as manufacturing, financing, distribution, and exchange) resulting in decentralization and automation; markets and labor processes have been reorganized (emphasizing a multiskilled, involved labor force); unions have declined, with increases in subcontracting and part-time labor; economies of scope have risen (consumption-driven small-batch production runs with high levels of product differentiation) to replace economies of scale.

If modernity is about mass production, mass culture, everything mass, then postmodernity is about returning to the small and the flexible (flexible specialization of labor, flexible production). If capitalism in modernity is committed to maximizing profit by producing more for less and then attempting to persuade consumers to buy the products, capitalism in postmodernity is committed to maximizing profit by developing systems of production and distribution that can respond quickly to the different demands of smaller groups of consumers (obviously such demands may still be shaped by advertising). If modernity focuses on people as laborers, consumers, and family members, then postmodernity constructs and celebrates identities as multiple, fragmented subjects defined entirely by consumer and lifestyle choices.

In postmodernity, there is no human activity that is free from capitalism, commodification, and the profit motive. No space in people's everyday life remains outside these economic processes. This is most apparent in the case of culture and communication, which have become totally commercialized. The result is that "no society, indeed, has ever been saturated with signs and messages like this one," according to the American literary critic Fredric Jameson (1992, p. 22). This "omnipresence of culture" has important consequences for the experience of postmodernity.

Another mark of postmodernity is the increasing mobility, both voluntary and forced, of human populations around the world. The migration of whole societies, the problem of refugees, the incorporation of migrant workers, have created a global, multicultural society that challenges the ability of any nation to define a reasonably homogeneous cultural identity or a set of cultural norms. The case of the failure of America's "melting pot" image is a telling example. Although the United States has always been a nation of immigrants, it managed, at least until World War II, to maintain a sense of itself as a whole, a European-derived, English-speaking nation. But new migrations— Asian, African, and Latino—have challenged this image and made it almost impossible to define a central cultural identity for the nation. Moreover, the American experience has become the norm in other parts of the world as well. People's identities have become fractured, pluralized, and hybridized, and populations that were silent and marginalized in the past have suddenly moved to the center of the historical and cultural stage.

The rapid development of new communication technologies, in particular the computer and other information media, is essential to postmodernity. According to the French social philosopher Jean Baudrillard (1988), who echoes McLuhan's (1964; McLuhan & Fiore, 1967) technological determinism, this is the most important factor bringing about the postmodern era.

Postmodernism as a set of cultural practices or a new aesthetic norm was first used in the field of architecture as a challenge to the high modernist form of the urban skyscraper, which typified most of twentieth-century urban building. Jameson (1991) has offered the most commonly used description of postmodernism by describing features that cut across many cultural forms and media.

First is the *disappearance of depth.* By this, Jameson refers to the irrelevance of anything outside of the text, of the normal assumption that cultural texts refer to something else—such as deeper meanings or the expression of an author's intention or the representation of an external reality. In postmodern texts, only surfaces matter, only images are real.

Second is what Jameson describes as *pastiche,* which refers to the absence of any normative rules and definitions of coherent styles and forms. Perhaps the easiest examples to illustrate this are buildings by such postmodern architects as Philip Johnson and Michael Graves. Both of these architects combine elements from a wide range of historical architectural styles, from Greek arches to Gothic spires and modern glass walls, in one structure.

Third, Jameson points to the *schizophrenic* character of postmodernist works; such texts are frequently fragmented, both formally and temporally. Characters themselves are often inconsistent and seem utterly incapable of unifying past, present, and future into coherent stories, and authors seem unwilling to create coherent narratives.

Fourth, both history and the sense of history have been reduced to an experience of *nostalgia,* a romanticized longing for the past. The attempt to appropriate a missing past comes increasingly to resemble a search for a lost fashion, according to Jameson.

Last, and perhaps most controversially, is what Jameson calls the *postmodern sublime.* By this, he refers to that experience which cannot be represented in contemporary cultural codes. For Jameson, this unrepresentable dimension is the inability to construct maps of the contemporary spaces of everyday life within capitalism. As the world is changing so rapidly, under the influence of global, multinational capitalism and decentered communication networks, it has become more and more difficult to locate oneself within the system of social relationships and political geography. Jameson thinks that people need "cognitive maps" of the space of their social lives, where they fit in some idealized social structure. But these cognitive maps are ever harder and harder to maintain or even construct. If you have ever walked into a postmodern building, perhaps you can better understand this idea. One of the most common reactions to such buildings is that people often find it difficult to navigate—they can't quite figure out how to get from the lobby to their room, or from their room back to the lobby. Oddly enough, having made the trip once does not seem to make it any easier the second time.

Other critics have described the postmodern sublime in different terms. Perhaps the most important of these, and perhaps the most powerful description of the nature of the experience of postmodernity, is given in the work of Jean Baudrillard (1983b) and, in particular, in his notion of the *simulacrum.* According to Baudrillard, in the postmodern world, the difference between an image (or code) and reality is no longer important. In fact, if anything, reality is measured against images rather than images against reality. Consider the image of a Boston sports bar on the television show *Cheers*. When the network wanted to go to such a bar during the World Series to interview local fans, what they ended up doing was going to the set of *Cheers* and interviewing the cast. Baudrillard would view this as perfectly reasonable and sensible in the postmodern age. How many times has someone seen a movie and said to him- or herself, *Didn't I read about this, or hear about this on the news, sometime in the past?* And then a few months later, they read about it or see it on the news and say to themselves, *Didn't I see this in a movie?* Baudrillard's point is that as the ability to distinguish reality from its images disappears, so does the difference between them.[2]

Consider Baudrillard's description of Disneyland:

> Disneyland is there to conceal the fact that it is the "real" country, all of "real" America, which is Disneyland (just as prisons are there to conceal the fact that it is the social in its entirety, in its banal omnipresence, which is carceral). Disneyland is presented as imaginary in order to make us believe that the rest is real when in fact all of Los Angeles and the America surrounding it are no longer real, but of the order of the hyperreal and of simulation. It is no longer a question of a false representation of reality (ideology), but of concealing the fact that the real is no longer real and thus of saving the reality principle. (1983b, p. 25)

Finally, Baudrillard (1983a), drawing on McLuhan (1964), argues that this historical transformation has significant implications for the very nature of media and the possibilities of communication:

> In short, the medium is the message signifies not only the end of the message, but also the end of the medium. There are no longer media in the literal sense of the term (I am talking above all about the electronic mass media)—that is to say, a power mediating between one reality and another, between one state of the real and another— neither in content nor in form. (p. 102)

Baudrillard's version of postmodernity depends on the power of the computer and other new information technologies to erase the distinction between the virtual and the real worlds. As a result, his theory of postmodernity is open to the charge of technological determinism. Other postmodernist visions, although not determinist, do tend to portray the future in rather apocalyptic and cataclysmic terms.

The problem with the narrative of the modern and the postmodern, and indeed the problem with any grand narrative that attempts to describe the world and its history on such a scale, is that it tends to assume that its descriptions are universal in character and that they are shared by everyone. This narrative assumes that everyone now living shares the experience of postmodernity, but this is not so. Modernity and postmodernity are relevant particularly to industrialized western nations and do not necessarily describe life in other places. Also, between industrialized nations, such notions vary: Japanese modernity and postmodernity (if these terms can even apply in the context of Japan) are different from that of the United States or Europe, for example. Also, even within a nation, different populations may have different experiences of the same events and spaces. For example, though the business traveler or tourist may get confused on the way from the lobby to his or her room in a postmodern hotel, the cleaning staff may suffer from no such confusion (indeed, they cannot if they expect to get their jobs done). In short, what narratives of the *longue duree* lack are the specificities of social forces that we get with narratives on the level of the conjuncture.

## CONCLUSION

These narratives of media history offer insights into the role of the forms and modes of communication in human history. As we discuss the power and influence of today's media on modern life, we should keep these narratives in mind because debates about the power of the media are often debates about the future—about the futures we fear and the futures we desire. Every new form of communication has given rise to both optimistic and pessimistic visions of the future. The conclusions often depend upon conflicting definitions of what is important and what is trivial about the media, about what is fundamentally reshaping social life and what is a passing fad. We need to keep in mind then the relative scale of the changes that are occurring (from daily events to epochal transformations) and the different stories of power that are told in different narratives. We also need to recognize that stories of future fear and future desire are often rooted in the stories we tell of our past.

## NOTES

1. Indeed, Fiske (1989) makes the distinction that popular culture is culture that people themselves make (which encompasses what we have called folk culture). He contrasts this with mass culture, which consists of the mass-manufactured products distributed to markets. One way of thinking about popular culture is that it is not the mass culture product, but what people do with it. For example, popular culture is not an episode of *Alias*, but it would be *Alias*-watching parties, fan fiction based on the world of the series, and also practices of everyday life in which people draw on the characters and references to the show. This is obviously a different use of the terms than we have followed in this chapter.

2. Baudrillard (1983b) argues that there have been three stages of human history. He describes each stage by the nature of the assumed relationship between the image and reality. In the first stage, the image was seen as a counterfeit, as the approximation of a world whose truth always remained outside of the image. Thus there was assumed to be a natural truth—the law of god, for example—which images could only dimly copy. In the second stage, the image was taken to be the source of reality. Language produces reality, in much the way that we have described it in this text. But in the third, postmodern stage, neither term—language or reality—can be privileged, and the difference between them has disappeared or, in Baudrillard's terms, *imploded*. This is the simulacrum: the model against which both reality and its image are judged. The simulacrum is a model, like the genetic code.

## SUGGESTED READINGS

Adorno, T. W. (1990). *The culture industry: Selected essays on mass culture* (Ed. J. M. Bernstein). London: Routledge.

Berman, M. (1988). *All that is solid melts into air: The experience of modernity.* New York: Penguin.

Eisenstein, E. L. (1978). *The printing press as an agent of change* (2 Vols.). New York: Cambridge University Press.

Innis, H. A. (1950). *Empire and communications.* New York: Oxford University Press.

Jameson, F. (1991). *Postmodernism or the cultural logic of late capitalism.* Durham, NC: Duke University Press.

McLuhan, M. (1964). *Understanding media: The extensions of man.* New York: McGraw-Hill.

Ong, W. (1982). *Orality and literacy: The technologizing of the word.* New York: Methuen.

Williams, R. (1958). *Culture and society 1780–1950.* New York: Harper & Row.

# Media People and Organizations | 3

Nothing could be more important in understanding the processes of making media than understanding *who makes the media* and *how the media are "made"*—the rules, practices, and procedures that govern what we see, read, and hear.

## MEDIAMAKING AND LEVELS OF ANALYSIS

A key to understanding who makes the media is the idea of levels of analysis. By this, we mean that production of just about anything in an organized society involves phenomena at different strata, and at each of those strata or levels, variations are reflected in what is produced. As we ascend a "ladder of abstraction," we can think of media products as the creations of individual people, of media organizations, or of media industries. Furthermore, the media together constitute an institution, and the ultimate shape of media is influenced by the interaction of the media institution with other social institutions. Finally, media are influenced by the culture in which they are produced: American media, for example, are similar to the media of other industrial countries, but there are important differences between U.S. media and those elsewhere. Understanding who makes the media, then, prompts us to ask different sorts of questions, and get different answers, at several different levels of analysis—the individual, the organizational, the industrial, the institutional, and the cultural.

## Media People

More than a million people are directly engaged in the creation of media in the United States. Some—Sheryl Crow, Jon Stewart, or David Letterman, for example—are well known and instantly recognizable, and they impart a particular flavor or spin to their products: A Sheryl Crow song covered by someone else isn't the same song; *The Daily Show* with Jon Stewart is recognizably different than *The Daily Show* with Craig Kilborn. What makes them different are individual differences among their creators: differences in talent, creativity, energy, and a host of other "individual difference" variables—the interests, values, gender, and ethnicities of the individuals creating them. Sometimes, in fact, even in very complex media organizations, the persona of the star becomes virtually identified with the product itself: For example, though the title of his show is *Late Show With David Letterman*, the show is popularly referred to either as "David Letterman" or just "Letterman" (as in, "I saw Green Day on Letterman last night").

## Media Organizations

However, *The Tonight Show*, starring Johnny Carson or Jay Leno, isn't just Johnny or Jay. Although Johnny or Jay (or David Letterman, Conan O'Brien, or Jon Stewart) is each obviously the linchpin of his program, these late night talk shows would not go on without a hundred other people in different roles to get the show on the air. In addition to the star, we need an announcer, a bandleader and band, a producer and director, three or more camera operators, lighting and audio personnel, makeup artists, joke writers, researchers, gaffers (electricians), interns, receptionists, custodians, and so on, not to mention the guests. Each performs a particular and essential role, and some clearly have more influence on the particular look or sound of the product than others. Moreover, *The Tonight Show Starring Jay Leno* is not just the product of these people *as individuals;* it is the product of an organization. The fact that media products are almost all created by complex organizations is important for several reasons. First, when something is the creation of a single individual (for example, Stephen King), he or she has virtually total control over its creation and the shape the product takes. When products, however, are the creatures of organizations, "authorship" becomes more complicated, and interesting questions about creativity, control, and coordination of production can be asked.

And, as we note below, we actually know quite a lot about rules and regularities that govern the processes of media created by organizations. In *The Tonight Show* case, several organizations are necessary to get that program on the air—starting with its production company and the NBC Television network (a corporate division of the General Electric Company, Inc. [GE]). The show is piped into homes via a local television station and possibly a cable television organization as well (and the local TV station and cable company are likely owned by larger media chains). Some of these organizations have a great deal of control over both the overall shape of the program and what is on any particular program, and some have almost none. Equally important, organizations are bureaucracies, which means that they are hierarchically structured so that some people are superiors and others are inferiors; that they are governed by rules and routines that must be followed by all individuals; and that they strive for efficiency. We cannot account for how a particular program takes exactly the shape it does, even a particular Wednesday night *Tonight Show* episode, just by knowing all there is to know about the people preparing it. Characteristics of the organization, and of organizations in general, also help explain that. Put another way, a particular Wednesday night episode would be quite similar, although not exactly the same, regardless of whether the host was Leno or someone else, whether the first guest was Jennifer Lopez, Denzel Washington, or Lindsay Lohan.

## Media Industries

Still a third layer must be described to begin to talk about how the media product takes the shape it does. At the *industrial* level, we would note that certain elements characterize the products of an industry, regardless of the people *and* the organizations within the industry. We all have expectations about what a newspaper looks like, what it contains, that are different from our expectations about a book, magazine, or television show. The differences are in content, style, and form, and they flow from the different expectations, practices, and routines that the makers of media products in each industry must follow; the differences also flow from cultural forms.

Each media industry, too, is characterized by different *genres* of product (see Chapters 5 and 6) that make the production of content predictable for both its producers and consumers. In the television industry, for example, we all have a very good idea what the "typical" television evening news program is like: *Channel 7 Eyewitness News* looks remarkably similar, whether we are watching Channel 7 in New York, Boise, or Sacramento. It will open with a teaser of the top few stories and a brief tape clip, and after a commercial break, it will feature half a dozen hard-news stories, all or almost all with tape; none of the stories will be longer than 90 seconds. There will be a male and a female anchor (the male will be older than the female), a weather person, and a sports anchor. One or two will be members of a minority group. Weather will be after the midprogram commercial break, and sports after the next break, and the "news team" will send us off with a "feel good" feature. The form is set and so familiar that we rarely notice it, much less stop to ask *why*.

A large part of the answer to why TV programs are so similar is that there are industrywide constraints—unwritten "rules" that characterize what TV is. Note that these rules are not chiseled in stone: They are not inherent in the medium itself, but evolve from complex interactions over time. They maintain themselves because they are familiar, taken for granted, and usually unquestioned, by both those in the industry and the audience. The format allows for a degree of predictability that is an important characteristic of the mass media, both for the audience and the producers. Even with a new medium such as the World Wide Web, there is pressure for content to look like it does on old media because these are comfortable and expected. For example, the online version of *The New York Times* still looks like a newspaper; in fact, the site gives you the option to view the news exactly as it is laid out in the print version of the newspaper.

New media are complex organizations, but can be complex in different ways from traditional media. Indeed, the Internet has allowed a great diversity of content to be made available, but much of this was not produced within the hierarchical, corporate organizations that shaped the mass media a decade ago. A different set of personnel is involved, including computer programmers and Web page designers, though with the technology now available many of these tasks can be carried out by a single person.

## Media as Institutions

There are two points we would like to make about the media as institutions. One is that it is often argued that the media constitute an institution in their own right; that despite their differences there are enough commonalities in what they do for people to be comfortable making statements like, "The media are . . . ." However, such statements are usually generalities that reveal more about the assumptions of the speaker about what the media are than about what actually is going on. The speaker might be speaking only about news organizations, or television, or corporate media.

The second point is that what media are—the roles and functions they fulfill, what they say—is shaped or constrained by the relationships that the media institution has with other institutions. When we get to this level of analysis, however, we usually can only infer institutional influence from interpreting the real behaviors of individuals or organizations representing those institutions—by doing history, as we describe in Chapter 2. We will discuss the relationship of media to other institutions later in this chapter. This is the level of analysis that looks at how the media in general influence and are influenced by institutions of government, religion, medicine, and so on.

## Media and Culture

At the "highest" level of analysis, there are aspects of any culture, above, beyond, and outside its media, that are reflected in media content and form. The media do not reside outside their own society and culture, but are a part of them, both influencing them and being influenced by them in turn.

Probably the easiest way to see this is by using a comparative approach. If culture did *not* affect media, then media would be very similar in every society. TV news, for example, would be pretty much the same in, say, Italy as it is in the United States. But this clearly is not the case; not only is TV news different, but most other media are as well, not necessarily in broad form (even in other languages, we would recognize a Japanese newspaper or magazine as a newspaper or magazine, a Russian news broadcast as a news broadcast) but in other ways—in content, in treatment of content, and even in the assumed relationship that writers have with their audience. (See Box 3.1, "Cultural Differences in Media.")

---

**BOX 3.1**

**Cultural Differences in Media: U.S. and Italian TV News**

An analysis of a week's worth of Italian and American television network newscasts during then-President Reagan's trip to Europe in June 1982 found that news broadcasts in the two nations varied dramatically, both in content and in *representational form.*

In both content and form, the differences are consistent with each nation's culture and institutions. The content of American television paid far more attention to international news and to the nation's chief executive, and slightly more attention to the national executive branch of government, compared to Italian TV news. Italian TV news, on the other hand, paid far more attention than American TV news to political parties and to labor unions (during the week, no American air time at all was given to unions). These differences reflect political reality: The center of national political power in the United States is the president and his administration, whereas in Italy, which has changed administrations slightly more often than once a year since World War II, the political parties and unions are the center of power.

One might have expected American TV news to devote more time to international news because it is an international power with extensive foreign interests and commitments, whereas Italy is not.

Even more interesting are differences in forms of representation. American network news programs tend to be thematic: TV news producers make a concerted effort to link stories together, to provide a common theme to keep audience attention. In the study by American scholar Dan Hallin and Italian researcher Paolo Mancini (Hallin & Mancini, 1985), Italian TV news tended to be disjointed, with one story wholly unrelated to the one preceding or following it. The same held true within stories: American stories tended to be unified by a common theme, and journalists tended to be interpretive; to our eyes, an Italian story would seem to be disconnected, and interpretation was usually left to the sources in the story rather than to the journalist. The unity, or lack of it, could be seen in the way each medium used visual images: In American TV news, the visual image was intimately connected to the spoken text; in Italian TV, the moving image was usually literally background. The two also varied in their use of "the common man": In their study period, Hallin and Mancini found that one third of the people appearing on U.S. evening news programs were "nonofficials"—for example, protesters or families of soldiers—selected by journalists to portray average citizens. On Italian TV news, virtually all sources were people deliberately selected to represent the views of organized social and political groups.

Finally, the relationship between the news organization and its audience differed. When an American TV journalist uses the first person, especially the first-person plural ("we"), it is almost always to refer to the news organization: "Up the road at *our* foreign desk in London," Peter Jennings would say. But when an Italian journalist uses the first-person plural, it is to refer to himself or herself *and* to the audience: "Let's see what is going on in Lebanon." Moreover, they note, first-person usage by American TV journalists is rare; for Italian journalists, it is commonplace:

> The television journalist in the United States, in other words, will not normally "cross the screen" to put himself "on the side" of the audience in relation to events; while the Italian announcer routinely moves back and forth across that invisible boundary. (Hallin & Mancini, 1985, p. 215)

Why were the narrative forms in each so different? Hallin and Mancini argue that part of the explanation derives from economic differences: American network TV news is highly commercialized, and its producers must fight for an audience by presenting an attractive, visually engaging package; Italian network TV news was not so constrained. But perhaps more important is that the programs reflect very different political cultures. In Italy, the "public sphere" in which ideology and policy are debated is very much filled by political parties, unions, and industrial associations, and on Italian TV, it is their representatives who provide meaning and interpretation of the day's events. In America, political parties are no longer strong or central enough to do this, and most other organized political groups—trade unions, industrial associations, and other interest groups—generally pursue narrow, not broad, political agendas. In the United States, Hallin and Mancini argued, the press and the presidency are the only two institutions strong enough and able to serve as the interpreters, the arbiters of political meanings, hence American TV news was more active and more autonomous than its Italian counterpart.

71

## MEDIAMAKING IN CONTEXT

Our discussion of levels of analysis should make clearer that media are "made" in a specific context. Individuals and groups do creative production work, but that work is guided and shaped by the organizations they work in. The individuals and organizations, in turn, are shaped and guided by the industries they inhabit, and the individuals, organizations, and industries reside in a society that shapes and guides them as well.

At each of these levels, different influences operate on the making of media.

### People

The many individual characteristics of mass communicators can indeed influence the content and character of the products they create. At least since the 1960s, women and minority groups have actively argued and worked against their underrepresentation in the media industries. For example, the American Society of Newspaper Editors reported that in 2005, only 13.42% of daily newspaper newsroom workers were members of minority groups (5.5% African American, 4.3% Hispanic, 3.1% Asian American, and 0.6% Native American), a slight increase from the prior year, and women comprise about three eighths of the newsroom labor force, as they have for a number of years. Why is this a matter of concern? For at least two reasons: the desire of members of minority groups for equal access to jobs and fair consideration for promotion and advancement, and the belief that if minority groups are to receive fair and accurate portrayal in the news, minorities must be represented in newsrooms. In other words, this argument is that a personal characteristic of the journalist—in this case, ethnicity or race—can make a difference in *what* news gets covered and *how*. (See Box 3.2, "Media People.")

---

**BOX 3.2**

**Media People**

In May 2003, the Bureau of Labor Statistics (www.bls.gov) estimated that more than 1.5 million people were employed (either full time, part time, or as freelancers) in mass communication. These included the following:

---

60,230 reporters, correspondents, and news analysts

43,740 writers and authors

108,990 editors

147,970 public relations specialists and an additional 58,490 public relations managers

182,600 marketing managers

71,100 advertising and promotion managers

57,740 photographers

21,430 camera operators

51,840 actors

54,370 directors and producers

15,100 film and video editors

32,750 art directors, fine artists, multimedia artists, animators, designers, musicians, and broadcast technicians.

These numbers do not include many others who are employed by the media, from delivery drivers to secretaries, or amateurs creating Web pages or fanzines.

Similarly, conservative critics of the news media have argued for many years that the media are liberally biased. Among the evidence they offer is survey data showing that American journalists, and especially "elite" journalists at the television networks and major newspapers, are more likely to identify themselves as political liberals than are Americans in general (see, for example, Lichter, Rothman, & Lichter, 1986). (We will see shortly that liberal critics argue that the media are conservatively biased, but their evidence comes from a higher level of analysis.) And several writers have suggested that the big-city and Jewish backgrounds of Hollywood producers and screenwriters have shaped the content of American motion pictures and television programs (Gabler, 1988; Stein, 1979).

There are two views about how individual differences influence media content. First is the view that individual creators derive from their backgrounds and experiences the attitudes and ideas that shape what they create. This is clearly the case, for example, in fiction writing, when authors may derive their characters and stories from people and events in their own lives. Second is the view that, to the degree that *groups* share a characteristic, then that characteristic may show up in much of the content produced by that group. In *The View From Sunset Boulevard*, for example, writer Ben Stein (1979) argues that big business is portrayed as corrupt or criminal on American television because the small number of TV writers and writer-producers (he estimates that no more than 200 people work steadily in the business) overwhelmingly share antibusiness attitudes.

These two arguments lead us in two directions. First, we need to divide values, attitudes, and norms that shape media content into two categories: those that are *occupational* or *professional,* those sets of values related to a person's media job, and those that are *general,* pertaining to someone's overall view of the world. In the former case, for example, public relations specialists certified by the Public Relations Society of America subscribe to a code of ethics that requires them not to intentionally deceive others. Second, we need to elaborate on the influence of work environment and professional background: How much—and how—an individual can shape a media product depends a lot on the power resources she or he can bring to bear when that product is created. Because most media are produced within complex organizations with hierarchical structures (that is, a boss makes and enforces the rules, and the subordinates follow them), we would expect that those higher up the organizational ladder should have the power: Presidents give orders, and those below carry them out, and this is the rule—sometimes. But the power to shape media products is not just top-down; media professionals do have some resources in making messages the way they think they should be made. In general, the power or autonomy that any worker has is directly related to that worker's indispensability to the organization in creating a media product.

Media scholar Joseph Turow (1984), borrowing from industrial sociologist Howard Aldrich, says that a useful way of understanding how media are made is a *resource dependence perspective.* By this, he means that we can better understand how media producers—individuals, organizations, and industries—behave by understanding how their resources are allocated. Many resources are necessary to produce anything complex—time and money, talent and creativity, expertise and energy, raw materials and prepackaged components. The act of creating media is one of bringing these resources together, and anyone who controls a resource that a media organization or industry needs has some power over the shape of the finished product.

74

In a case study of a California daily newspaper, sociologist Rodney Stark (1962) observed many years ago that reporters and editors could be divided into two groups, one of which—the "Locals"—supported the paper's conservative politics, and a second group which did not. The "Pros," the professionalized reporters, were able to keep their jobs and subvert some of the publishers' biases because they controlled resources upon which the paper depended. Among these resources were reporting and writing talent, a sophisticated knowledge of the paper's deadlines and editing routines, and expert knowledge of their "beat" specialties. In short, control of resources gave them a degree of power, independence, and autonomy; the greater the control over a resource on which a producer is dependent, the greater the power. In the recorded music industry, for example, established "track-record" artists can flex far more muscle in terms of creative control over their music than can newcomers.

The eminent German social thinker Karl Mannheim once observed that "strictly speaking it is incorrect to say that the single individual thinks. Rather it is more correct to insist that the individual participates in thinking further what other individuals have thought before" (cited in Shoemaker & Reese, 1991, p. 85). What this means is that, in all we do, we operate inside social systems that predispose us to think and act in ways that are patterned by that social system. The newspaper example shows that whereas some control over the product resides at the individual or "people" level, the product must be described in an organizational context.

Likewise, in a study of the creation of *Freestyle,* an educational TV program for public television, James Ettema (1982) noted that three groups—educators, evaluation researchers, and television production professionals—were supposedly granted equal power in making decisions about the show's content, style, and format. On the planning committee to create the series, each had equal representation, and representatives of each group argued strongly to craft the show to suit its own interests. Over time, however, the TV production group, represented by the executive producer, won most of the arguments. He did so, Ettema argues, by appealing to his expertise about what makes "good TV," a subject about which the educators and evaluators were ignorant, and his knowledge of what could be done given a set budget. Although his knowledge was an individual characteristic, the rules concerning TV technique and budget constraints belong at the higher, organizational, level of analysis, and to that, we now turn.

## Organizations and Industries

At the level of organizations and industries, there is some blurring of the lines. *All* organizations and *all* industries, media and otherwise, are characterized by roles, rules, and routines as they attempt to cope with their environments, to bring order where there seems to be none: Where they vary is in their solutions to problems. Most TV production houses, for example, will have very similar structures and roles—people will have the same or similar job titles—and similar routines for writing and casting, production, and postproduction, but particular differences will show up in the shows they produce. Dick Wolf's Wolf Film Productions (*Law & Order, Law & Order: Special Victims Unit, Law & Order: Criminal Intent, Law & Order: Trial by Jury, Crime & Punishment*) are known to be gritty, "realistic" views of big-city crime, for example. We turn next to why and how rules, roles, and routines are used within organizations and industries, and how these ultimately shape the media, often in ways that are subtle and nonobvious.

### Routines and Rules

For most of us, the first time we were assigned to write a term paper or research paper was a scary experience. What's a suitable topic? How long should it be? Where can I get information? How much do I need? How do I organize it? How much detail should I go into? How much of it should be my opinion and how much should be "just the facts"? When do I need to use a footnote? The teacher could answer some questions fairly specifically ("It should be 15 pages. It should open with a thesis statement stating a point of view, provide sufficient information to support the point of view, and close with a summary-and-conclusion."). Other answers were open-ended ("I'm not going to assign a topic; write on something you're interested in." [Yeah, right.]) Whereas writing that first term paper was hard, writing the second one was somewhat easier, and the third, a bit easier than that. That is so because we not only write the term paper but begin to learn the rules for researching, organizing, and writing them.

The same holds true for media organizations and industries. No creator ever sits down with a blank sheet of paper (or a blank computer screen) and says, "Now, what am I going to create for the media today?" The creator sits down with a set of ideas—and, as Mannheim noted, these ideas are not new ones but rather ones that are inherited (cited in Shoemaker & Reese, 1991)—and in these ideas are the rules and routines for getting to work. The rules and routines, then, are what make media creative practices *efficient*.

In putting together any particular *Tonight Show*, the show's production team begins not with a blank slate, but with a lot of information—even before the first joke is written or the first guest invited—and a number of strategies for creating the show (for a more detailed discussion, see Tuchman, 1974). These unwritten rules and routines allow the team to organize its time productively: Months in advance, the producers and writers will know what nights the show will appear and what nights the host will be available or on vacation so that a replacement must be booked. At least two weeks in advance, the main star/guest must be booked so that her or his name will make the deadlines for *TV Guide*, newspaper television listings, and other promotional material. Lesser guests can be booked later, depending on availability and currency. Jokes for the monologue are written on the day of the show.

In one critical respect, TV talk shows are different from most other media products in that "outsiders" who contribute to the show—guests—are not directly motivated by money, because the union-scale appearance fee is nominal. Most celebrity guests appear on such shows to further careers, to promote themselves and their latest products: "Celebrities," Marshall McLuhan (McLuhan & Fiore, 1968) once commented, "are well known for their well-knownness."

How do guests make it onto the show? Not by chance. Established stars have established track records—they are familiar to audiences and "known" to the show's producers and host. Part of what they are known for, as sociologist Gaye Tuchman (1974) has noted, is for being "good TV." That is, they will, predictably, be humorous, attractive, nonpolitical, personable, and personal (but not *too* personal). All but the top few repeat talk-show celebrities will be "preinterviewed" by researchers and writers twice: Once to steer them toward topics that the host can later ask them about and to steer them away from taboo topics such as politics and the details of their breakup with ex-spouses, and a second time to prepare them for the night's show (the "spontaneous" dialogue between host and guest is largely scripted). All potential guests who are not big stars are preinterviewed, to be sure that the potential guest will be "good TV."

How does the program staff learn about potential guests in the first place? Celebrity helps, but researchers and staffers are always on the lookout for "new" faces to add some variety. Where do they find them? There are two principal sources: first, bookers and especially agents who want to place their clients—comedians, actors, recording artists, and book authors—on the shows for the favorable publicity to be garnered. Second, *other media* are a rich source of the offbeat, bizarre, and unusual performer or character.

This extended example shows several aspects of media organizations' rule-boundedness: First, the rules and routines help to assure that production will be smooth, efficient, and *predictable,* with few surprises for the producers. Second, the media end up being interdependent, relying on each other for the "raw material" that becomes their content. Third, not everybody is treated in the same way, as "stars" are governed by different rules than are unknowns. And, finally, the rules and routines that make putting media products together easier, more predictable, and efficient for their producers also makes them predictable for audiences. However, intermedia "borrowing" and predictability hinder novelty, spontaneity, and creativity.

A second example from the organizational-industrial level is the decision making that goes into getting TV programs on the air in the first place. There is no way to guarantee that a new product will be a hit. Given this uncertainty, however, media organizations do have rules for deciding what new programs will air: First, "track-record" producers (like Dick Wolf) have a decided edge, and production companies with successful shows will have an easier time getting new shows on the networks than will newcomers. Second, spin-offs and shows that imitate successful shows will also have an easier time. Third, shows featuring established stars (Matt LeBlanc, Pamela Anderson) are more likely to appear than shows featuring all new talent. Fourth, conventional and predictable shows will be most likely to air, in large part because the rules are enforced by cautious, risk-aversive network program executives. However, occasionally, unconventional shows do get picked up by the networks, and occasionally (*All in the Family* in the

1970s, *Hill Street Blues* in the 1980s, *The Simpsons* in 1990, *Queer Eye for the Straight Guy* in 2003), they become hits.

Turow (1982) has shown that even for unconventional TV shows, the conventional rules apply. In a study of how three conventional TV programs and three unconventional programs made it onto the network program schedules, Turow found that the conventional shows had conventional origins—they were the products of studios and production companies that already had shows on the networks,[1] and they were approved by network program executives who were well established in the business. By contrast, the unconventional shows tended to be the creations of writer-producers whose track records, although extensive, were outside television, largely in films and theatrical productions. An important point is that established network executives and networks doing well in the ratings are not interested in unconventional, innovative shows: Truly new shows are championed by executives new to their jobs and willing to take risks to make their marks. Columbia Broadcasting System (CBS) president Rob Wood told Turow that his ideas in his first few years as network president "were the freshest." Later, he said, "You learn the rules too well and don't think in new directions" (Turow, 1982, p. 121). And innovative shows tended to appear on networks either trailing in the ratings or anxious to appeal to attractive demographic groups to which that network was not presently appealing. Finally, Turow learned that unconventional shows took longer from their initial conception to airing—an indicator that networks were dragging their feet—and were far more likely to be placed in unattractive time slots than were more conventional shows. Thus breaking the rules is difficult, and programming executives sometimes set up unconventional programs to fail.

There are other values to routines and rules in that the process usually ensures some level of quality of the product. Content produced outside of traditional media organizations may be quite innovative and may provide alternative perspectives not heard elsewhere, but they often do not benefit from the cross-checking, editing, or even credibility of more mainstream media organizations. This is especially true in news, where rules for fact checking, cross-referencing multiple sources, and in-depth background research ensure the accuracy and credibility of what is reported. Nontraditional online news sources may or may not follow these routines. (See Box 3.3, "Indymedia," and Box 3.4, "Matt Drudge: Trading Accuracy for Speed.")

**BOX 3.3**

## Indymedia

The following is from Kidd (2003):

Indymedia is made up of over sixty autonomously operated and linked Web sites in North America and Europe, with a smaller number in Africa, Latin America, and Asia. The first IMC [Independent Media Center] was started in Seattle in 1999, just before the encounter between the World Trade Organization (WTO) and the social movements opposed to its policies. Early on in the counter-WTO planning, several different groups had recognized the strategic importance of making an "end-run around the information gatekeepers" to produce their own autonomous media (Tarleton, 2000, p. 53). They were well aware of the limitations of depending on the corporate media to provide coverage, especially the necessary analyses and context for the complex changes threatened by the WTO regime. In fact, before the event, only a handful of articles in the U.S. corporate media had discussed the implications of the WTO meetings.

The IMC would not have been possible without the convergence of new levels of social movement organization and technology. In three short months in the fall of 1999, and with only $30,000 in donations and borrowed equipment, Seattle organizers created a "multimedia peoples' newsroom," with a physical presence in a renovated downtown storefront and in cyberspace on the Web (Tarleton, 2000, p. 53). The IMC enabled independent journalists and media producers of print, radio, video, and photos from around the world to produce and distribute stories from the perspectives of the growing anti-corporate globalization movement. The IMC was the child of collaboration between local housing and media activists; journalists, independent media producers, and media and democracy activists from national and international arenas; and local, national, and international organizations active in the burgeoning anti-corporate globalization movement.

Second, the Seattle IMC drew from the technical expertise and resources of computer programmers, many of whom came from the open-source movement. While Bill Gates of Microsoft played a major role in bringing the WTO to Seattle, Rob Glaser, who made his millions at Microsoft, donated technical support and expertise, and in particular the latest streaming technologies, to the Indymedia Web site. "From the standpoint of all these independent media, the WTO couldn't have picked a worse place to hold their meeting," according to local media activist Bob Siegel. "I mean it's Seattle—we've got all the techies you'll ever want. . . . It's perfect that the WTO came here. Perfect" (quoted in Paton, 1999, p. 3). Indymedia.org allowed real-time distribution of video, audio, text, and photos, with the potential for real interactivity through "open publishing," in which anyone with access to the Internet could both receive and send information.

In just two years, the IMC network has become a critical resource for activists and audiences around the world, providing an extraordinary bounty of news reports and commentaries, first-person narratives, longer analyses, links to activist resources, and interactive discussion opportunities from around the world. In the beginning, they focused primarily on the anti-globalization mobilizations at the multilateral summits of neoliberal governance. At each of these meetings, they provided innovative international coverage, which often included collaborative initiatives with other media and social-movement activists. In the last year, and particularly since September 11, the network has added several new member sites and widened the scope of its coverage to include local, national, and international campaigns concerning anti-corporate globalization. (pp. 49–51)

Source: © 2003 from *Cyberactivism: Online Activism in Theory and Practice* by Martha McCaughey and Michael D. Ayers. Reproduced by permission of Routledge/Taylor & Francis Books, Inc.

However, we should also note that routines and rules change over time. Currently new technologies are putting pressure on the news routines discussed above. News Web sites and 24-hour news channels emphasize the need to either break a story first or keep up with the up-to-the-second headlines from other sites. This pressure for speed often works against routines of double-checking facts and sources. As Howard Gardner, Mihaly Csikszentmihalyi, and William Damon (2001) put it,

The news industry has always placed a premium on speed. The question is not whether it is desirable in general for the news industry to hold workers to a standard of timeliness but rather whether recent changes in the profession have added a corrosive element to this perennial source of journalistic pride and pressure. (p. 140)

---

**BOX 3.4**

**Matt Drudge: Trading Accuracy for Speed**

The following is from Gardner, Csikszentmihalyi, and Damon (2001):

The Internet is a uniquely democratic news medium, with nothing—not time, not money, not editorial supervision—standing in between Internet newscasters and the material they wish to post. Nothing, that is, but the scruples of the

*(Continued)*

(Continued)

person who does the posting. Hence the unique importance of journalistic standards in the Internet age.

If all Internet newscasters interpreted the standard of truth in the same manner as the leading journalists [. . .] this new medium would pose little challenge to the domain. But many Internet newscasters have little journalism training and little respect for the domain's codes and traditions. The most prominent of this new breed is Matt Drudge, a "one-man gossip and news agency," according to one recent account.[1] Drudge managed to first break the Clinton-Lewinsky scandal, because he was willing to go with a story that *Newsweek,* among others, considered not yet adequately confirmed. In subsequent months, Drudge continued to scoop the established media on many juicy components of the story, including the telling proof of semen stains on Monica's blue dress. Drudge turned out to be right about most of the material that he posted, but he also made errors. His fame and notoriety grew with every scoop, and his *Drudgereport.com* gained a multimillion "circulation" that outnumbered every newspaper's in the land.

In a rare appearance before the National Press Club, Drudge repeated a statement that had scandalized the mainstream press corps when *Newsweek* first quoted it: "Oh, I guess I'm about 80 percent accurate, the body of my work." Earlier, Doug Harbrecht of the Press Club had asked Drudge, "Could you succeed as a journalist if you worked for an organization which required an accuracy rate of 100 percent, instead of 70 or 80 percent." Drudge was having none of it. "I'd rather stay in my dirty Hollywood apartment," he quipped.

Drudge painted a picture of an entrenched mainstream press that, prior to the Internet, monopolized the news and kept important information from the public. Editors have biases, as do the corporate chieftains that editors work for. "Clearly there is a hunger for unedited information, absent corporate considerations." What about the role of editors in making sure that a news story consists of confirmed facts rather than gossip? Drudge replied: "Well, all truths begin as hearsay, as far as I'm concerned. And some of the best news stories start in gossip. Monica Lewinsky certainly was gossip in the beginning. . . . At what point does it become news? This is the indefinable thing in this current atmosphere, where every reporter will be operating out of their homes with Web sites for free, as I do."

In the supercharged world of today's electronic media, Drudge may be winning the argument. And his influence is by no means confined to the Internet alone. According to the 1999 book *Warp Speed,* written by two journalists,[2] Drudge and his ilk have spawned a "journalism of assertion" that is forcing other mass media outlets to air sensational rumors before they can be properly verified, all in the name of keeping up with the competition.

The authors of *Warp Speed* believe that the "journalism of assertion" is eating away at the foundations of public trust for the press—a trust necessary for the survival of the extraordinary freedoms and privileges that the press requires in order to serve a democracy. Other journalists concur. In a *Brill's Content* cover story on Drudge, Jules Witcover of the *Baltimore Sun* was quoted as calling Drudge "a reckless trader in rumor and gossip—[an] abomination of the Internet."[3] And Joan Konner, the publisher of the *Columbia Journalism Review,* asserted that "by no reasonable measure [is Drudge] working in the public interest."[4]

In the same piece, *Brill's Content* estimated that, of the thirty-one exclusive stories broken by Drudge in 1998, ten (or 32 percent) were untrue or never happened, eleven (36 percent) were true, and the accuracy of the rest was in doubt.[5] These figures make Drudge's claim to 80 percent accuracy look wildly exaggerated, and no reputable journalist would accept even that percentage as an adequate standard. The *Brill's Content* article concluded that, "in Drudge's case, he must achieve a higher level of accuracy in his reporting to gain genuine credibility." To which Drudge replied: "Screw journalism! The whole thing's a fraud anyway."[6]

Yet Drudge's work has not been entirely without value. He has shown us the potential of an astonishing technology—the Internet—to open up vast informational territories. Drudge is right when he claims that the "balanced" accounts provided by a small circle of mass media powerhouses can be a narrow balance indeed: in fact, it has sometimes led to an *im*balance fostered by a closed set of unexamined establishment assumptions.

But Internet reporting, like any other news source, needs both internal standards and editorial monitoring if it is to become a moral force in its own right. The universal standard of truthfulness cannot be slighted in any sustained news endeavor, not for the sake of speed, nor for the sake of any other marketplace advantage. And news reporters will not be able to dismiss the editorial function without eventually suffering a ruinous loss of credibility, because the editorial function is the primary means the domain has evolved for checking its work against its accepted standards. In the end, if the Drudges of the world are to succeed in expanding journalism's capacity to accomplish its noble purposes, they will do so only by arming themselves with the best traditions of the domain. (pp. 146–148)

## Notes

1. Kovach & Rosenstiel, 1999, p. 11
2. Ibid.
3. McClintick, 1998
4. Ibid.
5. Ibid.
6. Ibid., p. 127

## Roles and Reference Groups

Within media organizations and industries, roles and reference groups serve important functions. A *role* is the set of attitudes, values, and behaviors expected of any occupant of a position. A role can be a job title or occupation. A film editor does certain kinds of work—splicing different segments of film into each other to attain a meaningful narrative. However, how the film is edited—what the narrative is supposed to mean—is dictated by the film's director.

Similarly, a *reference group* is any group of which one is a member and to which one orients his or her thinking and actions. We saw in the earlier example of the California newspaper that two sets of reporters (a role) allied themselves in two different reference groups, the Pros and the Locals.

Roles and reference groups are important for two principal reasons. First, doing anything as complex as assembling a media product requires people in multiple roles; each role carries with it different sets of behaviors and especially attitudes and values. Second, the existence of different reference groups helps us to understand the circumstances under which conflicts are more, or less, serious.

Role conflicts are inevitable because of the differences in values and attitudes implicit in different roles. In general, media production requires a three-tier structure. At the front end are "raw material" processors—the creative staffers such as writers, artists, or reporters who do the initial processing of media materials. In the middle are managers, editors, directors, and producers who coordinate the production and mediate between the front-end staff and top management. The top tier of executives sets budgets, makes corporate policy, sets organizational goals, and occasionally defends the organization's employees from outside pressures (Shoemaker & Reese, 1996). Most media organizations, and hence their top managements, are most interested in making money: For a media enterprise to survive, it must do so, and thus top management generally has the strongest and most direct interest in questions of profit. Management's vision of how to attain profit (or to meet other organization goals, such as respectability or prestige) may well not square with front-end staff. An example of such tension is that between news organization management and reporters and editors. A focus on profits often means cuts in newsroom staff, hampering their ability to cover the news adequately, and also pressures to report on stories that will increase readership or viewership, regardless of newsworthiness (Gardner, Csikszentmihalyi, & Damon, 2001).

## Institutions

We noted earlier that within a society or culture, various institutions shape media content. This is only half the equation: The media help influence the society and its institutions as well. If media content did *not* have an impact on a society and its institutions, then those institutions would have no interest in shaping the media. But the constant barrage of criticism media face from the government, the military, religious groups, and organized interest groups of all sorts is vivid testimony to the belief that the media have major impacts on public and private life.

### The Nature of Institutional Relationships

In discussing the relationships between media and other institutions, we need to make two sets of critical distinctions. First is the degree to which the nature of the relationships is passive—that is, how much do the media *mirror or reflect the societies in which they exist*—or active—how much do media themselves *shape and change the society?* Second is the distinction between *formal* and *informal* constraints on media. Formal constraints are those codified into laws and regulations by the state. Informal constraints are all other mechanisms—ethical, social, economic, and cultural—that govern the media and shape their content.

In a comparison of U.S. and Italian TV news (Box 3.1), Hallin and Mancini (1985) argue that the cultural practices serve as *informal* constraints on the news people of each country: TV journalists' expectations of the implied relationship they have with the audience, for example, lead them to address their audiences in different ways. At the same time, Hallin and Mancini do not argue persuasively either way whether this relationship is active or passive; that is, whether the Italian media practice of addressing the audience in the first-person plural—*we* and *us*—results from a wider social practice, or whether it is actively used by journalists to encourage an audience bond, thus reinforcing a culturally familiar form of address. In large part, this is because extricating such practices from their context, and deciding whether one leads to the other or vice versa, is extraordinarily difficult.

85

The line between formal and informal rules is a bit clearer. Laws are codified, written down. We can tell a great deal about any society by seeing how the law books and court cases say things run. Moreover, this division points out several other important factors in the relationships between media and other institutions:

1. Formal, institutional relationships are perhaps the most important ones for understanding how the media operate. They account, in large part, for relationships between government and the media, and they explain how a society views the nature of the public.

2. Formal relationships change over time. Historically, the relationship between media and government has varied. In the United States, for example, the long-term trend has been toward less formal restraint of the media—at the same time that informal control of the media, especially by the economic institution, has grown.

3. Formal relationships do not in and of themselves explain how the media are regulated; we must consider informal relationships as well.

### Government-Media Relations

Among all institutions that media confront, government is most important. This is true for several reasons. First, worldwide, government control is direct—the government is the only institution that can legitimately use force to assure compliance. In other words, if an enterprise breaks a law, it will pay a fine, or its officers or employees might go to jail. To ignore the commandment of any other institution usually means only that organizations within the institution censure or expel you—or use the law, the government—to punish the offender. Second, government exerts control not only over media, but over other institutions as well, and control over other institutions may be indirectly reflected back into regulation of mass media. For example, the 1996 Telecommunications Law has enabled businesses previously not in mass media–related businesses—primarily telephone companies previously excluded from being content providers—to begin competing directly with television and cable; this provision was part of a complex lobbying effort with the Congress and the White House that also allows cable operators to compete with the phone companies for telephone business. Third, the relationship between the state, or government, and the media is undergoing radical transformation worldwide. Increasingly, formal governmental control of the media is being supplanted by informal regulation by other forces, primarily those of capitalism, as governments substitute market forces for regulatory pressures. Expanding on these themes suggests a brief history of the nature of the relationship between the state and the media.

Government and media have always—at least since the development of truly mass media—had a rocky relationship. In 1690, a Boston printer, Benjamin Harris, published the first issue of the first newspaper in America, *Publick Occurrences both Foreign and Domestick.* As it happened, this issue included a story about brutalities committed by Indian allies of the colonial military. This first issue was also the last: Harris was forbidden by the colonial governor not only from printing any more issues of the newspaper but, for that matter, from printing *anything at all* without prior permission. Such *prior restraint* is unquestionably the most effective form of censorship, and it was typical not only in Boston but elsewhere in the American colonies, in Britain, and in Europe. It works not only directly—authorities can prevent the publication of anything critical of or offensive to the government—but also indirectly; as printers quickly figure out the sorts of material that censors are unlikely to allow through, they precensor it, not bothering to submit it to review.

A second and related form of censorship is *licensing.* Colonial printers were granted a royal or governmental license to print, but the license could be withdrawn—effectively forcing them out of business—if they printed anything the authorities did not like. Unlike direct prior restraint, licensing does not directly prevent a printer from publishing critical materials, but the cost of guessing wrong about what the authorities will tolerate is so high—loss of one's livelihood—that licensing serves about as well as prior restraint in stifling free expression.

A third form of censorship comes in punishing the publisher after something is published. Two forms were powerful means of suppression in the colonial period: criminal prosecutions for treason or giving aid or comfort to an enemy of the state and prosecutions for seditious libel, or any published material that, without justification, cast blame on any public man, law, or institution established by law (see Rivers, Peterson, & Jensen, 1971). Both seek to punish publishers for material that to some people's eyes does no more than inform people about or criticize the government. Both were infrequently used. The mere threat of imprisonment or death was generally sufficient to keep publishers from being too critical. Printing presses were so scarce in colonial days that it did not usually take much effort for officials to find out who had printed something; today, of course, anyone with a computer and a printer and/or an Internet connection, or a two-way radio can be a publisher.

How could the government get away with these forms of censorship? The prevailing political ideology of the day was fully supportive. The authority of the state—the crown, colonial officials, governors—was absolute. Neither the press nor any other institution had any "rights" with respect to the state or governing authority. In the United States, development of the philosophy of libertarianism was intermixed with a steadily increasing desire among the American colonists to free themselves from British rule. The press ultimately freed itself from direct governmental control.

In 1735—still 41 years before the American Revolution—a New York printer, John Peter Zenger, was charged with seditious libel for printing a series of scathing articles about the governor of New York. Zenger did not write the articles, but because they were anonymous, the officials had no one to prosecute but the printer. As the law was written, Zenger was clearly guilty. Truth (the governor, history suggests, *was* a lying, pompous scalawag) was no defense under the law, and the judge instructed the jury that in fact, the greater the truth, the more the harm, and thus the greater the libel. But Zenger's attorney argued to the contrary, that the people should decide what is true and that a sovereign people should have the right to criticize those in authority. Zenger's acquittal technically did not change the law, but seditious libel thereafter was no serious threat to colonial printers, and the idea that a sovereign people could decide what was true became a part of the American ideology.

The 1791 ratification of the Bill of Rights brought with it the First Amendment, which says in part, "Congress shall make no law abridging freedom of speech, or of the press." Interpreted literally, this would mean that the press had become free from government interference. However, this was not to be, for several reasons at several levels. First, from the beginning of the republic until the early part of the twentieth century, the First Amendment was a restraint only on the federal government, not on the states. Second, even at the federal level, Congress managed to pass laws, especially the 1798 Alien and Sedition Acts, which managed to muffle publishers and writers by threatening criminal prosecutions for sedition. Third, freedom of the press can mean different things to different people. True, the American press was in 1791, and is today, pretty much free from prior restraint or censorship by the government.[2] But courts have interpreted the First Amendment to say that some *classes* of expression are not constitutionally protected, including obscenity, libel and slander, and violations of national security.[3] This basically means that some things that could be printed are subject to subsequent punishment, which serves, as we've noted, as a damper on their publication in the first place.

Nonetheless, the range of things that the government can prevent or punish through the application of law is quite narrow; virtually any criticism can be written, spoken, or broadcast; material that is tasteless, sensational, and even inaccurate (with a few exceptions[4]) is constitutionally protected as well. The most obvious exception involves over-the-air broadcasting, where the Federal Communications Commission (FCC) has authority to fine broadcasters for crudities and sexual titillation that don't rise to the legal level of obscenity and pornography—the "seven dirty words" of George Carlin's classic routine, and, in 2004, the flashing of Janet Jackson's breast at the Super Bowl halftime show and Howard Stern's radio program. The 2004 episodes led to a firestorm of criticism of TV and the FCC, calls in Congress for much heavier fines on offending broadcasters (CBS was eventually fined a record $550,000), and media conglomerate Clear Channel's dropping of Stern's program from six of its radio stations. (See Box 3.5, "Clearing the Air.") To repeat, the law—in the colonial period and today—covers only what the government can prevent or punish. As we'll see, that's only a small part of this important institutional relationship.

---

**BOX 3.5**

**Clearing the Air**

Events in 2004 brought the relationships of government and the media into strong focus. In a matter of a few weeks early in the year, Janet Jackson suffered a "wardrobe malfunction" in a Super Bowl halftime show produced for CBS by Music Television (MTV) and Howard Stern aired a radio show featuring a discussion of anal sex. Shortly thereafter—and after tens of

*(Continued)*

---

(Continued)

thousands of individuals and scores of conservative, religious, and child-advocacy religious groups registered complaints with the networks, the FCC and individual stations, the FCC reversed an earlier decision that a spontaneous outburst by U2's Bono at the televised 2003 Golden Globe awards ("This is really, really fucking brilliant!") didn't violate its offensiveness standards, and fined NBC. As noted, after Clear Channel (still, at this writing, contesting a $495,000 FCC fine for the Stern radio program on six of its outlets) dropped the Howard Stern radio program from six stations, Stern very publicly accused the FCC of buckling to efforts to censor him for his repeated editorial attacks on President George Bush.

Broadcasters responded by tape delaying virtually every major live broadcast (including the 2004 Academy Awards, watched worldwide by at least a half billion people), and even the Public Broadcasting Service (PBS) agreed to recut "foul" language in the "quality" British import miniseries *Prime Suspect*. In the meantime, in Congress—which writes the outlines of regulations the FCC then enforces—a number of bills were proposed to raise the dollar value of fines for episodes of indecency and, in one proposal, to include cable programming—never before regulated for content on the theory that since people pay to subscribe to it they want and know what they're getting—in indecency regulations.

However, by the summer of 2004, the move to tighten up on content regulation had begun to bog down: Public attention had moved away from the issue toward other concerns, especially after Abu Ghraib and other concerns about the Iraqi War. Government as an *institution* was also divided, with the executive branch more concerned with ownership rules, siding with media conglomerates. The *media* were not of one mind, either: The broadcast media were, by and large, compliant with toning down their content, largely because, as many argued, it was difficult to tell precisely what the rules were, while virtually all media, and many other groups, were concerned about overregulation of public expression—especially since the rules were not yet clear.

If earlier U.S. media history serves as any guide (the recurrent violence issue has tracked this way as well), we should expect to see the continuation of a cycle: Media pushing the limits of the allowable, followed by vocal elements of the public expressing outrage, followed by a flurry of governmental attention, followed by declining concern and inaction—and no tangible change in public policy. The political sociologist Murray Edelman (1964) also described this cycle in his classic book *The Symbolic Uses of Politics* some 40 years ago. Not much has changed.

Sources: Edelman (1964), Steinberg (2004).

The key word in understanding how the media and government interact is *relationship*. In a relationship, each party typically has something to give and something it wants to get, and relationships are reciprocal: To get something you want from someone else, you give something you have in exchange. Recall our earlier discussion of the resource-dependence perspective: What one party has to give is its resources; what it wants to get is the other party's resources. And by definition, in a reciprocal relationship, your resource is my need (if I didn't need it, it wouldn't be a resource for you, at least in dealing with me).

The major resource the media have is *publicity*, the ability to focus public attention on a topic or issue or person. The government and government officials need access to the public to focus public attention on problems and issues and especially to marshal public support for present policies and actions. This can be seen very clearly in election campaigns; a candidate needs media exposure to be seen as "viable," as having a chance of winning. The 1992 presidential campaign of Larry Agran, the Democratic mayor of Irvine, California, is a case in point. Virtually unknown to the national press and hence unreported on by them, Agran campaigned hard in New Hampshire but failed to attract much media attention. Why? Because he was an "unknown" and thus an "unviable" candidate. The evidence that he was unknown was easy to come by: Public opinion polls failed to find more than 1% or 2% of potential Democratic primary voters who expressed a preference for him. Early pre-election polls always favor candidates with high name recognition. In the early 1992 Democratic primaries, New York governor Mario Cuomo, who wasn't even a candidate, was leading in the preference polls. Agran was frequently excluded from media events, especially debates among the contending candidates, because he was viewed as not being viable. A similar situation was that of Ralph Nader's bid for the presidency as nominee of the Green Party in 2000. He was excluded from all televised debates despite a growing following. When one votes in presidential elections, one is likely to note any number of names on the ballot of whom one has never heard mention in the media, all of whom qualified for inclusion on the ballot. In brief, voter preference comes from publicity, the media provide the publicity, and their decision rule about news coverage largely comes from their estimate of viability, determined by voter preference polls and election results.

If the media's major resource in dealing with government and political life is publicity, the government's and politics' major resources are the ability to supply "raw material" to the media, especially the news media, and their ability to set the rules of the game for the way the media operate.

Clearly, those in political and governmental circles are interested not only in getting publicity but also in having it be favorable publicity, what has come to be known as *spin control.* Governmental and political officials attempt to influence what is said, and how it is said, by controlling the access that the news media have to them and their activities. The media's need—and the officials' resource—is news. Sociologist Herbert Gans (1979), in a content-analysis study of national TV news and newsmagazines, estimated that three fourths of all news came from government sources.[5] The dominance of the government as a source of news is understandable: The government acts on policies that affect us all, and hence its activities are news. Moreover, the media—and government—have adopted rules and routines that make covering government relatively efficient and predictable.

Government, political officials, and the military can control access in a number of ways. Getting favorable coverage means accentuating the positive and shrouding the negative by making access to symbols and messages that support your position easy and by making access to anything else difficult. Sources having great power—people such as the president, whom the press virtually must report on—enjoy a great resource advantage. The Gulf War of 1991 was another case in point. Although the nation's press corps complained bitterly over Defense Department restrictions on coverage, they by and large went along with these restrictions, for *not* reporting on the day's biggest news story was literally unthinkable, and General Norman Schwartzkopf and his staff controlled all access to the field. By the same token, those who have no such guaranteed access simply do not have it as a resource.

We noted earlier that the First Amendment protects freedom of expression—of speech and of the press—but under current court interpretations, this freedom basically covers what Americans say and print, but does not extend very far in covering anyone's ability, including the press's, to get access to information that the government, or other institutions, prefers to keep secret.

## Relations With Other Institutions

We've noted before that the First Amendment grants the media substantial latitude in what they can say. It's important to remember, however, that it protects media only from government censorship; it does not apply to relationships the media have with other institutions (like advertisers) or with members of the public, who remain free to censor what they will.[6] As may become clear from our discussions, whereas the history of formal control—control by government—of the news media is one of increasing freedom, the history of influence on the media by other social institutions shows no such pattern; the give-and-take pattern of fluctuating degrees of freedom enjoyed by the media depends on who has the upper hand in informal interactions between the media and other institutions.

The media clearly have important relationships with other institutions, and resource dependence marks these relationships as well. As is the case with government and the political sphere, the resources the media have are essentially publicity and legitimization, and the ones they seek are support, for attention, money, and content—the stuff of which media are made.

In the following pages, we look at media relationships with two other institutions—education and medicine. Two later chapters concern the media's interaction with two other critically important institutions—the economy and the public sector.

### Education

The relationships between media and education are particularly close and complex. In the first place, much of our education is mediated; indeed, textbooks and educational materials account for almost a third of the $36.6 billion spent annually on books in the United States.[7] And if media are implicated in education, the reverse is true as well. Let's suppose that you're 20 years old and have watched—since you were 2—three and a half hours of TV a day, actually an hour less than the national average of four and a half hours a day. That means you've now watched about 29,900 hours of TV, or a bit under 3 ½ years of 24-hour days; that's about 1.8 times as much time as the approximately 16,000 hours you've spent in school (as a matter of fact, if you're an average American, you've spent more time watching TV than engaging in *any* activity other than sleeping).[8] At least part of the time we're watching TV, we're also learning—education is not just the formal education we get in school.

At any rate, media may be used directly for education, with educators involved in planning and producing media, as the many programs of the Children's Television Workshop (*Sesame Street, Dragontales, Sagwa the Chinese Siamese Cat*) attest. Media may also function incidentally as an educational outlet, as we learn much about the world beyond our immediate experience from the media.

Many educators are wary of TV and other media, feeling that watching television is negatively related to school achievement. Studies of the relationship show that it is neither simple nor straightforward. Some studies find this, but others don't; the best studies suggest that watching moderate amounts of TV has no relationship to how well students do in school, but watching 5 hours or more is hazardous to kids' grades. We may remind ourselves that the one nation in which kids watch more TV than in the United States is Japan, where students almost always score higher than American children on standardized tests.

The controversy over the use of Whittle Communications' *Channel One* in the nation's high school classrooms illustrates one relationship between the media and education. *Channel One* represents a media challenge to the traditional structure of the schools, which until recently have not been commercialized. Because *Channel One* carries age-appropriate advertising during its 12-minute daily newscast, it has focused attention on American schools as a site for marketers to reach student consumers. A Harris Poll estimates that the youth market (ages 8–21) is now a $172 billion per year market, with preteens (8–12) spending $19.1 billion of that ("Generation Y," 2003). *Channel One* is not alone in this regard. A continuing issue is the increasing presence of advertisements and corporate sponsorship in cash-strapped public schools. Corporations even produce education media such as videotapes and textbooks that are provided to the schools gratis, but that act as subtle and not-so-subtle advertisements for their sponsors.

Education is, however, dependent on the media, most particularly the news media, for information and viewpoints about how schools run, from basic questions of educational policy to mundane matters of what the school cafeterias will serve.

## Medicine

Medicine and health care make up one of the largest and most important sectors of American social life and its economy: Health care costs now are almost one sixth of the Gross National Product (GNP), and the proportion of GNP devoted to health care is steadily rising. The monetary stakes alone, in what American health care is and what it will become, are enormous and likewise growing. Where do the media fit in? The networks and most large newspapers have correspondents who cover medicine and health as a regular beat, and a listing of magazines that accept advertising classifies more than 150 magazines under Health and Nutrition and more than 400 others under Medicine, Dentistry, and Nursing. (By comparison, Journalism and Writing has fewer than two dozen entries; see *Magazine Industry Market Place,* 1996.) While television news and newspapers tend to aim their coverage at explaining medicine and health to a mass audience and hence serve boundary-crossing functions (that is, they tell one institution, the public, about the workings of another), the vast majority of the magazines are specialized, or *intrainstitutional* media, informing an institution, or a specialized segment within it, about itself. But perhaps the most interesting place to look at the relationships between media and medicine is in television entertainment.

Doctor shows did not begin with *ER* and *Chicago Hope.* The genre has a history that predates the medium. *Dr. Kildare* began as a short story and became a radio show and series of movies (there were, in the 1930s and 1940s, fifteen *Dr. Kildare* movies) before it became the No. 1 television show in the 1960s. *M\*A\*S\*H*, a variation on the genre, became the longest-running No. 1 show in TV history in the 1970s. Television studios and networks are attracted to medical shows because of their wide popularity, although, like shows of any other genre, not all succeed: Joseph Turow (1991) demonstrates that whereas 32 network medical shows ran for a full season or more from the 1950s through 1987, 22 others lasted less than a full season. TV writers and producers like medical shows because doctors and nurses (and even coroners, such as on *Crossing Jordan* or *Quincy*) are "good" central figures for a show. It's easier to write drama or comedy when the main characters are people who routinely and credibly come into contact with a wide and changing variety of secondary characters. Turow argues that this interaction helps explain why professionals in general—lawyers, writers, and teachers as well as doctors—are overrepresented in TV entertainment programming. Besides, medical stories almost by definition involve life-and-death situations, easy for high drama.

The popularity of the genre, moreover, has not been lost on the medical establishment. Early on, from the doctor movies of the 1930s to the 1954 debut of the series *Medic,* the American Medical Association and the Los Angeles County Medical Association had enormous influence on the content of medical programs. The associations and the industry depended on each other: The TV producers got free technical advice to make shows accurate and realistic; in exchange, the medical associations were able to influence the portrayal of medicine on television—another example of the resource-dependence perspective.

## CONCLUSION

The media do not exist "out there": They are *made.* And understanding how they are made is somewhat like peeling an onion—to understand mediamaking requires us to look at more than one level. People—individuals—make media, but they do so in an organizational context: That is, to make media requires rules, roles, and routines, and each of these influences what can be made. Moreover, organizations exist within industries that shape or constrain them. Furthermore, that understanding is fostered by paying attention to the way media people, organizations, industries, and institutions share resources with others in what we label a resource-dependence perspective. Alternative or radical mediamaking focuses on reorganizing the ways information is processed and distributed to the public, creating new contexts and allowing for new voices and opinions to be heard.

## NOTES

1. Until 1995, TV networks were barred by Federal Communication Commission regulations from producing their own prime-time entertainment programming. The regulations, aimed at fostering competition in entertainment production, meant that most prime-time network shows were purchased from Hollywood-based production companies, many of them affiliated with

movie studios. In 1997, networks owned or had ownership interests in 29 of 80 prime-time entertainment programs (for example, *Ellen* on ABC, *The Single Guy* on NBC), with the remainder produced by independent houses and studios (Sterngold, 1997). We must note that the formula for *All in the Family* was copied from a British sitcom, *'Til Death Us Do Part,* and *The Simpsons* was spun off from Fox's *The Tracey Ullman Show.*

2. This freedom was upheld most famously in the 1971 Pentagon Papers cases, in which President Richard Nixon's attorney general, John Mitchell, sought to keep *The New York Times, Washington Post,* and *Boston Globe* from printing excerpts of a secret Defense Department multivolume document on the origins and history of the Vietnam War. The papers had been surreptitiously photo-copied by Daniel Ellsberg, who then made them available to the three news-papers. The U.S. Supreme Court said that prior restraints on the press were unconstitutional unless an extremely strong case could be made that publica-tion would damage national security, and that the government had not been able to show that. It should also be noted that this prior restraint doctrine applies with greatest force to news; the Supreme Court as late as the 1950s was willing to say that local communities could prescreen motion pictures and decide whether they were suitable for local showing.

3. In trying a case involving freedom of the press, a court must decide whether material is or is not obscene, libelous, or slanderous; the publisher is protected if the material is found not to meet the legal definition but is subject to crimi-nal prosecution, in obscenity cases, or to recovery of damages in libel cases. In theory, at least, prior restraints of material that would damage national secu-rity are still possible, although the government has not been able since the Pentagon Papers cases to prove any media publication would damage national security. It came close in 1979, when *The Progressive* magazine was prevented from publishing an article outlining how to make a hydrogen bomb. The gov-ernment, however, dropped the case when the magazine was able to demon-strate that all the information contained in the article was already available in libraries and previously published articles, and the article appeared in the magazine.

4. The principal exceptions are in libel, slander, and deceptive advertising. Libel and slander are published or spoken, respectively, falsehoods that defame a person or corporation. Defamation, legally, is anything that exposes persons to hatred, contempt, ridicule; lowers them in the esteem of others; causes them to be shunned; or damages them in their business or calling. At present, the law of libel requires that, for a private individual to collect damages for libel, she or he must show that a defamatory falsehood was published either with knowl-edge that it was false or with lack of due care for whether it was true or false.

Reflecting the concern that public debate should be, in the words of the U.S. Supreme Court, "uninhibited, robust and wide-open," the standards applied to public figures (who presumably place themselves in the public eye on purpose) and government officials are even higher. To collect damages, they must prove that a defamatory falsehood was published with knowledge that it was false or with "reckless disregard" for whether or not it was. In deceptive advertising cases in the recent past, the federal government has moved largely against only flagrantly inaccurate advertising.

5. And fully one fifth of the news came from the president of the United States (Gans, 1979, Chapter 1). Virtually every subsequent content analysis of major news media has calculated similar proportions.

6. Legally, censorship applies only to restrictions by government. Thus, if Clear Channel drops Howard Stern from its stations, it may keep him from being heard in those communities, but that's not true censorship (and the Internet makes it ineffective, since Stern's program is available worldwide to anyone who can do basic audio streaming from a radio station carrying the program).

7. In 2002, they accounted for $10.149 billion, according to the *Statistical Abstract of the United States 2003*. The percentage includes elementary, secondary, and college texts; standardized tests; and subscription reference services but excludes audiovisual media.

8. In addition, let's assume that you'll go to work at age 22 and work a 40-hour week until you're 65, and that from 22 until age 72, you watch the national average of four and a half hours a day of TV (1,661 hours per year in 2001). That means that over the course of an average life, you'll spend about 83,050 hours watching TV, about 86,000 hours working and about 16,000 hours in school. These TV use estimates are from the *Statistical Abstract of the United States 2003*; the school estimate is based on 6.5 hours a day for 180 days a year from age 6 to age 20; the work estimate includes a two-week vacation yearly.

## SUGGESTED READINGS

Gardner, H., Csikszentmihalyi, M., & Damon, W. (2001). *Good work: When excellence and ethics meet*. New York: Basic Books.

Tuchman, G. (1978). *Making news: A study in the construction of reality*. New York: Free Press.

Turow, J. (1984). *Media industries: The production of news and entertainment*. New York: Longman.

# Media and Money

4

I t is not possible to think of the modern mass media without also thinking about money, economics, and profit. The media are, for the most part, made up of and controlled by corporations that both invest an enormous amount of money in their media operations and expect to make at least a reasonable profit. After all, the media are big business, one of the biggest in the world. In 2002, the average American household spent over $2,000 on entertainment (Bureau of Labor Statistics, 2004); the *Statistical Abstract of the United States* for 2004–2005, produced by the U.S. Census Bureau (2004), stated that in 2001 consumer spending on media was $673 per person per year, projected to increase to $941 by 2007. It is worth remembering, however, that there are millions of people, even in America, who simply cannot afford to purchase many media products.

In fact, how the media are organized institutionally and how they operate to produce the particular kinds of products they do are significantly influenced, if not determined, by their relationship to money and profit. In the United States, people take it for granted that the media operate within and are part of a capitalist economy, in which they must compete for profit in the marketplace. But people are not always aware of the differences the system makes. For example, scholars and critics persistently argue about the extent to which, and how, the organization of media as largely profit-making ventures influences the sort of media products that are made available to the audience. On the one hand, there are numerous examples of media corporations producing messages that are critical of mainstream society and even of the capitalist economy from which they profit. Whether it is CBS Records releasing records by the Clash advocating revolution, or the conservative Italian media mogul Silvio Berlusconi publishing a Communist newspaper, the bottom line is money. On the other hand, there are many accounts of how media corporations have suppressed products (news stories, films) that were critical of their own actions (or those of their parent companies) and, more generally, of how they make products intended to defend their interests and points of view. In addition, critics commonly point out that the commitment to profit has, perhaps more than anything else, limited the range and quality of messages produced by the media. More generally, the question is whether the media's reliance on and commitment to profit conflicts with its important role in society.

This chapter will describe the economy of the media—what it looks like, how it behaves, how the money side of mediamaking influences the rest of mediamaking. Although there are significant economic differences among the various media industries, there are important similarities. We will stress the common economic factors that shape how the media operate.

## A PRIMER OF ECONOMIC TERMS

From Adam Smith in the eighteenth century and David Ricardo and Karl Marx in the nineteenth century to John Maynard Keynes and Paul Samuelson in the twentieth century, we have come to accept a number of basic economic concepts and principles as fundamental. Because contemporary media operate within a capitalist economy, it is necessary to understand some of these basic concepts and principles.

The founding principle of any economy is the distinction between two forms of value. Every good has some *use value*, which describes its function in our lives. Most of the time, the use value of a product is obvious, but other times—think about designer jeans—it is not quite so obvious. Perhaps we wear designer jeans because they give us a certain status, or define for us a certain image and style. Every product also has an *exchange value*, which is its value (measured loosely in its cost) in the market. Notice that there is no necessary correlation between use value and exchange value. Water has a very high use value, but for most people, unless they live in a desert, it has a very low exchange value. On the other hand, designer labels may have relatively low use value, but very high exchange value. Insofar as products are made primarily to be sold in the market, they are referred to as *commodities*. When people purchase a commodity, they treat it only in terms of its exchange value, its monetary worth, and forget about the fact that it was made by the labor of real people. *Money* is a kind of universal abstract measure against which we measure the exchange value of different commodities. Otherwise, money does not exist, and certainly it has no value of its own, especially because the government no longer guarantees that it can be traded in for gold (the gold standard was supposed to guarantee the value of money).

People don't usually think about the production of the commodity, only about its place within the market. But it is precisely its production—or, more accurately, the labor that goes into it—that gives a commodity its exchange value. This is known as the *labor theory of value.*

The aim of the capitalist marketplace is to sell the commodity at a higher price than the cost of the labor (and materials) necessary to produce it. This is profit or *surplus value.* The real aim of capitalism is to increase the rate at which profit is generated. Ideally, capitalists—the people who own the factories (the means of production), the banks, and so on—accumulate surplus value as capital to be reinvested, thus increasing both their profit and the rate of profit.

How does a capitalist create surplus value? The simplest way would be to create systems within which particular kinds of labor simply go unpaid: For example, think about the domestic labor of housework, which women have traditionally had to carry out "for free." But, of course, this is not the primary way in which capitalism operates. On the contrary, a key feature of capitalism is that it makes labor into a commodity that can be bought and sold on a supposedly competitive market. Consequently, the most likely way for capitalists to increase their profit is to buy labor at the cheapest possible cost and to seek ways to increase the efficiency of labor.

The capitalist charges more for the commodity that is produced than he or she pays for the total labor, material, and machinery and thus generates surplus value. It is as if the worker were contributing a certain amount of unpaid labor to the capitalist.

*Profit* is what's left over after one subtracts the cost of producing the product from the price one sells it for. There are two ways of increasing profit: lowering the cost of producing something and increasing the price at which it is sold. We have already discussed the most direct way of lowering costs. The latter is somewhat difficult to manipulate, for as economists like to point out, when a competitive market is working well, price is determined by the laws of supply and demand: As supply increases, price decreases, and as demand increases, price increases. Moreover, there is a complex relation in the market between supply and demand themselves. One of the most powerful ways of increasing profit is to participate in what economists call an *economy of scale*. In an economy of scale, after a very high initial cost of starting up, the cost of producing each unit of product declines rapidly as the number of units produced increases. That is, the more products that can be produced, the higher the *rate of profit* and the larger the profit on the last item that has been produced.[1] For items involving a lot of hand labor or very expensive materials, there are few economies of scale; it costs, per item, about as much to produce 100 television programs as it does to produce one. However, for products that can be mass produced, such as CDs, economies of scale are an attractive and powerful way to keep the cost down.

Of course, economies of scale only work to increase profits if one can increase the market demand for the product. Thus, once again, we return to the problem of trying to influence people's desire for specific products, a problem that has, as much as anything, contributed to the enormous growth of the media as industries responsible not only for promoting their own products but also for serving as the means of promoting the demand for other kinds of capitalist product as well.

## ECONOMICS AND THE MEDIA

The media, particularly in capitalist societies such as the United States, operate to produce and even to maximize profit for their owners. Profit, generated from the sale of media products, can be increased in a number of different ways. The key to media profits is *access*, which can take either of two forms: selling products directly or indirectly to consumers or selling access to the audience to advertisers. Let us begin with the simplest questions: What is the basis or source of the media's profits? In what different senses do the media exist as commodities? How are they economically supported?

## The Sources of Media Support

People in the industrialized world are surrounded by media almost everywhere they go. Every day, there are many occasions on which they use different media, both mindfully and absentmindedly. In every case, someone has to pay for the production and distribution of the media products. These different media are supported in various ways.

Some media products are paid for fully and directly by consumers. Most such media products are tangible physical entities that consumers take home with them, such as books, tapes, and CDs. The price of the commodity covers its full cost plus a profit. You pay directly for the media product you consume; by controlling the price, the producers can make the product more or less affordable for the consumer. The producers are not entirely free to set any price. They have to recoup their costs;[2] at the same time, they have to recognize that higher prices are likely to reduce the total demand. Small demand may dictate higher prices, but higher prices may also lead to lower demand.

Direct purchases may come in a series of one-time sales, as when a consumer purchases records and books, or in the form of a longer commitment through subscriptions. In fact, in most media, subscriptions do not cover the full cost of the commodity, but in a few, such as community radio and some alternative newspapers, which refuse or seriously limit advertisements, subscriptions may in fact provide almost the entire income for the business. Similarly, some cable stations (such as premier movie channels) rely entirely upon subscription fees.

Other media products are sold as access instead of ownership. Control of access is by "turnstile": One pays to go through the gate, as with a movie or concert or Internet provider. As unlikely as it may seem given the costs of such tickets, the price of admission usually covers only part of the total cost and profit. Concessions and secondary merchandising (which we shall discuss shortly) often generate a significant part of the income. According to *Screen Digest* (Cinema concessions, 2002),

> In the U.S. cinema companies reap 85 cents on the dollar for concessions, compared to 70 cents per dollar on ticket sales. . . . A rough rule of thumb . . . is that if concessions account for 25 percent of a cinema's revenues, they will represent around 50 percent of its profits. (n.p.)

That helps explain why a few cents worth of popcorn costs $4. Similarly, although the price of admission to rock concerts has apparently gotten out of hand, rarely does the gate profit cover the cost of touring. Bands and promoters make profits largely by selling merchandise at the concerts.

Some media are delivered "free," so that there is no direct cost to the consumer at all. In the United States, at least, broadcast radio and television have developed as media that are supported entirely by advertising. Advertisers buy time in and around programming in hopes that the audience will be stimulated by the advertising to buy a product or service (or even to vote for a politician). Direct mail ("junk mail") advertising operates in the same way: The cost of producing and distributing it is borne directly by the advertisers. In the long run, advertising is not free to consumers insofar as the cost of advertising a product is usually added into the price of the product. Sometimes the advertising is paid for indirectly, as when bookstores get a commission for subscriptions to magazines entered with the ads they distribute with all purchases.

Some media are paid for in several ways combined: They may be purchased, but they are also subsidized by other means so that consumers share the cost with others. For example, the price of buying or subscribing to a newspaper or magazine is only a fraction of what it costs the publisher to produce it. In fact, the newsstand cost of a newspaper is just a bit less than what it costs the publisher to buy the paper on which one copy is printed. The rest of the money comes from advertising. Two thirds of a typical newspaper publisher's revenue comes from selling space in the paper to individuals and companies to print ads in hopes that consumers will see the ads and buy whatever goods or services they are advertising. Cable television is similarly supported: Subscription fees (both for basic services and for premium channels) are shared between the local cable operator and the various program suppliers. But increasingly, both the local cable system and the cable networks depend on advertising sales for their profit. Similarly, it was hoped that advertising would subsidize costs for Web sites on the Internet. Thus we have had to deal with annoying flashing banner ads, pop-up ads, and pop-under ads. Despite all of these, advertising on the Internet, though still a $6 billion industry in the United States (Elkin, 2002), has not proved as lucrative as was hoped. Many Web sites are exploring other funding options, such as leaving the basic Web site free but charging for access to enhanced information and features, or charging micropayments for access to a page, or complete corporate sponsorship of a site.

Why would advertisers subsidize consumers' access to media such as television, radio, newspapers, and magazines? The answer is that, from the point of view of the advertisers, they are purchasing access to the consumers or audiences themselves. In television, for example, the advertiser buys something called "impressions" or the estimated number of people who see their television advertisement. In this sense, the television network can be said to deliver an audience to the advertiser ("We sell eyeballs," a Chicago television executive told a student) at the same time it delivers an advertisement and other programming to the audience. (See Box 4.1, "Advertising Spending.") Television news is both subsidized by advertising and underwritten by the networks. Thus, for example, special news broadcasts are always difficult for networks to manage because of the complex negotiations necessary to cover the cost. Consider again the events of September 11, 2001: By the end of the extraordinary coverage (three days of broadcasting without commercials), the networks had lost millions of dollars, because extra programming costs were associated with the news coverage and especially because advertisers did not want to advertise during the coverage, fearing that they would be considered insensitive or that their products would be associated with the events. (That's just a little ironic, given the amount of violence on network television.)

---

**BOX 4.1**

**Advertising Spending**

The following table presents total advertising spending for 2002. Dollars are in billions. *Per capita* figures are arrived at by dividing expenditures by U.S. population (estimated at 283 million); figures may not sum exactly due to rounding. *Percentage change* is since 2001.

*(Continued)*

---

105

(Continued)

| Medium | Ad Spending | Percentage of Total | Percentage Change | Per Capita |
|---|---|---|---|---|
| Newspapers | | | | |
|   National | $6.81 | 2.9% | 2.9% | $24.03 |
|   Local | 37.23 | 15.7 | −1.1 | 131.55 |
|   Newspapers total | 44.03 | 18.6 | −0.5 | 155.58 |
|   Magazines | 11.00 | 4.6 | −0.9 | 38.87 |
| Broadcast TV | | | | |
|   Four TV networks | 15.00 | 6.3 | 4.9 | 53.00 |
|   Syndication* | 3.03 | 1.3 | −2.2 | 10.71 |
|   Spot (national) | 10.92 | 4.6 | 18.4 | 38.59 |
|   Spot (local) | 13.11 | 5.6 | 7.0 | 46.33 |
|   Broadcast total | 42.07 | 17.8 | 8.2 | 148.66 |
| Cable TV | | | | |
|   Cable networks | 12.07 | 5.1 | 2.5 | 42.65 |
|   Spot (local) | 4.23 | 1.8 | 7.5 | 14.94 |
|   Cable total | 16.30 | 6.9 | 3.6 | 57.59 |
| Radio | | | | |
|   Network | 0.78 | 0.3 | 9.0 | 2.76 |
|   Spot (national) | 3.34 | 1.4 | 13.0 | 11.80 |
|   Spot (local) | 14.76 | 6.2 | 4.0 | 52.16 |
|   Radio total | 18.88 | 7.9 | 5.7 | 66.71 |
|   Yellow pages | 13.78 | 5.8 | 1.4 | 48.70 |
|   Direct mail | 46.07 | 19.4 | 3.0 | 162.80 |
|   Business publications | 3.98 | 1.7 | −11.0 | 14.06 |
|   Out of home | 5.18 | 2.2 | 0.8 | 81.30 |
|   Internet | 4.88 | 2.1 | −13.5 | 17.24 |
| Miscellaneous | | | | |
|   National | 23.41 | 9.9 | 1.0 | 82.72 |
|   Local | 7.32 | 3.1 | 6.6 | 25.87 |
|   Miscellaneous total | 30.73 | 13.0 | 2.8 | 108.59 |
|   National total | 145.43 | 61.4 | 2.6 | 513.89 |
|   Local total | 91.45 | 38.6 | 2.2 | 323.14 |
|   Total | $236.88 | 100.0 | 2.4 | $837.03 |

*includes United Paramount Network (UPN), Warner Brothers (WB), and Paxson TV (PAX).

Source: Reprinted with permission from *Advertising Age*, copyright © 2004 Crain Communications, Inc.

Over the years, a number of different groups have argued that the underrepresentation of various social groups on television—for example, Blacks, Hispanics, and the elderly—is a consequence of this need for television programmers to deliver those audiences that advertisers most desire. Thus the fact that, until quite recently, advertisers did not see Blacks as a "most wanted" market segment for their specific products (because they were not thought to have a lot of disposable income) meant that the networks were reluctant to program shows aimed specifically at Black people. Programs about Blacks often are constructed in ways that are intended to attract both specifically middle-class segments of the Black population and White audiences as well (for example, *The Jeffersons, Good Times, A Different World, Cosby,* and *The Wayans Brothers*). At other times, Blacks were kept off the air because programmers were afraid that their presence would offend other—White—segments of their market (this was particularly the case in the 1950s). Currently, however, advertisers are finding it necessary to define more and more specific market segments, and to redefine their often-taken-for-granted assumptions about which are the most desirable market segments for which products.

Traditionally, given the specific products that were advertised on television (household goods, food products, cosmetics), advertisers assumed that the best market segment was defined by housewives ages 18 to 49, those people who were thought to do the shopping for such goods for the entire family. Now, network advertisers want even younger audiences, those 18 to 34. Moreover, as the number of available cable channels increases (to over 500 channels per cable or satellite system), advertisers want to reach ever more specific target audiences for their products and are demanding programming geared to such specifically defined audiences (such as professional women ages 25 to 34 or upper-middle-class male teenagers).

There are many new market segments available today as well. The structure of American families has changed significantly in the past 30 years. Fewer than 25% of American families fit the typical image of the nuclear family: a father, a mother, and some children living together. Furthermore, women's roles in the family have changed, and as income has been generally redistributed across the society, there are many new consumer groups of interest to advertisers: children, older people, single people, single parents, Blacks, Hispanics, and other minorities. (See Box 4.2, "The Hispanic Market.") In fact, advertisers find that they must develop strategies to identify who their potential markets are, where they can be found, and how best to appeal to them. This market segmentation has led to what is commonly known as *niche marketing* in advertising or *narrowcasting* in the broadcasting industry, in which the same product is marketed in distinctively different ways to different audiences, or different products (often only slightly different, with different brand names or labels) are marketed to different audiences.

---

**BOX 4.2**

**The Hispanic Market**

One of the new niche markets in the United States is the Hispanic market. Currently constituting just over 13% of the U.S. population, the number of Hispanic Americans is expected to increase to 50 million people in 2007 with a buying power of almost a trillion dollars (Nucifora, 2003). This rapidly expanding market segment is attractive to those who have goods to advertise, which means a higher media profile for Hispanics on mainstream television and film screens and a growing presence of Spanish language channels. But this niche-market land rush also has important implications for the cultural identity of those within the Hispanic market, because marketers and media companies are making decisions about what makes someone Hispanic: Marketers decide what images they will present (Are Hispanics more dark or more fair?); what language they use (Do all Hispanics speak Spanish?); what cultural references are made (Is Spain a common referent? What of those not of Spanish heritage?), and these choices all work to define a common Hispanic identity (Dávila, 2002). Even the decision by marketers to refer to this segment as *Hispanic* (those of Spanish descent) rather than *Latino* (those with origins in Latin America) is significant.

The following excerpt from Dávila (2001) addresses the marketing to (and of) Latinos in terms of the negotiation of a common group identity:

"Latinos are hot, and we are not the only ones to think so. Everyone wants to jump on the bandwagon, and why not? We have the greatest art, music, and literature. It's time we tell our stories." With these words, actor Antonio Banderas welcomed all to the first advertising "Up-Front" presentation by the Spanish TV network Telemundo. Summoning advertisers to "jump on the

---

bandwagon," he echoed a promise that is repeatedly heard in corporate head-quarters and at advertising conventions alike: that Latinos are the hottest new market and that those who target them will not regret it. That Latinos are hot is not at all surprising. It is becoming increasingly common to see aspects of Latino culture popularized in mainstream culture, with salsa outselling ketchup and taking over dance floors, and a growing number of corporate sponsors interested in Latinos as a target market. That a famous Spaniard like Antonio Banderas should become the spokesman of U.S. Latino culture, which is overwhelmingly Mexican, Puerto Rican, Hispanic Caribbean, and Central American, is also not surprising. Although Latino social movements in the 1960s defined themselves against anything Spanish, such distinctions have since been countered by the growing consolidation of a common Latino/Hispanic identity that encompasses anyone from a Spanish/Latin American background in the United States.

Central to this development is Hispanic marketing and advertising. Long before the current popularization of Latin culture, this industry first advanced the idea of a common "Hispanic market" by selling and promoting generalized ideas about "Hispanics" to be readily marketed by corporate America. Thirty years later, the existence and profitability of this culture-specific market feeds one of the fastest growing sectors of the marketing industry in the United States. Over eighty Hispanic advertising agencies and branches of transnational advertising conglomerates spread across cities with sizable Hispanic populations now sell consumer products by shaping and projecting images of and for Latinos.

[. . .] Although these populations have historically lacked access to public venues of self-representation, it is in the market and through marketing discourse that they are increasingly debating their social identities and public standing. These issues are consequently reduced and correlated with their "advertising worthiness and marketability," cautioning us against the facile celebration of Latinos' commercial popularity as an infallible sign of their "coming of age" and political standing. (pp. 1–2)

A niche market that has gained considerable attention is the youth market, especially teens. A recent poll puts American teen spending at $94.7 billion annually ("Generation Y," 2003), and teen spending globally would obviously be much more than this. It is not surprising then that teens are a major market for films, TV shows, CDs, videogames, and many other products from fashion to fast food. In addition, an entire industry called *cool hunting* has grown up in recent years to focus on teen spending. Cool hunters monitor youth culture closely, looking for the next trend in fashion or culture by finding the most innovative teens. Cool hunters' findings are then made available (for a substantial fee) to marketers and corporations that make products for the teen market. In essence, teens provide the corporations with innovations, which the corporations then manufacture and sell back to the teens. (See Box 4.3, "Cool Hunters.")

---

**BOX 4.3**

**Cool Hunters**

The following is from Klein (1999):

> While the change agents were getting set to cool the corporate world from the inside out, a new industry of "cool hunters" was promising to cool the companies from the outside in. The major corporate cool consultancies—Sputnik, *The L. Report,* Bureau de Style—were all founded between 1994 and 1996, just in time to present themselves as the brands' personal cool shoppers. The idea was simple: they would search out pockets of cutting-edge lifestyle, capture them on videotape and return to clients like Reebok, Absolut Vodka and Levi's with such bold pronouncements as "Monks are cool."[1] They would advise their clients to use irony in their ad campaigns, to get surreal, to use "viral communications."
>
> In their book *Street Trends,* Sputnik founders Janine Lopiano-Misdom and Joanne De Luca concede that almost anyone can interview a bunch of young people and make generalizations, "but how do you know they are the 'right' ones–have you been in their closets? Trailed their daily routines? Hung out with them socially? . . . Are they the core consumers, or the mainstream followers?"[2] Unlike the market researchers who use focus groups and one-way glass to watch kids as if they were overgrown lab rats, Sputnik is "one of them"—it is in with the in-crowd.
>
> Of course all of this has to be taken with a grain of salt. Cool hunters and their corporate clients are locked in a slightly S/M, symbiotic dance: the clients are desperate to believe in a just-beyond-their-reach well of untapped cool, and the hunters, in order to make their advice more valuable, exaggerate the crisis of credibility the brands face. On the off chance of Brand X becoming the next Nike, however, many corporations have been more than willing to pay up. And so, armed with their change agents and their cool hunters, the super-brands became the perennial teenage followers, trailing the scent of cool wherever it led.
>
> In 1974, Norman Mailer described the paint sprayed by urban graffiti artists as artillery fired in a war between the street and the establishment. "You hit your name and maybe something in the whole scheme of the system

---

gives a death rattle. For now your name is over their name . . . your presence is on their Presence, your alias hangs over their scene."[3] Twenty-five years later, a complete inversion of this relationship has taken place. Gathering tips from the graffiti artists of old, the superbrands have tagged everyone–including the graffiti writers themselves. No space has been left unbranded. (pp. 72–73)

**Notes**

1. Sullivan, 1997, pp. 182, 187–88
2. Lopiano-Misdom & De Luca, 1997, p. 11
3. Mailer, 1974, p. 77

Some "free" (and even some paid) media are supported partly or fully by nonadvertising revenue. That is, they are literally subsidized. Many organizations—unions, universities, companies—wholly or partly subsidize their own publications, often called *house organs*, although they may also sell advertising to contribute to the costs. University publications, such as the telephone directory and the class schedule, were traditionally distributed free (although that seems to be changing). Similarly, universities subsidize their faculty's and students' access to the Internet. Public radio and television are supported through taxes, through corporate and foundation support, and by viewer and listener contributions solicited primarily by what some people in the business call "beg-a-thons."

Many countries in the world established state-owned and supported "public" broadcasting systems for both radio and television, rather than the competitive profit-making system put into place in the United States. In Great Britain, for example, the state-owned British Broadcasting Corporation (BBC) had a radio and television monopoly financed by an annual tax on all television and radio sets. (Incidentally, taxing receivers limits access to over-the-air broadcasting.) British people could choose among several BBC-Radio and two BBC-TV channels. The tax—and the BBC—remain; but since 1954, private, advertiser-supported broadcasting has grown up alongside it (though this is highly regulated). And the private broadcasting sector has put increasing pressure on the state to privatize the remaining public networks. More recently, this pattern has been repeated in most of Western Europe, and trends suggest it will be the pattern for most of the rest of the world.

Even in the United States, other forms of subsidy exist. Many magazines, particularly journals of opinion such as *The Nation* and *National Review,* often operate for long periods at a loss, a loss that must be made up by "angels" or wealthy individuals who underwrite the journal because they support its editorial positions. Government subsidy is more widespread: By issuing second-class mailing permits for printed matter such as magazines, the U.S. Post Office is using profits from the higher prices of other categories to cover the lower price of these subsidized permits. Various tax credits serve a similar purpose: More than two thirds of the states exempt newspapers from state sales taxes, and some exempt textbooks and magazines as well.

Many of the challenges facing companies that invest in Internet content involve questions of how to charge money and earn profits through this new medium. The big dot-com bust of the late 1990s (when many of the new Internet start-up companies went bankrupt) was based on just such lack of profits. Indeed, this problem points to a contradiction in the capitalist approach to managing the Internet. The Internet was established as a medium for the sharing of data, and a culture has continued online that values the free exchange of information from file sharing to open-source software (in which anyone can make improvements and come up with new versions, but which no one truly owns). This runs in the face of companies asserting ownership of data or software and trying to profit from its exchange. The case that emphasized this contrast in approaches is that of Napster.

Napster was a program that allowed online users to download MP3 versions of their favorite songs. It allowed users to upload copies of music as well, so that others could download it. Needless to say, all of this free copying of songs upset the music industry, which saw such exchange as a loss of revenue (one less CD sold). Napster was sued by the recording industry and the company was shut down. However, other file-sharing software is still in use and so the story is not over yet. And it is not just music that can be traded online but any electronic file, including films that have been digitized. The potential loss of revenue if it becomes much easier for fans to download and exchange entire films has Hollywood's attention. The Motion Picture Association of America (MPAA), a motion picture industry trade group, estimated it lost $3.5 billion in revenues to downloaders; while this number may be self-servingly inflated, the amount likely is in the billions.

## Competition Among the Media

Capitalism assumes that any product enters into a freely competitive market. Whatever the reality of the degree of that competition in any particular market, any producer attempting to create and distribute a new media product has to consider the marketplace, where the product will almost certainly compete with other products. There are different forms of competition. First, there is direct competition for an audience: A new newspaper, for example, will compete directly with all the other newspapers already in the market. Similarly, a new album competes with other albums. When a single item, say a book or a CD, is brought on the market, it competes with other products much like it—other books and other CDs, especially those with the same target audience.

Second, there are forms of indirect competition both within and across media. Within a medium, products compete for resources necessary for their existence—for example, airtime or advertising. A new newspaper has to attract advertisers that otherwise might have gone to another newspaper or to some other medium, such as radio. A new television program has to compete with other programs to find a place in a network's schedule so that it has the possibility of finding its audience.

In addition, a new media product has to find an audience, and sometimes that involves convincing an audience to buy that product (and spend the time necessary to use it) *instead* of buying and spending time with something else. After all, everybody's time and energy, and most people's money, are limited. Scholars analyzing economic data from the 1920s until 1979 argued that a *principle of relative constancy* was operating. After correcting for inflation, this principle suggests that, over time, individuals spend a constant portion of their disposable income (income left over after taxes and essentials such as food, clothing, and shelter) on media. If some media product is purchased, some other is not. In the more recent past, however, the fraction of disposable income spent on media has increased, largely because of increased spending on electronic and video media. In other words, people are spending relatively more on media and relatively less on other nonessential items than they did in the past. Hence the attempt to introduce a new media product into an existing market may not face quite the same constraints as such endeavors did in the past. Instead, new products might be creating new markets and new categories of consumers (for example, the traveler as a primary reader of *USA Today*).

Different conditions are involved when competition is between media themselves, when the new product is a new media technology. In discussing how media compete with other existing media, both for dollars and for attention, media economists have borrowed from population biologists the notion of an ecological niche, or a space that some entity successfully occupies because it has some competitive advantage over other, somewhat different entities. A local newspaper enjoys a couple of competitive advantages for its niche over competing media: It's a more efficient (cheaper and broader) vehicle for classified advertising (such as help-wanted, personal, and auto ads) and generally reports local news in more detail than television or radio. Television and radio, however, occupy slightly different niches and likewise enjoy competitive advantages over newspapers (such as breaking news coverage, video and audio reports, and so on).

What happens when a new *medium* appears? Sometimes, a new medium wholly supplants or replaces an existing one: Motion pictures began life as peephole Kinetoscopes. People paid admission to a nickelodeon, a forerunner of the video arcade, where they, by themselves and for a nickel, watched a one-reel short subject on a single machine; for 100 people to watch a film at the same time required 100 Kinetoscopes. Enter the film projector: With it, 100—soon 1,000 and more—people could watch the same film at the same time using just one machine. This was a lot more economically efficient (cheaper) for exhibitors, and capital flowed away from the Kinetoscope and toward movie palaces.

The Kinetoscope and the movie projector occupied the same niche—popular light entertainment—and, in the process, helped to kill off still another "mass medium," vaudeville live performance. Furthermore, the projected movie altered the medium itself: Film watching became a social experience; we watch films in groups, and we react not only to the film but to the other members of the audience as well. Groucho Marx of the Marx Brothers used to go to premieres of his movies with a stopwatch, and he would re-edit the movie if he found that too much, or too little, time had been left after punch lines for the audience to laugh: If too much time had been left, the movie dragged; if too little, the audience would be laughing too loud to hear the next line of dialogue.

Recorded music provides another dramatic and more recent example of media replacement. Vinyl records were supplanted by audiocassettes, which have since had to compete with the introduction of CDs. Along the way, eight-track cassettes failed to find a niche. No one can predict what medium will replace CDs, but it is clear that something—such as portable MP3 players—will. At the same time, although it appeared that tapes and discs would drive records off the shelves, it seems that vinyl is making a limited comeback. The point is that such media relations are too complex to predict in advance, and investment in media economies remains a highly risky business.

Some media continue on while the world changes around them. The American magazine began life in the eighteenth century, much as American newspapers did: a high-priced, locally circulated medium supported by and catering to the tastes and interests of elites. Only in the 1890s, half a century after newspapers went through a similar process, did magazines evolve to what they would become for the next 60 years: large, nationally circulated journals, supported by advertising and appealing to the widest, "massest" interests possible, with audiences that in some cases numbered in the millions. Cultural changes that made such magazines viable included increasing literacy in the population; increasingly efficient mass production, which allowed per-copy prices to drop dramatically; improved modes of distribution and communication; and the development of modern marketing. Not until about 100 years ago were there national brands of merchandise—before that virtually everything was generic—and without such national brands, national advertising was literally unthinkable.

Magazines such as *Life, Look,* and *The Saturday Evening Post* dominated their niche: For a 35-year period, the mass circulation magazine had no competition as a national mass medium. Radio changed that a bit, but television changed everything. In 1950, *Life, Look,* and *The Saturday Evening Post* each had a national circulation exceeding 5 million. As such, the magazines were important advertising vehicles, for no other visual medium reached so many eyeballs. Radio could tell you about a Pontiac or a Studebaker, but it couldn't show you one. TV could show (like magazines) and tell (like radio), and it added motion (like cinema). More important, it could reach a larger audience. By 1955, TV reached 47.8 million American homes—78% of the total—and a modestly rated network television program was viewed by millions more people than any mass circulation magazine. Circulation of mass magazines, as one might expect, declined. *The Saturday Evening Post,* for example, slipped from 6.2 million at its peak in 1959 to just under a million when it ceased publication 10 years later. But more important than the readers deserting was that the advertisers deserted as well. TV was a more efficient (cheaper) media buy for advertisers; mass circulation magazines were driven out of their niche and had to evolve.

The introduction of television as a commercial medium affected not only magazines but the motion picture and radio industries as well. Roughly one third as many people go to the movies in a typical week today, compared to the mid-1940s, for example, and only in the early 1980s did motion picture revenues surpass the industry's heyday of the 1940s. This increase was largely the result of the sharp increase in the price of tickets, which more than tripled between the 1940s and the 1980s. The movie industry also adapted by specializing. Movie makers shifted from making films directed to a mass audience, in which adults and families were the primary market, to a set of genre markets— science fiction, martial arts, and especially horror/slasher films—aimed more at adolescents: In 1985, people ages 12 to 24 accounted for only 27% of the population but 53% of movie tickets sold. Today, however, with Baby Boomers making up a third of the audience, we are seeing more independent films or more intelligent, quality films, which appeal to an older audience ("Baby Boomers," 2003). The movie industry also stressed its competitive advantage: a bigger and better picture than television's. Cinemascope and other large screen formats were developed to bring audiences back to the theater.

As with movies, the advent of television signaled the end of radio as it had been known. Television appropriated not only the niche but literally the form of radio as well, and many of radio's most popular programs and performers migrated to TV: Jack Benny and Bob Hope, George Burns and Gracie Allen. Radio networks—CBS, NBC, the American Broadcasting Company (ABC)—became television networks. The result was that between 1949 and 1959 radio lost most of its mass audience and the national advertisers who marketed to this generalized audience. Radio adapted by specializing and reformatting: Instead of programming for everybody (conceived as a market of families), local stations began programming for more specialized audiences, initially almost exclusively along lines of musical taste—middle-of-the-road

116

pop, rock, classical, country and western, rhythm and blues. By the 1970s, however, these musical formats were further fragmented and specialized (rock, for example, fragmented into dozens of different genres and formats), and other formats based on ethnicity or nonmusical programming (talk and all news stations) emerged. Many of these formats were available as relatively cheap prepackaged programming (Casey Kasem's *Top 40 Countdown* is a good example). Radio's survival was also made possible by two technological advances that broadened its audience: the development of the transistor, which allowed for smaller, cheaper, and more reliable receivers, and the opening to broadcasters of the FM spectrum, which enabled not only clearer signals but also stereophonic transmission, both of which were especially important for its increasing musical orientation. And so radio "downsized": Expensive, network-produced musical variety and dramatic programs were replaced with self-sufficient local stations and packaged programming. At the same time, radio expanded: More stations came on the air to chase after various specialized audiences.

Interestingly, as other media were specializing in response to television's threat to their market share, television's content between the late 1940s and the 1970s become less diverse, at least in the genres of programs it offered (Dominick & Pearce, 1976). In the early "Golden Age of Television," prime-time programming included many categories, such as quiz programs, westerns, serious drama, and musical variety, which had all but vanished by the 1970s, when TV programming consisted largely of situation comedies and action-adventures. This can be understood as a result of television's search for the largest possible mass audience: The result was that decision makers repeated the most successful genres, reducing much of the variety of early television.

Recently, network television's control of the broadly defined mass-audience niche is being challenged by a host of competitors: cable and satellite systems (which now reach approximately 70% of U.S. television homes), video games (which compete with programming for the use of the television set), videocassette recorders (which can be used either to "time shift"—to allow viewers to record a program and view it at a more convenient time—or to play prerecorded tapes), DVD players, and now even Web surfing. The network share of the television audience during prime time has fallen from a high of 91% in 1978–1979 to 40% in 1996–1997, which network executives attribute mostly to the encroachments of cable. These developments mark an interesting reversal in the history of media, for unlike other niche battles, what we have here are specialized formats challenging a mass medium, rather than a struggle between mass media.

In the 1990s and 2000s, the FCC greatly lessened its restrictions on cross-media ownership (whether one can own both radio stations and a newspaper in the same market) and on the portion of a market one owner could dominate (the stations one could own could only dominate a limited percentage of the total market in that area). With this deregulation came major consolidations in the media industry, especially in radio (where half the stations in the United States have been sold since 1996). Large national corporations, like Clear Channel, purchased rival independent stations leaving the radio dial in most cities dominated by a couple of different corporations, and driving independent and family-owned business out of business and local voices off the air. We will discuss the potential consequences of such consolidation at the end of the chapter.

## Profit in the Media Industries

Media economics, like capitalist economics in general, focuses on efficiency and the generation of profit. There are significant differences across the various media industries: A large number of different factors help shape routes to profit in relation to each media. Still, one can identify the general economic principles that influence the content of media and the role of the media in society.

Many media industries, being capital intensive (they require large initial investments in fixed costs such as machinery), provide almost classic examples of economies of scale. For example, in the music industry, the cost of manufacturing each album declines as the number of albums manufactured increases. That is, the marginal cost of an additional album is small. Thus it is to the company's advantage to produce and market only those records that can be expected to sell in sufficiently large numbers. Economies of scale are most pronounced for those media where materials and distribution costs are negligible. Think about media "hardware," such as CD players, DVD players, large screen televisions, and personal computers: The initial prices on these items are always exorbitantly high; as demand increases, prices drop rapidly. The price change follows the law of supply and demand, but it is also the result of the economy of scale in the manufacture of these goods.

Yet there are important ways in which media industries are more complex and significantly different from other types of industries, especially because some of them are involved simultaneously in two economic transactions: selling something to an audience and selling that audience to advertisers. In newspapers, for example, the initial investment is huge, but the marginal costs of adding each additional copy are negligible. At the same time, one has to take into account the costs and profits of adding additional advertising pages against the additional profits. Radio and TV differ: Adding any number of listeners or viewers adds no cost, though there are real material limits to the number of advertising minutes that can be added. Obviously, a larger audience does allow a station to lower its cost per thousand listeners/viewers, generating more income than competitors, but there are always constraints and limits: Competition comes not only from other media outlets, but from different media forms as well. Finally, in some media, such as cable or telephone, the economy of scale is so strong that it tends to produce natural monopolies.

The profits of the media industries are constrained by a number of other factors that serve to both strengthen and mitigate the influence of economies of scale and the laws of supply and demand. One of the most important and powerful of these factors is audience size. In television and other media, two key measures—ratings and shares—are used to calculate the size of the audience; advertisers use these measures to estimate how many people will see their commercials, and television networks use them to calculate the popularity of their programs and thus how much they can charge advertisers to advertise on the programs—the larger the rating, the larger the charge. *Ratings* estimate the total number of households viewing any particular program. Ratings are expressed in *ratings points,* and each rating point is equivalent to 931,000 households with television. Hence a program with an 18.8 rating is estimated to have been viewed in 17.5 million homes. *Shares* provide an estimate of the percentage of all households, among those viewing television, that viewed a particular program. Shares are expressed in *percentage points.* A program with a 31 share, for example, is estimated to have been viewed by 31% of all households watching TV at the time.

The number of people watching TV varies across the day. More watch in prime time (which is why it's "prime" for advertisers) than watch in the morning, afternoon, or late at night. Thus both the ratings and share numbers are important measures. A program in the afternoon, for example, could have a large share of the audience but a modest rating; a soap opera with a 3.4 rating but a 38 share might be a smashing success. Yet a prime-time show might have a much larger rating but a more modest share: A series with a 6.8 rating and an 11 share would be seen in twice as many households as the soap opera, but it would be a prime candidate for cancellation.

Because a television network's profits depend on its advertising revenues, which in turn depend on its market share (its proportion of the viewing audience), it needs to attract as large an audience as it can. But market share does not influence the production cost of making a television show. It costs about the same amount to produce and air each episode of a show (and currently a 1-hour television pilot costs about $2.8 million ["Budget," 2003]) whether it is watched by 25 million people or no one at all, although a network might be willing to make a larger investment (more per episode or more episodes) if it is confident about the future size of the audience. Similarly, the cost of producing a master tape for a record does not vary with the size of its potential audience, although a record company might be willing to invest more in the production of such a tape if they believe it is likely to sell well. Hence one of the most basic principles in media economics is this: The larger the audience, the larger the income (whether from sales of the product, of advertising, or of admission) and usually, the larger the profit. For truly *mass* media, such as television, motion pictures, newspapers, and the like, this makes trying to reach the largest possible audience the primary goal.

A third factor that influences media profits is the specific shape of the profit curve in such industries, often described as the *break-even point* and the *hit-to-release ratio*. In the profit curve of a typical industry operating within an economy of scale, profits are calculated by subtracting marginal cost (the difference between the cost of producing the last and the next to the last product or good) from marginal price (the difference between the price of the last and the next to the last product or good). However, in many media industries, almost the total cost of the product is up front; that is, almost all of the total cost is the cost of producing the first item (the actual television program or the master tape for a record or the first print of the film). Beyond the first item, the cost of subsequent copies or impressions is minimal and follows the principles of an economy of scale. This leads the media to calculate their profits on the basis of a break-even point: They attempt to recoup all of their initial costs as quickly as possible. Companies will often include the high cost of promotion and advertising media products in calculating these initial costs, because such promotion is necessary to begin the process of sales. But once a product becomes a hit, promotion costs decrease sharply. Thus, for example, all of what would be the profits from the sale of a record are charged against the initial costs of producing the master tape or the first copy. Once those initial costs are recouped, the record is said to have reached the break-even point, and every record sold after that creates pure profit for the company, minus the small marginal cost of producing the physical object itself. It is only after a record reaches the break-even point that the artists begin to collect royalties (their share of the profits).

For these reasons, the ratio of hits to releases is extremely important when a media corporation calculates its profits. The hit-to-release ratio simply describes the percentage of media products that reach and sur-pass their break-even points. It is not simply a matter of hits versus bombs, because a product with high initial costs might well sell a large number of copies or do well in the box office but fail to reach its break-even point. For a company releasing a large number of products, the profits from the hits (which surpass their break-even points) can be used to offset the losses from the other products. The result is that a company not only will attempt to produce as many smash hits as it can, but also will prefer to have a small number of mega-hits rather than a large number of smaller hits. Hit-to-release ratios are particularly impor-tant in the music, film, television, and book publishing industries.

One recent change has significantly affected the media industries: An increasing percentage of their profits come from *secondary markets;* these are profits derived from sources other than advertising or the direct sale of the product. There are a number of different ways in which such secondary profits are generated. One such source is the sale of merchandise associated with the original product: T-shirts and other clothing, toys, posters, and all manner of products with media logos. A second source involves licensing the rights to the product or its image to other media industries: Record companies license the use of their music to film companies for soundtracks, and sometimes original film soundtracks are released separately as records. Record companies also license the use of their music to television commercials. A third source involves the sale of the product to secondary markets, such as when television programs are syndicated or released on videotape or DVD, when films are sold for broadcast or videotape distribution, or when any product is distributed outside the primary market of the United States.

## Risk and Media

The unique ways in which profits are generated and calculated in media industries mean that, in general, media products are quite risky ventures; producers cannot know for certain in advance whether a particular product—a movie, a television series, a book, a record—will be popular or whether that popularity will translate into profits. In the case of most individual media products, as a matter of fact, the odds are against success. Ninety percent of all new TV series are gone after one season, 90% of new magazine titles fail within a year, and 90% of pop CDs do not break even. Nonetheless, a producer can, if sufficiently well capitalized (if starting out with a big enough cash cushion or credit line) underwrite a number of flops because successes can be spectacularly profitable. Thus large and well-capitalized producers enjoy a decided advantage over newcomers.

One of the most important reasons for the high risk in these industries is that consumers have little brand loyalty in their media tastes. Rarely do people watch a program because it is the latest ABC offering or read a book because it is published by Random House or buy a record because it is on Polygram. (There are exceptions: small companies that have developed specific identities—Harlequin in the field of romance novels, Rounder for Blues records.) Rather, consumers are making choices for individual products from the wide range of offerings.

This uncertainty and inability to predict smash hits is an example of unique risks involved in mediamaking. The various forms of market testing that guide consumer products have not proven very helpful to the media industries so far.

The other reason for the high risk in media industries is that the industries cannot control the creative process. The songwriter, the screenwriter, the author, and the actor—all of them determine to some extent the success of the product. Yet there is little the industry can do to guarantee the quality (and appeal) of what they produce.

Most media industries face similar problems of trying to manage the risk involved in producing hits, and they employ similar strategies. If the risk is the result of various features of the media economies in general, it is also the case that not all media producers or potential producers face the same odds. A number of strategies exist that allow a producer to maximize the chances of success; almost all favor the trends toward corporate consolidation—toward smaller numbers of larger media companies—that have marked the past few decades and that virtually all observers expect to continue into the future.

The first strategy is to *maximize the investment capital.* The more money available to invest in the product in the first place, the better the chance of making a successful product. Clearly, corporations with lots of their own money to invest have a competitive advantage. If a company is short on investment capital, there are a number of options. One can borrow it from someone else. But most lenders—banks, venture capitalists, investment groups—want assurances that the product will be a success. They are likely to look for a product that looks familiar—one that looks pretty much like other successful products in the niche—produced by people with successful track records. This formula favors already successful companies, superstars, and bland, imitative products. A second way to obtain capital is to sell one's company or part of it to a company with more capital or a better credit line. But, often, the new parent company, like any investor, will demand some control over the product that is being planned. A broader, mediawide strategy may involve lobbying the government for favorable tax laws or regulations. This is a complex relationship, because the increasing connections between government and media result in both a reluctance on the part of politicians to stand up to the media and a reluctance on the part of the media to do anything that might offend those in the government who can pass such legislation.

The second strategy for reducing risk and maximizing success is to *integrate the production process.* A producer who can control the entire process of producing, marketing, and distributing the product enjoys two principal advantages over a producer who does not. The first is that it might give him or her some creative control. Suppose a group wants to produce a record. The group might choose to turn the process over to a record company or attempt to do it on their own, renting a studio, mixing the master, designing the package, and advertising themselves. The group would have to hire out the physical production and the distribution of the product (though the Internet is potentially an effective alternative medium in this regard). The album is more likely to turn out to be what the group wants it to be—this is the attraction of various do-it-yourself and independent record companies. But such choices also carry the risk of reducing the potential market for the product: Who's going to know about your music and who's going to buy it, and where? In attics and basements all over the world are unsold copies of bands' efforts to do this.

So, the band may opt for the more prudent course, taking its demo tape to a record company that is *vertically integrated*. A vertically integrated enterprise is one that controls the entire production and distribution process. A vertically integrated record company would control everything: the creation of the music, its physical reproduction and packaging, its marketing and promotion, and its distribution to wholesalers and retailers. When a young band goes to such a record company, its contract basically turns over complete control of the product to the company. The band may have to adapt its music to the company's ideas about what will sell. Until it is successful, the band may not get to choose its own producer or engineer, or the director of its music video, or the designer of its package cover.

A second advantage of vertical integration is profit. With the steps done separately, the recording studio makes a profit in renting the studio, the manufacturer profits in producing the tape or CD, and the distributor profits in moving the product to wholesalers. If a single company controls all the steps, it gets to participate in additional sources of profit (and economies of scale) and to keep all the profits for itself.

Third, to maximize profits and minimize risks, a company can attempt to *rationalize the consumption process.* Although there are no guarantees that the public will buy any particular media product, there are myriad ways that a producer can increase the odds. Just as the production process can be integrated, so too can the consumption process. The company can try to maximize the potential market. The more people who have the opportunity to buy the product, the more who are likely to do so. For example, television networks are highly motivated to increase the number of stations affiliated with them. An affiliated television station is a local television station that has an exclusive agreement with one of the major networks to carry only that network's television shows. In return for carrying the television programs, the local television station—which is paid by the network a share of the network's advertising income—gives to the network an audience for the network's program. And because the size of the audience a network has across the country determines advertising revenues for any program, networks want to have as many affiliates providing audiences as possible. A record company will want its products in as many retail outlets as possible. Discount and wholesale chain stores like Wal-Mart can sell large numbers of products, giving them some influence over what is released (Wal-Mart refusing to sell a CD can significantly hurt the album's overall sales).

A company can also try to integrate the consumption process by creating a product that is assumed to have the best chance of appealing to the largest possible audience. As a former NBC vice president, Paul Klein, noted in the early 1970s, television programming proceeds on the L-O-P formula: Least Objectionable Program (interview in *TV Guide*, July 24, 1971, pp. 6–10, cited in Clark & Blankenburg, 1973). Programmers assume that people watch what's left over after they've rejected the other alternatives, rather than what they really want to watch: That attitude is hardly a strategy for innovative or novel products. The company can also maximize the potential market by rethinking the product itself. A product can be created for multiple media and at multiple sites of possible consumption. What, for example, is Charles Schulz's *Peanuts?* Is it the comic strip syndicated to a thousand U.S. newspapers, or the CBS television specials, or the characters licensed for stuffed toys, party favors, greeting cards, and Metropolitan Life Insurance commercials?

The ability to profit by transporting products across media takes advantage of *horizontal integration,* or the control of markets across media. The 1980s saw an acceleration of media consolidations aimed at horizontal integration. In late 1989 and early 1990, Time, Inc., went into $10.7 billion debt to buy Warner Communications and thereby create the world's largest media company. In 2001, Time Warner was purchased by America Online (AOL) in a $165 billion merger, making AOL Time Warner the largest media company in the world (at the time of this writing, at least). A principal reason for this mega-merger was the synergy executives (and large lenders) thought it would produce. Time, for example, runs ads for its *Entertainment Weekly* magazine on Warner videocassettes; Warner Looney Tunes cassettes are now marketed through Time's aggressive direct-mail unit (the same folks who sell *Sports Illustrated* and all those home-repair and occult book series). The combined company is also the largest U.S. cable television operator, which, not coincidentally, owns Home Box Office (HBO) and Cinemax, and now owns Turner Broadcasting and its CNN.

This synergy can also be turned on competitors in an attempt to drive them out of the market. In the fall of 2003, Time Warner officially dropped "AOL" from its company name (although it is still part of the company), indicating that the synergy might not have been all that the company expected.

Finally, the consumption process can be integrated by "rationalizing" the audience itself. This refers to the practices by which media corporations try to condition people to expect and desire certain kinds of products. Media corporations attempt to make audience choices or tastes more predictable. They may use familiar categories to guide them: For example, producers have at least some idea of how large the market for a particular film genre might be and can budget the film accordingly. Although staying within the genre increases the predictability of revenue, it also dampens both creativity and audience expectations. Media corporations may also attempt to use market research (a set of tools to gauge audience interest and taste, and thereby attempt to rationalize audiences) on potential products and audiences.

## ALTERNATIVES

When we write of alternative media in the context of this chapter, we mean media that do not follow the dominant capitalist model of private, for-profit media organizations. Globally, there are still examples of such models, including state-run media (and we could even include here stations like the Voice of America, which is entirely funded by the government). In the U.S. context, the most prominent alternative to for-profit media is the Public Broadcasting System—both PBS for television and National Public Radio (NPR) and Public Radio International (PRI) for radio. Funded through a collection of government grants, audience pledges, and corporate and charitable foundation sponsorship, these networks do not rely directly on advertising for support. As a consequence of this funding arrangement, it is easier for the public networks to air educational, informational, or controversial programs that do not have mass-market appeal. However, government funding has all but dried up for public broadcasting and as a result these networks are more reliant on audience support (and have begun programming more for mass appeal) and corporate sponsorship (and potentially steering clear of controversy).

There are other alternative media as well. Drawing on the work of John Downing, Australian media scholar Graham Meikle (2002) summarizes the key characteristics of alternative media:

> First, they are independently owned and managed; second, they artic-
> ulate viewpoints which are in some sense dissonant from those of the
> wider media; and third, they foster horizontal linkages between their
> audiences, in contrast to the top-down vertical flows of established
> print and broadcast media. (p. 60)

Downing's discussions of such alternative media include public speeches, graffiti, street theater, performance art, flyers, posters, newspapers, magazines, radio, film, video, and the Internet. What differentiates these media from established media, apart from content, are organization and funding. Alternative media tend to be either individual and personal expression or grassroots (at times ad hoc) network of peers and like-minded individuals. We considered the example of Indymedia as an alternative media organization in Chapter 3. An example of alternative funding would be Paper Tiger TV, a New York–based media collective which produces television programs for broadcast on independent stations, cable television, and for video distribution. The programs are produced by volunteers. In 1985, Paper Tiger established a national satellite network called Deep Dish TV for the distribution of their programs (and others) to cable television systems. Another example is the Pacifica Radio Network, which is entirely listener supported; it's a radio network committed to educational and community-produced programming and to allowing voices and information to be heard that aren't found on mainstream radio. But even Pacifica has been tempted in recent years to cash in on their brand name and possibly become a commercial entity (despite an audience revolt at the prospect [Meikle, 2002]). And there are also a number of media movements worldwide which Clemencia Rodriguez (2001) has termed "citizen's media," where citizens actively intervene in their society by producing their own media. Since many of the movements described above tend to be political in nature, we will be dealing with them more in Chapter 11 when we discuss media and politics.

But not all alternative media are explicitly politically motivated. Fan clubs produce their own home-made magazines (fan magazines or *fanzines*) including fan-produced art and fiction written by fans that feature characters from whatever they are fans of (such as *Star Trek* or

*Buffy the Vampire Slayer*). These fanzines are circulated among the fans themselves (either in print form or now on the Internet). Local bands also produce cassette tapes and home-burned CDs for distribution at concerts (and nowadays also MP3s for distribution online). There's also independent filmmaking and the independent music scene (which, more often than not, are far from independent of the corporate media structure, but some are), and community radio and alternative newspapers. And there are also pirate radio and television stations that broadcast without FCC license. Some pirate stations cover only a few square blocks, some send out more powerful signals, and some even broadcast from international waters, outside the jurisdiction of any government.

## PROBLEMS

Although the problems facing the media industries are, in some ways, typical of any capitalist industry, they also have unique problems in that the industries can most efficiently control the process of distribution (rather than either production or consumption). That is precisely what the media are: a distribution system for culture, for communication, and for information. They cannot completely control the production of their products, since they rely on artists of various sorts (writers, musicians), or how these products are consumed, or what meanings people make of them (see Chapter 5). A consequence of the media industry's control over the distribution of culture and information is that these industries may shape much of the communication to which the audience is exposed. Media critics like Ben Bagdikian (2004), Edward Herman and Robert McChesney (1997), and Herbert Schiller (1992) have argued passionately that the increasing concentration of media ownership leads to increasingly tight corporate control over information and ideas. The ideas aired or published will predominantly be those that benefit the corporation as a whole at the expense of benefiting the public as a whole.

A handful of media corporations control most of the business in newspapers, television, magazines, books, motion pictures, and music not just nationally but internationally. The top five media corporations are Time Warner, Disney, NewsCorp, Viacom, and Bertelsmann. Time Warner owns a number of online services, book publishers, cable television channels, cable television systems, film and television production and distribution companies, magazines, music labels, theme parks, sports teams, and others. (For a more full list, see Box 4.4, "Time Warner Holdings.") In addition to each corporation owning a number of media companies, they also own shares of each other. And these corporations also frequently enter into joint ventures where two or more of them own a media firm. These multiple connections between media giants could be seen as decreasing competition between them, and therefore decreasing the need to be creative or unique.

---

**BOX 4.4**

**Time Warner Holdings**

The respected journal *The Columbia Journalism Review* maintains on its Web site (www.chr.org/tools/owners) a current listing of the holdings of major media companies. As of August, 2004, for Time Warner they list, among others, the following:

*Time Warner Book Group:* Warner Books, Warner Faith, Little, Brown and Company, Time Warner Book Group UK, Time Warner Audio Books, and Time, Inc. (which owns Southern Progress Corporation which publishes Sunset Books).

*Time Warner Cable:* HBO, CNN, CNN International, CNN en Español, CNN Headline News, CNN Airport Network, CNN fn, CNN Radio, CNN Interactive, Court TV, Time Warner Cable, Road Runner, New York 1 News, and over half of Kablevision (in Hungary).

*In Demand:* Metro Sports (in Kansas City).

*Time Warner Inc. Film and Television:* Warner Bros., Warner Bros. Studios, Warner Bros. Television, The WB Television Network, Warner Bros. Television Animation, Hanna-Barbera Cartoons, Telepictures Productions, Witt-Thomas Productions, Castle Rock Entertainment, Warner Home Video, Warner Bros. Domestic Pay-TV, Warner Bros. Domestic Television Distribution, Warner Bros. International Television Distribution, The Warner Channel (Latin America, Asia-Pacific, Australia, and Germany), and Warner Bros. International Theaters (in over 12 countries).

*Time Warner Inc. Magazines: Time* (including five international editions, *Time Money,* and *Time Kids*), *Fortune, Business 2.0, Life,*

*(Continued)*

---

(Continued)

> *Sports Illustrated* (and related titles), *Inside Stuff, Money, People* (including *People en Español* and other variations), *Entertainment Weekly, In Style, Southern Living, Progressive Farmer, Southern Accents, Cooking Light, The Parent Group* (including *Parenting*), *This Old House, Sunset, The Health Publishing Group* (including *Health* and *Weight Watchers*), *Real Simple, Asiaweek, Field & Stream, Golf Magazine, Outdoor Life, Popular Science, Ski, Snowboard Life, Verge,* and others—not to mention *DC Comics, Vertigo,* and *Mad Magazine.*
>
> *Online Services:* CompuServe Interactive Services, AOL Instant Messanger, AOL.com, Digital City, AOL Europe, Spinner.com, and Winamp.
>
> *Time Warner Inc.-Turner Entertainment:* Turner Broadcasting System (TBS) Superstation, Turner Network Television (TNT), Cartoon Network, Turner Classic Movies, New Line Cinema, Fine Line Features, Turner Original Productions, and the Atlanta Braves among other things.

There are also Time Warner consumer products, the Warner Brothers Recreation Enterprises (which owns theme parks), Netscape Communications, AOL MovieFone, and others.

The precise effects of such unprecedented media concentration are subject to intense debate. Such large corporations cannot control every program, article, or song they put out. Indeed, it sometimes makes good business sense to release products that openly critique the company or others like it if that product, in the end, will make the company money. But at times corporations will kill a product or a story if it conflicts with prominent advertisers or the future business prospects of the corporation. For example, in 1998 Rupert Murdoch, owner of News Corporation, stopped its subsidiary HarperCollins' publication of the memoir of Christopher Patten, the last governor of Hong Kong, since the book was critical of the Chinese government with whom Murdoch was eager to do business (Bagdikian, 2000). (The book was later published by Times Books.) Alternatively, corporations will use their multiple media subsidiaries to reinforce each other. A film produced by one company gets advertised in company-owned magazines; "behind the scenes" programs of the making of the film appear on company-owned cable television channel; the soundtrack from the film is released on a company-owned record label, and so on. This synergy crowds out other products from other companies. For example, in 1996, more than half of the books excerpted in the *New Yorker* magazine were published by Random House, both of which were owned at the time by Advance Publications (M. Miller, 1997).

The Internet is not immune from such concentration. The September–October 2003 issue of *Adbusters*, for example, noted that in 2001 Internet users' time online was dominated by less than 20 companies (compared with over 100 companies just two years before.)

A consequence of the corporate concentration is that each component of the company is looked at according to its bottom line: how much profit it generates. The pressure on media companies to be profitable has begun to erode the wall between the news production aspects of some media companies (with their values of truth and objectivity) and the marketing divisions (focused on advertising and market share). Pressures to write stories that have broad market appeal (and that are not too upsetting to major advertisers or shareholders) are challenging the profession of journalism. Howard Gardner, Mihaly Csikszentmihalyi, and William Damon (2001) write,

> In the news media today, ferocious competition has created pressures that are strongly felt throughout the field. Nearly every editor feels impelled to lean more toward entertaining coverage and less toward more serious probing. Dazzling video techniques that capture the public's eye have led producers to forego the thoughtful effort needed to prepare careful or profound presentations. All this has thrown the basic question of "What is news?" up for debate. Material deemed obscure, difficult, or distant has lost out to local "human interest" stories. (p. 130)

In addition to corporate concentration and its effects on the distribution of culture and information, a second problem more unique to the media is that of obsolescence. Most capitalist industries have to plan a certain degree of obsolescence into their products. Let's face it: It wouldn't do much for the auto industry if the car you purchased lasted a lifetime. One way of planning obsolescence is to emphasize the novelty of each new product, to focus on minor innovations that do not basically change the product. But too much novelty, too much innovation, is likely to act against the principles of mass production. These problems are particularly important in the media industries, where there has to be a continuous demand for, and supply of, new products.

A third problem more unique to the media concerns consumption. Although many of the media's products are sold to individuals or families, the industry cannot guarantee what is done with a product once it is owned. Television and radio programs can be taped and shared with others, just as the tapes and records we purchase can be shared with and even reproduced for other people. Books can be photocopied; magazines can be passed from one person to another. What the industries can control is the production of hardware and consumable materials (such as blank tapes) in attempts to limit or control consumers' behaviors. But the industry cannot guarantee the meaning that the media audiences make with their product.

These are some of the problems facing the media industries. Moreover, the media play a central role in contemporary society: They shape our desire for goods, they control the information we receive around the world, they organize our leisure activities, and they provide many of the interpretations of reality we use in our everyday lives. The media help to create and shape our investment in certain lifestyles, images, and commodities.

## NOTES

1. In fact, technically, when economists describe such relations it is in terms of the marginal rate of profit, which describes the profit made on the next to the last item produced.

2. The totality of the cost increases with the number produced, even though the amount of increased cost for each marginal product decreases.

## SUGGESTED READINGS

Atton, C. (2002). *Alternative media.* Thousand Oaks, CA: Sage.
Bagdikian, B. H. (2004). *The new media monopoly.* Boston: Beacon.
Downing, J. (with Ford, T. V., Gil, G., & Stein, L.). (2001). *Radical media: Rebellious communication and social movements.* Thousand Oaks, CA: Sage.
Pearson, R. E., & Uricchio, W. (Eds.). (1991). *The many lives of Batman: Critical approaches to a superhero and his media.* New York: Routledge.

# PART II

# Making Sense of the Media

# Meaning | 5

I n 1985, President Ronald Reagan caused a minor sensation when he attempted to link Bruce Springsteen, and especially Springsteen's song "Born in the USA," to his own conservative agenda and his own definition of patriotism. A national debate ensued, carried on not only in conversations but even in the national print and television press. What was the "real" meaning of the song? Many fans obviously interpreted the song as a celebration of American patriotism, carrying and waving flags at Springsteen's concerts. Others offered the lyrics of the song as "proof" that Springsteen was in fact quite critical of the way the United States, and its government in particular, had treated both the Vietnamese people and the military veterans who had fought in the Vietnam War. The issue was never resolved. "Born in the USA" today stands as both a patriotic anthem and an indictment of American injustice. In 1991 with the Persian Gulf War and in 2003–2004 with the war in Iraq, radio stations again played it in both contexts, as a show of support for the war effort and as a challenge to the Bush administrations of the day to confront inequalities in American society.

Competing definitions are not as rare as we might think. In the 1990s, debates over rap—especially so-called gangsta rap—raised the same issue. Rap's critics claimed that it celebrated and promoted drugs and violence; its defenders claimed that it offered a critical portrait of the street life to which an entire generation of Black youth is condemned. And here's another example: In 2003, the fifth book in the bestselling Harry Potter series, *Harry Potter and the Order of the Phoenix,* set records by selling 5 million copies in its opening weekend (in dollar amounts it made more money that weekend than the top grossing film in the United States, *Hulk*). But the book (and the series) has not been without controversy. Is this just the tale of a plucky young wizard struggling against the forces of evil, a book series that has got millions of young people reading again? Or is this a story that actively promotes witchcraft and needs to be banned? And a final example: Is Michael Moore's 2004 film *Fahrenheit 9/11* a documentary or a piece of propaganda, journalism, or polemic?

These cases point to the more difficult question of how we go about interpreting the variety of messages we receive through the media. More important, why do we even bother interpreting such messages? Consider the following examples:

▌ The president gives a speech and when it's over, news commentators describe "what he said," even though the audience already heard it. Do the news commentators do so just to make a living?

▌ A teenager has a fight with his parents over the CD he brings home because they're convinced that the lyrics are advocating Satanism or drugs or perhaps sexual abuse of women. Whether it is true or not, it probably had little to do with why the youth bought the album or what he hears when he listens to it.

▌ You watch a sporting event on television and are inundated by the "color commentary"—announcers who continually describe, evaluate, and interpret what we're seeing. They also provide additional information such as statistics and are able to put current play in somewhat of a historical context (the home team has never lost to this visiting team in this stadium, or a player is returning from an injury).

▌ Two friends are talking about movies they like and one of them starts analyzing the symbolism of Bruce Willis's bare feet in *Die Hard,* or perhaps starts talking about *Mean Girls* as a powerful metaphor for the difficulties of growing up in the contemporary world. Are these comments on the film just the result of taking a film class?

▌ A couple begins arguing about the Police song "Every Breath You Take." One says that it's a love song and really romantic, whereas the other says that it is about an obsessive stalker surveilling the girlfriend who dumped him and therefore more creepy than romantic.

Failures of communication occur in the most common everyday interactions when we don't understand what we see or hear. Problems in *interpretation,* the process by which people understand or make sense of something, are not limited to problems of communication; they can occur in people's daily lives whenever they try to make sense of the world. For example, two people are struggling in the street. To decide whether and how to respond, an observer must first figure out what is going on. Are they simply fooling around or having a serious fight? Is there a crime in progress?

Interpretation problems in mass communication are especially difficult. In interpersonal contexts, one can always ask for help. One can ask the teacher to explain what he or she is talking about. In any conversation or face-to-face situation, if one doesn't understand, one can raise questions.

Even if the President were speaking to 3,000 students in a campus auditorium, it is at least possible to ask a question, "Mr. President, what did you mean . . . ?" When the communication comes through mass media, help is not generally available. Even if we do talk back to the television at times, we really don't expect to get a response. And although a fan might dream about asking Gwen Stefani, Jay-Z, or Dave Matthews what his or her song is really about, most kids know better than to expect to do so. We could call a television station, or a record company, or a movie theater, but they are not likely to be able to explain the meaning of these various messages.

Most people are not aware that they are always interpreting messages from the media. For instance, people would say that most television programs present no problems of interpretation at all. Everything a viewer needs or wants to know appears to be right on the screen. *The Brady Bunch* is "a story of a lovely lady who was bringing up three very lovely girls. . . ." Yet viewers are likely to recognize that whereas *The Simpsons* is also a good story, as easy to follow as *The Brady Bunch,* there is always something more going on. Its episodes seem to be commenting on society and social issues, or perhaps saying something about the difficulty of love and family in the 1990s.

Then, there are always some programs, such as *Twin Peaks* in the 1980s, *The X-Files* in the 1990s, or *Lost* in 2005, that appear on first glance to be somewhat incomprehensible. Some viewers hated them because they were too "weird" and unstructured; other viewers became devoted fans. It is obvious that these shows were not simply, respectively, a soap opera mystery about who killed Laura Palmer, a story about government conspiracies concerning alien invasions, or a series about survivors of a plane crash stranded on an island. Even the appearance of these shows was different from what people had come to expect from commercial television. There was, one might assume, some deeper meaning, something going on "below the surface." Not everyone understood the shows or cared enough about them to try to understand. After all, what many people want from television is entertainment, a chance *not* to think.

The conclusion that we want to draw from all of these examples is that we are always interpreting, although we are not always aware that we are doing so. The complexity of some messages makes it obvious that a variety of interpretations are possible. And we have to work harder to interpret some messages than others.

## THE MEANING OF MEANING

Meaning is both the most and the least obvious of all the things the media make. In fact, the most difficult fact to grasp about human existence is that the world people live in is always meaningful or, if one prefers, that people are always involved in messages about the meaningfulness of that world.

### Where Is Meaning?

One can begin to see the magic and mystery of meaning. For it is not only people's languages and their systems of communication that are meaningful: The world itself is also meaningful. Someone walks into a classroom and instantly knows that it is a classroom. All of the objects in the room—the blackboard, the chairs and desks, even the way they are arranged—serve as messages that tell the observer the meaning of this space. The same person would be dazed and confused if, on entering a room for a class, he or she found a stove, a bed, or perhaps a trapeze and a barred area all together. No one would identify such a room as "a classroom." It would not be clear what sort of room it was.

There are two domains of meaning. The world itself—at least to anyone beyond infancy—is meaningful. And the languages people use to describe it are themselves meaningful. In fact, language and the world are so closely intertwined that they are, for all practical purposes, inseparable. This is what distinguishes humans from other animals.

Certainly, in one sense, an animal's world is full of meanings. This is food, that is a friend, and that is an enemy. Animals must rely on their ability to understand, to make sense of their world. Yet the information that enables them to make such meaningful distinctions is either innate (through such biological mechanisms as instincts) or learned by rather simple processes of behavior reinforcement, both positive and negative. For example, when a dog is repeatedly punished for doing something, it soon learns not to do that; it learns that the particular behavior is "bad."

Although some behavioral psychologists have tried to explain human behavior through such processes of reinforcement and conditioning, most students of human behavior agree that instinctual knowledge and behavior reinforcement are not sufficient to explain the complexity of human action and experience. Instead, humans learn the meaning of the various parts and relations of the world through the messages that create their cultural and communicative environment. It is easy to ignore this important fact. For, in most cases, the entire process is taken for granted. Understanding what is going on in the world or what something is or what some message means, seems to come as naturally as walking or talking or using the toilet, none of which actually comes very naturally to people. Everyone forgets how much effort it takes for children to learn to walk, to talk, and to use the toilet, and how much trouble their parents go to in teaching these tasks. By the same token, rarely do people have to stop and ask what something means.

Most of the time, the meaning of the various objects, places, and relationships people encounter seems so obvious, so natural, that only a very young child or a space alien or some sort of cave person would not understand. We can recognize a classroom when we see one.

Unless some dispute arises, there is usually no reason to make explicit our understanding of an event or a message. People take this meaning making for granted. But the meanings that surround us are not part of our genetic pattern: They are not fixed in place, once and for all. And it is this flexibility or *polysemy*—the fact that anything can have a variety of different meanings and interpretations—that may be the most human characteristic of all. This underlies the human ability to laugh and to cry, to seek the truth of the world and the meaning of life.

Meaning organizes the human world. Human beings live in a world of meanings. That is, the maps they have "in their heads" that tell them how to survive in the world, that tell them what to do with different things, that tell them where to find the things they need and want, are maps of meaning. By telling people what things mean, these maps make the world understandable.

So, how do people know what something means? Where do they find meaning? In other words, where do the maps of meaning come from? Where do people get the meanings from which these maps are constructed? Are they out there in the world, to be picked up and collected like shells or cassettes? Or are they already inside people's heads, as Humpty Dumpty declares in *Through the Looking Glass:* "Words mean exactly what we want them to mean, no more and no less"? Who is, after all, in control of the meanings of words, and of the world?

In a brilliant satire, Mark Twain describes Adam and Eve's arguments as they walked through the Garden of Eden. Eve wanted to give everything whatever name came to mind; Adam retorted that things were what they were and hence that their names had already been assigned. Of course, it was Adam and not Eve who could "see" these correct names, who could read the correct use of words as if they were transparently written upon the face of the various objects and animals in the world. It is no coincidence in a patriarchal society that it is the male who claims to have this power (see Chapter 9).

The fact is that people do not find meanings in the world, nor are meanings already inside their heads. People *make* meaning. They make multiple and often competing meanings. But they are not entirely free to make any meaning they want. There is a history and a way of life behind the interpretations of the world and of languages that they make. This relationship between meaning, history, and ways of life is precisely what is meant by *culture*. People are not free to ignore the culture in which they live. There is a reality outside of language, even if they can only know it through their language and culture. The relationship between culture and reality cannot be easily grasped. It must remain something of a dilemma, for meaning is both something people find in the world awaiting them and something they imagine in their heads and project upon that world.

## What Is Meaning?

What precisely is this stuff called meaning? How does it work? The most common way of thinking about meaning is that it is *representational.* To describe meaning as representational is to say that any language (or any system of meaning) always points or refers to the real world. Thus the meaning of the word *dog* is obvious: It is a certain kind of object—a four-legged barking domestic animal—in the real world. In this sense, meaning always involves a process of naming. The word names that kind of object a dog.

But what about such notions as *justice* or *truth?* What do they mean? And what about *Superman?* Surely, none of these have any concrete existence in the real world. One can't hold truth or justice in one's hands, and Superman is only a character in a comic book. At this point, it becomes necessary to think of meaning as *conceptual.* That is, language refers to or points to thoughts inside our minds. The word *dog* means the particular image, picture, or set of associations that come to mind whenever the word appears. The following diagram captures representational and conceptual meaning:

Representational Word → Object

Conceptual Word → Concept

What is the relationship between two different people's thought objects (or concepts)? How is communication possible unless people know or at least assume that they share a common set of meanings when they talk with each other? After all, when Person A says, "Dogs are nice," she may be thinking of a cute, cuddly, lovable thing, but someone else, Person B, may think that A is crazy because B's concept of a dog is a snarling, aggressive, wolflike creature. Notice that one implication of this example is that communication may involve more than meaning understood simply as information; it also involves people's emotional and affective relations to whatever it is they are talking about.

Philosophers have pointed out that if meaning is conceptual, then every individual has a "private language," and any communication or intersubjectivity is really an illusion, for only the individual has access to the meaningfulness of his or her words. Moreover, the private language argument states that if meaning is conceptual, if the meaning of a word is a picture inside an individual's head, then how can anyone know that the picture referred to today by *dog* is the same as the picture referred to yesterday by *dog*. That is, not only is communication with a private language impossible, but a private language itself is impossible; it could not work as a language even for talking to oneself.

The theories of meaning as representational and as conceptual both describe aspects of how meaning functions in the human world. But neither can explain the capacity, bestowed on people by their systems of meaning, to distance themselves from the world, to think and talk about things that are not present at the moment, or to imagine things that do not yet exist. Nor can they explain how communication between people is possible. That requires a theory that begins with the social nature of meaning systems: People seem to share common codes that provide common maps of the meaningfulness of the world. A *code* is a systematic structure or organization of *signs*, where a sign is something that stands in for something else; we shall return to these notions shortly.

Both meaning as representation and meaning as concept locate meaning in a direct relationship between the code and something outside of the code. To assume that meanings are either in the world (that is, representational) or in someone's head (conceptual) is to make the mistake of assuming that there is a simple and direct relationship between language and meaning, that there is an identity between the languages or systems of meaning people use and what meaning refers to. A representational or realist theory of meaning assumes that for every word there is an object and for every object there is a word. A conceptual or intentional theory of meaning assumes that for every word, there is a mental image or thought and that every mental image or thought has its own appropriate word. These two commonsense views of meaning assume that there is a necessary correspondence between a particular word or sign and its meaning. These theories assume that meaning is made up of discrete entities that are captured and embodied in systems of meaning but that ultimately exist outside of the system of meaning itself. Hence using a language correctly involves learning what the proper word is for some visually perceived object (*horse*), or for some experience (*soft*), or for some thought (*friendly*).

Because people live within a particular culture's maps of meaning, it is easy to assume that every word has its own meaning (whether as an object in the world or a concept in our minds). But it is difficult to confront those situations in which the particular word or object has more than one meaning. If we talk about *democracy* or *art* or *rock and roll*, we will encounter disagreement over the meaning of these terms. And particular messages also often seem to have different meanings for different audiences. What is a love song for one person can be, for another person, a statement that love stinks. To one person, a news report on a drug bust can be proof of the effectiveness of the war on drugs, and to another, evidence of the failure of the government's policy. Ads for condoms can be viewed as advocating sex or addressing a serious social problem. *The Brady Bunch* can be an innocent program about an imaginary family, or it can be another example of male domination. How do we explain the disagreements that take place all the time over the meaning of different messages? Is Springsteen's "Born in the USA" a patriotic anthem? Does gangsta rap advocate drugs and violence? Is "death metal" music about Satanism? Why does your teacher want you to analyze the already obvious meaning of some television program?

## SEMIOTICS AND THE MEANING OF MEANING

We can begin to answer some of these questions by turning to *semiotics*, the discipline that studies the nature of any system of meaning. Semiotics begins by identifying the *sign* as the elementary unit of a code and a *code* as any system of meaning. A code can be very large, like the English language, or very small, like the system of traffic light colors. It can be simple (as in the code that says good guys wear white hats and bad guys black) or very complex (as in the world of fashion, where black takes on various meanings, from chic simplicity to mourning clothes).

## Codes and Meaning

*A code is a systematic organization or structure of signs.* This meaning is not very different from the everyday understanding of codes, especially codes as something to be broken. A code may appear to be different from a language, but in fact, they are both the same, although human languages clearly are among the most complex codes.

In semiotics, meaning has a certain autonomy, or independence, both from the world out there and from the pictures in people's heads. *Meaning is located in the codes of society.* Semiotics argues that this autonomy can be difficult to recognize because people live inside of their codes and thus take their systems of meaning for granted. According to semiotics, it is emphatically not the case that the languages or the systems of meaning people use provide a picture or mirror of their world and their thoughts. Rather, people expect the world to resemble the pictures that their codes create of it; in fact, they demand that the world mirror the codes of their language. Earlier in the twentieth century, two linguistic anthropologists, Edward Sapir (1921) and Benjamin Whorf (1956), argued that the world as people live and experience it always copies the grammatical structure of the language they speak. But semiotics goes even further. Consider the following example of a society and culture very different from the one most Americans live in today.

Anthropologists first studying the people of the Trobriand Islands in the South Pacific in the early twentieth century found that the Trobriand Islanders had a society built on what seemed to the anthropologists to be a rather odd interpretation of the water and its role in reproduction. These people lived in something of a tropical paradise. They apparently believed that sexual relations had nothing to do with reproduction. After all, sex was so pleasurable that it had to be a gift from the gods. If it were primarily serving a necessary biological function, it need not have been so pleasurable. And so they enjoyed rather free sexual relations. They also believed that when someone died, their soul lived on, swimming in the ocean. And when a woman went swimming, one of these free souls would enter her body and cause her to become pregnant. Hence the Trobriand Islanders had strict regulations about when women could swim but few about sexuality. This system of beliefs, an interpretation of their reality, was real to them. It functioned well enough for them to survive for many centuries.

The issue is not whether the Trobriand Islanders were "correct" in their meanings of swimming and sexual relations. Their meaning code was both coherent and functional. In fact, as the impact of Western civilization increasingly forced the Trobriand Islanders to adopt new and, to them, alien maps of meaning, their culture and their society gradually disappeared. They did not know how to live successfully as a society in this new reality.

People in what are sometimes called "exotic cultures" (by which is meant cultures that are significantly different from our own) are not the only ones who make the world mean something beyond "rational" or "concrete" reality. Every society not only believes that its culture, its codes, are rational and coherent, it also believes that it can explain events that appear to violate the natural rational order. In the cultures of the Western industrialized nations, people commonly offer interpretations that make use of meanings such as *market forces* when the economy acts in ways they don't understand, or *quarks* when the universe acts in strange ways. And despite all the rationality and scientificity of these modern cultures, the majority of the people still believe in the reality of sacred and irrational events (such as miracles) or in the necessity of appealing to God.

Every society lives within the codes of meaning that it produces for itself. These codes produce the maps by which and in which people live their lives and through which they interpret the world as a rational place. And, to a great extent, every society is continuously forcing reality to fit into its maps, rather than face the more threatening possibility that its maps may be inadequate. Or, to put it another way, every culture is made up of multiple codes and languages that are often incompatible and contradictory. Different people in the society may invest more credibility in one or another of these codes, but, more often, people simply invest differently in any number of these codes. Sometimes codes are assigned to particular places, making those places into distinct "life worlds," as when people find that their work life or home life are quite different from their church life. And sometimes codes slip out of their places, as when a person appeals to God in the face of a tragedy.

What is crucial is how real people's interpretations are to them. Interpretations may have immediate and physical consequences. Consider a hypothetical female anthropologist who plans to study the Inuit of northern Canada. She knows that, when she arrives, she will be invited to partake of a ritual supper of whale blubber, something that does not strike her as particularly appetizing. However, she also knows she cannot refuse the offer of food without insulting her hosts, probably ruining any chance of establishing the rapport she will need. And when she arrives, she is invited to supper and offered a bowl of what she takes to be whale blubber. The anthropologist eats the food that is offered and promptly throws up. Her hosts are confused and say to her, "We thought Americans liked chicken pot pie." Her interpretation of the food and not the reality of it made her sick.

Is this merely a case of expectations taking over? Well, in part. But it is the codes of meaning that define the structure of expectations with which people live their lives and act in the world and with others. In that sense, *the codes of meaning not only represent the world, they produce it*. Or, if you prefer, they produce another reality, a reality that is defined by its difference from the material world, a reality that is a world of meanings, a human reality.

## Meaning and Difference

Following the work of Swiss linguist Ferdinand de Saussure (1983), the semiotic theory of codes sees meaning as a function of absence and difference. Semiotics starts with the recognition that a sign is always about something else, that it represents something other than itself. The sign must always be different from what it represents. The chair one sits on is not a sign of a chair. But the word *chair* is a sign of what one can sit on. We cannot put the chair, the object itself, on this page. We can put the sign *chair* on this page. A sign is always a sign of absence. If people want to talk about a chair in their office, they only need a sign when the chair is not present in front of them. The sign *the chair in my office* allows them to talk about that which is absent; otherwise, they would have to pick up the chair and bring it with them wherever they went just in case they wanted to talk about it.

Because a sign must be different from what it represents, semiotics separates the question of meaning from that of representation. Semiotics, in fact, has little to say about representation because it is interested in how codes produce meaning, which in turn produces the reality people live in. But it has a great deal to say about the production of meaning in codes. Codes have a double reality. A string of numbers is only a code when it is assumed that there is another level of interpretation of the numbers in that sequence, that there is another string that can be related to the first. Similarly, when we see a red light, we know that it is red and that it is part of what the traffic code tells us. But the red light also tells us about something entirely different—namely, it conveys a set of legal constraints that demands a certain behavior from us: Red means stop; green means go.

Codes depend, then, on two different systems, each made of different and differentiable elements, being brought together. Because codes are built upon these differences, they are able to construct meaning, and they enable us to see differences in the world. Without codes of meaning, we could not distinguish one sort of object from another, a man from a woman, an *Aedes vexans* (the common pest mosquito) from an *Aedes communis* (the northern common mosquito), because there would be no categories for such distinctions. We would not even be able to identify an object, because there would be no maps allowing us to distinguish an object from its background, a painting from the wall, or a tree from the forest.

A code is a system of signs, each of which is distinct from every other. A sign is itself made up of two different parts: a *signifier* and a *signified*. These are the two levels that make up any system of meaning or code:

$$\text{Sign} = \frac{\text{Signifier}}{\text{Signified}}$$

What is a signifier? A signifier is a material form—a sensuous marker like a sound or a visual mark. Obviously, a sign has to have some mark of its presence; it has to announce itself. But not every mark, not every sound, not every squiggle on a page, functions as a signifier. *Qstk* is not a signifier in English. Similarly, while :-) is a signifier in a code in which it represents a happy face,))) is not a signifier and thus not part of a sign. For something to be a signifier, it has to be located within a code in which its uniqueness, its difference from any other possible signifier, can be recognized. Its uniqueness and its existence as a signifier are defined by its differences from the other signifiers within the code. For example, Americans have no difficulty distinguishing *cot* from *cat* when they hear them. Moreover, English speakers recognize them as signifiers, both written and aural. But *cet* is a different matter. These letters look like a typographical error or perhaps a new word.

147

This "word" is certainly not a signifier in English. But if we were to hear the sound, we would probably assume it to be the same as *cat*. This kind of difference would not register the sound as a unique signifier, unless it signified a regional accent. Similarly, if you are driving and see a traffic signal that has a blue light on the bottom, you might reasonably assume that, as a signifier, it is no different from green. But if you saw a purple light, you might wonder whether it meant anything at all, whether it was a signifier. Thus, for something to be a signifier, it must already exist in at least one system of difference, within a code that makes its existence as a signifier possible. Public relations campaigns often recognize this fact. For example, when Standard Oil Co. of New Jersey wanted a new trade name, the company purposely chose one that was not a signifier in any known human language so that it could become a unique signifier in the code of trade names: *Exxon* was chosen because *xx* is a feature of virtually no written language. Not so fortunate was Chevrolet, which in the 1970s unsuccessfully marketed its compact car, the Nova, in Latin America: In Spanish, *no va* means, roughly, "doesn't go."

Think about the line from the famous song by George Gershwin: "You say *tomayto*, and I say *tomahto*." In one code, there is no difference between the two signifiers, "tomayto" and "tomahto." They both mean a round, red fruit or vegetable, and they are the same signifier. But in the code of the movie *Shall We Dance*, with Fred Astaire and Ginger Rogers, the difference between the signifiers is crucial, pointing to class differences between the Astaire and Rogers characters and to a certain friction in their romance. Hence, "Let's call the whole thing off." In ordinary speech, the difference between "tomayto" and "tomahto" may identify no more than regional dialects.

Something is a signifier only by virtue of its location within a socially defined system of differences. There is a story commonly told about the armed forces' attempts to enlist the aid of the natives of the South Pacific islands in the battle against malaria. Mounting a large audiovisual campaign, including photographic blowups, the War Department had attempted to explain to these people how insects can carry the disease and why the mosquitoes therefore needed to be eradicated. After the war, investigators returned to try to understand why their media campaigns had failed. The local people told them that they did not have any insects that large; if they did, they would certainly think them dangerous. But they only had small, harmless mosquitoes.

Here is an example of the socially coded nature of a signifier. A picture is an example of an *iconic sign*—a sign that functions by virtue of its resemblance to its referent, what it refers to. Yet, even here, the natives, who did not share the appropriate codes, never having seen a photograph, could not understand the manipulation of the signifier implicit in the blowup.

A system of signifiers, then, is an organization of any material or perceptual variables: It can be colors, sounds, spatial arrangements, or shapes. The code tells those using the code where to draw the line between the elements. The code divides the universe of perception into a series of different elements. In that sense, the different elements do not exist as separable, identifiable entities except insofar as they are located within a code. The light spectrum is continuous, but we distinguish different colors in digital terms, separating, for example, red from orange, blue from violet. Similarly, we make distinctions (between *b* and *p*) to mark significant differences out of the spectrum of sounds. In other languages, *b* and *p* might not be marked as different.

But a code of signifiers by itself is not a code of meaning, for signs, language, and meaning are produced only when two such systems of differences are brought together. The second system of differences is the second level of a code or sign, the level of the signified or meaning. To use a simple example, the code of colors simultaneously establishes a system of different words (*red, green, blue, yellow*) and a system of differences within the electromagnetic spectrum. The differences are related to one another to create a single meaningful code of colors. The words can be a code of signifiers for the spectrum, or they can become a code of signifiers for another language of colors (red means love). Another example results from mapping a system of different sounds—words—onto the physical world of animals. Now we can label horses and mules, cats and dogs, cats and lions. Without the codes to mark the differences, there would be no way to think about the difference between a mule and a horse. People might certainly see a difference, just as they might see differences between different kinds of horses or between different horses, even if they had no signifiers for these differences.

Thus the traffic code tells people that red is linked to stop, green to go, and yellow to caution. But what is the status of these so-called meanings or signifieds? Are they actual descriptions of our behavior? Obviously not, or we would not need traffic cops. Nor are they concepts within people's heads or real objects in the world. Like signifiers, they are the product of, and only exist within, the semiotic codes of the society. The meaning that is linked to a signifier is always another signifier. Think about it: Whenever you try to come up with the meaning of a word or message, you can only come up with another word or message. It is like looking up a word in a dictionary: All the dictionary gives you is another word, which you can look up, to find another word. Sooner or later, you are led back to the original word you tried to look up. The meaning of a sign is always another sign; the signified is another signifier.

## Signs and Meaning

Thus a sign is more than a signifier; it is a signifier linked to a signified or meaning. But the signified is not a concept or referent, but is another signifier, itself defined within its own system of difference. The sign, then, is the interaction of two systems of signifiers. In the sign, the two signifiers are stitched together, one on top of the other as it were. The first signifier is the signifier of the sign, and the second signifier becomes the signified of the sign.

Within a code of meaning, the signified is always subordinate to, or conditioned upon, the signifier. The differences of the system of the signifier become a map or template for the system of the signified, defining its differences, in the same way that our color words are mapped onto locations of the electromagnetic spectrum. There is a classic example of this relationship between signifier and signifieds within a code of meaning, which will enable us to try a short experiment. First, think of the codes of meaning that make sense of the animal kingdom for us. Now, erase them from your mind and try to imagine living in a universe organized by a different code, the codes of a "certain Chinese encyclopedia" described by the Latin American writer, Jorge Luis Borges:

> Animals are divided into: (a) belonging to the Emperor, (b) embalmed, (c) tame, (d) suckling pigs, (e) sirens, (f) fabulous, (g) stray dogs, (h) included in the present classification, (i) frenzied, (j) innumerable, (k) drawn with a fine camelhair brush, (1) et cetera, (m) having just broken the water pitcher, (n) that from a long way off look like flies. (Cited in Foucault, 1970, p. xv)

150

Can you imagine what this world would look like? Can you imagine what it would be like to live in this world?

Codes organize the world into categories, telling us what is a significant relationship, what similarities and what differences are meaningful and matter. The organization of identity and difference (what things are to be considered the same and what are to be considered not the same) offered by the Chinese encyclopedia is very strange to us, but it is a viable code and it establishes a meaningful universe for someone. Recall now the codes of modern English-speaking culture that organize the animal kingdom. In fact, there are a number of different, overlapping codes. In American culture, we distinguish animals on the basis of size, danger, utility (domesticated pets, farm animals, game animals), and number (we mark extinct species), as well as by a hierarchical biological classification scheme of phylum, family, genus, and species (within which we distinguish mammals, reptiles, fish, and birds). This system would no doubt strike the author of the ancient Chinese encyclopedia as weird. The Chinese encyclopedia categories define common identities that may be very different from the ones we are used to; similarly, they make distinctions that we do not normally make. But the code still establishes a system by which we could give meaning to the world and to our experience of it.

The codes of meaning tell people what events are worthy of note, what events can be said to exist at all, what is to count as an event. Most Americans or Europeans would be unlikely to take stories blaming our troubles on leprechauns very seriously, although many people are likely to live within codes that take the role of God in human history seriously. And even more people are likely to accept codes that explain the universe in terms of subatomic particles. No one has seen leprechauns, God, or subatomic particles. Why certain codes appear reasonable to particular groups of people is a matter we will take up in Chapter 7.

The ability to watch and understand television depends on an individual's knowledge of and familiarity with the relevant codes. Sometimes the codes are very simple. It does not take a lot of effort to explain the codes operating in a Roadrunner cartoon. There are two major characters: the bad Wile E. Coyote and the cute Roadrunner (a code of characters). Wile E. Coyote always attempts to catch Roadrunner and always fails (a narrative code). Usually, some gizmo such as rocket roller skates Coyote has purchased from the Acme Co. backfires on him (codes about technology), leaving Roadrunner to "beep-beep" into the sunset. But imagine explaining this cartoon to someone who had never seen a cartoon. Imagine how much work it would take to explain the necessary codes to understand what is significant and what is merely irrelevant detail on MTV.

Conversely, some codes of meaning that seem quite familiar and reasonable can seem quite strange when scrutinized. For instance, in almost all visual media—film, photography, television, news, commercials—black and white is used to signify documentary reality. How odd: Most people see reality in color.

This example illustrates an important point about codes of meaning: They are *arbitrary*. To say that codes are arbitrary does not deny that there may have been—and continue to be—good social, functional, and historical reasons why specific codes were constructed in specific ways. Nor does it deny that, once an individual born into a social world learns to inhabit the world defined by the codes of meaning of that society, she or he sees nothing arbitrary about the codes. On the contrary, the codes (of signifiers, of signified, and of signs linking the two) appear natural, inevitable, logical, rational, commonsensical. Someone who refuses to accept the codes can only be an alien, or a threat. In fact, this is the theme of a number of popular films and television series, for example, *Men in Black*. The ubiquity of the codes is, unfortunately, often responsible for our attitudes toward people from significantly different cultures.

Codes (or any sign within a code) are arbitrary because they are the product of the joining of two systems of differences. No natural law says systems have to be linked (instead of colors, we could use shapes to control traffic flow). No natural law says systems have to be linked in just the way they were (red could mean go). No natural law says the world has to be divided up the way it is: A continuously changing system of colors could control traffic speed. Instead of dividing the world of water by size (oceans, seas, lakes, ponds; rivers, streams, creeks), the English language could have been more concerned with the content of the water (salty, dirty, full of fish) or the source of the water. For example, in French, the difference between *riviere* and *fleuve* is that one flows into the sea and one does not, a distinction not emphasized as much in the English terms *river* and *stream*. There is no natural or inevitable correspondence between the two structures of differences that make up a code of meaning. It is not inevitable that the word *horse* refers to that particular animal instead of what is commonly called a *cow.* Similarly, it is not inevitable that the animal kingdom be divided up into Western scientific categories. In fact, the scientific system of classification has changed significantly over the past century, although the latest usages have not entered into common sense. The organization of differences, the maps of meanings that any culture's codes produce, are not some inevitable reflection of the way things are, but the product of human history and, as we shall see, of relations of power.

## Semiotic View of Meaning

A semiotic view of meaning has important implications for thinking about the meaning of any message or text. If a sign is always produced by temporarily linking together two signifiers, then it is perhaps not accurate to see this process as making connections between two independent chains or codes of signifiers. Rather, as C. S. Peirce (1958), the founder of both American pragmatism and semiotics, argued, a signifier is always sliding into another signifier in an endless production of meaning. The French philosopher Jacques Derrida (1981) calls this process *dissemination,* the endless movement and proliferation of signifiers. This notion opens up two possible misinterpretations. First, perhaps, dissemination implies that the movement from one signifier to the next is inevitable and natural, rather than social, as if the line of dissemination were determined in advance. Second, it might seem that the meaning of any signifier is not determined at all and thus is infinite. The line of signifiers extends into infinity so that, in the final analysis, there is no meaning.

*Polysemy* implies a different understanding of this sliding of signifiers. The movement of one signifier into another might be thought of as a game of musical chairs. It is only infinite and without meaning as long as the music doesn't stop; but, of course, the music is always stopped. (Asking how the music is stopped and who stops it raises real questions of power and points toward questions of ideology, to be considered in Chapter 7.) When the music is stopped, some signifiers find a seat—in other words, they slide into the position of signified (meaning). In this way, the potentially infinite sliding of signifiers into other signifiers (which is the process of language production) is

153

transformed into the production of meaning by a particular articulation of signifiers.

*Articulation* is the process by which different elements are connected. In England, a 16-wheel semi-truck is described as an *articulated* lorry, referring to the link between the cab and the trailer. The cab and the trailer can be separated, although neither piece would be very useful alone. The two pieces can be linked to other cabs or trailers to form a different truck, but neither half is "a truck" itself. The production of signs, texts, and meanings can be seen in similar terms. Signifiers are linked to produce signs; signs are linked to produce texts; texts are linked to produce interpretations. When someone uses language, he or she articulates signifiers together and codes together; this is how language makes signs, texts, and meanings. Meanings involve the articulation of relations between signifiers, relations that are themselves described in terms of codes. This process, at a broader level, implies that texts themselves have meaning only in relationship to the codes with which they are articulated or located, and hence in relationship to the broader set of other texts that carry those codes with them. The meaning of a message depends on the ways these codes are linked or articulated to other codes in and through texts. Hence meanings are always *intertextual*. Articulation also implies that codes of meaning can transcend any particular message. Every message refers to other instances of the codes that have produced it. For example, as simple as the code of Roadrunner cartoons is, we would not recognize it except for the fact that it appears in so many other common texts in our culture.

If meaning does not exist outside of the structure of differences produced by the codes, then meaning is not movable from one language to another. *Translatability* becomes something of an illusion. In fact, the same signifiers, located within different codes, can become entirely different signs. For example, consider the following anthropological experience (Bohannon, 1967).

A female anthropologist is studying an African culture in which storytelling is an important social ritual, normally reserved for the elders—always male—of the tribe. As a sign of their acceptance, the elders invite the anthropologist to tell a story. Searching her memory for an appropriate story, one that would demonstrate her wisdom and the wisdom of Western European culture, the anthropologist decides to recount the story of *Hamlet*. She tells it in great detail. But from the very beginning, she realizes that it is not going well. As soon as the tribal elders hear that Hamlet is visited by the ghost of his dead father, they become convinced that it is a story about witches. After all, the only explanation for ghosts is the spell of a witch. As the story continues, they become even more convinced that the story contains the wisdom of Anglo-American culture concerning the procedures for hunting and identifying witches. Despite the anthropologist's protests, they are not shaken from this interpretation and, in fact, offer a cogent and coherent interpretation of the story. Furthermore, they are convinced that the fact that the anthropologist is unaware of the true meaning of the story is merely a sign that the elders of her own culture have kept it from her, not surprising given that she is a woman.

The African elders clearly articulated the narrative of *Hamlet* to a set of codes and texts different from those the anthropologist was taking for granted. This is not some unusual case. Although many critics would argue that it is precisely the very richness of *Hamlet*, its openness to many interpretations, that makes it a great work of art, a semiotic theory of meaning defines every signifier, every sign, and every text as polysemic. What differs is only the degree of ambiguity that is recognized and tolerated in the various institutions assigned the responsibility of policing the possibilities of interpretation and misinterpretation (such as the institutions of literary criticism). Any text can be articulated to a wide variety of codes and texts, but no society ever tolerates every possible articulation of every text. Consider the names of the Teenage Mutant Ninja Turtles: Donatello, Raphael, Michaelangelo [*sic*], and Leonardo. For children, the names may signal a code of unfamiliar and therefore somewhat exotic names; for others, the names are part of the code of Italian Renaissance painters; and, for still others, they are part of the code of famous artists who were gay. Each of these articulations changes the text and its meaning. Nor does anyone know for sure whether the creatures' creators intended people to notice all these codes; that is, whether they intentionally selected the names of gay Renaissance artists. The Turtles' creators, Kevin Eastman and Peter Laird, note in their official history of their creation (www.ninjaturtles.com) only that they'd studied art history and selected European artists' names because they thought Japanese ninja names would be "too strange to American readers."

## MEANING AND COMPETENCE

In this discussion of meaning, we have assumed an adult model of competence. By *competence*, we mean the ability to decode or understand messages with sufficient skill to function relatively normally in society. Differences in interpretation are not thought to reside in the basic cognitive ability of the meaning maker, but in codes that are brought to bear on a sign. However, in the case of children, we cannot assume this level of competence. A substantial body of research examines how children come to interpret and make sense of media content, especially television programming. This literature draws upon theories of cognitive development, how children come to understand the world. Concern about the making of meaning is not exclusively the province of a cultural tradition of interpretation. Psychology, and particularly an emerging branch of the discipline known as cognitive psychology, has more than a little to say about how humans interpret symbols. Though there are some similarities with semiotics, there are substantial differences as well. Semiotics, for example, focuses on the social processes of meaning making, but does not consider individual psychology. The literature on children's interpretations of television has been used in the creation of educational children's television programs, starting with *Sesame Street*.

Children gradually become competent, and adultlike, in their meaning making of television programming. As they grow older, child viewers acquire the ability to understand the narrative contents, distinguish among program genres and formats, and correctly interpret the production forms (such as instant replays) of television. Chronological age is a fairly good gauge of children's competence, with children younger than ages 5 or 6 generally more idiosyncratic in their interpretations of the meaning of the television program than older children or adults. (See Box 5.1, "Children's Interpretation of Television.")

---

**BOX 5.1**

**Children's Interpretation of Television**

I sat down last Thursday to watch an episode of *The Simpsons* with my sons David, 8, and Stephen, 3. This episode was about the family's trip to a new Japanese restaurant for sushi where Homer ate *fugu*, a Japanese

---

blowfish, which was presumably prepared wrong and therefore deadly within 24 hours to anyone who eats it. The rest of the episode revolves around Homer's likely last day of life and his attempts to say good-bye to the people he loves: his wife, Marge; his children Bart, Lisa, and Maggie; his father and his boss and friends.

Clearly, David, Stephen, and I were interpreting this show differently. Stephen had very little understanding of the plot of the show: He could tell me that Homer was sick, but he didn't know why or how. "Sushi" was lost on him. His favorite part of the show was when Homer showed his son Bart how to shave: Stephen likes to watch his own father shave, and Stephen particularly likes Bart. To Stephen, Bart is "cool." Apart from laughing when Bart is on the screen, Stephen shows little understanding of the program outside of a few scenes: He laughs when the policemen pull Homer over for speeding and when Homer runs home after his car breaks down. What's the show about? Stephen's not quite sure; his attempts to tell me about it or answer my questions suggest that he has a very rudimentary under-standing of the plot—a lot of disconnected and discrete events are all that he can describe. What else happens? Stephen's not sure.

David had a much better understanding of most of the plot elements I thought were important for understanding the narrative: He knew that the fish Homer ate at the restaurant (he thinks it's a Chinese restaurant) was thought to be "deadly," he understood that Homer and Marge thought Homer was going to die and so Homer was planning all of the things he would do before he dies—"he has a list of stuff to do to make his family happy," says David. Here's David's description of the story: "He [Homer] went to a sushi place with his family and he ate something poisonous and he went to the doctor and he says he's going to die so he has a list of stuff to do before he dies to make his family happy. And so he does lots of things like play ball with his father, talks to Bart his son, listens to Lisa play her saxophone, makes a videotape for Maggie, and goes to the bar with his friends. And he doesn't die after all."

These differences between Stephen and David's comprehension of the narrative of *The Simpsons* illustrate that children have to develop an understanding of narrative and have to come to learn how to interpret television stories. Younger children, usually those in preschool or below age 5, tend to have difficulty understanding plot lines, particularly those events adults consider central or main points of the story. Consequently, younger children like Stephen tend to develop very idiosyncratic inter-pretations of the story. For Stephen, this episode of *The Simpsons* was

*(Continued)*

(Continued)

about "Homer and Bart shaving." At Stephen's age, children have difficulty distinguishing reality and fantasy on television. (Stephen thinks that Bart and Homer live inside the TV set. He's not sure what happens to them when you turn off the set.) They have difficulty identifying the characters' motivations for their actions; they have difficulty understanding the plot lines; and they have difficulty distinguishing the different kinds of content, in particular commercials and programs, of television.

As children grow older, they become more adept at understanding narratives in general and television narratives in particular. David at age 8 and I agreed on the central events of what happened in the show. He is much better at distinguishing reality and fantasy, and he certainly knows the difference between the ads and the programs (on Saturday morning, he pays particular attention to the ads to decide which fast-food restaurant he should ask to go to for lunch; he chooses the one giving the best prize in their kids' meals). But even David has difficulty making sense of some of the characters' motivations, and he doesn't understand some of the more adultlike depictions, in particular, Marge and Homer's discussion about "being intimate" is completely lost on David (for which both Mom and Dad are happy; they would rather address *that* question later). He brings a limited understanding about the social world and people to his interpretations of the television plot, and therefore he, too, compared to an adult viewer, has a different interpretation of the program. He sometimes looks quizzically at what I find funny about the show.

Children only gradually come to interpret television in the way adults do. That's why child advocates argue that children need programs specially designed with their needs and abilities taken into account. Adult programs, or shows that appeal to both adults and kids (such as *The Simpsons*) are interpreted differently by children of different ages and by adults.

Note: This essay was written by Ellen Wartella, an author of this text, as she watched a television program with her two children.

Up to about age 5 or 6, young children tend to interact with television as though it were a "magic window on the world," not a construction acted out by actors. They are less skillful at recognizing the scenes of a plot, which adults consider central to understanding the story. They tend to focus more on the appearance of characters than the characters' behaviors in making interpretive judgments about the character and in forming beliefs about the outcome of a story. They have difficulty connecting events that are separated in time. And the production characteristics of zooms, fast pace, rapid cuts, for instance, influence their comprehension. Moreover, young children must come to understand the purpose of such content as advertising: that advertisers are trying to sell them a product and therefore may present the product in its best light. Preschool children typically have difficulty identifying which is the program and which is the commercial; where program characters such as the Power Rangers are also toy products sold in advertisements, distinguishing programs from advertising becomes more difficult.

Young children, however, can be aided in their meaning making. When adults and older children watch television with a preschooler, identifying important aspects of the narrative and making interpretive comments, they can aid the younger child's understanding of the program. Also, educational television producers have demonstrated that when there is congruency between the audio and visual tracks of a program and, even better, when there is redundancy between what is seen and what is heard, younger children understand the content better and learn more from television. Also, the use of program separators (such as "And now for these messages" or "And now back to our show"), required by the FCC during children's programs, help young children distinguish programs from commercials. That young children differ from older children and adults in their ability to understand and make meaning from television and other media is the underlying assumption of federal requirements that television broadcasters must identify their educational and informational programs for children. Young children are a special audience of meaning makers.

## CONCLUSION

People live in a world of meanings and interpretations, organized by codes of differences. They do not make those meanings; they do not interpret their world for themselves. Nor does the world come already interpreted apart from human activity. People live within the codes, the systems of differences, and the articulations by which those codes have been stitched together in particular ways. They live within a culture, and, to paraphrase James W. Carey (1989), the process by which that culture is produced, maintained, repaired, and transformed is communication (p. 23). To speak of culture as produced and transformed is to also speak of reality as produced and transformed. People always live in a world made by the codes with which that world is made meaningful.

It is in and through communication that humans create the reality that they then inhabit. The codes of meaning that make up our common culture produce the very reality they represent. Communication cannot be separated from the world that it communicates, or from the codes that make it possible to communicate. For this reason, it is important to understand the codes and meanings that are communicated in the most public and visibly shared forms of communication in our society: the various texts of the mass media and popular culture. These texts clearly play an important role in producing the shared codes and maps of meaning that come to define the world we live in.

## SUGGESTED READINGS

Chandler, D. (2002). *Semiotics: The basics.* New York: Routledge.

Fiske, J., & Hartley, J. (1978). *Reading television.* New York: Methuen.

Hall, S. (Ed.). (1997). *Representation: Cultural representations and signifying practices.* Thousand Oaks, CA: Sage.

# The Interpretation of Meaning | 6

I n this chapter, we consider ways to analyze and interpret the messages or texts of the media in all their diverse forms. People are interpreting what they see and hear all of the time, but they usually take their interpretations, and the ways they arrive at them, for granted. We will make explicit the kinds of questions people ask of these texts and the sorts of answers they expect. Then, we will begin to develop analytic tools for examining texts.

Whatever the text—a film, an album, or a comic book—different readers are likely to have different interpretations and evaluations. Some people may find a particular text aesthetically progressive and engaging; others may find it boring, derivative, and unoriginal. Some people will argue that a particular text is somehow subversive and rebellious, others that it is more of the same old message (about war, politics, money, or social relations of gender or race). Interpretation and evaluation are not the same thing, although they are often closely related in everyday practice. In the following discussion, we shall be less concerned with evaluation than with interpretation, with how people arrive at an understanding of a text.

Some people will focus on their relationship to the performer and his or her image. Others will approach the text more traditionally. They talk about the text itself and consider how the artist may have intended it. Sometimes, people will refer to information beyond the text, such as interviews with the artist or their background knowledge of the history of the author, the medium, or the subject. Some people rely on knowledge or experience that most fans (and critics) would not think to bring to the text in question; their interpretations may seem particularly strange to others. Still others may be less concerned with the performer or the text than with the fans themselves and with their responses to the texts. Most people are familiar with the diverse forms of enthusiasm that have greeted such performers as Frank Sinatra, Bruce Springsteen, Michael Jackson, and Madonna, or such films as *Star Wars* and *Jurassic Park*, or such television programs as *Star Trek*, or the numerous successful soap operas on daytime television, or the *Harry Potter* books.

In its simplest form, the transmission model of communication assumes that the aim of all communication is to maximize the likelihood that the receiver receives the exact same message (that is, meaning) as the sender sends. Hence communication is assumed to function in such a way that the two ends of the process are somehow necessarily tied together; if they are not, the process fails. The British cultural critic Stuart Hall (1980), using semiotics, argues to the contrary that communication has to be seen as an articulation of two distinct processes, *encoding* and *decoding*, which do not have any necessary relationship to each other. Hall argues that although the two processes should be studied together, they are nevertheless distinguishable; therefore, the process of communication, and its success or failure, cannot be judged by some comparison test. Audiences interpret messages by articulating them into their own codes. It is thus reasonable to assume that the decoded meaning will differ from the encoded meaning, which describes the ways the text is articulated within the institutional contexts of its production.

## THE NATURE OF INTERPRETATION

We have shown that interpretation is itself a complicated and varied practice. Before someone decides what a text means, before he or she can interpret a text, at least three different questions must already have been answered, at least implicitly:

- What is the text to be interpreted?
- Why have we turned to this text?
- How does a text communicate?

## What Is the Text to Be Interpreted?

The task of interpreting a text is made even more difficult by the fact that, however simple a text may appear, it is actually quite complex. For the actual text—the signs and the codes—are themselves located in and cannot be separated from a complex set of relations: relations to the artist or author and his or her image; relations to the audience; relations to other texts and to the history of popular culture; relations to knowledge that people bring from a wide range of fields (including other media); relations to other forms of behavior (styles of dance, sexual attitudes, fashion); relations to the media (such as radio or MTV, which constantly repeat commercially successful texts) in which the text is itself communicated; and, finally, relations to different audiences and their various structures of taste (for example, how a fan of Tobey Maguire sees the *Spiderman* movies will be different from how a fan of the comic books sees them).

In fact, one has to realize that there is no single text that can be isolated for the sake of analysis. There are the signifiers themselves, the sounds and words and images that make up any text, any song or film or TV program. But the meaning of these signifiers, and hence of the text, does not exist outside of the codes, the relations of difference, which the text produces, to which the text is articulated, and in which the text itself is located. In that sense, every text is an *intertext*; that is, it consists of connections to other texts. This characteristic helps to explain the radically polysemic nature of media messages. Every text, every organization of signifiers, is potentially a number of different texts, each with its own set of possible meanings.

## Why Have We Turned to This Text?

Let us turn, then, to ask what kinds of questions can be asked about a text. What kinds of things do people expect a text to provide them with or do for them? In different interpretations of a text, people are not always looking for the same thing, not always asking the same questions. There are two sorts of common things people might look for in a text, two reasons they might be interested in it: behavior and meaning. Both of these reasons for interpreting a text (behavior and meaning) can also be considered within the broader question of why someone attends to a particular text in the first place. First, one can look for models of behavior, which might take the form of role models or "rules for living" or implicit instructions on how to do something. People learn everything, from dance steps to how to treat members of the opposite sex to a variety of different poses and attitudes, from media texts. People can learn ethical maxims and illegal practices; they can learn how to make love, or use drugs, or even kill someone. Note that one can find such models of behavior in media texts even if one hasn't gone looking for it. Whether or not people act upon any of this knowledge is a different question, which we will take up in Chapter 10.

More commonly, when interpreting a text, one looks for some meaning that is not obvious to everyone, some meaning that is, as critics often say, "below the surface." In such interpretations, all of the obvious visible and audible signifiers are interpreted as if they point to some underlying, "deeper," and less obvious, meaning. This need not deny that many people can and do make sense of the text by taking its surface literally. And although they may even be aware of a deeper meaning, in many cases, this is because the interpretations of the deeper meaning of a text have already become so accepted and commonsensical that they no longer appear to be below the surface. Instead, they appear for all practical purposes to be obvious and intentional. An example of this is the case of M*A*S*H, first a movie and then a television program set during the Korean War of the early 1950s. The show's popularity in the 1970s was built on an interpretation of it as a comment on the Vietnam War. This interpretation became so commonly held that most discussions of the program took at face value that M*A*S*H was "about" Vietnam. In another example, because the original 1960s television program *Star Trek* was seen on the surface to be only a far-out science fiction program, the show's writers were able to make quite pointed comments about current issues of the day: racism, colonialism and imperialism, the cold war, and Vietnam, among others. In the 1990s hit, *The X-Files*, this ambiguity is coded into the text itself: Whereas Scully always sees scientific questions on the surface, Mulder always sees conspiracies and aliens hidden below the surface. And was the 2004 film *Troy* "really" about the siege of that ancient city, or was it a commentary on the folly and savagery of a modern empire's foreign adventures?

In many cases, including that of M*A*S*H, the deeper meaning of the text is identified with questions about the political and social organization of reality. Such questions need not be explicitly political— M*A*S*H was often read as an argument against war in general and against the United States acting as the world's police agency in particular. It could be about disputed values or attitudes (Christianity, capitalism, or drugs); it could embody the experiences, hopes, and desires of a community (for example, much of 1960s music is about youth culture); it could challenge or defend an existing set of social relations (those between Whites and African Americans); or, in fact, it could be about the way a particular culture has constructed an entire world.

## How Does a Text Communicate?

Sometimes, when we interpret a text, we are not looking for its meaning. Instead, having already decided what its meaning is, we might be more interested in understanding how the text *produces* the particular meaning we assume it has. The question becomes less *what* the text communicates than *how* it communicates. Does a text rely heavily on genre conventions, or on a star's personality, or on assumed fan knowledge? Particular television programs might operate by using familiar clichés to demolish viewers' expectations of traditional television. Both *Saturday Night Live* and David Letterman, as well as *The Daily Show*, work precisely by violating the rules that normally enable television to communicate.

## INTERPRETATION AND THE AUTHOR

Perhaps the most commonsensical view of the meaning of a text is that it means exactly what its author intended it to mean, no more and no less. Most people operate with this view most of the time, both when they have no problem understanding a text and when they do not understand it at all. (Two psychiatrists meet on the street: Each says "Good morning!" As they pass, each asks herself silently, "I wonder what she meant by *that?*") Whether watching something that the viewer thinks makes the author's meaning very transparent, such as Steven Spielberg's *Saving Private Ryan,* or something completely opaque, such as David Lynch's *Mulholland Drive,* people tend to assume that the task of interpretation is to identify with or get into the mind of the author to discover what is really going on. Understanding a text is taken to require that the interpreter become one with the author. Thus, when people look at and quite un-self-consciously interpret a *Doonesbury* cartoon, they often assume that the meaning they find there (or is it the meaning they have given it?) is what Garry Trudeau placed there for them to find. Or they assume that Amy Lee can explain what an Evanescence song is really about. On the other hand, listening to a song by Radiohead, someone might assume just as easily that any inability to understand the song is a direct result of something going on inside the mind of Thom Yorke: He is too avant-garde (intentionally making it unnecessarily difficult), too self-involved, or at least too serious.

There are, however, a number of problems with this view of media meanings. First, why should the author of a text have the last say regarding its meaning? Imagine that two people in love have a favorite film that they think is very romantic and hopeful. Now, imagine that the director (who may or may not be the film's author, but we'll come to that in a moment) tells them that they have it all wrong; according to him, the film is really about the difficulties of sustaining love today. Do the lovers decide that they have been wrong all these years and that they have to give up "their" favorite film? Probably not, no more than Ronald Reagan could be convinced that because Bruce Springsteen's politics (and his statements) placed the singer in rather direct opposition to him, Reagan could not use the song as a statement of patriotism. (For another example, see Box 6.1, "The Wizard of Oz.")

---

**BOX 6.1**

*The Wizard of Oz*

For almost all of us, *The Wizard of Oz* is a pleasant "family movie," and most of us know it from one of the frequent reruns of the 1939 Metro Goldwyn Mayer (MGM) version featuring Judy Garland, Ray Bolger, and Bert Lahr. But it's more than that. L. Frank Baum's 1900 story, *The Wonderful Wizard of Oz*, was, according to writer Henry M. Littlefield (1964), a political allegory of U.S. national politics around the turn of the century. The "yellow brick road," for instance, referred to the gold standard, which populist Democrats wanted overturned in favor of the free coinage of silver, represented in *Oz* as the magical silver slippers. The Emerald City was Washington, D.C., the cowardly lion was Democratic presidential candidate William Jennings Bryan, and so on. The *political* meaning of this story is now virtually completely forgotten, but we still enjoy the movie, and "understand" it with no reference at all to its politics.

---

In fact, appealing to the author as if he or she could guarantee the meaning of the text contradicts the conclusions we have already reached: that texts are polysemic and intertextual. The fact that media texts are so widely and rapidly dispersed only magnifies the difficulties of trying to identify their meaning with the author's meaning. Often, authors do intend to, attempt to, and succeed in placing meanings in their texts. We have referred to this as the encoded meaning. But there is no reason to privilege such meanings. In most cases, people are simply unable to know what the author may have intended. The song "Yankee Doodle" was originally composed by British soldiers as a sarcastic put-down of the loutish American revolutionary soldiers. The Yankees, however, appropriated it as a patriotic song of their own. Today, it's mostly just a song that children sing. Similarly, Woody Guthrie wrote "This Land Is Your Land" as an angry socialist retort to—a protest against—the sentimental celebration of the country in Irving Berlin's "God Bless America"; now, it has become merely another benign patriotic anthem. Appealing to the intentions of the author also assumes that the author is completely aware of everything in his or her text. An author may not realize his or her own prejudices or biases or even intentions.

The second problem with assuming that the meaning of a text is determined by the author is figuring out who the author is. Take a television program or film. Is the author the scriptwriter? The series creator? The director? The actors? The producer? The cinematographer? The studio or network executives who control the budget and who may often directly intervene into (censor) particular programs? Is it the corporate owners, who also may intervene into the content of particular programs (including the news)? Or is it the banks, who are willing to finance some kind of media products and not others? Why are some films identified with their stars (for example, an Adam Sandler movie), others with their directors (for example, a Martin Scorsese film), and still others with their studios (for example, an MGM screwball comedy or a Disney animated cartoon)?

Can we isolate one single author? What if the different participants have different meanings in mind when they are working on the same text? Clearly, on a metropolitan newspaper or a feature film, hundreds of people contribute to the creative content of the product. The situation is not much better in a music album. People tend to identify the author with the performer, even when he or she does not write many of the songs. Many performers are groups, and writing credits are divided among them. Every performer plays songs written by others, including some ("covers") that have already been recorded. But, in addition to performers and composers, there are managers (who often control the careers of all but the most successful stars), producers, engineers, and record company executives (not to mention all the people involved in video production and the marketing of other image paraphernalia). The traditional thinking that the creative artists are entirely responsible for their creations is no longer appropriate in the age of the mass media and the mass production of popular culture. Today's "artist" is a group of people, all with their own intentions and responsibilities, all with their own agendas and constraints. In this rather chaotic context of creation, how can one possibly hope to identify the actual author?

Many questions can be raised about the relationship between authorship and the production of media texts; we will address these in other chapters. For now, the difficulty of identifying an author for most media texts makes it reasonable to assume that texts can be analyzed as if they had no author at all. After all, even if we are convinced that the real secret in understanding a text lies in what the author intended to say, in most cases, our only evidence will be what is available in the text. And if we give up the deeply held and romantic image of the creative artist, we are still left facing the text itself.

## TECHNIQUES OF INTERPRETATION

There are many different techniques for interpreting the meaning of a text and for understanding how the text constructs and communicates that meaning. In this chapter, we are concerned with techniques that focus on the encoded meaning—that is, that start with the text itself. Even if the text cannot be said to have a single, definitive meaning, the text does offer us certain organizations and structures of meaning that can be identified. We can understand the encoded meaning of a text to be what is "in" the codes and structures that can be identified in the text itself, putting aside all but the most obvious and culturally shared links between the signifiers of the text and other texts to which it might be connected.

Usually, people do not stop to analyze the system of signifiers that enable the text to signify in particular ways. Because they are quite familiar with the vast majority of codes employed in the mass media, people do not need to pause to inspect the text. But that is precisely what one must do to get a better understanding of how the media work to produce a meaningful world, and what specific meanings they produce. So, we will explore some of the different techniques for interpreting or, as it is called, *reading* a text of any type.

We are arguing that the author's meaning is not the meaning of a text. There is no *one* meaning of a text. However, it does not follow that just any interpretation of a text is valid. The signifiers of the text, their organization by and into particular codes, the intertextual relations of this text with other texts, and the questions and methods we bring to analyzing the text all limit or constrain our interpretations. Not every text lends itself equally well to all methods of analysis.

Most of the time, when people reflect on their interpretation of a text, they focus either on the themes or on the symbols that are most obvious in the text. We look for a theme in the content or subject matter of the text; examples of themes range from love and family relations to war and social responsibility. *Cinderella* is a story about romantic love. *Alias* is a spy thriller that also might be seen as a study in family relationships. After identifying the theme, the interpreter's task is to describe the way the theme is presented in the text. For example, in *Cinderella,* romantic love is not only highly prized, it wins out over all obstacles: Love conquers all. In *Alias,* Sydney's work is complicated by her relationships with her father, mother, and boyfriend.

Another way to interpret the meaning of a text is to look at the symbols that organize and give shape to the text itself. People talk about the various symbols of Christianity in the songs of Madonna and U2. Or, in the classic film *Citizen Kane,* the entire film is organized around the symbol of the sled, Rosebud; understanding the movie might depend upon understanding the meaning of the symbol. Does Kane's memory of Rosebud signify the loss of innocence and youth? Is it an Oedipal rejection of his father? The task of symbolic analysis is to figure out how the particular symbol is working in the text: What is it doing or saying? The meaning of the text becomes the meaning of the symbol.

169

The problem with both theme and symbol analysis is that they are largely intuitive. They offer little in the way of new insights into how the text is constructing meanings or into the range of possible encoded meanings that can be identified in the text. Both depend on prior assumptions the analyst makes about the meaning of the signifiers and symbols in the text. For example, in certain versions of psychoanalytic criticism, every vertical image refers to male sexuality. In an ad for Time-Life books, this kind of interpretive technique is used: A wife wakes up her husband and tells him she dreamed she was being chased. He offers to look up the various meanings of this symbol in his Time-Life book on dreams. Clearly, the strength of both theme and symbol analysis is to provide important ways of describing and clarifying people's taken-for-granted perception of the content and principal signifiers of the text.

It is important, however, to try to get beyond such intuitive approaches to interpretation. In what follows, we will consider four different ways of examining the text that go beyond intuitive interpretations to give us a better grasp of the encoded meaning of the text: narrative analysis, genre theory, semiotics, and content analysis.

## Narrative Analysis

One of the major ways in which a text can organize meaning—which is the same as saying one of the major forms of codes—is narrative. Narratives are the stories people tell. They are usually, either directly or indirectly, stories about themselves and their world. Narratives tell people who they are and where they came from; they tell them about their possible futures and the forms of social relationships they value. They explain the structure of the world and the relations between different events within it. They tell people how to act in different circumstances, and about their own abilities to act within and upon the world. Narratives are the most common codes of the mass media. They are everywhere, in advertisements and just about every form of entertainment. Narrative structure is central to movies, television, comics, and most popular songs. Even the news transforms events into stories: Elections become horse races, international crises become wars of nerve, riots become criminal adventures, and so forth. (See Box 6.2, "Watergate and the News as Narrative.")

## BOX 6.2

### Watergate and the News as Narrative

Media scholar Michael Cornfield (1988) argues that media coverage of Watergate, the 1972 break-in at Democratic National Committee headquarters in the Watergate office complex in Washington, which ultimately led to the 1974 resignation of President Richard Nixon, "became, through journalism, a real-life tale of crime and detection" (p. 183).

Cornfield underscores that journalists

> bind the news into narrative forms through framing devices that specify a time sequence (beginning, middle, end) and a space for the characters to interact (setting). Framing devices surface in chronological sidebars and charts, in such phrases as "questions remain" and "only time will tell," and in references to time spans outside the one automatically established by the journal's periodicity (i.e., daily for newspapers, weekly for newsmagazines). (p. 184)

Moreover, the press, where convenient or appropriate, organizes stories around themes. Watergate becomes a detective story through repetition in the coverage of Watergate as a "caper," through the labeling of the firing of special prosecutor Archibald Cox and the resignation of Attorney General Elliott Richardson as "the Saturday Night Massacre," and through the discovery of incriminating evidence in the White House tapes as "the smoking gun."

What is the *importance* of the press's characterization of the continuing Watergate story as a detective story? We think there are two important outcomes. First, by labeling it a detective story, the press led itself to some sorts of coverage (looking for "clues" to unravel the mystery) at the expense of others. If Watergate, early on, had been framed, for example, as a beleaguered individual (Nixon) against a misguided society, the press might well have been inspired to look for other sorts of "facts." Second, because Watergate *became* in popular lore the prototypical news-as-detective-story case, subsequent events have been held to its standards: The political fallout of the Bert Lance affair in the Carter administration and of the Iran-Contra scandal in the Reagan presidency was considerably lessened because in each of those cases, no "smoking gun," or irrefutable evidence of presidential involvement was ever found. Before Watergate, the president might have had to resign just because such political crises occurred on his watch.

Narratives are the easiest thing to take for granted, because everyone is always immersed in stories—stories about our family, about where we come from, about our country, and about our identity. Everyone is made comfortable listening to and following stories. Most conversations about particular texts in the mass media involve recounting the narrative—the plot—of some text or set of texts. When anyone walks into the room in the middle of a television show or movie or even the news, the first question is "What's happening?" Or even more directly, "What's the story?"

Narrative analysis goes beyond the simple and straightforward plot summaries that circulate among friends and even within the various media industries (for example, in *TV Guide*). It begins by making a distinction between the *story* and the *discourse*. The story is the actual progression of events through time that makes up the substance and the content of the narrative. The discourse is the way the text describes or tells the story (the way it is plotted, for example).

## *Story*

The story is the content of the text: the events and the characters involved in them. Every story has a beginning, a middle, and an end. Presumably, there is some point—some conflict to be resolved, some goal to be achieved, some mystery to be solved. Some events will be more central and crucial than others, just as some characters will be more involved in the narrative. The events presumably are linked, and they come one after another. But also, in narratives, it is usually assumed that events are linked by some causal connections. That is, people assume that because someone did this, then that happened, and so on.

Narrative *characters* are not real people; they are only players or roles in a story. They serve a specific set of story *functions* by doing certain things. For instance, a function of the character Princess Leia in *Star Wars* is to create tension between Luke Skywalker and Han Solo (she also functions as a goal for Luke's quest—rescue the Princess—and also as a means of rewarding his achievement at the end by giving him gifts and a medal). Characters have a variety of physical, social, and psychological characteristics assigned to them by the narrative, although not all of these may be necessary to the story. The fact that Lando Calrissian is played by a Black man, Billy Dee Williams, makes no difference in the story itself. Sometimes, however, the fact that a star is playing a particular character makes it more difficult to separate the character as a narrative function from the real actor playing the part. For example, in any role Harrison Ford plays, he brings the swaggering Han Solo along with him. And when he seems not to, critics always note in their reviews that he is "playing against type" and often the movie flops.

The mass media use and manipulate stories in many ways. Obviously, the story is one of the "hooks" that attract and sustain an audience's interest. Anyone who watches a lot of television, however, soon realizes that television programs often tell the same basic stories over and over. The programs spend more time on the minute differences within the same plots than on developing new plots. What becomes central in these repetitive stories are the characters and the relationships among them. This helps us understand why people might watch the same program or film again and again, and it partly explains the rapid syndication of successful programs (and the sales of program episodes on video and DVD): People *are* willing to watch the same program again.

In many series, the story is manipulated in ways to make it ever more suspenseful. One need only think of the preponderance of cliffhangers (where the program or even series ends with a major narrative question unanswered: *Will they get married? Who shot that character? Did they lose their jobs?*). Even television news relies on cliffhangers, called *teasers,* to keep you watching the program (*"How hot will it get? We'll tell you after this"* or *"Police have a suspect in that murder case. Details after the break"*). Another way of manipulating stories is characteristic of soap operas: Many story lines interweave within the same program, each with its own narrative interest.

Stories can be used also to help set up an apparently real world within which the story itself exists. Thus characters from one TV program will often significantly enter into the narrative of another, as when Mannix appeared on *Diagnosis Murder.* The 1970s TV sleuth and the 1990s TV doctor cooperated to solve a crime. In other instances, a series may make reference to another series, when a story line on *L.A. Law* has Douglas Brackman date Vanna White from *Wheel of Fortune,* or when shows like *Law and Order* and *Homicide* have cross-over episodes where characters from both series join together to solve a case. Within that alternative reality, events are often as predictable and meaningful as they are within the world of our own everyday lives. Think of how realistically the Bob Hoskins character, Eddie Valiant, entered the world of the 'toons in *Who Framed Roger Rabbit?* Audiences sometimes get into the act, as in the case of fans of *Star Trek,* who often "live" within *Star Trek's* universe during *Star Trek* conventions. And it is part of the folklore of television that many soap opera fans live within the world of, say, *General Hospital* and *The Guiding Light,* sending wedding presents and get-well cards to the characters.

## Discourse

The narrative is more than a story, however, because rarely is a story told straightforwardly. *Discourse* is the way the story is told in a particular text. The same story can be told in many different ways, depending on who is telling it and to whom. Narrative theory, then, is primarily a way of examining how a story is told and figuring out what difference it makes that it is told one way and not another.

*Narrator and Narratee.* Every narrative (the story in discourse) has a *narrator,* someone who is telling the story, and a *narratee,* someone to whom the story is being told. The narrator is always, in some sense, inside of the story. It is often, for example, the voice of a character. In *Star Trek,* the captain narrates the story, speaking into his log. The narrator defines the *point of view* that the audience has on the story, on what is taking place. In *Star Trek,* the viewer sees the world through the captain's eyes. This is certainly a common ploy in much television (for example, Bernie Mac, of *The Bernie Mac Show,* addresses the camera directly, discussing the events of the episode). Viewers see the story through the eyes and hear through the voice of the main character. Sometimes the audience does not know who the narrator is; such an anonymous narrator is not usually a major character in the story itself. Some narratives play off this feature of discourse by not revealing that the narrator is in fact a major character. For example, we find out at the end of Agatha Christie's *The Murder of Roger Ackroyd* that the narrator is the guilty party. In the dramatic film *Sunset Boulevard,* the narrator dies at the end with the death of the narrator's character. Akira Kurosawa's classic film *Rashomon* presents the same story narrated by different characters to make the point that, told from different of view, the "same" story is really four different stories.

174

In visual narratives, the narrator is almost always identified with the camera. That is, the camera's angle of vision, its perception of the world, defines the narrator's point of view. In that sense, the old adage that the camera doesn't lie is only partially true, because the camera may indeed lie by its identification with a single character and its consequent involvement in the story itself. The traditional Hollywood film uses the camera to establish a "third person" narrator who apparently exists outside the story. Occasionally, however, within such traditional films, the camera takes a position in the story. Viewers suddenly find themselves looking at a character (usually a woman) from a hidden position (outside a window or from a closet). They know someone is likely to enter into the action. This technique creates much of the suspense in films such as *Wait Until Dark* and many of Alfred Hitchcock's films. It's a technique that's also been parodied in *Scary Movie* and its many imitators.

Much of so-called avant garde cinema violates the tradition of a third-person or anonymous narrator by placing the camera in the position of a major character within the story. This is a typical strategy in most of Ingmar Bergman's films, such as *Wild Strawberries*. In another example, on the television cartoon *Rugrats*, the camera presents a kid's-eye view of the world.

Narrators can be described by their relationship to the story and by their knowledge of it. A narrator can be speaking as a character within the story (a *diegetic* narrator, such as Angela in *My So-Called Life* or Malcolm in *Malcolm in the Middle* or Bernie Mac) or from outside of the story (a *nondiegetic* narrator, as in the news and most documentaries). A narrator can be telling us a partial story (usually if he or she is acting within it, he or she will have only limited knowledge) or the narrator can be framing the entire thing (as, for example, a detective who has already solved the mystery). A narrator can have more information than any character could possibly have: An *omniscient narrator* knows what is going on everywhere (as in many fairy tales). Narrators can have different degrees of reliability, which may or may not be intentional. The criminal, narrating his or her own crime, obviously has an ulterior motive in presenting actions in a certain light. On the other hand, perhaps the narrator has only been told the criminal's side of the story and, not realizing that this character was the criminal, recounts the discourse as if it were the truth. In another example, the narrators of the TV program *The Wonder Years* and the film *A Christmas Story* are adults looking back on their childhood with nostalgia and so may not present the most accurate interpretation of the events.

Just as there is a narrator within the narrative, someone is there to receive the narration. Often, in television, this receiver is a live audience. Television critic Robert Allen (1992b) calls this the ideal audience or exemplary viewer: the audience is included in the show (as a studio audience or audience member who asks a question or even just a laugh track) to model how we, the audience at home, should be reacting to the show (when to laugh, gasp, applaud, and so on). Sometimes, the story itself makes it clear that the entire discourse is a conversation between two people, one of whom is narrating the story to another. Sometimes, the story makes it clear that someone is there but does not identify who it is. This is the effect, for example, of a canned laughter track. Or the internal audience may be identified but remain absent from the discourse of the text itself. For example, in *Twin Peaks*, Agent Cooper is constantly recording messages, reflections, and notes to "Diane" on a pocket tape recorder.

The narrator and narratee are not the same as the author and the audience. In fact, insofar as the author and the audience are real people, the interpreter of the text can have little or no access to them through the narration itself. But the discourse does create what critics refer to as an *implied* author and an implied reader. We may decide, for example, that the narrator is a rather shady character; we can also infer that we are supposed to know that and hence mistrust what the narrator says. The implied author gives another perspective on the story. The implied author is the image of the author constructed from the information in the text; it is the reader's imagination of who the author of this text must have been. What does one make, for example, of Stephen King or J. K. Rowling or Danielle Steele from their texts? Describing a movie as "a woman's movie" suggests that its perspective—not merely that of the narrator but of the implied author, as well—seems to represent women's feelings, concerns, and so on; it makes no difference whether the actual author is a man or a woman.

The implied reader, on the other hand, is usually assumed to be on the side of law and order, justice, and authority. The way in which the starship captains in all the *Star Trek* series are cast as narrators suggests not only a very sympathetic implied author, but also that their audience should be sympathetic to these authority figures as well. The implied reader or audience is, then, the audience that one imagines the implied author wants for his or her narrative. Feminists often argue that whomever the narratee may be, the implied audience of most commercial entertainment is male, judging by the way women are portrayed. Sometimes, the narrator will seem to address the implied audience directly, so that the implied audience and the narratee are one and the same. This is the case, for example, with almost all pornography. All of these levels of authors, narrators, narratees, and readers are summarized in the diagram below.

Real Author → Implied Author → Narrator → Narratee → Implied Reader → Real Reader

(Kozloff, 1992)

*Time.* The relationship between the story and the discourse is further complicated by the temporal relationship between the two. Is the narrative told while the events are unfolding, or immediately after, or at a much later time? The discourse of the narrative is free to change the organization of events within the story. Using flashforwards and flashbacks (when the future and the past, respectively, are represented in the present), the discourse can make connections that might be otherwise unavailable, or it can confuse and conflate events. Sometimes, these techniques are responses to the fact that simultaneous events cannot be represented simultaneously in a linear narrative, and discourses must always face the problem of how to represent such events. Events that recur in the story may be told only once in the discourse, whereas events that occur only once may be repeated for emphasis.

The narration may take longer than the story (as when it is stretched out for effect), or the story and discourse may be told in the same time (as in the TV show *24*), or the discourse may merely summarize the events that occurred. Most discourses are summaries, and it is easy to forget that a selection was made. For example, the investigations and trials that form the plot of *Law & Order* typically take months if not years to complete, yet are summarized in an hour. One of the most interesting things about the reporting of the Second Iraq War in 2003 was that the news was taking place in real time (at times being reported live by reporters embedded with the troops), not only as it unfolded but also lasting as long as the events that were being described.

Occasionally, the discourse may simply skip over entire scenes of the story (an *ellipsis*), creating a gap in knowledge, for example, when the discourse skips from the protagonist's past to the present, leaving out what happened in between. For example, the 2004 TV series *Jack and Bobby* takes place in present day with the title characters as teenagers, but also skips ahead into the future (the 2040s) to have characters comment on the presidency of one of the brothers. We are left to speculate about the intervening years, how one of these boys becomes President of the United States.

It is in these relations between the story and the discourse that we can discover the narrative and gain a more critical perspective on it. Narrative theory allows anyone to see how the telling of the story constructs the story itself and to identify the perspective that is taken on the story. In this way, it can give one a better view of how meanings are produced and communicated.

## Genre Theory

A genre is a class of texts that have something in common. We can interpret texts based on their genre. There are as many ways to define a genre as there are theories of meaning, but three are most commonly used. The first defines a genre by a shared set of conventions (such as conventions about narrative, characters, location, styles). The western, for example, is not merely defined by its setting in the nineteenth-century American West, but also by certain stock characters (the strong, silent hero-gunfighter, the evil businessman or gang leader, the school-marm, the saloon girl) and by certain events (the card game, the swindle, the gunfight, the saloon brawl). In this sense, the genre specifies both the formula that is reproduced in every western and the limits within which each new example of the genre has to find its own individuality.

The second approach defines genre as the underlying structure of values that the genre puts into play. The western is often about the conflict between culture and nature, embodied in the competing images of eastern and western life (W. Wright, 1975). Similarly, heavy metal music might be thought of as the embodiment of the conflict between angry youth (sexuality, violence, and noise) and creative adulthood (musical mastery).

Finally, and perhaps most flexibly, genres can be seen as articulations of texts that define a particular set of intertextual relations. For example, one can say that there is a genre of adult/children's programs, which brings together such programs as *Rocky and Bullwinkle, PeeWee's Playhouse, The Simpsons,* and *Beavis and Butthead.* Locating these texts in this genre would direct an analyst to compare these programs and find contradictory codes within them. For example, the same signs may mean different things to adult and child viewers. These programs are double coded; they are understood one way by a child and another way by an adult. This difference is crucial to the genre and to the way the individual programs construct meaning. In this sense, genres tell us how to read a particular text by placing it into more familiar structures of meaning. Film theorist Graeme Turner (1993) argues that genre acts as a kind of shorthand. If the audience understands the rules and features of a genre, then the writer or director can avoid spending time explaining the general setting, characters, and action and get right down to the story at hand. Without genre expectations, each Western would have to explain what life was like on a frontier town, the role of the sheriff, and so on.

The real challenge of genre analysis is to look at the relationship between a genre (as some general structure or set of expectations that describes a range of texts) and a particular example of the genre. One can explore how the particular text embodies the features of the genre, and also how it reshapes them; how it defines its own individuality and uniqueness within the genre, and even how it transforms the genre itself. Family situation comedies by Norman Lear in the 1970s, such as *All in the Family* and its spin-offs, *The Jeffersons* and *Maude,* changed the genre itself, by, for example, making dialogue more like the "real world" and introducing social-issue controversies (for example, Maude's abortion) that the bland sitcoms of the 1950s and 1960s had studiously avoided. Likewise, the 1970s blockbuster science fiction films, such as *Star Wars,* changed people's expectations about sci-fi films: The wizardry of George Lucas's Industrial Light & Magic technical crew made earlier sci-fi films seem amateurish, not "real" representatives of the genre. It is not always clear whether a text belongs in a genre. Many critics, for example, have argued that the *Star Wars* movies are more accurately seen as examples of the western genre, only set in space, than as science fiction movies. Some texts deliberately display a mix of genres. The television series *Buffy the Vampire Slayer* is comedy, horror, and teen drama all at once. But such an analysis depends upon developing a definition of the genre under discussion, and that depends in part on the analysis of the specific texts that make up the genre.

Genres are invented by people in the industry, by critics, and by audiences. For the industry as well as for writers, they are a way of defining, measuring, and sustaining taste. For instance, the networks may decide that westerns are popular again, or that family sitcoms are declining. This alerts programming executives to be on the lookout for proposed western series and to avoid new comedies. Similarly, record companies may decide that hard rock is not selling as much as techno or rap. Fans often use genres to describe their tastes, although rarely is anyone a fan of every instance of a genre. Genres can be very broad, encompassing a great deal of diversity, such as the genre of westerns or war movies or even heavy metal, or they can be narrow, as in "spaghetti" westerns or "speedmetal" or gritty police series (such as *Homicide: Life on the Streets*) or forensic procedurals (such as *CSI: Miami*). Genres are not simple and stable categories; they are historical: The family sitcom of today (for example, *According to Jim* or *The King of Queens*) differs markedly from those of the 1970s. Nor do they have any reality apart from the ways they are used by the industry, by critics, and by fans.

In any case, genre analysis is often a fruitful and powerful tool to describe the specific ways in which a text can both resemble many other texts and yet maintain its own sense of difference.

## Semiotics

We have already discussed many of the basic premises of semiotic analysis. Here, we want to describe some of the analytic tools that semiotics makes available for the interpretation of specific texts. Remember that meaning is produced when one signifier enters into a relationship with or is articulated to another, and every signifier in a text implies another signifier, and so on. Through this process—which is referred to as *connotation*—chains of meaning are established: *a* means *b* means *c* means *d*. . . . This red, white, and blue cloth means the flag of the United States, which means the country itself, which means the love and respect one should feel for the country. As these chains of connotation are reiterated within a culture, they can become fixed and frozen, as if calling up the first signifier opens the door into which come rushing all the meanings that have been linked to it. Such chains become codes that then structure future texts and interpretations. When this happens, we can speak of what French critic Roland Barthes (1970/1974) called *myths,* such as the Cinderella myth, and the myth of rags-to-riches. By myth, he doesn't mean that these codes are necessarily false, but that myths are the stories societies tell to explain the world. The myth of rags-to-riches describes a world where upward mobility and success are all possible with hard work.

A distinction that will prove very useful in semiotic analysis is that between *syntagm* and *paradigm.* These describe the two dimensions along which any text is organized. The syntagmatic dimension of a text describes its organization, how its signs are connected in time or space: This is next to that, this follows that. For example, in the previous sentence, *this* precedes *is.* If one were to reverse this order, so that *is* preceded *this,* this would change the phrase from a statement to a question. Changing the syntagmatic organization of a narrative or a photograph can seriously alter the ways in which meanings are produced, as well as the specific meanings produced. For instance, taking a photograph of the current president standing next to a portrait of Abraham Lincoln is most likely an attempt to connect Americans' positive associations with Lincoln to the president.

A paradigm describes possibilities rather than what is actually in the text. A paradigm describes the potential substitutions that one can make without changing the syntagmatic relationship. For any element, there are substitutions that can be made, that are allowed by particular codes within the culture. For example, watching a story in which a boy is bitten by a dog, one can imagine substituting different breeds of dog, or a wolf, or perhaps a cat, for the dog. But could one substitute a horse? And what about an elephant? Or a train? In the example of the photograph of the president, would a picture of the president's family behind him work as well? What about a picture of Moscow's Red Square or of Bart Simpson? A simple paradigm within American culture says that one could substitute a picture of George Washington or John Fitzgerald Kennedy, because they have similarly positive connotations. On the other hand, one would probably be well advised by our paradigms not to use a picture of Richard Nixon.

For example, take the sentence, "The girl drives the car." The syntagmatic dimension is the organization of the sentence (think of it as the grammar). Reorganizing the sentence changes its emphasis ("The car the girl drives") or makes it nonsensical ("Car the drives

181

girl the"). The paradigmatic dimension is the set of choices available for each element, and the difference those choices make. Why "girl" and not "woman" or "female"? Why "car" and not "automobile" or "Hummer"? Think of syntagm as the horizontal organization, and paradigm as a vertical set of choices for each element.

The existence of paradigmatic and syntagmatic codes can be useful in analyzing a text, especially through the *commutation* test. The commutation test simply asks whether a difference makes a difference. If this were changed, how would the meaning of the text be affected? Does it matter if the good guy wears black? If a heavy metal band does not play guitar solos? If Bart Simpson had ordinary hair? This is the power of semiotic analysis: to allow us to identify the ways in which texts establish meaningful differences that produce different meanings.

### Semiotic Analysis

Let's consider a simple example of a semiotic analysis. Consider a portrait of the Simpson family.

A number of iconic codes tell us that this is a cartoon. How do we recognize something as a cartoon? For one thing, notice that Matt

Groening, *The Simpsons'* creator, observes a cartoon convention: The characters have four fingers (drawing goes faster). Cartoons simplify and exaggerate the iconicity of signs. What changes would affect our assumption about whether this is a cartoon?

What other codes are operating? There is a code of gender marking: Anyone (that is, anyone familiar with the codes operating here) can tell which are the male and which are the female figures (as one almost always can in all cartoons and animated films, even when the characters are small, cuddly animals). They are marked by a number of different signifiers: size (males are larger than females), hairstyle, dress, accessories, and eyelashes (apparently men don't have any). The presence of accessories and eyelashes on the females suggests as well that they are more concerned with their appearance. The adults are marked not only by size but by distinctive hairstyles, as well as Homer's ever-present five-o-clock shadow.

The group is clearly a family. There are male and female adults with children (what would we conclude if there were no adults, or two women instead?). They are standing close to one another, perhaps gathering for a family portrait (when else do families stand in such a formation?). Marge is kneeling down to give Bart a big motherly kiss on the cheek (note that her eyes are closed, a sign of love and deep feeling). Bart, in stereotypical boyish fashion, is squirming away from this display of affection. Warmly, Homer, Lisa, and Maggie look on. The family seems relatively affectionate and "normal."

Homer stands behind his son, cradling Maggie in his arms, suggesting the image of a good father. His girth, balding pate (with scraggly comb-over), and unshaven overbite (notice that the entire family has a pronounced overbite) suggest a certain stupidity. But could we also read Homer through the codes of class? Is he working class (one of a long line of such television representations from *The Honeymooner's* Ralph Kramden to Roseanne's husband Dan) or perhaps as lower middle class (depending on how we read the style of his shirt and collar)?

The most obvious signifiers in the picture are the round bulging eyes—certainly warning any viewer that this family is not normal—and the hairstyles. The two girls' spiky hair may just be a cartoon representation of curly hair, although their appearance gives them other connotations as well: their starlike quality perhaps suggests positive (angelic) features. Marge's rather spectacular blue hair certainly stands out. Is it dyed? Presumably, at least one hopes. It resembles a grossly exaggerated beehive hairdo, popular in the 1950s. Certainly, this hairstyle tells the viewer something, not only about Marge, but about the class and tastes of the family.

Finally, there is Bart. In other images of the Simpsons, Bart is often separated from the rest of the family, signaling his difference and importance. (Although we have gone beyond the particular image, this is justified because most people in this culture will have seen other images of the Simpsons as well.) Bart is usually the only character allowed to speak (in the balloons that mark cartoon speech)—such phrases as "Hey, Dude," "Don't have a cow, man," "Ay Caramba," and "An underachiever and proud of it." Similarly, in the animated cartoons, Bart is frequently positioned as the narrator. Bart is often presented with or on his skateboard, an important sign in contemporary youth cultures.

The most central signifier in Bart is his hair. Like Marge's, it is not like the rest of the family's. Its spiked quality suggests punk culture, but its height makes it look more like a crown. It could even resemble popular African American hairstyles.

Two other aspects or possibilities of semiotic analysis are important here. First, semiotics often finds (or assumes, depending on your point of view) that texts are organized around a series of binary oppositions or binary codes: black/white, individual/social, good/bad, male/female, young/old, beautiful/ugly, strong/weak, work/play, nature/culture. Such codes create structures of meaning by establishing equivalencies between the terms of different binary oppositions (woman = young = beautiful = weak = play = nature) and then privileging one side of the opposition over the other. In this way, cultural codes create hierarchies or pecking orders—male over female, strong over weak. Think about the western, which often divides the world into good versus bad, white versus black, East versus West, culture versus nature, individual versus community, violence versus talk, civilization versus crime. Different westerns will create different systems of identity among these various binary codes and weight the two resulting systems of meaning differently. In *Shane*, individuality and violence are necessary to save the family and community, but in the end, they cannot be integrated into its harmonious existence. In *High Noon*, violence is only legitimated by its integration into the family and community. The binary oppositions that such a semiotic analysis identifies are themselves part of a code in which they are made meaningful. Notions such as bad/good or man/woman

184

are only meaningful within the codes of society; they have no independent existence outside of people's maps of meaning.

Such analyses also fail to recognize and challenge the assumption that each of the terms within a binary opposition exists independently of the other, that each term has its own meaning and definition. Women exist, men exist; they can be defined independently of one another and then compared. Yet, by the very terms of semiotic theory, this is impossible. *Deconstruction,* the invention of the French philosopher Jacques Derrida (1981), is a theoretical extension of semiotics and a critical practice that criticizes the tendency in semiotics to believe that codes are organized according to simple binary oppositions (or that such oppositions are simply equivalent to the semiotic notion of difference). Deconstruction undermines the ability to draw such simple dichotomies in which one side is made superior (male) to the other (female). Deconstruction argues that the terms in such binary oppositions depend on each other (as in a system of differences). That is, deconstruction extends the argument that difference is more fundamental than identity. The very meaning of the two terms, of *male* and *female,* depend upon each other; apart from their relationship, they have no meaning. The meaning of *female* is *not-male,* but at the same time, the meaning of *male* is *not-female.* The meaning of the terms is defined by the relationship between them and does not exist apart from that relation. Each term is tainted or contaminated by the other term, because the other term is already present and active within it. Deconstruction cautions us not to glibly assume that the western is about the value of civilization over violence or the individual over the community. Instead, a deconstructionist would argue that every western is about the complex ways in which nature and culture, civilization and violence, individuality and community, are always implicated together and constitute one another.

Second, because semiotics argues that the meaning of a text is the product of its articulation to and by a set of cultural codes, one can analyze a text by isolating the various codes that intersect to produce its most obvious readings. To put it another way, because the polysemy of any text suggests the possibility of many interpretations, one has to wonder (and explain) why most people (in the same culture) arrive at what are basically the same interpretations for the vast majority of cultural texts, especially media texts. If so many meanings are possible, why do people arrive at so few, and why do they usually arrive at the same one, a meaning that is not only taken for granted but is assumed

185

to be obvious and transparent? According to semiotics, the answer is that a relatively small number of very powerful semiotic codes transect in the text itself and thus produce the accepted meaning.

The classic example of such an analysis is that offered by Roland Barthes (1970/1974) in his book *S/Z*. Barthes takes a classic realist short story (realism here refers to an aesthetic genre) and analyzes it by identifying the various codes, five in all, that construct it precisely as a realist text. The precise nature of each of these codes is not important here; the point is that a complex structure of codes constructs and produces the meaning of a text. There is, however, a weakness in the analysis, and Barthes not only recognizes it, he makes it central to the analysis itself. It is the point where Barthes' analysis meets deconstruction. Like Derrida, Barthes argues that every text has a certain point where it falls apart, where it falls in upon itself, where its assumptions appear, if only by their effects. This *aporia* is a gap in the logic of the text, an absence on which it builds its entire textual edifice. This aporia disrupts the fluidity of the narrative and undermines the transparency of the taken-for-granted interpretation, even as it remains taken for granted. The point is simple: Even when polysemy seems to be totally under control, there is always at least one point in the text when it is threatening to reappear, and that point can never be totally sealed up.

## Content Analysis

The previous methods of analysis (narrative, genre, and semiotics) are rigorous means of investigating how meaning is constructed, but they still require some subjective insight into the text. Our final method here, content analysis, is sometimes defined as a more systematic and objective method of describing the manifest or surface content of a text. According to this perspective, by rigidly categorizing or quantifying aspects of a text we can more readily observe patterns that we otherwise would have missed. In its usual form, content analysis begins by defining a set of categories to describe the various elements of the content of the text. Next, the analyst counts the instances of each category that appear in the text. For instance, suppose we want to describe television programs. One way to describe them is in terms of how violent they are. To do this, we might count the number of acts of violence in each program. But, first, an act of violence must be defined. Perhaps violence is "the infliction of harm by one person on another." We might further want to distinguish between verbal and physical violence and between intentional and accidental violence. We would have to define each of these categories or types of violence as well. However many categories there are in the system, the task of the analyst is to identify the number of occurrences of each category in the text. The problem is to provide a clear enough definition of each category in the analytic system so that different analysts can agree on each instance of the category. For example, when Wile E. Coyote's traps backfire on him, is that an example of intentional or accidental violence? Is calling someone stupid an act of verbal violence? These are questions of the definition of content analytic categories. (See Box 6.3, "Content Analysis of TV Violence.")

---

**BOX 6.3**

**Content Analysis of TV Violence**

In a three-year content analysis study of violence on network and cable television, the National Television Violence Study (1997) defined violence as follows:

> Our fundamental definition of violence places emphasis on three key elements: Intention to harm, the physical nature of harm, and the involvement of animate beings. Violence is defined as *any overt depiction of a credible threat of physical force or the actual use of such force intended to physically harm an animate being or group of beings. Violence also includes certain depictions of physically harmful consequences against an animate being or group that occur as a result of unseen violent means* [italics added]. Thus, there are three primary types of violent depictions: credible threats, behavioral acts, and harmful consequences. (p. 41)

This definition lays out the parameters not only for what the content coders *are* to consider violence (credible threats of violence, actual violent acts, and circumstances—such as finding a dead body with a gun next to it), but also, by exclusion, what is *not* considered violence—accidents, disasters, and discussions of acts of violence without visual depictions. Elsewhere, the researchers exclude from violence activities by animals that might be gory and perhaps frightening to children, such as a hawk catching or killing and eating a rabbit.

Using this definition, the NTVS researchers found that about three of five U.S. television programs contained one or more instances of violence.

We discuss the issue of violence on television further in Chapter 10.

---

More typically, content analysts find it necessary to use a number of different category systems, each describing a different dimension, in order to more fully capture the content of the text. For instance, if they want to describe a television news story, they might begin by devising a coding system with several dimensions. They might consider its location in the newscast, whether it is first or last or in between; its length in seconds; its overall topic—whether it's about war or government or sports; who produced, prepared, or delivered it—the anchorman reading it, a reporter on the scene; where the news depicted took place—in Washington, D.C. (such a story might be coded as national), or Paris, France (such a story might be coded as international or European or French, depending on why the story is assumed to be interesting in the first place), or Paris, Illinois (U.S., local, Midwest, or Illinois); who was quoted or cited in the story—and here there might be several dimensions as well, such as whether sources are male or female, Black or White, governmental officials or private individuals, and so on. There are obviously many dimensions and, within each, large numbers of categories that one might use to describe the content of a television news show. And so the content analyst has to begin by deciding which questions about the text he or she wants to answer, and these questions in turn define which dimensions will be examined.

Another important part of content analysis is deciding what texts will be analyzed to answer the questions. For instance, if a researcher wants to know how violent television is, he or she must decide what is meant by "television." What will the sample be? That is, what television programs will be analyzed and for how long? Will the researcher analyze every program in prime time on every network and cable channel for a year? Does this include or exclude news programs? Imagine how large the sample could be. But if, for practical reasons, the researcher studies only a week's worth of prime-time programming on the four major networks (ABC, CBS, Fox, and NBC), can he or she claim to be describing "television"?

Choosing the sample is often as pivotal as defining the categories of analysis. In fact, the most common criticisms of examples of content analysis often focus on these aspects: What does the sample represent? Can the study be generalized beyond this sample? After all, in content analysis, the sample should be representative of the object of study. Similarly, categories should capture the significant or important aspects of the texts, and categories should be defined specifically enough to capture all the important differences. (For example, would coding the order of presentation of a news story give a real measure or even an indication of the importance of the story?) These are questions about the *validity* of the study. Content analysts are also concerned about the *reliability* of their content analysis; that is, whether a different set of coders would code the content in exactly the same way, or whether the same set of coders would code the same content the same way if they did it a second time. Similar questions can be raised about every method of interpretation and analysis of texts.

Unlike the other methods of interpretation, content analysis claims to be systematic and objective. It is made systematic by making the categories mutually exclusive (so that any element can be coded in only one way) and collectively exhaustive (so that every element can be coded in some way, even if it is only put into a general category called "other"). Content analysis is made objective by training different analysts to apply the same set of categories in the same way. This is called *content coding*. That is, any two people should *code* Tom slugging Jerry in the same category of the coding system for TV violence: as an intentional physical act of violence. Note that the word *code* is used in content analysis in a way that is different from its use in semiotics, although it is in some ways similar. Like a semiotic code, a content-analytic code uses one set of signifiers to mark the differences in a second set of signifiers. In semiotics, for example, colors mark different behaviors at traffic lights. In content analysis, one assigns numbers to categories and maps them onto another set of signifiers, the content.

## The Analysis of Visual Texts

A lot of mass media is visual, and there are techniques of interpretation that can help us analyze visual texts. For the sake of time and space, we will focus here primarily but not entirely on semiotics. Semiotics is particularly useful in visual analysis because people often assume that visual images are somehow closer to reality, as if they were less subject to manipulation and less structured by codes. Semiotics explains that this is not so by revealing the choices made in the construction of an image and the significance those choices have for the meaning of the text. These choices are both syntagmatic and paradigmatic choices. A full description of all the possible choices that are made with visual texts would encompass another full chapter. Here, we just highlight some quick questions that can get one analyzing a visual text.

As in any other text, one can begin the analysis of a visual text by examining the appearance of *themes or repeated visual motifs and symbols*. The depiction of a man with his arms outstretched (the crucifixion) is a common visual symbol in our Christian iconography. Similarly, the eagle flying overhead is commonly used as a symbol of freedom. We can describe *the structure and the content* of the visual image. Is the composition balanced? Symmetrical? Harmonious? What sort of contrasts appear? What is foreground and what is background? These differences describe visual codes: For example, in Anglo-European culture, people assume that what is in the foreground is more important than what is in the background. Different structures of composition direct people's eyes to see different parts of a picture in a different order with different emphases. A disharmonious composition often places its subject in a negative point of view to contemporary eyes.

We can also begin by examining *the mise-en-scene*, what is in the frame itself. We can describe the time and place, the appearance and spatial organization of the setting, and the camera's point of view. We can look at the way in which the scene is constructed, at the presentation of characters (their costumes and makeup). We can consider how the lighting both illuminates and hides particular aspects of the scene, and how it gives other elements a specific emotional tone (soft lighting is often used to present someone in a rather romantic light). We can see which characters are most frequently lighted and from what angles. We can observe the actions of the character.

A *shot* is a single frame of a moving image or a single photograph. Every shot is framed in particular ways, defined by the manner in which it has been photographed. Does it look flat or deep? Where is the line of sight, and where does the horizon appear? How is the shot focused? Where is the camera positioned? Is the hero, for example, shot from above, from below, or from straight on? Shot from below, for example, the hero will look larger than life. Are the characters shot from far away (a long shot) or from up close? Returning to moving images, one can ask whether the camera pans (moves horizontally) or tilts (moves up or down), or whether the camera tracks—moves with—the action. Are the camera's movements rough or smooth, in time with the action or working against it?

Finally, we have to look at *editing,* the process by which shots are connected to each other. The editor chooses shots, their order, their respective lengths, and how they are joined. Shots can be connected by fading out into black; by fading in from black; by superimposition (in which one shot fades in while the other fades out); by having the frame of the new image literally push the old image off the screen; or by simply splicing the two shots together in what is called the cut. For example, most Hollywood films are dominated by what has come to be called *continuity editing,* which ensures that the viewer feels the narrative continuity reproduced on the screen. In such editing, a shot establishing a scene is usually followed by a reverse shot of someone looking at the scene (the scene is now no longer visible, and the viewer assumes that the previous establishing shot was filmed from this position). Also, scenes can be intercut with each other at different tempos. Finally, editing can be organized according to various principles, including rhythmic, spatial, or temporal relations among the images. TV journalists hate to use jump cuts (cutting from one shot to another shot of the same person) largely because this calls attention to the fact that the news film has been edited. This editing reminds the viewer that something has been left out, that the account is not verbatim, and that someone (the journalist) comes between the story and the viewer.

The issue of editing raises some obvious questions: Who gets to be the editor? On what bases do editors make their editing decisions? What effects do these editing decisions have on the "meaning" of the texts? What effects do these meanings have on the audience? These questions point to the role of the media, the role of power in the media, and the power of the media. Throughout this book, we will continue to try to get a better understanding of these complex processes of meaning and power making: *Who makes meaning? Who is entitled to make meaning? Who makes this text apparently mean that? Who stops the endless flow of meaning? Are some people or groups more able to get their message across? Who are they and why do they have this ability?*

## CONCLUSION

We have introduced the notion of meaning as one of the primary products of media communication. Meaning is the process by which people organize the world into significant differences. This process is accomplished through the construction of codes (and of signs within the codes) that are socially, culturally, and historically specific. We have argued that there is no single meaning to any media text; texts are inter-textual and polysemic. Every text can be located within a number of codes, and each articulation produces not only a different meaning, but a different text. The four modes of analyzing texts—narrative, genre, semiotics, and content analysis—are tools we can use to obtain a more reflective and rigorous reading of particular media texts.

## SUGGESTED READINGS

Allen, R. C. (Ed.). (1992). *Channels of discourse, reassembled: Television and contemporary criticism.* Chapel Hill: University of North Carolina Press.

Chatman, S. (1978). *Story and discourse: Narrative structure in fiction and film.* Ithaca, NY: Cornell University Press.

Ellis, J. (1992). *Visible fictions: Cinema, television, video* (Rev. ed.). New York: Routledge.

McCloud, S. (1993). *Understanding comics: The invisible art.* Northampton, MA: Kitchen Sink Press.

Stuken, M., & Cartwright, L. (2001). *Practices of looking: An introduction to visual culture.* New York: Oxford University Press.

# Ideology | 7

T his chapter brings together two notions that we have already introduced but left rather underdeveloped: power and the social construction of reality. Every society attempts to guarantee its own continuing existence. A society maintains itself by reproducing its institutions and its structure of social relationships. To do so, it has to continuously reproduce the things necessary for its existence, from the resources to produce food and shelter for its people, to the labor necessary to transform these resources into commodities, to the individuals willing and able to participate in the institutions and occupy their assigned roles in the social relationships. But we have been suggesting throughout this book that the institutions and relationships that constitute a society always embody structures of power and inequality. If a society is to continue existing, it must, therefore, ensure that its particular relations of power—its particular hierarchies of economic, political, and cultural power—continue to operate with some appearance of legitimacy in the lives of the general population. One way of doing that is to use force to control people's lives and to actively suppress opposition.

A less troubling and more efficient way involves getting people to accept an *ideology*, a particular way of thinking and seeing the world that makes the existing organization of social relations appear natural and inevitable. Although such *ideological power*—the attempt to define reality in particular ways—has always been part of social life, its

193

importance increased significantly in the eighteenth and nineteenth centuries, as part of the processes of modernization in Europe and America. Historically, becoming modern involved the democratization of both political and cultural life. As "the masses" gained political power and cultural literacy, partly as a result of the development of new communication media, the use of force became more difficult, costly, and visible, and thus it became an instrument only of last resort. Instead, society came to rely more and more on the ideological possibilities of communication and culture.

## IDEOLOGY, REALITY, AND REPRESENTATION

The issue of ideology is closely tied to the discussion in the previous two chapters: The media make meanings and organize them into various codes and systems. Implicit in these arguments is the assumption that these codes interpret reality; they make the world meaningful and comprehensible. The introduction of terms like *reality* and the *world* signals the move from questions of meaning to questions of representation, from culture to ideology. After all, there are lots of meaningful texts that do not necessarily claim to describe an actual reality. Much of the time, people assume they know the difference between fact and fiction, although, as we shall see, this assumption is very problematic. Many meaningful statements explicitly describe a world that is not actual (for example, a world in which a man with super strength and X-ray vision constantly saves the world from bad guys). That world might be one that we can imagine; it might even be one that we assume to be plausible. Or there may be certain features of that world that we take to be descriptive of our own world. For example, we might agree that the legitimate law enforcement agencies need help, or that the difference between the good guys and the bad guys is obvious. Other meaningful texts describe fantasies that people may take to be describing impossible realities or at least realities that they would not want to see actualized.

People experience the world only through the cultural codes of meaning that enable them to interpret or make sense of the world. Yet people are capable of understanding many codes of meaning that they are incapable of experiencing as possible or even imaginable realities. In other words, certain codes of meaning are not only intelligible, they

194

are also assumed to be descriptions or possible descriptions of the world. As descriptions or representations, particular codes appear obvious, commonsensical, and even natural. They are assumed to be objective descriptions of how things are and, more often than not, of how things have to be.

The word *representation* literally means "re-presentation." To re-present something means to take an original, mediate it, and "play it back." But, again, this process almost necessarily alters the reality of the original. Representation involves making a claim on and about reality; but it is not the same as realism. It is not merely a matter of realistically constructing an imagined world; it is not merely a matter of what critics have called "the willful suspension of disbelief." In this sense of realism, the producer of a text will try to maximize the experience and impact of the text on the audience by drawing the audience into the universe that the text has created. Hence, as we have noted, films use continuity editing to create the illusion, not that this is the *real* world, but that the world the film creates has a reality of its own, a reality that acts in much the same way as the reality of the world outside the text behaves. Even so-called reality TV is a representation. The producers use a variety of techniques (such as hand held cameras, "confessional" type interviews, or "surveillance camera" type images) to convince the audience that what is presented is unmediated, or at least less mediated than what is on television the rest of the time.

To make a realistic text, producers have to try to hide their own presence in and operation on the text. As we have already suggested, a producer who is aiming for realism will avoid editing practices that emphasize his or her own interventions; for example, audiences notice such things as jump cuts, when cinematographers and video editors keep a camera and subjects in the same position but edit out a portion of a filmed or videotaped sequence. They not only notice that something is missing but are also reminded that the world they are seeing is not "real" because it has been produced. The illusion of realism is broken. And for just this reason, media producers seek to avoid jump cuts: They aim for a seamless, involving presentation that draws the audience's attention into the content. The audience must "forget" for a moment that the text is "just a text" producing meaning: Its realism, which may or may not necessitate that the world of the text has specific relations to the audience's everyday reality, depends on the audience's ability to imagine the actualization of that world.

For example, when two of the authors were watching the first *Batman* movie in 1990, we were startled midway through the movie, as Batman is scaling a building, when a college student sitting behind us blurted out, "Cheez, is that fakey!" Up to then, we guess, he had found the portrayal of a grown-up dressed in a bat costume and hopping off skyscrapers perfectly plausible. Or, as Dennis Muren, the supervisor of special effects for *Terminator 2* and a six-time Academy Award winner in that category, put it, "Reality is so touchy. Everyone can tell if something isn't real. Once something is unbelievable, you've lost the audience" (quoted in Pollak, 1991, p. B2).

Representation, on the other hand, is not necessarily realistic, although it is always staking a claim on reality. Realism as a genre is only the most obvious way in which particular texts might attempt to operate ideologically—that is, to make claims about reality. But even the most fantastic texts—think of all the Disney animated movies—can still be effective ideologically. *For ideology is not a characteristic of texts themselves but of the ways they are located and deployed in society. Insofar as a text, through whatever means, makes a claim about the world that its audience lives in—about what is real and possible—then a text is ideological.*

Consider the following example: In April of 1992, "riots" erupted in Los Angeles after a Ventura County, California, jury acquitted four police officers on charges stemming from the beating of motorist Rodney King. Virtually every person in the nation, and many across the world, had repeatedly seen a home video of the beating, in which King was struck 58 times by police officers. No one challenged the "truth" of the videotape: It did capture real events. But to render a verdict, the jurors in the King trial had to interpret the reality of the videotape. The prosecuting attorneys pressed on them one version, that King was savagely beaten by police officers out of control; the defense's version of reality was that the police officers acted reasonably under the circumstances. One picture, two different ideological articulations, two different realities. But also notice that the very description of the events following the trial as "riots"—rather than as "protests," or "demonstrations," or even an "uprising"—is an ideological choice.

Ideology is not only a matter of meaning becoming representation; it is also about the question of power and inequality. Although the concept of ideology originated with the French *philosophes* of the Enlightenment in the eighteenth century, it was the German philosopher and political economist Karl Marx who developed the concept in its present form. Writing in the nineteenth century, Marx wanted to understand how minorities were able to maintain power and why the vast majority of people accepted a system and even acted in ways the consequences of which seemed to be against their own interests. Why did subordinated populations accept their subordination and even act in ways that continue that status? Quoting Marx (1975),

> In the social production which men carry on they enter into definite relations that are indispensable and independent of their will; these relations of production correspond to a definite stage of development of their material powers of production. The totality of these relations of production constitutes the economic structure of society, the real foundation on which legal and political superstructure arise and to which definite forms of social consciousness correspond. The mode of production of material life determines the general character of the social, political, and spiritual processes of life. It is not the consciousness of men that determines their being, but, on the contrary, their social being determines their consciousness. (p. 425)

Marx is concerned here with simple questions. How do societies maintain and reproduce structures of social difference and power? Why do some people see themselves as superior and thus justify their privileged position in society? More important, why do people who are subordinated *accept* their subordination? In some societies, hierarchy is maintained through the use of force; you may be surprised to learn that even less than a hundred years ago, factory owners often used force to subdue workers and to compel them to accept their exploitation (Ewen, 1976). Even today, force is often used against illegal immigrants and in many Third World countries. However, most modern democracies eschew the use of force in favor of ideology. If those in power can succeed in constructing a dominant vision that justifies social inequalities, and they can win agreement to this vision, then their position of power is reasonably secure; force becomes unnecessary. The construction of such a consensus is thus always tied to the particular interest groups that struggle for power in society. Creation and maintenance of such a consensus is called *hegemony.*

Let's take a simple example: In the nineteenth-century American South, the dominant ideology represented Blacks as inferior, often not quite human, beings. To the extent that both Blacks and Whites agreed to this ideology (and notice that this agreement was often unconscious because it seemed so commonsensical), the system of subordination and subjugation endured. Of course, not everyone—certainly not all Blacks and not all Whites—accepted race-based subordination as a natural fact, and some struggled against it. And often force was used to subdue such disagreements. Still, the ideology was largely successful for many decades. Paradoxically, this ideology often was more humane in its consequences than less discriminatory ideologies; in treating Blacks as not fully and rationally human, it allowed for interracial relationships of a fairly wide range, and it usually protected Blacks as if they were like children. For all of the horrors of this period, then, we should not forget that Northerners who staked out the moral high ground often ended up treating Blacks worse than did southern Whites. Nonetheless, and certainly by today's standards in the United States, any ideology that justifies the enslavement of any human by another is unjustifiable.

In the contemporary world, the media are involved in the production of ideology all the time. After all, they are, as we have suggested, perhaps the most important producers of meaning and the codes of meaning in contemporary society. Furthermore, they are often a central and important part of people's everyday lives. They have the potential, then, to become the site at which meanings become more than meaning. When the media become representations, when they make claims about the way the world is, they become powerful ideological institutions. And they are, therefore, potentially a source of great conflict and struggle.

Almost all media texts, from the news to *Everybody Loves Raymond*, can be seen as ideological. Although it is true that not all media texts (whether apparently factual news reports or obviously fictional entertainment programs) support the status quo or the power structure, what is often presupposed or taken for granted is a set of relationships that usually do: The dominant codes of the media in the United States, for example, rarely if ever question whether a business enterprise should make a profit or whether politics is defined solely by the electoral system as opposed, for example, to organized protest. Similarly, the media seem to regularly present the world in a way that makes assumptions about such things as the primacy of the nuclear family, the necessity of working for wages, and the relative value of various segments of the population; in these media portrayals, these values seem commonsensical, universal, and even unquestionable. That is, the media, like other ideological operators, are constantly hiding the gap between reality and their representations of it. Even alternative media operate ideologically. They just may not share the mainstream ideology.

But ideology cannot be understood simply in terms of particular unrelated acts of representation, or particular unrelated codes of meaning, applied to particular events, people, relations, or practices. It always involves *ways* of representing, seeing, and thinking about reality. In *Ways of Seeing,* John Berger (1972) gives a number of examples of the new ways of seeing the world that characterized the emergence of modern society in Europe. Berger points, for example, to artists' practice of representing people with their possessions as a new perceptual system for thinking about the value of individuals. Similarly, he points to the ways in which women are represented in visual arts (from painting to advertising) as the passive objects of an unseen man's gaze.

Another example of a "way of seeing" the world touches some of the deepest assumptions about reality in the United States, where the laws, economy, and value system all seem to be centered on the "natural" priority of the individual. Americans tend to see individuals as the most basic and valued unit of social life. Perhaps this in part explains Americans' hostility to socialism, as well as the effectiveness of negative rhetorical appeals that attack social alternatives (from single-source health care to labor unions) as socialist. It might also explain most Americans' suspicion of religious cults, because they are based on the community as the basic unit of social life.

Ideologies are not merely particular systems of representation or ways of seeing. They are also ways of excluding and limiting, for they set the boundaries on what we are able to understand as possible. Ideologies are also not neutral. In defining the terms within which reality is experienced, perceived, and interpreted, they are always articulated or connected to the struggle of one group or another to maintain or challenge particular social organizations, particular relations of power. Ideology is, then, about trying to get people to see the world according to the terms or codes that have been set by one or more groups of people, usually those who control the power within a society. Although some ideological codes are explicitly linked to political positions and philosophies (think of the ideologies of communism and capitalism, or of the Democrats and the Republicans), ideology is a much more pervasive and common feature of social existence.

Capitalist societies, for example, need to have people who are willing to sell their labor so that someone else can profit from it. Capitalist ideology needs to have people believe that anyone can be economically successful who is willing to apply himself or herself. People who "fail" must have something wrong with them. (What must constantly remain hidden is the fact that there are structural inequalities in the system and that the system in fact needs such inequalities.) Similarly, the two-party system depends upon people's unshakable belief that the two-party system guarantees them a real say in the governance of their country. Patriarchy—the assumed superiority of men and the masculine over women and the feminine—requires that all people take as "natural and obvious" that men are stronger, more rational, better rulers, natural family heads, and so on. An example of an ideological or taken-for-granted assumption about the natural way of organizing television can be seen in the fact that American television programs are always interrupted by commercials. Whereas Americans find watching this unproblematic and have no problems connecting the segments into a single narrative, people from other cultures often complain that they find it difficult to follow the story and distinguish the program segments from commercials. As we shall see in Chapter 9, ideology is always involved in the way that the media treat various segments of the society.

## REALITY AND THEORIES OF IDEOLOGY

Reality is a somewhat paradoxical concept because reality is what most people assume exists independently of any concept or representation. Reality is what exists, end of discussion. Thousands of years of argument in metaphysics (the theory of the nature of reality) and epistemology (the theory of knowledge of reality) quickly disproves the commonsense assumption that reality is not a problem. Even if reality is what it seems, however, the question remains how human beings can know and talk about it. The most common theory, and the most commonsensical, assumes that reality is a collection of material facts (what actually exists or happens), that human beings accurately perceive such facts, and that these perceptions (and the facts they correspond to) can be accurately described, captured, or even mirrored by the various verbal and visual languages of human culture. Every society assumes that its own perceptions and languages provide the only and most accurate representation of reality. These sorts of realism have two great flaws: They are ethnocentric and they cannot explain misperceptions, hallucinations, disagreements, and so forth.

A second theory goes back at least as far as the Greek philosopher Plato, who, in *The Republic,* offered the following fable to describe humans' relationship to reality. Imagine that some people have always been prisoners in a cave, chained so that they can only see the back wall. Behind them, figures move and dance in front of a fire, casting shadows on the back wall. The prisoners, having never been out of the cave and never having seen the figures, assume both that the shadows are real and that they are all of reality. Plato was suggesting that people confuse appearances (which do have some causal or indexical relation to reality) for reality itself. Plato drew an absolute distinction between people's experience of the world—an experience of images and appearances—and reality itself. The latter exists behind the former as its cause, but without an understanding of the nature of this causal relationship, people are incapable of knowing reality itself. Such a "phenomenal" theory makes experience the other inferior half of reality.

A third theory asserts that reality is not real in any obvious and direct sense. It is, rather, the product of human invention—something people create and re-create (produce, maintain, repair, and transform). In this view, no independent reality is ever available to human beings; rather, the things that are taken to be real are real because they are socially constructed, or represented as real. According to this view, *reality has to be made to mean.* The claim that reality is socially constructed implies that communication is always doubly articulated: First, the chain or sliding of signifiers is stopped to produce meaning, and, second, particular meanings are themselves articulated to other practices and events as their representations. The first is the production of meaning or significance; the second, the representation and construction of reality. And insofar as each of these articulations is possible only from a position of power, then, the social construction of reality is always a process inextricably related to the relations of power in a society. Notice that such a theory does not necessarily imply that there is nothing that is not language or culture, that there is no material reality. It does, however, imply that insofar as human beings experience any reality, such reality is always the double articulation of culture, an ideological product.

Each of these theories of reality and knowledge offers a different account of the operation of ideology. Because human existence is always more complicated than its theoretical description, each of them has a certain truth and describes at least certain moments of the relations of power constructed within and by the cultural and communication environments in which people live.

## A Realistic Theory of Ideology

The most commonly held theory of ideology, a realist theory, defines ideology as "false consciousness." For example, Marx and Engels (1970) claimed that the dominant ideas of a society are the ideas of the dominant class. That is, the class that holds power (for example, the capitalist class) attempts to impose its ideas, its version of reality, on the rest of society. These ideas intentionally misrepresent the world, at least from the point of view of the real interests of the working class. The capitalist class tells the world that it is the natural order of things that labor power be sold as a commodity on the market, that the quality of one's being is measured by one's life, that the family is where one lives out one's real life, and so on. The fact that workers believe them means that, in one way or another (and Marx never quite figured out how), they are brainwashed. They are suffering from false consciousness because they are taking as true knowledge ideas that are false. (This formulation assumes that there must exist true knowledge and that there must be some way to tell the difference.)

This theory of ideology also implies that there is a direct correspondence between social position (such as class membership) and knowledge and interests. Thus there is something called "the interests" of the working class, which can be defined independently of any particular social struggle and defined solely by the fact that workers sell their labor as a commodity. Moreover, there is a truth that would describe their reality. Similarly, the capitalist class has its own interests and its own truth. The problem comes when the truth of the capitalist class is universalized and naturalized, then offered as the truth for everyone, as if it were both the way the world is and the way it has to be. In other words, ideas, knowledge, and culture are simply a reflection of the social position of those who produce them. They are not real; they are nothing but the effect of more real and determining social and economic relations.

Such a view of ideology is common in the contemporary world. As we shall see in Chapter 9, it plays a central role in many discussions about the politics of identity, as when one member of a group accuses another of having bought into the mindset of the dominant group. Equally common, some critics of contemporary society assume that the media are consciously and intentionally feeding the population false information and a false set of attitudes about the way the world is and has to be. In fact, some critics assume that, on the basis of the social identity of the producer of a particular text (by which they usually mean the board of directors of the responsible corporation), one can know the ideological bias of a text. Capitalists produce procapitalist texts that intentionally misrepresent reality to the audience for the sake of maintaining their own power. Male-run corporations produce promasculine texts that intentionally misrepresent reality to the audience for the sake of maintaining their own power.

## Experience and Ideology

A phenomenal theory of reality adds a layer to the analysis of ideology. Experience is always in some sense false, only a shadow of reality; it always exists at a distance from reality. And yet experience has its own sort of truth. It is, at the very least, the necessary starting point for any attempt to discover the truth of reality. Experience is the dimension through which human beings live the meaningfulness of their culture. That is, a phenomenal theory emphasizes the fact that human beings live in a meaningful world, but it still privileges the real world as if it could be accessed outside of the codes of meaning that define people's experience of it. A phenomenal theory of reality gives rise to a humanistic theory of ideology.

This theory of ideology emphasizes the more humanistic and less economistic side of Marx's (1975) writings. It refuses to reduce culture and knowledge to a mirror image of reality or to a direct effect of something else; it refuses to ignore the active role of meaning in human life. Instead, this theory begins with the assumption that people's position in the social world determines their experience of the world through the mediation of the cultural and communication forms that have emerged naturally and *authentically* from that position. That is, rather than assuming that there is a natural correspondence between social position and truth, a humanistic theory of ideology assumes a natural correspondence between social position, cultural forms, and experience. First, social position determines experience. By virtue of being working class, a worker is alienated from his or her labor, whether or not he or she knows it. By virtue of being a woman or a person of color, one inevitably has certain experiences of the world. For example, every woman has had the experience of being "sized up" by men, and any person of color has had the experience of being treated differently from White people. Second, left to their own devices, groups produce their own cultural forms and institutions, which accurately express and represent their experience.

However, precisely because these social groups are politically and economically subordinated, their culture is also subordinated to the cultural institutions and forms of the dominant class. The dominant culture tries, through any number of means, to replace and displace the authentic culture of the subordinate. It may simply drive or crowd their institutions out of business in the name of profit, in the way that the record and radio industries basically defeated and erased the music hall tradition of the working class. It may marginalize the cultural products and practices of the subordinate groups by constructing them as unworthy of serious consideration, or of social support. It may castigate them as vulgar, profane, obscene, dangerous, and even unpatriotic. Or it may appropriate them by making them a part of the dominant cultural codes so that these authentic expressions of subordinate experience are transformed from a challenge to the dominant values into a reaffirmation. This is called *recuperation*. For example, during the protests against the Vietnam War, dominant news media reporting on demonstrations would often emphasize that the very fact of such protests confirmed the unique privilege (freedom) of American society. In the process, the actual object of the protest (for example, the war in Vietnam or the disproportionate number of Blacks serving in the armed forces) was forgotten or ignored (Gitlin, 1980).

The result of this contest between an authentic culture and a dominant culture is that the subordinate group's ability to express and represent its authentic experience is negated. The dominant culture misrepresents and redefines others' experience. Thus the subordinate group comes to experience the world in the codes of the dominant group; its experience is made inauthentic because of the mediating power of cultural or communicative codes. While the truth of knowledge (as an authentic relation to the world through experience) and ideological misrepresentation are still at stake, the key terms are no longer truth and reality but experience and culture.

The correspondence that such a theory assumes—a correspondence between one's position in and perspective on reality, experience, and cultural forms—is reflected in the assumption that there is a structural homology or parallelism that operates and can be read across these diverse dimensions. It is as if, everywhere one looks, one sees a particular message that can be taken to describe the structure of culture and experience, whether the authentic or the dominant. For example, consider Raymond Williams's (1992) discovery of the structure of mobile privatization. Mobile privatization, in its simplest terms, defines a structure in which the individual avoids the hostile world by retreating into the privacy and safety of the home. The outside world is beamed into the home via the mass media; no longer do individuals need to foray out into the world to gather information. Williams argues that this "structure of feeling" describes at least a significant part of the culture and experience of contemporary life and that it can be read from a wide range of texts and aspects of the mass media.[1]

## Social Constructionism and Ideology

Both of these theories of ideology assume that ideology is in some sense a distortion or correctable misrepresentation of reality. In the end, ideology is a kind of bias operating within culture and knowledge. But social constructionism denies that there is any access to a reality outside of representations that would allow one to measure the truth or falsity of representations. Ideology is not "bias" because it cannot be measured against something that is not ideological, or that exists outside of ideology. One can only compare one ideological representation to another. Phenomenal theories of reality that contrast it to "mere appearance" assume that people (or at least the critic or scholar) have at some level an unmediated (nonideological) experience of the world that can serve as a normative yardstick against which to judge specific ideologies.[2]

People live within the systems of representation; they experience the world according to their codes of meaning. There is nothing outside of them that allows them to measure or judge their truth. Ideologies, then, are the systems of meaning within which people live in reality or, to put it differently, live their relationship to reality. They define how people experience the world, what they take for granted. Ideologies define what is taken to be common sense; the truth of ideological statements appears obvious and even natural. But people are often unaware of many of these ideological codes, because the codes are unconscious and often unchallengeable.

If realist theories deny experience any significance, and humanistic theories make experience into the privileged access to truth, a social constructionist theory argues that experience itself is what ideology produces. It suggests that the most powerful and important effect of ideological representations is that they construct our most fundamental and basic experiences of the world. When Richard Nixon and even Robert Kennedy went hunting for Communists in the 1950s, they honestly saw such figures everywhere and viewed them as a real menace. There was no way to argue against this ideology by appealing to some experience outside of another ideology. In other words, an ideology is self-contained and nonfalsifiable.

The twentieth-century French philosopher Louis Althusser (1970) was the leading proponent of such a theory of ideology, arrived at, he argued, by bringing the insights and arguments of semiotics and structuralism to bear on the question of ideology. Althusser defined ideology as the systems of representation in which people live out their imaginary relationship to their real conditions of existence. Notice: What is at stake here is not people's relations to reality but their relationship to a relationship. What is this imaginary relationship if not people's already meaningfully interpreted relations to the world? To put it simply, there is no way out of experience. Experience is the beginning and end of ideology. It is the world in which human beings always exist, and it is the product of ideological experiences.

If this theory is accurate, then it would seem to follow that the more obvious the truth of an experience is and the more certain people are of that truth, the more ideological that experience is. Consider the following analogy: Two people are talking. Person A says that his arm is broken. Person B says that it is not. Only one is right in this matter of fact. (Even judgments of such matters of fact involve relations of power. As Michel Foucault [1973] has demonstrated, the history of medicine is partly a history of the reorganization of power: For example, who has the power to diagnose such things?) But suppose Person A had said that he was in pain, and B had challenged this claim. There is an obvious problem here, because Person A made a statement of experience and not fact; we assume that people do have some privileged empirical access to their own experience. I cannot be mistaken that I see red, although I can be mistaken that there is something red there. Yet a constructionist theory of ideology seems to suggest that just such experiential statements, statements that seem to be the most secure, are in fact the most ideological.

How does this production of experience work? It works by pulling individuals into its signifying systems in such a way as to make them responsible for those representations; individuals become the authors of their own experiences. You know when you "see" a red car. That is, you *authorize* your own interpretation as the truth because you are the source and author of the statement and hence of the experience. Ideology works in just this way. It positions individuals as the subjects of their own ideological statements and hence of their experiences. People believe themselves to be the arbiters of an experience that is in fact constructed by ideological codes. Althusser (1970) describes this process as *interpellation.* Interpellation is ideology's ability to assign individuals to specific positions within its own communicative (semiotic) representations of reality.

We can further explicate this rather difficult notion by suggesting two experiments. First, pick up something that someone else has written in the first-person singular, such as a letter or a report. Now read it aloud. You will find that you begin to identify with the *I* in the text, that you feel yourself living what the person who wrote it lived, and that it seems to become part of you, or rather, you seem to become part of it. Through an identification with the *I*, it begins to become part of your identity, but, of course, this will only be temporary because you know what is going on.

Now, try a second experiment: The next time you go to a movie, imagine that the world that is represented on the screen is real and that you are in it. Ask yourself where are you standing in that world. Think about your field of vision, what you can and cannot see;

that will pretty clearly define where you are. Then, ask yourself if you could be standing anywhere else. Even if you can imagine other positions, you will still be unable to actually put yourself in them; you remain firmly rooted where you are. Why? You are positioned by the camera. Because the camera that filmed the scene is your only source of information about the world of the movie, you are basically forced to identify with the camera and to be in the place it defines for you.

Films represent a reality that does not exist outside the film. Viewers experience it according to the way they are positioned in relation to what appears on the screen. They can see only what the camera shows them. More important, in most commercial Hollywood films, the camera never violates people's sense of their perceptual position in the world by showing them something that it would be impossible for them to see. They cannot see what is going on behind a wall or in another place or behind their backs. The camera may turn around, but it must always do so in predictable ways that do not violate the viewers' sense of where they are standing in relation to the film's world.

These two experiments illustrate the process of interpellation. Interpellation literally means "putting into the space." Theorists use it to describe the way in which different codes—the codes of language or the codes of the cinema, for example—place people into particular positions that define their subjectivity and experience of the world. It is a bit like walking down the street and hearing someone say, "Hey you." You turn around thinking that perhaps they have called to you. In that instance, you have been hailed and positioned—interpellated by that single simple utterance. Interpellation makes the individual into a subject (a speaker of language) responsible for every word that he or she speaks and for the reality that these words imply. Return to the image in Chapter 5 of a game of musical chairs: Meaning is created when the moving signifiers stop moving, and some signifiers slide below others into the chairs, taking on the function of signifieds. Interpellation answers the question of why the music stops. The individual speaker stops the music; it is his or her apparent intention that creates the meaning. To put it another way, it is the *I* who is both inside and outside of language that draws the line between the signifier and the signified. (See Box 7.1, "Interpellation and Advertising.")

## BOX 7.1

### Interpellation and Advertising

A series of advertisements ran on television a few years ago for Soloflex home exercise equipment. One advertisement featured an attractive male model and another an attractive female model. Both contained similar voiceovers and imagery. A voiceover would intone, "This could be your arm," accompanied by a close-up shot of a finely muscled arm. The advertisement would continue with other body parts such as "your leg," "your shoulders," and "your stomach," and end with, "This could be you" accompanied by a medium-shot of the model from the waist up. This final image was the closest the advertisement came to showing the entire model, and was the only time you saw the person's face.

What we would like to focus on here is the explicit use of ideological interpellation by the advertisement. Television scholar Mimi White (1992) reminds us that ideologies are systems of representations that "function to construct individuals as social subjects, contributing to the production and recognition of one's very sense of identity" (p. 169). Now, all advertising implicitly hails the audience, but this advertisement was more explicit: "This could be *you*." What, then, happens if an audience member responds to the hailing and says, implicitly, "That could be me"? In other words, what is the ad asking you to do? What is it asking you to believe or value? If this is "you," who are you? What set of assumptions does one make about the world, one's place in it, and how one gets things done?

At its most basic, to say "That could be me" to this particular ad could mean that one is or identifies with being white, middle class, with a certain disposable income. It could mean that one values appearance over personality, intelligence, integrity, and so on; it could mean that one sees one's body and one's life as a continuing project to be worked on ("I need to work on my abs, and also on my relationships; and on my decorating; and on my education; and . . ."). It could mean that one buys into a culturally based assumption of what is considered attractive: not only the whiteness of the models, but their build, lack of body hair, and so on. And it could mean that one buys into the notion that purchasing things solves problems (in this case, the problem of not looking like the models).

Television interpellates its audience in many ways, especially through direct address. We are hailed as "you" or perhaps as part of "we" in news broadcasts, game shows, talk shows, and across the spectrum (Allen, 1992a). We are hailed when a television host looks directly in the camera and talks as if to us. Each of these instances can be viewed as an attempt to position the audience member within the terms of reference of the program. Who is it asking us to be? What is it asking us to believe? What is it asking us to value? What is it asking us to do? And, finally, we should ask, Who benefits if we see the world this way?

In this way, by having reporters "embedded" with the troops during the second Iraq War, and reporting live from the battlefront, the Pentagon sought to interpellate the audience by increasing the audience's identification with the troops (and therefore with the war effort itself) by placing them in the shoes of a person in combat. Positioning the audience in this way makes them feel more directly a part of the war itself. The reality of the war that was presented was that as experienced by some of the U.S. troops, and not the reality of others (such as the Iraqi troops or civilians, or diplomats, or others).

If ideologies are somehow linked to particular power relations and interests, then it appears that one has to assume that ideologies somehow distort reality for the sake of the interests of those in power. Returning to the example above, it is in the interest of capitalists to construct an ideology of the free market of labor, but such a market does not actually exist, or so it would seem. But, according to social constructionism, an ideology is not a biased view of a reality that can be described outside of ideology. This problem is known as *mystification*.

Ideology mystifies in two ways. First, because an ideology presents itself as natural and universal, it hides its connection to the interests of particular social groups or power blocs in society. By making the labor market, as it functions in capitalism, appear to be the only rational and natural form of labor, for example, the ideology of capitalism hides the ways in which this particular form of the labor market exploits workers for the benefit of capitalists. Second, ideology is mystifying precisely because it does create the reality it represents. For example, the ideology of patriarchy represents women as the weaker sex and thus continues the privileged position of men in society. Precisely because of the commonsensical nature of this ideological representation, parents often treat boys and girls differently. Boys will be encouraged to participate in activities that augment their strength, and they are allowed to be rough, whereas girls will be guided toward more passive pursuits. Or consider a different example: Marx (1977) said that the major figure of capitalist ideology is the commodity, something made to be sold. Capitalist ideology represents everything, including labor, as a commodity. Through the power of this ideology, everything in capitalism—including workers—*becomes* a commodity. The mystification arises not because things are not commodities (they are) but because they need not be. In a different ideology, such as the communism Marx envisioned, labor need not be rewarded on the basis of its value, but on the basis of people's requirements for a humane life.

Or, to return to the question of patriarchy, one can imagine a different system of child rearing that would, among other things, disprove the apparently natural differences between the sexes. But this new system would not actually disprove patriarchy so much as replace patriarchy with a different construction or representation of reality, which would in turn create its own reality.

## IDEOLOGY AND STRUGGLE

One need not choose among these theories of ideologies, for each can be seen to have different uses. The social constructionist theory describes the broad terrain on which a society's communication and cultural life actively determine both the structure of social relationships (power) and their relationship to the world. Still, it has little to say about specific situations in which ideology becomes a more conscious and explicit site of struggle. A humanistic theory of ideology describes the struggle between attempts on the part of subordinated minorities to define a part of their life outside of the control of the dominant majority, a space of authenticity to which they assign a direct relationship to their subordination. It also describes some of the processes (such as incorporation) by which a dominant ideological code might attempt to deal with such moments that might escape or even resist its domination. Both of these theories are concerned with the way domination is achieved and maintained through the construction of a cultural consensus using the means of communication. But neither theory addresses those situations where the existing consensus is precarious enough that it can be maintained only by an explicit ideological war that often consciously dissimulates to the audience. A realist theory of ideology is often useful for describing explicitly political economic battles (for example, capitalism vs. communism).

A social constructionist theory maintains that ideology always involves practices of articulation. In Chapter 5, we argued that any event or media product can have multiple meanings or interpretations. The same media product can be read as telling a number of different stories. We argued that meaning was produced by linking or articulating signifiers, signs, or texts. Similarly, there exist at any moment a number of different stories about reality or about specific events that

211

occur. Ideology is then the product of a double articulation: First, a text is articulated to a certain meaning, and then a meaning has to be articulated to reality to become an ideological code. Consider any government scandal (from Watergate to Irangate to the latest one): Every scandal elicits a number of stories, each of which seems to make sense of the "facts." Each version has different consequences, and each is related to different political interest groups. For example, Watergate was a scandal of the corruption of a small group within the Republican Party; Watergate was a phony scandal invented by Democrats to embarrass the Republicans; Watergate was a sign of the corruption that has become pervasive in American politics; Watergate was a "nonevent," no different from the way politics has ever been conducted.

Notice that it *does* make a difference which of these stories becomes the accepted one, which becomes "knowledge" that most Americans share. It is this struggle to make specific meanings and stories into taken-for-granted representations of reality that defines the struggle over ideology. If articulation describes the way specific meanings can be attached to specific signs or texts, it also describes the way a particular set of meanings can be linked to material or nondiscursive practices and events. Remember the example of the Trobriand Islanders, who believed that sex has nothing to do with reproduction: As a story, it can be humorous and entertaining to Westerners; but, as an ideology, that story had been successfully articulated to reality so that the islanders actually experienced the world in its terms.

The question of how reality is represented, the choice between different stories or pictures of reality, is not random. Nor is the decision freely made by each individual in isolation. Individuals do not get to decide that reality is this way, even though the rest of the world disagrees with them. The construction of a socially shared representation of reality is always implicated in society's attempt to reproduce its own existence and to ensure the continued viability of the particular relations of power characterizing that society.

On the other hand, although one ideology (or more accurately, an ideological formation, because it is composed of numerous statements that might not fit seamlessly together) is usually dominant, there are always competing stories about events and reality in a society. The *dominant* ideology defines the taken-for-granted or commonsense reality of the vast majority of people in the society. How does this work? Ideology can be effective only if it appears to be unquestionably true, to be so obvious and natural that any rational human would assent to its interpretations. Recreational drugs, for example, have become demonized by contemporary conservative ideologies, and increasingly the common sense of American society. To stand up and speak for *certain* drugs, to argue that they are not the evil force that we have been led to believe, seems almost impossible. Indeed, the demonization of marijuana is quite clear in the debates about the use of marijuana for medicinal purposes. In this way, specific ideological representations of reality become both natural and universal. Those living within an ideology assume that any rational being would share their common-sense perceptions; if they do not, then something must be wrong with them. The construction of "welfare queens" as lazy parents out to cheat the American public provides a further example.

There are always multiple ideologies within any given society. This is not quite the same as saying, as we did in Chapter 5, that there are always many meanings or stories. For an ideology is more than a story: *It is a representation.* An ideology embodies the claim by a particular group that this meaning or story represents reality. Consequently, ideologies are always in competition with each other. There is always a struggle between ideologies to achieve dominance. In that sense, people cannot be seen as passive "dopes" who unknowingly are manipulated by a single dominant ideology. Because there is no sure way to establish how reality will or must be represented, people are constantly involved in the struggle over ideology. The British media critic Stuart Hall (1985) tells a story about when his young son was learning the colors and simultaneously something about his own identity. The son could not understand why he was "black," because, in fact, he was brown. But a particular color has been articulated to a particular social identity. That color carries with it a particular set of meanings: In Western cultures, these are largely negative, as in black magic, black humor, the wearing of black at funerals. And these meanings are carried into the articulation. This articulation is part and parcel of a racist ideology that naturalizes and legitimates the subordination of Blacks. But Hall also points out that one of the most important parts of the civil rights struggle was the ideological struggle to disarticulate black from its negative connotations and to rearticulate it to a more positive image: "Black is beautiful." Or consider another example of the articulation of color and race: When the authors were growing up, one of the crayons in the Crayola box was labeled *flesh.* Today that color is *peach.*

Culture involves constant struggles between competing ideological codes, each attempting to gain the upper hand, to somehow win people into seeing the world in terms of its particular meanings, to experiencing the world in its terms. Ideological formations are not as coherent and systematic as the discussion thus far may have made it appear. As the Italian journalist and critic Antonio Gramsci (1971) argued, common sense is not a systematic structure. On the contrary, it is made up of contradictory fragments of meaning and understanding, assumptions about the world that a society inherits from any number of different sources. Often, no one can remember where these bits of knowledge originated or how their truth was established. They are now, as Gramsci describes them, traces without an inventory; we have lost the ability to remember where they came from and why they seemed so reasonable at some time.

Thus the ideological effects of a particular text need not be determined only by the totality of the program or narrative. One can watch the *Batman* movies, find many aspects of the films unacceptable and certainly unrealistic, but leave the theater finding notions of vigilantism and the incompetence of the police strongly articulated (or rearticulated) in one's common sense. Similarly, consider the *Rambo* films: Looking at the narrative as a whole, one might argue that at least one possible ideological articulation of the movies makes the federal government into the enemy. But that is probably not the most common ideological effect of these movies, which were more likely linked to various notions of violence and individualism and even jingoistic patriotism. More recently, *Independence Day* displaced the Cold War fear of communism by relocating the enemy as the feared Other into outer space. But, as in the sci-fi movies of the 1950s, one can ask whether the film is really about new threats facing the United States here on Earth or is, as some critics have suggested, less about particular enemies and more about the need to reassert a strong sense of identity against a common enemy in the face of political challenges to the established system of identities and differences. To put it simply, is the current revival of sci-fi movies about alien species really a backlash against feminism, antiracism, new immigrants, and the end of the Cold War? On the other hand, the *Men in Black* films seem to undermine any ability to represent aliens as uniformly threatening others.

One of the most interesting recent public spectacles presents a good opportunity for thinking about the complexity of ideological struggle and the differences between the theories of ideology we have discussed here. On August 31, 1997, Diana, Princess of Wales, was killed in an automobile accident in Paris while fleeing with her lover from the paparazzi. The world media coverage was unrivaled, and the public response unprecedented. Over a billion people watched the funeral; millions of people sent flowers or waited for hours to sign books of condolences from all over the world. The death of Diana, the "people's princess," was the occasion for a worldwide collective act of public and private mourning.

Let us begin by considering how each of the three theories of ideology might be used to enlighten our understanding of this event. An ideological realist might interpret this event as another media spectacle that distracts public attention from the serious problems of contemporary society by focusing on the life of another member of the rich and famous. After all, Diana's worldwide celebrity was itself a construction of the media. Diana's image as the people's princess is false consciousness, because, in reality, she was a wealthy member of the ruling elite who used most of her time and money in conspicuous consumption of exorbitantly priced designer fashion.

A humanistic theorist might talk about the ritual aspects of her life and her death. Beginning with her marriage and ending, for the moment, with her funeral, Diana's entire life and image as Princess of Wales was a media ritual celebrating all sorts of common values and dreams. Like the mythic Cinderella, the fairy tale that was Princess Diana's marriage reaffirmed our faith in love, marriage, and the apparently happy ending suggested by the myth that Prince Charming is waiting around the corner for every woman. Diana's life reaffirmed our belief in the importance of compassion, charity, and, in the contemporary political climate, volunteerism. But the events leading up to her divorce and her death were a spectacle of another order, reaffirming our worst fears about dysfunctional marriages, unsupportive families, and the victimization of women in contemporary society.

The social constructionist might make a number of observations. First, he or she might raise the question of Diana's relationship to contemporary notions of royalty and the power of the monarchy in contemporary British life. Diana's death seems to have challenged the monarchy in new and powerful ways that threaten to either reform or end its power. Second, a social constructionist might want to inquire into the grounds for the very real and powerful emotional identification with

215

Diana that marked the worldwide response to her death. Psychiatrists reported that women patients talked about her life and death as public parables about the changing nature of life for women in contemporary society, from eating disorders to abuse. Finally, the social constructionist could use Diana's life and death to talk about the changing nature and role of celebrity in the media; how the traditional and tabloid press are implicated in the development of the paparazzi and journalists who spend their lives stalking celebrities to provide the apparently insatiable demand for coverage. Are these changes in the media themselves related to other aspects of contemporary definitions of entertainment and news, and the blurring of the distinction between them?

The question remains, *Where is ideology produced?* Where is it found? Where are the struggles over ideology taking place? The answer is simple: wherever language, culture, and media are found. For it is in the shared culture of a society that ideology resides. And as the media have grown to be the most important and visible cultural institutions of the society, they have become the most important ideological battlefield. It is in the media that one finds not only the dominant ideology—from which people learn the commonsense view of reality—but also subordinate ideologies struggling to change that commonsense view.

## NOTES

1. In fact, Williams discovers this structure through an analysis of the economics, technology, and cultural forms of television.

2. See Marx's *Das Kapital* (*Capital*, 1977), where he describes ideology as a necessary misrepresentation.

## SUGGESTED READINGS

Althusser, L. (1971). *Lenin and philosophy, and other essays* (B. Brewster, Trans.). London: New Left Books.

Berger, J. (1972). *Ways of seeing*. London: Penguin.

Gramsci, A. (1971). *Selections from* The prison notebooks (Q. Hoare & G. Nowell-Smith, Trans.). New York: International Publishers.

Marx, K., & Engels, F. (1972). *The German ideology*. New York: International Publishers.

# PART III

# The Power of the Media

# Producing Identities    8

People have always needed a sense of who they are and a place to ground that sense of their identity in one or more of the institutions or activities of their lives: the Church (and their soul or some core values), their work (and their labor or skills), their families (and their sense of a generational past and future), and, increasingly in the twentieth century, their leisure and consumption activities. (Thus it seems reasonable to work at an unrewarding job so that one can afford to enjoy the weekends.) Moreover, every person can be described as and has a sense of himself or herself as both an individual and a member of various social groups (which can range from the very broad, such as Black or White or male or female, to the very narrow, such as a graduate of a particular university or a member of a particular club). That sense of individuality, whether grounded in the religious spirit or simply in some personal essence, involves some sense of transcendence, some sense that we are not only the sum of the various social roles that we play, the various social groups to which we belong.

By the 1950s, the issue of identity had become not only politically and culturally but also psychologically dominant in American culture, especially among youth. In fact, a new psychological "disorder" was "discovered" among college students, some of whom began to feel

219

anxious about who they were. They apparently worried that their individuality, that which made them unique, was nothing more than the sum of the various social groups to which they belonged and the images they took on. In fact, many of the most powerful images from 1950s popular culture—James Dean in *Rebel Without a Cause,* Marlon Brando in *The Wild One,* Jack Kerouac's novel of the "beat generation," *On the Road,* and even the later parody of a beatnik, Maynard G. Krebs, from the TV show *Dobie Gillis*—revolved around this common search by young people for a stable individual identity. By the 1980s, this anxiety had become a taken-for-granted part of growing up. Calvin Klein could even use it as the theme for his commercial with Brooke Shields: *"Is there a real me? Or am I just what you see?"*

This identity crisis was often assumed to be linked to the growing power of the media (and media images) in the lives of these youths. In fact, there can be little doubt that the strength of the traditional sources of identity—religion, family, and work—has declined in proportion to the growing power of the mass media, leisure activities, and the consumer lifestyles in which media and leisure are bound up even as they define and promote such lifestyles. More than anything, what nearly everyone in America shares, whatever school or church or job they go to, is the mass media. Despite differences in taste and access, there are significant commonalities in our shared experience of the most "mass" of the mass media: television, popular music, and blockbuster movies. At the same time, the sense of unity among people, created by such powerful identities as were defined by religion, nationality, and work, have themselves been increasingly undermined by the powerful representations of difference that have come to define the media's cultural content, even as the media have come to shape social life. Ultimately, the media's ability to produce people's social identities, in terms of both a sense of unity and difference, may be their most powerful and important effect.

In this chapter, we will explore the ways in which the media produce people's sense of who they are and who others are. There are many dimensions on which people have a sense of themselves, a sense of their own identity:

- ▍ Politically, people exist as citizens and as members of a public.
- ▍ Socially, people exist as exemplars of social roles (fathers, children, teachers, and so on).

■ Culturally, people exist as exemplars of social groups (often defined within semiotic systems of differences, such as Black or White, male or female).

■ Economically, people exist as consumers and members of an audience.

It is perhaps most common in the American context to conceive of the audience as a market or as consumers, and then to treat them as such. In other contexts, such as the British model of public service broadcasting, the dominant concept of the audience is as a public. We will consider the relation of media to public more fully in Chapter 12.

It would be a mistake to conceive of the concept of the audience as only an economic category, where the audience is understood as the *market* for media (and other) products. Not only is the concept of the audience intricately bound up with the dimensions of social and cultural identity, there is at least one other dimension that has to be accounted for: the audience as *fans* and members of subcultures.

A fan is not simply a person who uses or enjoys the media. Fans identify themselves with a particular media product, star, or style. They may be members of a particular subculture or followers of media fads or fashions. We shall postpone a discussion of the significance of fandom and subcultures until the next chapter.

In this chapter, we shall discuss the remaining dimensions of the audience and identity: the audience as market and as a set of social and cultural identities. We are ignoring the differences between social and cultural identities because we will be treating all of these in relationship to the media, as questions of audiences and representations rather than of social relationships between people per se. That is, we are not going to address the ways in which one's identity is shaped in specific social relationships: You learn that you are a student, and how to be a student, in relation to the activities of teachers and other students in a classroom; you learn that you are a girl and how to be female in relating to boys and other girls and observing how they relate to each other. But you also learn that you are a student or a girl and what that means through the variety of cultural and media texts that represent such identities and place or interpellate you in specific relations to those representations.

Thus we are concerned with how notions of the audience and of identity actually involve an image of the entire process of communication. Talking about the audience in a particular way already makes

221

assumptions about why certain media products are produced, what those products do, and how audiences are affected by them. Media products produced as a service to the public can be quite different from those produced to sell advertising, for example. The two dimensions of audience and identity discussed here—market and cultural identity—are all used by most of the groups involved in communication, including media producers, economic institutions, and the people who use media. At various moments, audience members may think of themselves as markets and as having specific cultural identities.

## CONSTRUCTING THE AUDIENCE AS MARKET

*media gives us what they want to give us, not what we want/need, + we buy into it*

The *audience* as such does not actually exist except as an idealization. That is, the audience is itself constructed by people who use the term for a particular purpose. The chief executive officer of a television network may claim that he or she is simply supplying the audience with what it wants, even though only a fraction of the potential viewing population is watching (and even fewer claim that what they get is what they actually want). Nielsen Media Research claims, on the basis of an extraordinarily small sample, to know what the audience is watching; but audience meters cannot know what is actually taking place in front of the television set. Advertisers are trying not only to reach the audience, but to adjust their messages to fit the audience. *TV Guide* claims to speak for the audience, as do the talk show hosts who claim that "our viewers want to know ..." Various political advocates from the political right and left make all sorts of claims about the viewing habits and desires of something called *the audience*. Different notions of the audience are the creations of different economic, political, and cultural groups. There are different audiences for different media and cultural forms.

*Yes, ppl buy the paper + are consider as 'audience' but*

The concept of the audience is a social construction, a concept that can mean and be made to do many different things. Yes, there are real people out there watching a television program, or reading a newspaper, or buying an album, who can be said to be *in the audience* for a particular media product. However, the idea of an audience is never merely an innocent description of the sum total of individuals. The fact of the matter is that the audience does not exist out there in reality apart from the way in which it is defined by different groups for different purposes. How the concept of the audience is constructed determines how it can function and how the relationship between the media and their audiences can be described, measured, and evaluated.

## The Audience as Market: Consumers

The most common conception of the audience within the media industries is as a conglomeration of potential and potentially overlapping markets. *A market identifies a subset of the population as potential consumers of a particular identifiable product or set of products.* Markets may vary according to their size (the market for techno-dance is smaller than that for mainstream rock; the market for NSH speakers is smaller than that for all-in-one stereo systems), although, often, the general population has little sense of the size of various markets (for collectible cards, comic books, or *bhangra*—a mix of Indian film music and disco). For example, in July 2003, an Indian film, *Main Prem Ki Diwani Hoon*, playing for select audiences of primarily Indian Americans and Indian expatriates in the United States had the sixteenth highest grosses of the week according to *Entertainment Weekly* and made more money per screen in each of the 60 theaters where it was showing than the big blockbuster released that week (*Charlie's Angels: Full Throttle*, in just under 3,500 theaters). The market for Indian films in the United States, though obviously no direct competition with the Hollywood studios, is still larger than one might think, but only recently has that market begun to be measured. Markets may also vary according to their duration (the market for the latest hit film or album is quite fleeting compared to the market for films or albums in general) and to their stability and flexibility (the market for television is probably more stable and flexible than that for network television in particular). Markets can also have "identities" attached or articulated to them. In this sense, the market for heavy metal music is generally thought of as primarily composed of adolescent boys; the market for Saturday morning cartoons as preschool and grade school children; and the market for soap operas as adult women.

Increasingly, programmers seeking niche audiences (because advertisers want to focus their messages where they think they'll be maximally effective) will look for content they believe will keep certain potential viewers *out* of the audience. Joseph Turow (1997) noted that MTV specifically expected *Beavis and Butthead* to be offensive to older viewers to keep them from watching: Advertisers wanted to focus on young people.

223

There are two basic ways in which audiences are constructed and function as markets: as consumers and as commodities. The most common way that those involved in the media industries think of the audience is as made up of consumers: To sell a book, a film, a record, a videotape, or any media product, or even to get people to watch, listen, or read something, a media producer has in mind the type of person who will purchase or tune in to that product. That idea of the media consumer is what is referred to as a *market type*. As we described in Chapter 3, the media industries spend a great deal of time and money in the search for more and more information about media consumers and the appropriate appeals to make to convince media consumers to buy a particular media product. The people who purchase and enjoy the products of the media often think of themselves as consumers as well. And insofar as they are successfully constructed by the media as an audience for the media, as a particular market type, people will often think of themselves in these terms. That is, by linking individuals together within the category of a market, at least a part of their identity is defined by their participation in this market.

It is not enough for the industries to simply be able to describe specific market types; they have also attempted to develop better ways of understanding what is going on in such consumer groups and better ways of describing and categorizing the various types of such groups. The three most common and persistent ways of describing market types are through demographics, taste cultures, and lifestyle clusters.

*Demographics* is the quantitative description of a population according to a set of social or sociological variables. The American population can be described by counting the number of people who fit into a set of demographic categories such as age, race, gender, income level, education level, employment category (professional, sales, blue-collar, pink-collar), place of residence (urban, suburban, rural), geographic region (Northeast, Southeast, Midwest, Southwest, Northwest, and West) and type of residence (home owner, home renter, condo owner, apartment dweller).

Assumptions about consumers underlie marketing categories. Media corporations invest a great deal of money in market research to identify the likely market for their product. This information helps them determine marketing strategies and advertising styles. The Disney Channel is more likely to be marketed to families with children (say, through an ad in *Parent's* magazine or an ad during *SpongeBob*

*SquarePants*) than to single individuals. And TV commercials for herbicides used in farming are more likely to be found in less populous areas of the Midwest than in the cities of the Northeast.

A second way of understanding a market type is as *a taste culture.* In this case, the demographic identity of the audience members is less important than the continuing commitment of a group of people to some type of product. For example, science fiction producers want to appeal to the science fiction fans out there who are always seeking a new book or film to indulge their taste for this genre. Similarly, among music consumers, there are clear taste cultures that are not always easy to define demographically; yet, clearly, the market for classical music is different from that for country western or The Darkness or Ashlee Simpson. In fact, among even a fairly homogeneous group of people— at least in demographic terms—a wide range of musical taste cultures is probably represented.

*[handwritten margin note: music tastes differ + demographics have no effect on it, so it's tricky.]*

Whereas some taste cultures correspond to generic categories (the taste culture of science fiction fans), others are characterized by either multiple genres or by selective choices made from different genres. For example, radio programmers think of different formats as appealing to different taste cultures. Contemporary hits radio, one of the more popular formats, comprises some pop-punk (Good Charlotte and Green Day, but not the Strokes), some Latin-dance music (Shakira and Ricky Martin, but not the Buena Vista Social Club), most pop music (Justin Timberlake and Avril Lavigne, but not Fountains of Wayne), some rap (50 Cent and Jay-Z, but not The Roots), and so on. Producers operating with an understanding of the audience as taste cultures construct media products according to their understanding of the features of the product that hold the taste culture together, rather than according to their image of a particular demographic group of consumers.

The most recent way developed to describe market types has been used extensively by advertisers: *Lifestyle clusters* can be understood as a mixture of demographic categories and consumption habits or tastes. A lifestyle cluster represents a segment of the population that tends to purchase and use certain kinds of products or to make certain kinds of decisions, including voting. The best-known example of a lifestyle cluster is the *yuppie.* What's a yuppie? Originally, it referred to a small market segment of young urban professionals (y-u-p) with a great deal of disposable income who tended to display their wealth through the purchase of particular brands of consumer goods. For example,

*Newsweek* defined a yuppie as someone with five different kinds of mustard in the refrigerator.

A lifestyle cluster creates groups in the population whose members have several characteristics in common. Most important, the members of a particular group tend to spend their money and time in similar ways. The entire population of the country can be displayed as a number of lifestyle groups according to systems of consumption patterns and values. The most powerful of such descriptions takes the project one step further by attempting to correlate lifestyle clusters with geographic location (for example, as described by zip codes of home residences). Advertisers and media producers can then target a particular lifestyle cluster for their products: Sometimes, this takes the form of producing different versions of the same magazine with different advertisements directed at different lifestyle markets. Direct mail advertisers often now tailor their mailings according to zip codes and even specific block addresses.

*eg.*

Implicit in the very notion of the audience as consumers operating in a market is the need to continually make people think of themselves as consumers. Many historians and media scholars have observed that this is one of the major effects of the media in the twentieth century: to help construct a consumer society by encouraging people to locate their identity in their leisure tastes and consumer practices rather than in other roles, such as jobs and church membership. The ideological message is that what we buy says more about who we are than other facts, including where we get the money. Media programs and advertising are all about this redefinition of self-identity. The media are both a part of any lifestyle and one of the ways such lifestyles are produced and promoted. The media reinforce the power of the market over identity, even as they themselves produce the very identities that locate people in the market as consumers.

*Major effect of media on society*

*lots of control*

In most countries of the advanced industrial world, people take the existence of a consumer society for granted. It appears natural that everyone in these societies is part of a national market and that people's lives are defined and measured by, if not devoted to, the consumption of various goods and services. But, in fact, the notion of a consumer society is a very recent invention, and it took a great deal of work—not only economic, but political and cultural work as well—to establish it.

The origins of the American consumer society can be found in the social changes that were the product of economic developments between

1880 and 1920. In fact, many of the basic features of contemporary society came into existence in this period. Society was changing as economic, political, and cultural questions were increasingly transformed into bureaucratic decisions for experts. Mass production came into being as a result of the assembly line—using expensive single-purpose machinery with cheap, quickly trained single-purpose workers to inexpensively produce a large number of the same item—and Taylorism, a system for time studies that enabled any production line to be broken down into identifiable movements that could be performed in certain specifiable times.

An immediate and significant consequence of these changes was the new glut of cheaper products had to be sold; thus new and larger markets had to be discovered or opened up. As Henry Ford made more cars and made them more cheaply, he also had to find people who had the money to buy them and who wanted or believed they needed to buy an automobile. In one sense, the solution was obvious: Henry Ford is often quoted as having said, "If I could get my workers to all buy cars, I could make a fortune." And that is basically what happened. Higher wages allowed workers to become consumers of the goods they were mass-producing, and shorter hours allowed them the time and freedom to use their newly purchased goods. But higher wages alone were insufficient. Workers were often reluctant to spend their money on what seemed to be frivolous luxuries. The culture of many of those in the working class emphasized saving for a rainy day rather than spending. Moreover, it was not enough to convince workers and their families to spend their money. They had to spend it in predictable and controllable ways. It would do no good if all of Ford's workers decided they wanted Cadillacs when there were lots of Model Ts waiting to be sold. It is in this context that both advertising and marketing research were introduced as ways to maximize and rationalize the consumer habits of these new consumers who were apparently reaping the benefits of mass production. It is in the same context that department stores and national glossy magazines arose.

Advertising not only had to define the particular desires and needs of these new consumers, it had to make *them* think of themselves as consumers as well. People who for generations had lived on the edge of poverty, and whose identity was almost entirely built around their family and their work, had now to think of themselves as consumers rather than producers, as individuals with their own desires rather than as families. Work had to become less a source of identity and pride and more a means by which people could fulfill their desires through consumption.

But this new consumer society, and the communicative and cultural changes that helped to produce it, was responding as well to other serious changes and problems confronting the United States between 1880 and 1920: There was a sharp rise in labor protests, often aimed at the systems of industrial production and wage "slavery" themselves. New waves of immigration, especially from Eastern Europe and the Mediterranean, challenged the apparent homogeneity of the society, creating the need to find ways of integrating these new populations into the American way of life. And, finally, in the early twentieth century, there were a series of "Red scares" motivated by the fears of a domestic communist movement based in immigrant and labor populations.

Advertising, the mass media, and ultimately the new consumer society were placed into this crisis as a new source of social control and harmony. By giving all the people the sense that they had access to commodities that would improve their lifestyle and their social status, the new consumer society sought to undermine the conditions that led to social unrest. By bringing people's desires and needs under the control of the new culture of mass media, and hence under the control of science and industry, the new consumer society sought to "rational-ize" people's everyday lives. It was thought that the new culture could shape people's consciousness, leading them away from real social dissatisfactions toward individual desires, away from issues of class and inequality and toward questions of prestige, style, and status. In the new consumer society, apparently, all social problems could be solved by working on your "self."

In a sense, at least part of the function of modern mass media has been to change the way people have thought of themselves: to make people think of and even experience themselves as consumers. And it still remains part of the very effects of the media on audiences—to remind us that the value and purpose of our lives is defined by our existence as consumers, by what we buy and what we own. It is no accident that so much of the content of the media is directed to our consumer life, that the stage of the media's messages is always cluttered with products.

Notice that conceiving of the audience as consumers does not mean that people are entirely passive; on the contrary, the audience as consumer is very active. People must make decisions about which media to expose themselves to and which products to buy, and then to buy products, use them up, and buy more. A goal of the media is to constantly reproduce—and, along the way, influence—this activity of desiring and buying, not only of media products but of other products as well. The audience as a market is constantly working, gathering information on what products exist, deciding what is best for them to buy, and, eventually, going out and buying them. The audience need not always be consciously involved in such activity—except insofar as they choose to consume particular media messages rather than others—but they are always being reminded of their role as consumers and as potential markets for specific products and services.

At the same time, it is important to realize the limits of the claim that a part of people's identity is defined by their investment in consumption. People are aware of themselves as consumers, but there is far more to their self-conscious sense of their own identity. In addition, not every individual act of consumption necessarily defines one's identity. What we are describing is a general, culturally constructed sense of an economic identity, not a specific sense of lifestyle cluster or taste culture. For some people, the particular brand of jeans they buy and wear may be a part of their identity, whereas for others, it is a relatively minor issue in their lives. What we buy may reflect either our group identifications or our individual taste. Someone who refused to consume or who opposed consumption in American society would seem like an outsider, if not a crackpot.

## The Audience as Market: Commodity

The media not only created a consumer society by constructing the audience for its messages as a market, but it also constructed the audience as a commodity. Remember that a *commodity* is an object produced in order to be sold for a profit. It may seem odd to think of an audience as something that is produced and sold, something from which someone can make a profit. But think about how media work in their relation to advertising: The media produce an audience for their own media products, and then deliver that audience to another media producer, namely an advertiser. When people watch their favorite TV program, they are also watching the ads embedded in the show. Some people may enjoy watching ads for their own sake: For example, in Italy in the 1970s, the most popular prime-time show was a half-hour of

229

commercials. In the United States, it is not uncommon for advertisers to advertise forthcoming advertisements or to give advertisements a story line. The former is especially true of commercials aired during the Super Bowl each year. There is always prior speculation as to the nature and quality (and cost) of the commercials, and some tune in to the game simply for the commercials.

However, ads work only when their audience moves on to become the consumers of the product being advertised. Think about the discussion of advertising support for television in Chapter 4. Few people choose to watch TV programs for the advertising, and yet viewers are inevitably an audience for the ads. As we said, this is why ratings are so important in the relationship between the television networks and advertisers. Each wants to know the size of the audience as a potential market so that it knows how much to charge or pay for this particular commodity. In fact, networks program a particular series precisely to attract a specific market type so that it can sell that audience as a highly priced commodity to an advertiser. And, increasingly, advertisers (as well as other media producers) attempt to link their products to specific, highly desirable social groups and identities (consider, for example, the marketing campaigns of Pepsi, Toyota, or Levi's).

Media producers have to think about whom they want to attract as an audience for their shows because this is the audience they are selling to advertisers. A television network may decide to leave a program on the air even though it has a relatively small audience if it is a particularly attractive audience to advertisers. A radio station may decide to change formats to one already overrepresented in the local market because, again, its demographics are the most desirable to the local advertisers. On the other hand, a program that has a relatively large audience may be taken off the air if the particular market it attracts is decidedly unattractive to advertisers. Programs such as *Gunsmoke* and *The Beverly Hillbillies*, although both were still relatively successful in the early 1970s, were nevertheless canceled because their audiences were primarily rural and old, not particularly attractive audiences to TV advertisers. One of the major reasons that popular musical styles such as heavy metal and rap are so underrepresented on radio is that their audiences are not particularly attractive to advertisers. The long-term underrepresentation in the media of certain social groups, such as Blacks and Latinos, might similarly be partly explained by advertisers' assumptions about the desirability of such audiences.

As these groups' desirability changes, their representations on television and in the other media will change—witness the increased presence of Latinos on television in the early 2000s (and see Box 4.2).

Advertisements attempt to transform the audience for a particular program or media product into the potential market for the advertiser's product. For example, a television network or radio station sells the audience for each program to advertisers. It delivers this audience as a commodity to the advertisers so that the advertisers can get their message—*"Consume this product"*—to the audience. Advertisers are purchasing what they hope is the attention, the visual labor of watching and the labor of listening, of the audience. If the audience is not actually watching or listening and paying some minimal attention to the ad, then the advertiser has wasted money.

Television and radio are only the most obvious places where the audience is commodified. In the music industry, for example, the sale of actual musical commodities (records, tapes, CDs) accounts for a decreasing percentage of profits. Instead, music is increasingly used to deliver audiences to the sellers of other products and media, such as clothing with rock star insignia, and to films (where soundtracks are important). Also, music is used in advertising to sell other products. The identification of particular products with classic or contemporary music stars (for example recent car ads featuring music by Led Zeppelin or Celine Dion) has become very explicit in the 2000s: In 2002, Volkswagen was even selling a CD compilation of songs that had been used in their commercials. In short, even in those industries that we think of as not relying on "advertiser support," the audience is commodified indirectly.

*[margin note: music itself didn't make mad $, so its now used to sell other stuff (clothes, collectibles)!!!]*

Part of the reason audiences can be so easily commodified is because of audience loyalty to certain media celebrities and media products. Stars can supply their fans with a wide range of merchandise in addition to their albums; if an advertiser wants to reach a certain segment of the market, he or she might reasonably decide to hire a particular recording artist who has already proven to be attractive to the particular segment to provide the musical soundtrack for or even appear in its commercial.

*[margin note: endorsements]*

Technology has created serious problems for advertisers and the media. Consider television: Advertisers cannot be confident that the audience of a program is actually the audience for the commercials embedded in the program. With the remote control, audience members

*[margin note: Technology = huge problems]*

*[margin note: ↳ switch channels during commercials.]*

*[margin notes: —remote control, —mute, —videotaping, —TiVo, ∴ shorter commercials or more entertaining]*

can move ("graze") from program to program and avoid all commercials while they watch parts of several programs at a time. Moreover, recent audience research demonstrates that audience members who don't graze turn off the sound during commercials. And by videotaping programs, people can avoid watching all commercials as they fast-forward ("zap") past them. New technologies such as TiVo digitally record television programs and can automatically delete the ads. In response, advertisers try to devise means to keep the audience's attention (making commercials as short as 15 or 20 seconds, or making them more entertaining, more like mini-programs or mini–music videos).

## CULTURAL IDENTITIES

*[margin note: Audience as: – market – commodity – cultural identity]*

In addition to characterizing the audience as market and commodity, we can think of the audience as *cultural identities* represented in the media. The audience is composed of individuals who are each members of one or more social groups that define their identity. A part of your identity might be defined by the fact that you are a college student; but this identity is already quite complex, and the way it is lived may vary depending on your age, background, income, and so forth. Nevertheless, you are part of an entire generation of college students, both past (all college graduates) and present (the particular graduating class). You are also part of the population of a particular university or college; your affiliation may be expressed in any number of ways (wearing school colors or clothes, sporting the school insignia, supporting the athletic teams). You may also be a member of various groups on and off campus ("Greeks" or independents, commuters or dorm residents, different majors and classes).

Consequently, even something as apparently simple as your identity as a college student is itself the product of your particular position in a variety of social groups and social differences. In addition, everyone brings many affiliations with them to campus: religious, racial, ethnic, gender, and sexual identities, particular regional and economic origins (Midwest farming, Northeast working class, or Southwestern suburban middle class) as well as particular interests (for example, sports and musical tastes). One of the things that every university tries to accomplish is to bind students together into a common identity with common loyalties. Recent events have made this task even more difficult, as many universities and colleges have experienced an increasing sense of fracture among various gender, racial, and ethnic groups, each of which is likely to have its own associations on campus.

In fact, many of the major social and political problems facing the contemporary world involve the relationships between and among different social groups: among religious groups, racial groups (Black and White, brown, red, and yellow, as they are so crudely described), gender and sexual groups (men and women, straight and gay), age groups (children, youth, adults, and the aging), economic groups (working, middle, or upper classes), ethnic and national groups (whether Bosnian or Bosnian American), and so on.

The problems that these relations impose on the contemporary world cannot begin to be solved unless one first begins to understand the relationship between an individual and the social group or groups to which he or she belongs. This relationship defines the problem of *social identity*. In fact, social identity is a very complex notion that involves at least three different questions: First, exactly where do such categories of identity come from and what do they signify? Second, what does it mean to belong to or be a member of a particular social group? In other words, how is such membership determined? Is one biologically assigned, socially positioned, or culturally interpellated or perhaps a little bit of each? And third, what is the content or meaning of the categories and how are these meanings themselves determined? Implicit in all of these questions is the issue of the role of the media (and culture more generally) in the construction of people's social identities. What is the relationship between the images (visual and verbal) of the various categories of identity made available in the media and the ways in which people take up and live their own identities and relate to those inhabiting other identities? For example, images of Arabic men on television in connection with the September 11, 2001, terrorist attacks made everyday life in America very difficult for men and women of Arabic descent, for Muslims in general, and even for those who looked generally like them (Sikhs from India, for example).

There are two major schools of thought that respond to these questions, two major theories of identity, and each has distinctly different views of the role of the media in the politics of identity and of the relationship between media images and social identities. The first assumes that the categories of identity are natural, necessary, and universal. This *essentialist* view assumes that every category exists naturally, in

① Essentialist view     233
② Anti-Essentialist view

and of itself; Blackness exists whether or not any other racial category or group exists. And the meaning of the category is always intrinsic to the category itself, determined ahead of time. That meaning, and hence anyone's membership in the category, might be determined by genes, or by the anatomy and physiology of the body, or by some determining history (common roots in Africa or the common experience of a history of slavery). According to this theory, representation is a matter of accuracy versus stereotyping. The question, then, is how to contest negative images with positive ones, and how to discover and re-present the authentic and original content of the identity. Basically, the struggle over representation here takes the form of offering one fully constituted, separate, and distinct identity in place of another.

The second theory of identity completely rejects the assumptions of the first. There is no single physical trait or genetic marker that can be used to separate the human population into what we call "races." There are even greater genetic differences within races than between them. While many people still think along the lines of the first theory of identity, it has no basis in science. This does not mean that the discourse of the essentialist theory of identity doesn't have very real consequences for individuals. The second theory of identity therefore emphasizes the impossibility of such fully constituted, separate, and distinct identities. It denies the existence of authentic identities based in a universally shared origin or experience. Instead, it argues that the categories of identity are culturally constructed and can be understood only relationally. Consequently, they are always in process and incomplete. According to such an *anti-essentialist* view, the very existence of such categories, as well as the specific ways they function, the specific differences they mark, and the specific meanings they carry, are all culturally constructed. Identity is always an unstable and temporary effect of relations that define identities by marking differences. The theory recognizes that there are differences between people, but insists that which differences become important and visible (skin color rather than foot size), where the line is drawn (between Black and White, or male and female, or young and old), and the meanings of each category are the products of the communicative codes of a society.

There is no single, universal, or essential content to a category and, consequently, the question of whether any specific person belongs to a social group must also be the product of cultural processes. Moreover, to say that such categories are relational is to say that categories are only defined by their relations to or differences from other categories. To put it another way, the meaning of the categories of identity is largely the product of the ways that the members of the categories practice their relations to members of both their own category and to the members of other categories as well. The emphasis of the anti-essentialists is on the multiplicities of identities and differences and the interactions among identities. Obviously, representation is no longer a matter of accuracy and distortion but of identities that are produced and taken up in and through practices of representation.

## Representation as Stereotypes

The media provide pictures of people, descriptions of different social groups and of their social identities. If someone has never seen any member of a particular group—an Azerbaijani, for instance—then it is likely that what they think such people are like will be the result of what they have seen, heard, or read about them in the media. But what does anyone make of the media's representation of a group of which they are a member? Walter Lippmann (1922) referred to *stereotypes* as "pictures in our heads" of other people or, more accurately, of the identity or nature of other groups of people. Stereotypes can define some people's expectations of how, for example, women or Hispanics or other groups in the society are supposed to behave. In this sense, stereotypes are neither avoidable nor necessarily bad. They are a psychological means of dealing with the diversity of the world by categorizing the world into types and learning how to respond to types rather than how to respond to each individual. In the modern world, the media are obviously a major source of such pictures.

Typically, discussing the process by which the media re-present the various social identities in the world as stereotyping implies that there is some "correct" image of a social group's identity that is somehow distorted in the media's portrayal of that group. Sometimes, stereotyping is a matter of the absence of images of a particular social group; but it is more often a question of how the group is portrayed, of the content of the images themselves. We can take note of the extent to which various ethnic and social groups have been represented negatively in the mass media and how images of various groups have changed over time in accord to that group's changing position in the culture. Media images of women, minorities, New Yorkers, gays and lesbians, doctors, the handicapped, Southerners, and so forth are likely to elicit certain expectations about how members of these groups act. How social groups are portrayed in the mass media—particularly in films, on television, and in advertising—has been a long-standing concern of various representatives of those groups who feel they are being misrepresented or stereotyped. (See Box 8.1, "The Celluloid Closet.")

---

**BOX 8.1**

**The Celluloid Closet**

Hollywood films are directed at mainstream audiences. Their worldview is a heterosexual one and therefore representations of gays and lesbians reflect mainstream stereotypes and sensibilities. Hollywood films instruct the public in what to think about homosexuals and in many ways influence gay and lesbian audiences' own self-images. These audiences, especially in the 1940s through the 1970s, learned to read between the lines, to recognize subtle gestures, glances, or styles by which one might interpret a character or a situation as gay. Some of these were intentionally placed there by writers, actors, and/or directors; others were not. But this way of reframing the film image allows gay and lesbian audiences to affirm their own existence and identity.

Images of homosexuals have been present in cinema since its earliest days. And even in the early silent era, these images were stereotypical ones, for example images of mincing, swishy gay men appeared in cowboy films and even in Charlie Chaplin films. Hollywood films of the 1920s and 1930s became more bold: Marlene Dietrich could dress in male clothes and kiss another woman on the lips in *Morocco* (1930). But the Hays code effectively ended direct references to or appearances of homosexuality, though certain character types were implicitly coded as gay (the sissy, for example). As Hollywood films pushed beyond the Hays code in the 1960s, more direct references to homosexuality were allowed and could be a central plot issue (see *The Children's Hour* [1962]). However, these representations still reflected a mainstream sensibility. Gays and lesbians were presented as tortured, self-hating figures who either committed suicide or were murdered. Either that or they became the villains—lesbian vampires and transvestite murderers stalked the screen, to be killed off in spectacular fashion by the end of the film. Gay characters who actually survived to the end credits were rare until the 1970s. From the 1980s through the 1990s, more positive gay and lesbian

---

characters and situations were portrayed, though these were also made to be palatable to heterosexual audiences. The scourge of AIDS allowed gay characters to be portrayed sympathetically (for example, in *Longtime Companion* [1990] or *Philadelphia* [1993]) though gays remained tragic figures who died by the end of the film.

Vito Russo (1987), whose groundbreaking history of homosexuality in the movies is the basis of the summary above, wrote,

> The history of the portrayal of lesbians and gay men in mainstream cinema is politically indefensible and aesthetically revolting. There may be an abundance of gay characters floating around on various screens these days but *plus ça change.* . . . Gay visibility has never really been an issue in the movies. Gays have always been visible. It's *how* they have been visible that has remained offensive for almost a century. . . .
>
> The few times gay characters have worked well in mainstream film have been when filmmakers have had the courage to make no big deal out of them, when they have been implicitly gay in a film that was not about homosexuality.
>
> So, no more films about homosexuality. Instead, more films that explore people who happen to be gay in America and how their lives intersect with the dominant culture. (pp. 325–326)

Television presented a similar set of images to film throughout its history. Gays were the subject of humor, pity, and fear. Protests by gay activists in the mid-1970s led to more positive representations—for a while. But the 1980s saw a major anti-gay backlash. Throughout the 1990s until today, the numbers of representations of gay characters on television have been rising, and the representations themselves have been more positive. In particular, programming aimed at teenage and young adult audiences has more successfully integrated continuing gay and lesbian characters (as opposed to one-time guest appearances on "Very Special Episodes" of a series). *My So-Called Life* and *Buffy the Vampire Slayer* are but two examples here. By the late 1990s, *Ellen* and *Will & Grace* featured lesbian and gay characters in prime-time sitcoms, and today such shows as *The L-Word, Queer Eye for the Straight Guy, Queer as Folk,* and *Six Feet Under* regularly present much more nuanced and explicit representations of gay and lesbian lifestyles. But, are these representations of gays and lesbians on television, or even in contemporary cinema, ones that Russo would have said "worked well"? Or are they still representations of homosexuality framed for the comfort (or titillation) of mainstream heterosexual audiences?

*(Continued)*

(Continued)

### Suggested Reading

Capsuto, S. (2000). *Alternate channels: The uncensored story of gay and lesbian images on radio and television.* New York: Ballantine.

Dyer, R. (with Pidduck, J.). (2003). *Now you see it: Studies on lesbian and gay film* (2nd ed.). New York: Routledge.

Gross, L. (2001). *Up from invisibility: Lesbians, gay men, and the media in America.* New York: Columbia University Press.

Russo, V. (1987). *The celluloid closet: Homosexuality in the movies* (Rev. ed.). New York: Harper & Row.

Tropiano, S. (2002). *The prime time closet: A history of gays and lesbians on TV.* New York: Applause Theatre & Cinema Books.

### Suggested Viewing

Epstein, R., & Friedman, J. (Prod. & Dir.). (1996). *The celluloid closet.* HBO/Sony Pictures Classics.

In this sense, stereotyping is the process of distorting the portrayal of some social group in a media image. That media contribute to stereotypes (and even create stereotypes of groups) is assumed to be the result of systematic biases in the portrayals of social groups. One major research project in the United States, the Cultural Indicators Project at the University of Pennsylvania, has been systematically comparing the demographic profile of those who appear on prime-time television (via *content analysis;* see Chapter 6) to national demographics as shown in the U.S. Census since the late 1970s. Over time, the research has demonstrated that the world of television has been dominated by White males in traditionally powerful and adventurous occupations. Women, the old, children, and minority groups are systematically underrepresented (at least in terms of their numbers in the population) in the world of television (Gerbner, Gross, Jackson-Beeck, Jeffries-Fox, & Signorielli, 1978). George Gerbner, a leader of the project, argues that who is represented on television reflects the producers' wish for a particular audience (generally, white males of a certain age and income).

Perhaps the best example to provide here is the changing images of Blacks in the film industry and on television. In the very earliest days of film, Blacks were portrayed in a blatantly racist manner, perhaps best exemplified by the 1913 film *Birth of a Nation*. In the 1920s and 1930s, a few stereotypical Black roles appeared, such as Stepin Fetchit's "Black fool" and the "mammy" in *Gone with the Wind*. However, the majority of American films simply ignored and excluded the Black population. Similarly, the Hollywood studios ignored the work of a number of pioneering Black filmmakers (such as Oscar Micheaux), who produced all-Black films that have remained unknown to White audiences and often to Black audiences as well. A number of Black film production companies were set up in the 1910s and 1920s to make films more reflective of the Black experience. Alternative networks of film distribution and exhibition were also needed to avoid segregation laws in order to reach Black audiences, since the mainstream film industry would not handle such films. In the 1930s, Hollywood discovered the Black film market and made a few all-Black films, but such films generally fell back into the broad racist stereotypes that the Black producers had been trying to correct.

By the 1950s and 1960s, a few Black actors, such as Lena Horne, became Hollywood stars. Sidney Poitier, who won an Academy Award in 1963 for *Lilies of the Field*, opened the door to other actors, such as Bill Cosby, Ossie Davis, Ruby Dee, James Earl Jones, and Morgan Freeman. More important, as these actors became successful, they were able to demand less demeaning roles and less stereotypical images. Even in this period, however, Black actors did not fare particularly well: There were still few Black stars in the overwhelmingly White film industry, and the roles were still limited and racist. Even at the height of the civil rights movement in the 1960s and 1970s, "blaxploitation films" (such as *Shaft* with Richard Roundtree), although they created Black stars, were overtly racist and stereotypical.

By the late 1980s, the emergence of major Black filmmakers, such as Spike Lee (*Do the Right Thing*), Mario Von Peebles (*New Jack City*), John Singleton (*Boyz 'n the Hood*), Matty Rich (*Straight out of Brooklyn*), and lesser-known filmmakers such as Charles Burnett (*To Sleep With Anger*) and Julie Dash (*Daughters of the Dust*) provided a vibrant and challenging alternative portrait of Black life in America and the racist currents of American culture. These filmmakers have opened the door, not only to new generations of Black actors, but also to Black participation in the various aspects of film production.

This shift from an absence of Black people in film and overwhelmingly stereotypical images of Blacks to the production of films about

Black life and racial themes by Black producers, writers, and directors has taken most of the twentieth century. The year 2002 proved a landmark year in this regard when Halle Berry and Denzel Washington both won Academy Awards for Acting in Lead Roles.

Television, too, has shifted in its portrayals of Blacks and has followed a somewhat similar course. In the early days of television, with the exception of *Amos 'n' Andy's* stereotypical representation of happy-go-lucky hucksters, Black people were absent from prime-time drama. However, Black entertainers such as Pearl Bailey, Louis Armstrong, Johnny Mathis, and Nat King Cole did appear on variety shows in the 1950s. It wasn't, however, until 1965, when Bill Cosby was paired with Robert Culp in the series *I Spy,* that a Black actor emerged as the star of a network drama series. The 1970s saw the rise of a number of situation comedies featuring Black family life, shows such as *The Jeffersons, Sanford and Son,* and *Good Times.* And Black stars such as Bill Cosby, James Earl Jones, Arsenio Hall, Keenen Ivory Wayans, and Oprah Winfrey—often with creative and financial control (and, in some cases, their own independent production companies)—continue to increase the participation of Blacks in a wide variety of television genres.

These shifts in portrayals of Blacks in American media cannot be understood outside of the real struggles over civil rights in American society and the changes that have resulted. Not until the rise of the civil rights movement in the late 1950s and early 1960s did stereotypes begin to change in the media. At the same time, part of the success of the civil rights movement was that footage of peaceful marches as well as racist violence in the South was shown on television. The images of Blacks on television news in the 1960s stood in stark contrast with the images (and lack of images) of Blacks on the prime-time television entertainment shows that followed the news. As well, pressure groups began to confront racist images and demand more positive representation in television and in film. Last, and most strikingly in recent years, Black professionals have moved into creative and economic control as producers, writers, and directors in the film industry, as well as owners of radio, TV, and media properties. The fact that larger numbers of Blacks have moved into higher economic strata has helped to create a Black market for advertisers and media programmers. Moreover, youth of all races have become a significant market for Black cultural products across many media and genres. All of these factors have contributed to changing the stereotyping of Blacks in mass media.

This doesn't mean that stereotyping no longer exists. Some people have criticized many contemporary Black films on the grounds that the emphasis on urban gangs and crime continues many of the stereotypes of Black people. Other ethnic groups, such as Hispanics, Arab Americans, Italian Americans, Asian Americans, and others, have complained over the years about their representation in the media (such as Italians as mobsters on *The Sopranos* or Arabic men as terrorists post–September 11). The rise of the feminist movement since the 1960s has made us increasingly aware of the stereotyping of women in media images. And the horrors of the AIDS epidemic has made questions about the stereotypical representations of gay men and lesbians an important social concern. In each of these instances, fighting media's stereotypical representations has become a crucial part of the group's struggle for social equality.

For the fact is that stereotypes, even if they are only images, do have real and important consequences. They can affect the self-esteem of those being stereotyped, and they can often come close to determining the way some people think of and behave toward members of the groups being stereotyped. And, sometimes, if they are repeated often enough, people forget entirely that they are dealing with images; the images become the reality that determines the ways people, institutions, and even governments act in the world (for example, toward Muslims).

A good example of the potentially pernicious effects of stereotypes might be the representation of AIDS and of people with AIDS (PWAs). These images affect how many people think about this disease and those who suffer its consequences. Critics have documented the effects of such stereotypes on issues of education, funding, legislation, and even research and treatment. Remember the startling power of the image of the late Princess Diana holding hands with PWAs in a London hospital. AIDS activists have often complained about the way the disease is represented in the mass media. Thus the disease is often represented primarily in its association with homosexuality, concealing other equally pertinent facts: for example, that the majority of AIDS cases in New York City are among people of color, with a rising percentage among women. This misrepresentation perpetuates itself in that it affects the patterns of counseling and diagnosis. Moreover, they argue, the representation of PWAs as lonely victims passively awaiting death distorts the facts of the disease and how it is lived. It also distorts the

241

fact that PWAs are also suffering from government inaction, insurance companies' and corporate employers' greed, the unavailability of adequate health care, and institutionalized racism and homophobia.

Thinking of people in terms of stereotypes only enables us to ask whether a stereotype is an accurate portrayal of a particular group. But to ask this question already assumes that this grouping of people is inevitable and natural, that its identity is singular and stable and exists independently of how it is represented in cultural codes and the media. For example, to ask whether the image of Blacks on television is an accurate one assumes that all "Blacks" have the same identity, which can be compared to what is presented on television. But what happens if all Blacks do not have the same identity? Do we really want to assume that conservative Supreme Court Justice Clarence Thomas, Bill Cosby, Tiger Woods, P. Diddy, and a young urban unemployed Black man are really essentially and basically the same by virtue of being Black, that they are all representatives of the same identity? And what if Blacks' identity changes, as when, to use a simple example, heavyweight boxing champion Cassius Clay changed his name to Muhammad Ali? What if some Blacks do seem to fit the stereotype? For instance, what if there *are* kids out there who want to be like the stereotypical character J. J. from *Good Times* or the violent and sexist "gangstas" of the music group NWA? Does that make these kids somehow less real for how they behave?

Some critics have even argued that by continuously focusing on the question of race and stereotypes, other critics are reinforcing the tendency of our society to divide everyone into Black or White. After all, is it necessary that the world be divided up that way? Most people don't worry about stereotypes of people with big feet, and they don't assume that such people have some identity of their own or that they are suffering from the ways they are represented. Also, the tendency to see the race question as one of Black and White erases all other minorities (from Native Americans to Asian Americans to Latinos/as). Finally, as long as one is talking about stereotypes, it is too easy for some people to ignore that, for some people out there, the media are representing who they are; or, to put it in other terms, the stereotype is not of someone else but of *themselves*. This raises one of the most important questions about the role of the media in people's lives, for it deals with how people come to understand who and what they are, to view their identities and identifications, the positions that they occupy in society.

## Representation as Cultural Construction

By seeing media representations as actively involved in the ongoing construction of identities, one can begin to appreciate the complexity of the processes by which people's identities are produced by the culture they live in: How is a category of identity established? How are individuals assigned to it? How is its meaning determined?

Consider where the categories of identity come from. Aren't most distinctions found in nature? For example, people normally assume that racial and sexual distinctions are genetically based, but that is simply false. People do not somehow see through the body into the genetic code. What is being read as sex or race are signs on the surface of the body. Genetic diversity is much more complex and plural than our simple categories allow. Even physiology and anatomy cannot explain the systems of relations that define people's identities. Are all women capable of bearing children? If someone is not, is she then not a woman? Do all Black people have dark skin? Then how does one account for the history of "passing"?

To take one category, aren't all people born either male or female? Yes and no. Biologists used to believe that sex was determined by a simple combination of two chromosomes, creating only two possibilities. But they have discovered that there are more chromosomes and more possibilities involved; what remains true is that for purposes of biological reproduction, sexes can be functionally divided into two large groups. But biological reproduction among humans requires certain social relationships as well. People have to occupy certain social roles and practice certain behaviors. These roles and behaviors define what is called *gender identity*. Again, our common sense makes it seem reasonably easy to divide the world into two major gender groups—masculine and feminine—although many critics have argued that such classifications are too crude. In fact, much of feminist theory addresses the question of how certain characteristics, behaviors, and styles come to be thought of as either masculine or feminine.

The categories of identity are the products of cultural codes, which select some aspects of the body and make them significant (into signifiers) whereas others remain "mere anatomy." Such codes, as we described in Chapter 5, organize signifiers according to relations of difference, so that any signifier of identity is only significant insofar as its difference from other signifiers is provided by the code itself. Culture selects the relevant dimensions that will constitute people's identities and organizes them into relations of difference. It is not merely that to be White is to be not-Black; it is also that being not-Black is itself part of the very meaning of being White. And, by the same token, being Black always includes being not-White. The two categories are bound together, each always implicated in the very existence and meaning of the other. This means that more than a set of biological characteristics determines who is included within each category—an Asian woman may suddenly find herself placed in the position of a Black person by the cultural codes of race in contemporary America.

At the same time, one term is always dominant within the culture; one term defines the norm. The norm is not only positively valued, it is treated as if it were neutral. It does not appear to be an identity at all. It does not need to be named; it remains *ex-nominated*. For example, although we think of Black as a race with its own characteristics, it is usually measured against an assumed neutral Whiteness that is rarely marked as a race. The same argument can be made for most of the other major dimensions of people's identity, including sex, gender, class, and ethnicity. We talk about Polish Americans and African Americans but rarely about Anglo Americans.

Everyone occupies some positions in these various codes of difference. What is the process by which individuals are given identities by being placed into one of a binary pair, by becoming identified with one term? This process of being placed is called *interpellation*. Recall the discussion in Chapter 7 (and the two experiments we proposed). The process of interpellation occurs when individuals are placed into (and take up) particular (social) positions by and within cultural codes. Who we are, in one sense, is answered by where we are. I am the person standing here, the one who can see you looking at me but can't see me looking at you. *Subjectivity* is a useful term to capture this sense of the relationship between who and where we are. Subjectivity is the sense of existing both at the center of and apart from any particular experience. Subjectivity lets people reflect on their experience and their place in the world; it lets us carry on a conversation with ourselves about ourselves, as it were. It is what lets people use language creatively to say new things and to express their experiences. That is, part of what you are, your subjectivity, is defined by the fact that you occupy the center of your own field of vision and experience. You are always at the center of your experiential field. Because you are the subject of your experiences, because they are in fact *your* experiences, they seem quite natural and obviously true.

But what about someone whose experiences of the world are not legitimated, someone who is forced to see the world through someone else's eyes? What happens to someone for whom the world seems to deny their experience of who they are, their subjectivity? Consider the way many women who were raped were treated in our society (we can hope that this is now only rarely the case): Often, their own experience of having been violated, abused, victimized, was denied and the woman was treated as the cause of her own violation. She was not viewed by the society as the victim of violence (reinforced by systematic and structural sexism), but as the aggressor who—by how she dressed ("seductively") and by how she interacted with the man ("willingly")—asked for it. That is, her experience is recoded into the dominant codes of male experience. After all, if you are placed in the position of the subject through certain codes, then you can also be placed in the position of the object.

People occupy a variety of positions in language and social relationships depending upon how they are addressed and inter-pellated. A teacher says, "You have to . . . ." A friend says, "We feel like going . . . ." An older brother says, "Do I have to take it along . . . ?" Think about all the different ways people are addressed, even in the media, ways that may include them in or exclude them from certain identities. This same process works not only to produce people's sense of themselves as human subjects (capable of creativity and autonomy) but also to place people in the various culturally constructed categories of identity.

How is it that society interpellates people into these systems of cultural differences, guaranteeing that it reproduces the basic struc-tures of its organization of power? Some media critics draw upon Sigmund Freud's psychoanalytic theory, which tried to explain how children grow up as social subjects, reproducing the sexual and gender roles of their parents. According to Freud, this is accomplished by the child's renunciation and repression of specific desires, which results in the formation of an unconscious. People become subjects because they reject part of who they are (boys defer their desire for their mother by trying to become their father; girls renounce their desire for their father by bonding with their mother). There are enormously powerful social processes at work interpellating individuals into their "proper" places as "normal" members of society. Some feminist film theorists argue that the basic plot structure of Hollywood cinema reenacts the process by which people are interpellated into and accede to their appropriate gender and sexual identities. Different media continually address differently gendered and sexed audiences (for example, Lifetime, the channel for women; various women's magazines; soap operas).

In the media, women seem to be largely defined or placed as the object of male pleasure—both visual and physical. Many classic Hollywood films, television programs, and even commercials feature rather gratuitous shots of women in various stages of undress, as if they were placed there only for the viewer's pleasure in looking. This coding of pleasure means that the camera's position defines and embodies a male perspective on the world. The camera is masculine. Similarly, in most narratives—at least until recently—it is the male characters who define the action of the story, although it is often the woman who, as an object of desire, makes the story move. The hero sets out to win, to rescue the woman, or to find some object required to win or save the woman. The woman is rarely allowed to speak. If a strong woman character threatens to disrupt the masculine universe of the story, she will almost inevitably be subdued in the end, by either death or marriage. Similar processes are at work in all of the cultural processes of identity including, for example, race. People are interpellated by other people's language and behavior, as well as by the media texts that address them.

However, the actual people receiving this message are not necessarily as passive as this makes them sound. Interpellation can define someone into a subordinate position, but the person has to accede to that interpellation. He or she has to take up the position. People can struggle against specific interpellations, struggle to reject the experience, or try to find alternative positions within the text. Consider the following rather simple example: Someone tells a racist joke to a group of people. Everyone in that group is interpellated as White, and, insofar as they remain silent, they accept that interpellation. But what if one person were to suddenly say, "You only told that joke because you assumed that I am White." What would that do to the normally assumed processes of interpellation?

Cultural codes, and especially the media in the contemporary world, also articulate the meanings of the various positions people occupy. In this way, we can think of the media as actively constructing the meanings and expectations that are associated with, or linked to, particular social identities. For instance, the meaning of "young Black man" as an identity in America is often linked to a host of threatening associations: juvenile delinquent, drug user/dealer, potential mugger. The result is that people in the United States are often more nervous near a young Black man than near a young White man; even the police follow more closely the behavior of young Black men on the streets. The civil rights movement can be seen in part as an attempt to challenge the meanings that the dominant cultural codes articulated to Blackness, meanings that were almost entirely negative, and to construct new articulations: "Black is beautiful."

For example, consider what meanings have been linked to the identity of woman in American culture. Women have been seen as weak, emotional, nonassertive, and illogical. But there is nothing inherent in the position of women that makes them less aggressive, more emotional, or even weaker than men. The fact that women have different hormones cannot provide a sufficient explanation of these meanings. These meanings are not necessary. There is nothing inherent in women that determines these connotations of the identity of being a woman. These meanings can and do change. But they are also powerfully effective in society. The fact that the articulations have been made has a strong influence over the way people, both men and women, think about women and behave toward women. If people believe that women are weaker than men and that they are supposed to be less aggressive, this will certainly influence the way parents differentially treat boys and girls. The results will make the articulation even stronger, make it appear even more obvious, seemingly natural, and commonsensical. Because women "are" weaker, parents tend to discourage their little girls from roughhousing and playing in contact sports (although this is apparently changing). And because boys "are" tougher, parents are (often too) quick to discourage little boys from crying and to encourage their aggressive play in team sports. Parents encourage different cultural tastes, which reproduce certain articulations (and which also produce different interpellations). But these meanings are open to challenge; articulations can be disarticulated, and new links, new articulations, can be made.

Moreover, the links are never made in either simple terms or in isolation from other identities. For example, Spike Lee's 1988 film *School Daze* created a furor by opening up a debate about color differences, and the resulting racisms, within Blackness and among Black people. Identities are never simply Black or female, just as people never live their identities simply as Black or female. Real people are—they live their identities as—Black *and* female *and* middle-class *and* American *and* urban, and so forth. So the articulations that give depth to the categories of identities are always more specific, fragmented, and contradictory than theories of stereotypes assume. Sometimes, these different identities interact in a variety of ways to produce the particular, concrete identities that define who people are. Sometimes, these identities even conflict and produce competing demands on people. For example, Alice Walker's *The Color Purple* opened up a public debate within the Black community about the relationship between Black men and Black women, and among Black women.

The notion of articulation frees the struggle over representation from some stable and true external referent against which all meanings are measured. Rather, it makes the mutually determining conjunction of social reality and cultural representation the only game in town. The history of media representations is not a progression from stereotypes to truth, but a struggle to constantly articulate the meanings of people's identities and the ways they can live those cultural categories. There is no single narrative that can be told. There are always competing meanings and articulations struggling to win dominance or at least acceptance.

The history of representations of women on network television shows a complex and contested play of meanings circulating around the category of woman. During the 1950s, the common history argues that women occupied a subservient role to men, that women were almost always little more than window dressing or support for strong father figures on such family programs as *Father Knows Best* and *Leave It To Beaver*. Of course, women could sometimes be zany and incompetent, as was Lucille Ball's character in *I Love Lucy*. When women appeared in nonhousewife roles, they were still subservient to the men they served as secretaries or nurses or saloon girls.

And yet other critics have pointed out how much more complex this field of representations was: The comedian Lucille Ball was not zany and incompetent; she was assertive and brilliant (and, it turned out, astute in business). Sitcom mothers often turned out to be the real strength in the families. And working-class women, such as Alice Kramden in *The Honeymooners*, were important predecessors for contemporary images like Roseanne's. Not all the women of the 1950s were seductively attractive (*Our Miss Brooks*), and not all the men were competent ideal mates (Jackie Gleason or Milton Berle).

In the 1960s and 1970s, as the women's movement gained national attention, women's roles began to change on television as well. During the 1970s, women began to occupy more positions outside the home, as police officers (Angie Dickinson in *Police Woman*), as TV news producers, and more frequently on television news as correspondents and reporters. Yet women were still young, attractive, and secondary to more powerful male figures. Mary Tyler Moore's role in *The Mary Tyler Moore Show* represented a significant advance over her earlier role as the at-home housewife and mom on *The Dick Van Dyke Show* (and certainly a very significant advance over her appearance in *Richard Diamond*, a detective show in which only her legs were shown and her voice heard). It was the first network program to focus on an unmarried working woman. Yet the program continued to reaffirm many of the most common meanings of "single women" in our society. Mary was constantly looking for a husband, or at least a good date, and despite her growing power in the office where she worked, she always seemed subservient to Lou Grant in ways that the men in the office were not. (For instance, only Mary called her boss "Mr. Grant.") But such a typical narrative ignores the fact that there were many moments that outlived the 1950s, and even some moments that foreshadowed the decades yet to come.

By the 1980s and 1990s, however, women's roles on television had changed, and with new roles have come new images of the possibilities of what it means to be a woman in American society. It is impossible to answer the question of whether these new images reflected or brought about changes in society; the only possible answer is both. For instance, the success of the over-60 Jessica Fletcher character in *Murder, She Wrote* and of the *Golden Girls* validated new images of being older and female. Yet Jessica is a highly traditional woman in many ways, devoted to the memory of her dead husband and to sexual abstinence. Also, the development of the aggressive newscaster Murphy Brown, and the less-than-perfect housewife and mother Roseanne have broken many of the old stereotypes of both women in work and women at home. Yet Murphy Brown pays a price in sometimes being less than likable, and she still has to play male/female games, even as a single mother. And it is the case that, for each of these steps forward, one can point to programs that seem to have taken two steps back. Sure, Ellen came out as a lesbian, but there is more than enough homophobia on television. And what does one make of the success of programs such as *Married With Children?*

Identities never proceed in some linear and coherent story from falsity to truth, or from truth to falsity. The codes of identity are always complex and contradictory, defining a field in which different meanings battle to become the dominant articulations. The field is never entirely open, and it is often quite constrained, but it is also often contested. Sometimes, the story is one of an expanding field of competing meanings; other times, the story is one of shrinking possibilities. Ideology is always a matter of struggle rather than simple domination. Victories are sometimes won and new meanings become dominant; sometimes, victories are won when new meanings are simply allowed into the field. Just as women have advanced into new roles and occupations in American life over the past several decades, the cultural codes associated with the identity of woman in the media have developed, broadened, and become more complex. These changes are not simply the result or reflection of changes taking place in the "real world," for they are in part responsible for these very changes. As we have been suggesting throughout this book, the relationship between communication and reality is too complex to be described either as simply production or reflection.

We cannot talk about the image of women in television as if television were itself a simple homogeneous message. For example, do *60 Minutes, American Idol, The Bachelorette, Eve, Friends, The Gilmore Girls,* and *Judging Amy* all have the same message about women? Also, we cannot talk as if the image of women in television were somehow isolatable from other media. For the ideological struggle over the representations of woman takes place across all of the different cultural media, which have to be taken then as complex interactive systems of messages. The question of identity is not simply that of struggling with what is presented in the mainstream media. As in the case of Black films in the 1910s and 1920s, media makers can begin to produce their own media products to counter stereotypical images by presenting more nuanced alternatives. With cheap video recorders and, now, more powerful home computers and fast Internet connections, it has become more possible for people to produce images and texts that better represent their own experience of the world—potentially at least. Let us give you an example: Inexpensive digital cameras connected to the Internet (called *Webcams*) allow individuals to either display aspects of their everyday lives or environment or to create performances that can be viewed by others online. At times, these Webcams can challenge dominant stereotypes, as does performance artist Anna Voog's Webcam site, which seeks to rework notions of what it means to be female in contemporary society (see Snyder, 2000). But, more often than not, such Webcam sites that feature women simply reproduce and reinforce dominant stereotypes of how women should appear and behave.

The struggle over the ideology of woman cannot be limited to images of women per se and the roles they play, for the meaning of woman cannot be separated from a complex array of other social roles and practices. Thus the struggle over the meaning of woman can also take place in representations of the family and of domestic spaces (the household) and of the variety of practices that take place there. The ads on television in the 1950s, ads for new consumer goods usually marketed as labor-saving and convenience devices for the household, were all about "being a woman." But so were ads and programs about television itself. A number of media historians, most notably Lynn Spigel (1992), have argued that families had to be taught how to watch TV, just as much as they had to be taught, as did architects and builders, about how to redesign domestic spaces to accommodate the new medium into the family living space. Thus the ideological field of woman involves representations of issues as diverse as domesticity and domestic spaces, suburbia and the reorganization of urban spaces, the changing nature of labor in and out of the home, family relations and consumption, and the place and use of the new media such as television. But these are more than representations. Hence ideological articulations always involve realities that are not merely cultural; they also involve social and material practices (like the actual spatial organizations of houses and the material design of television sets), which may themselves be the object of other ideological struggles.

## CONCLUSION

In recent times, and partly as a result of the increasing importance of the media in constructing people's identities, people seem to have developed a much more fragmented and fluid sense of their own identities.

Some identities even become so contaminated by other identities that it is difficult to tell what they refer to. For example, when the British Commonwealth sponsored a photography exhibit asking amateur photographers to document their sense of national identity within the "British commonwealth," the results were baffling to say the least. People's sense of their national identity was composed of fragments of tradition, of American commercial culture, of British symbolism, and of the media. There was no pure identity, only the articulations of the variety of identifications that people made in their lives (Goldman & Hall, 1987). In fact, there has been a long history (which has only increased with time) of debate about what it means to be "American," about whether schools and the media should present a coherent (traditional) view of Americans and American history, or whether they should open the door to multicultural views of how various groups have come to be part of American life. People's identities are less stable and unified than they were in previous generations, and people tend to have less commitment to any single identity than did previous generations. Debates about multiculturalism may partly reflect the fact that the very nature of people's identities is changing as a result of the growing power of popular culture and the mass media.

## SUGGESTED READINGS

Douglas, S. (1994). *Where the girls are: Growing up female with the mass media.* New York: Times Books.

Dyson, M. E. (1993). *Reflecting black: African-American cultural criticism.* Minneapolis: University of Minnesota Press.

Ewen, S. (1999). *All consuming images: The politics of style in contemporary culture.* New York: Basic Books.

Gray, H. (1995). *Watching race: Television and the struggle for "blackness."* Minneapolis: University of Minnesota Press.

Hall, S., & Gay, P. du (Eds.). (1996). *Questions of cultural identity.* Thousand Oaks, CA: Sage.

# Consuming the Media | 9

I n the early 1970s, the novelist Jerzy Kosinski (1970) created one of
the most telling and powerful images of the omnipotence of television in our everyday lives: Chance, the gardener in *Being There*,
lives through the television screen. Television is not measured against
reality; his reality is measured against television. All that he knows is
what he observes on television—who he is and what the world is like.
But, even more startling, how Chance lives his life, how he reacts to
and with other people, how he feels, his pleasures and desires, and
even his moods place him inside a television world:

> Chance went inside and turned on the TV. . . . By changing the
> channel, he could change himself. He could go through phases, as
> garden plants went through phases, but he could change as rapidly as
> he wished by twisting the dial backward and forward. In some cases,
> he could spread out into the screen without stopping, just as on TV
> people spread out into the screen. By turning the dial, Chance could
> bring others inside his eyelids. Thus, he came to believe that it was he,
> Chance, and no one else, who made himself be. (p. 5)

> He did not know how to explain to her that he could not touch better
> or more fully with his hands than he could with his eyes. Seeing
> encompassed all at once; a touch was limited to one spot at a time.

>   She should no more have wanted to be touched by him than should
>   the TV screen have wanted it. . . .
>       "I know, I know," she cried. "I don't excite you!" Chance did not
>   know what she meant. . . .
>       He turned and looked at her. "I like to watch you," he said.
>   (pp. 94–95)

There are two ways of reading Kosinski's parable of modern life. Perhaps Kosinski is arguing that television defines reality in modern life. This interpretation raises crucial questions about the relationship between media and reality. Or perhaps Kosinski's parable is a description of the extent to which television—and by extension other media—increasingly occupy a central place in our everyday lives.

We have argued thus far that the media produce commodities (and money) and cultural products (meanings, ideologies, and identities). But the circuit of communication cannot end there. People have to purchase or acquire these commodities and then use (and eventually use up) such commodities. Media industries depend on the fact that people use up their products so that they will continue to buy new products. Similarly, meanings, ideologies, and identities can only be effective if they are interpreted and taken up by the audience members. In this chapter, we discuss the ways in which people make use of media products; that is, the ways they select them and attend to them, and especially the ways they locate them in different places and relations in everyday life. Understanding how we consume media in our everyday lives requires us to explore people's relationship to media and cultural products. Why do people choose to use certain media products, under what conditions do they use them, how do they use them, and what are the consequences of these choices and conditions of use?

Raymond Williams's (1965) image of the "long revolution" describes the enormous and significant changes that have produced the advanced industrial democracies. Williams traces these changes—economic, political, and cultural—to the moment when Europe was transformed by the emergence of capitalism, democracy, and mass literacy in the 1600s. In fact, each of these social forces fueled the others so that, Williams argues, developments in media, such as the advent of the printing press, are a crucial part of the emergence of modern society and modern life. It would be a mistake, however, not to recognize, as

Jerzy Kosinski does, that these social forces, including the media, affected not only the broader structures of society but also the more mundane and immediate ways people lived from day to day, from moment to moment.

Williams's argument has enormous implications for how we think about the media and their effects on us. Common sense may lead us to link, in a direct and simple line, the media or specific media products with the visible or identifiable results that they produce: For instance, we talk about television's effects on violent behavior or the effect of pornographic material on sexual attitudes or the influence of journalistic practices on election behavior. (We will discuss such matters in the next chapter.) But Williams would argue that this simple linkage is a mistake. Any attempt to understand the power of the media or specific media products requires us first to understand how these products are located and operate within people's everyday lives: That is, the effects of the media depend on or are *mediated* by where, why, and how people use or consume them.

For instance, research has demonstrated the different effects on children of television viewing depending on whom they are watching it with: Preschoolers who watch *Sesame Street* with an adult tend to learn more from the program than those who watch the program alone (Lesser, 1974). Or you may have had the experience of associating a certain song with an old girlfriend or boyfriend or perhaps a particularly emotional time of your life. Every time you hear this song now, your response to it is colored by that emotional association. Or just think of the difference between watching music videos in your home and in a dance club. All of these are examples of the ways everyday life, the context and psychology of media use, influence the effects of the media.

But there is an additional complication that Williams's argument forces us to recognize: The long revolution itself is responsible for shaping and changing people's everyday lives. To put it another way, the sociology and social psychology of media use are themselves historically influenced by the media whose effects they mediate. An obvious example of this interdependence comes from studies of how Americans spend their time. As sociologist John Robinson (1996) has pointed out, the advent of television has "colonized" leisure time in America, so much so that every additional minute of leisure (time not spent working or caring for family and household or sleeping) that

Americans gained between the 1960s and the 1980s was spent watching television. Newer media technologies, from portable media such as the Walkman, cellular phones, handheld TVs, and wireless portable computers, make it possible to carry media into places and spaces of everyday life hitherto closed to media and culture. Moreover, it is obvious that the Internet—the shorthand term we use to describe our increasingly computer-interlinked culture—is fundamentally changing our interactions in everyday life, as well as the context and psychology of media use and thus how the media affect us all. For example, the question of whether Internet use is more likely to bring us closer together, to create "social capital" by and through which people can shape their own lives, or, conversely, to turn us into social isolates has become a social concern. Early research (Kraut et al., 1998) suggested that Internet use led to social isolation and feelings of depression, but more recent research by the same researchers and many others (see DiMaggio, Hargittai, Neuman, & Robinson, 2001; Howard & Jones, 2004; Wellman & Haythornthwaite, 2002) suggests that, although it's complex, for most people, Internet use makes us a bit *more* social.

The introduction of almost every new media technology in this century has immediately given rise to considerable concern and widespread public discussion about who is using it, how often, and under what conditions. That is, before people have worried about the effects of movies or radio or television on their audiences, they first take notice of the size, shape, and character of the consuming public.

Oddly enough, the process of consumption has received little attention in economic theories, although it is generally acknowledged that consumption is the necessary completion of the process of exchange on which all economic relations are based. The production of anything, from a widget to a television program, makes no sense unless someone consumes it—that is, buys it and uses it up. Every product is designed and made on the basis of certain assumptions about how it is to be used, under what conditions, and for how long. Cars, for example, are produced with a certain life expectancy as well as with certain assumptions about the uses to which they will be put; most cars are not designed to be driven in races or demolition derbies. But, as we shall see, manufacturers cannot accurately predict how consumers will use their products.

As students of the media and culture, we need to ask to what degree the intended use of a product determines its actual use and effects; to put it the other way around, what is the contribution of the consumer in determining the actual use and effects of media products? This problem is often referred to as the question of the relative activity or passivity of media audiences. We also must consider the different functions that the consumption of media products serves for their users. What are the conditions under which people are able or unable to consume particular media products? Who can engage in particular acts of media consumption?

## THE ROLE OF THE AUDIENCE

It is obvious that, in some ways, consumption is an active process, even in the most apparently passive situations of media use. Consider a person—the stereotypical "couch potato"—vegging out in front of the TV screen, eyes glazed, shoes off, reclining on the couch with a bag of potato chips in hand and a drink on the coffee table. The person looks passive. Yet that person had to decide to watch television at this particular time, had to put the television on, had to get the bag of chips and the drink; maybe our couch potato read *TV Guide* to find out what was on or surfed through the channels to decide what to watch. And there's more.

A great deal of cognitive activity goes on. *Cognition* is the act of attending to and making sense of the world; it is the application of consciousness to the world. Even the couch potato is cognitively engaged with the television set: Couch potatoes have to focus attention on the screen, process the dots on the TV set into recognizable images, interpret those images as representations of some reality, fill in the blanks in the narratives presented by the television screen, and make sense of the messages coming from the screen. There is evidence that different people expend different amounts of mental effort to make sense of different programs. Nonetheless, this act of watching television can be said to be an active process because minds are engaged. The question is often raised whether the activity of watching television is as active, relatively speaking, as doing other things, such as reading a book, watching a live play, or writing a letter. (See Box 9.1, "Children and the Activity of Television Viewing.")

---

**BOX 9.1**

**Children and the Activity of Television Viewing**

Researchers who watch children watching television in laboratory studies or in home observations find that children seem to be very actively involved in attending to the set: The children move in and out of attention, monitoring the set until something comes on that they want to watch. Indeed, the one programming style researchers have found that seems to elicit a "transfixed" gaze among children is cartoon shows. Moreover, there is considerable evidence (from postviewing interviews, as well as observational studies of children playing) that children have to actively work to make sense of television messages. This, too, suggests that television watching is an active process for children.

According to communication researchers George Comstock and Haejung Paik (1991),

> The television experience cannot be described as either active or passive without reference to what each term is intended to denote. There is justification for both labels; no good rationale can be offered for giving either term precedence; and the appropriate term depends on what aspect of the experience is being described or emphasized. [Television watching] is typically passive in regard to involvement, but inherently active in regard to monitoring. (p. 23)

---

Another way the audience is active is in bending a medium and its messages to the audience's own purposes. In almost every instance, the producer of a media product has in mind some idea of about how the audience will understand and use the particular product. That is, the producer (which may be a corporation or an individual) intends for the product to have an effect. Indeed, researchers have to beware of what's called the *intentional fallacy,* the notion that what the creator of a message intended it to mean (its *encoded meaning*) is what the audience takes it to mean (its *decoded meaning*)—that what the author intended is the "real" meaning of the text (see Chapter 6). Research on audiences and what they do with the media they consume clearly demonstrates that people are very creative—they have their own interpretations of media products, and they will often do very surprising and unpredictable things with them. Let's consider a range of different examples.

Think about the intentions of those who produce a newspaper. The newspaper's reporters and editors prepare newspaper stories to be read, to provoke thought, and perhaps even to persuade their readers to act in a particular way or to change their minds. But the purchasers may not act as expected. A study by Barnhurst and Wartella (1992) had college students write autobiographical essays about their memories of using the newspaper from childhood to adulthood. The authors found that

> the newspaper played a role in a variety of activities—art projects, family, housework, do-it-yourself projects, and entertainment pastimes. Most of the uses mentioned for newspapers were predictable: hitting the dog with it, putting it in shoes that had holes, and the like. Few were at all unusual, but some students, like a White female frequent reader, implied that using the newspaper for anything other than reading was odd: "My parents have always found bizarre uses for the newspaper as well. My mother, a sincere plant lover, likes to spread newspaper over our countertops to shield them from soil when she repots her plants." Students reported making early use of newspapers as an implement (in 70 essays), an art medium (in 56 essays), and a protective covering (in 47 essays). These uses introduced a first frustration with newspapers: the ink rubs off. (p. 199)

A more consequential instance of the multiple and often unpredictable uses of the media can be found in many technological innovations. Industries introduce new technologies for a number of purposes, such as expanding their current markets or opening up new markets. As we have argued, in each instance, such new technologies are introduced to increase profit for the owners. However, in many cases, audiences use technologies in unintended ways, ways that had not been imagined and that often subvert the intentions of the producers. For example, audiocassettes have allowed people to make multiple copies for personal use and have allowed less scrupulous people to pirate recordings. Cheap recordable CDs and MP3s have done the same thing but without the same degradation in quality that one gets from dubbed tapes, making them even more an issue for the industry. Such practices have cut into the profit margins of the record companies.

Perhaps the most important dimension of the audience's activity, at least as far as audience researchers are concerned, is the extent to which audiences make meanings for the media products they consume. In a study by Australian communication researchers Bob Hodge and David Tripp (1986) of children's use of television, they report a particularly striking example. One of the most popular programs among Australian grade school children in the 1980s was a program called *The Prisoner in Cell-Block H,* a minimalist, black-and-white, half-hour dramatization of everyday life in a woman's prison. This is not a program one would expect young children to embrace, and Hodge and Tripp wondered why it was so popular with children. They suggest that the children used the specific relationships and dramatic situations of the program to describe their own feelings about school and their everyday life. The program became a kind of secret code with which the children could talk to each other about particular teachers and classes, and about the experience of school, without fear of being understood by adult authorities. Although this example may seem extreme, audience researchers argue that television audiences give their own meanings to the programs they watch in order to fit the programs into their everyday life.

Think about your own experiences: When you listen to a song on the radio or read a romance novel or a comic book, when you go to a movie on a date or watch a videotape in your room, or when you roam the Web on your computer, you help to determine or shape the meaning and significance of the particular media product. Your interpretation of a song does not necessarily match someone else's interpretation. Audience researchers argue that the meaning of a media text resides in the audiences, not in the messages. However, it is not always easy to sort out and distinguish the contributions of the producer, the message itself, and the audience to the meaning of any given text.

Much of this audience research is based on Stuart Hall's (1980) distinction between encoding and decoding. Hall argued that the production and the reception of media messages were two relatively autonomous or independent processes within the larger *circuit of communication.* Thus there was no basis for assuming that how a particular audience or audience member interpreted a text would correspond to the meaning that the producer of the message intended or hoped to communicate. Of course, this encoded meaning did define a *preferred meaning* and, presumably, at least some of the elements of the text would push the audience in the direction of the preferred meaning. But this cannot guarantee that this process will be successful. Decoding is not a matter of misunderstanding but of the nature of communication as a struggle, from different social positions, over the meaning of the text. How a particular audience interprets a text is determined in complex ways by its social position, by the interests and resources it brings to the text.

Hall's original work was directed toward the study of network public affairs programming; consequently, he assumed that the encoded meaning of these texts would support the dominant ideology of the society on the particular issues that defined the topic of the text. He then identified three broad possibilities for decoding. An audience's decoding can assent or correspond to the encoded or preferred meaning. Or a decoding can explicitly oppose the dominant ideology encoded into the text, at least on the particular topic of the text. Or a decoding can negotiate a position somewhere between assent and opposition, bending the text to the experiences and values of the audience. It is important to remember that these categories of decoded meaning—*preferred, oppositional,* and *negotiated*—were developed to talk about texts where politics was a central and visible aspect of a message. These categories are less useful if one is talking about an audience's decoding of texts where such explicit political commitments are more difficult to identify.

The significance of media products in everyday life includes a broader range of uses and effects than just questions of the material use of a medium (such as using newspapers to wrap fish) and the meanings of particular messages. Consider the Britney "wannabes" (or Avril Lavigne, Lindsey Lohan, or Hillary Duff wannabes) who construct elaborate images of themselves and a sense of their own identity (who they are, who they want to be, and how they want to be seen by others) through media products. In *Fast Times at Ridgemont High* (1982), a new student in the high school remarks that another student looks exactly like Sheena Easton. Her friend points to a number of different groups of students, both male and female, who seem to have taken on the identity of their favorite rock star or actor. Researchers are beginning to look at the ways in which the media provide the resources with which audiences construct their sense of their own identity. This surely is a media effect, but it is one that requires the active involvement and investment of the audience in the process.

Another example opens up yet another dimension of media effects and uses: soap operas. For real soap fans, just watching a favorite soap is not enough. They want to talk to other fans about the trials and tribulations of the TV characters, they want to actively be involved in predicting the characters' futures, and they often refer to the experiences of these characters to make sense of their own lives. Internet researcher

Nancy Baym (2000) has documented how some soap fans turn to the Internet to find communities of other soap fans and to discuss and debate the happenings on their favorite soaps. Television critics have long attempted to understand this powerful relationship. But it is very common for people to be fans of particular genres of television, movies, books, or music. People derive very real and complex pleasures and emotional experiences from media consumption. It is the emotional relationship to soaps that seems to dominate the fan's experience; it is the pleasure derived from particular media tastes that provides the foundation for other effects of media. All consumers derive some kinds of pleasure and emotional satisfaction from their media use; and, like the meanings we give to media products, the pleasures and emotions we experience as consumers are often quite unpredictable. They vary not only individually but also, as we shall see, across different social groups of consumers.

We have introduced here several of the major perspectives employed by audience researchers in understanding the place of the media in everyday life. In the rest of this chapter, we will elaborate each of these perspectives. First, we will consider one of the oldest and most commonsensical research perspectives, which looks at the social and psychological functions that media use serves for their audiences. This approach has been called *functionalism* or the *uses-and-gratifications perspective.* Second, we will investigate the *affective* or emotional experience of media audiences. Third, we will look at the *social context* of media use.

## FUNCTIONS OF THE MEDIA

Perhaps the most commonsensical way to think about the mass media is to ask what functions they serve. For individuals, the functions of media can be thought of as the satisfaction or gratification of individual needs. For the society as a whole, the functions of media can be thought of as the purposes served by media in the society. A function can refer to a purpose, a consequence, a requirement, or an expectation. Denis McQuail (1987) gives the following example: "The term 'information function' can refer to three quite separate things: that media try to inform people (purpose); that people learn from media (consequence); that media are supposed to inform people (requirement or expectation)" (p. 69).

It is important to separate a requirement from an expectation: For example, although we might expect and hope that the media inform the audience, as contemporary presidential campaigns have demonstrated, this is not a requirement for the continued existence of the society. Another distinction is that some media functions are manifest, visible on the surface and easily recognizable, and others are latent, hidden deep below the surface of everyday life and difficult to identify. For example, news broadcasts inform the public about presidential candidates; that is a manifest function. But the character of the news coverage may also more subtly shape people's attitudes and assumptions about the nature of the political process itself (M. Robinson, 1976). That is a latent function of news coverage. Similarly, the manifest function of listening to music may be to relax us, to give us something to dance or exercise to, and the like. But music may also serve a latent function: It may shape our expectations about romance and it may increase our tolerance for noise.

Functionalism is a perspective that assumes the existence of a closed system, whether a society or an individual or even an ecosystem, which has requirements for its continued survival. Media functionalism looks at the uses the media serve in the systems of society and individual lives.

## Social Functions

One of the earliest typologies of the social functions of the media was offered by Harold Lasswell (1948). He wrote that the mass media served three major functions for the society:

- *Surveillance* of the environment: providing information about events and conditions in society and the world
- *Correlation* of the various parts of society: explaining, interpreting, and commenting on the meaning of events and information; coordinating separate activities; socializing
- *Transmission* of the social heritage from one generation to the next.

In the 1950s, sociologist Charles Wright (1960) added *entertainment* as a social function of media. Denis McQuail (2000) added a fifth category, which he called *mobilization*, or the ability of the mass media to bring people into particular processes of change and development.

263

It's clear that these social functions of media are not always realized when any given media product is considered. There is no simple and direct relationship between specific acts of media consumption and any predictable function. Moreover, many acts of consumption involve multiple and sometimes even competing functions. For example, many of the television programs that are, on the surface, "mere" entertainment may entail other social functions as well. One could learn of current events through a joke in Jon Stewart's monologue, for example. Also, one could be entertained by programs designed to be informative or interpretive, like watching the McLaughlin Group debate for the personality clashes in addition to simply the opinions presented.

## Individual Functions

For individuals, the functions of media can be thought of as the motives or reasons why individuals use the media products they do and the sorts of satisfactions they receive from the use of these products. One of the earliest studies of the functions of media for individuals was conducted in the early 1940s by Herta Hertzog (1944), a sociologist at Columbia University's Bureau of Applied Social Research. She studied the motivations and gratifications of radio soap opera listeners. Her interest was to try to understand why women became such ardent fans of the radio soaps, serialized dramas about the trials and tribulations of people's relationships. The goal of the study was to determine what satisfactions listeners said they derived coupled with a psychological evaluation of these listeners' claims: The functional approach sought to account for why audiences attended to particular content on the assumption that the act of attending served some function for the individual. Hertzog found that such programs served two overarching functions for these women: They provided *emotional release* from the women's everyday lives, and they served as a *source of advice* concerning real-life problems. What sort of lessons did soap operas provide? Hertzog found that the lessons of the soaps often applied in unlikely situations. For example, one woman reported going to the doctor before she started her diet because someone on the soaps had done so. The chief lesson Hertzog identified was that if one remains calm and does nothing, everything will somehow come out all right in the end—perhaps a useful lesson.

264

In 1959, Elihu Katz, one of the founding figures of communication research and still one of the most active and influential figures in the field, relabeled the approach *uses and gratifications*. For Katz, uses-and-gratifications research would empirically test some of the critiques of popular culture that had been made in the 1950s: Were audience tastes being debased? Were audiences being entertained? What did people do with the media? What uses and gratifications did people find in mass-produced news and entertainment?

The assumptions of the uses-and-gratifications model as proposed by Katz and expanded in work with Jay Blumler and Michael Gurevitch (Katz, Blumler, & Gurevitch, 1974) are the following:

1. The audience is active, hence use of media is goal-directed.

2. Audience members have expectations of what certain kinds of content have to offer them and these expectations help shape their selections. That is, particular audience members can take the initiative in linking their needs to the ability of particular media products to gratify those needs.

3. The media compete with other sources of need satisfaction (such as talking with friends, taking a walk, sleeping). The needs potentially satisfied by the mass media are only part of a wider range of human needs.

4. People are sufficiently aware of their needs, media choices, and the gratifications they receive from media use to be able to tell researchers what motivates their media behavior.

The major work on uses-and-gratifications research for the past 25 years has been to catalog the various uses and gratifications that audience members report obtaining from their media consumption. These include the following:

- *Information:* finding out about relevant events and conditions in immediate surroundings, society, and the world; seeking advice; satisfying curiosity; learning
- *Personal identity:* finding reinforcement for personal values; finding models of behavior; identifying with valued others (in the media); gaining insight into one's self
- *Integration and social interaction:* gaining insight into circumstances of others; identifying with others; finding a basis for

  conversation and social interaction; having a substitute for real life companionship (*parasocial* relations)

 ■ *Entertainment:* escaping from problems; relaxing; filling time; emotional release; getting intrinsic cultural or aesthetic enjoyment.

## The Critique of Functionalism

Although uses-and-gratifications research has provided useful empirical evidence about audiences' consumption of the media, there have been serious criticisms of its theoretical assumptions and research programs. First, this approach ignores the social dimensions of media consumption and reduces media use to an individual psychological relationship. Yet we know that media consumption is very often socially *situated;* that is, it is something engaged in with others. In fact, uses-and-gratifications research offers no way of understanding the connection between individual psychological needs and social structures and processes. At best, the individual is conceptualized in terms of specific social roles, which apparently carry their own socially induced needs and tensions.

Second, the key term—*function*—of this approach remains ambiguous. Functional activities have many different meanings in the literature: as a useful activity, as an appropriate or normal activity, as a necessary activity, and as a valuable activity. Nor is it clear how to determine whether an activity is useful, normal, necessary, or valuable. And for whom? How do we define the "society" within which such decisions are to be made?

Third, uses-and-gratifications research offers no account for the origin of needs or the relations among them. Instead, it often slips into deterministic accounts that are inconsistent with the notion of an active audience. Finally, uses-and-gratifications theory suffers from two more general problems facing any functionalist theory: It is circular and conservative. It is circular because the only way to tell that a need is being gratified is to assume that the gratification provides evidence for the existence of the need. That is, if watching television distracts me from my problems, I must need such distraction. This perspective is thought to be conservative, because the system of needs assumes that the existing society is capable of satisfying any individual's needs—in this way, the status quo becomes the definition of the normal and only structure of society.[1] In short, uses-and-gratifications research allows no possibility for social criticism or social change.

## THE SOCIAL PSYCHOLOGY OF CONSUMPTION

If uses-and-gratifications research fails to adequately describe the psychological relationship between a media product and its audience, perhaps looking more directly at the psychological state of the audience would be more helpful. Here, we are going to consider some of the dimensions of an individual's psychological state, recognizing that such states are always in part the product of social conditions and relationships. In particular, we are concerned here with the *affective dimensions* of a person's psychology. Every affective state, such as feeling happy or being blue, varies in intensity and differs in character; thus you can be happy rather than sad, satisfied rather than desirous. You can also be more or less happy, more or less sad, more or less satisfied. We will consider three affective or noncognitive dimensions—emotions, moods, and pleasures—and their relationship to media use briefly.

### Emotions

First, let's consider emotions. Media products try both to manipulate our emotions and to use emotions to produce some other effect (such as when advertisers use emotional appeals to try to get us to buy a product). Audiences, in turn, clearly use the media to produce emotional experiences for themselves. Many of us seem to enjoy going to movies that make us cry or cringe in fear or laugh at other people's foibles.

Interestingly, audiences do not seem to tire of such emotional uses of media products, even of the same product. People will watch a movie over and over, each time experiencing the same emotions, no matter how prepared they may be for the particularly moving scenes. Audiences cry at all the same times, every time, while watching *E.T.: The Extraterrestrial*, and, even after 30 years, it takes only two musical notes in a darkened room for an audience to recognize and react to *Jaws*.

In fact, audiences sometimes seem to use the media to learn about their emotional lives or to produce certain emotional states. Simon Frith (1981), the leading writer on popular music in England, has argued, for example, that the narratives of popular songs provide ways for fans to make private experiences public through a musical language of emotions. We learn how to feel about romance or the breakup of a romance by listening to a shared set of musical texts.

Think about your own use of music: When you are in love, there are particular songs that you play that capture and interpret your intense feelings. Conversely, many music fans create a "hate tape," which is full of songs expressing and making sense of the anger and rage they feel at another person when that person has deserted them. Country music is particularly overt in its constant narration of emotions and love stories.

Sometimes the emotional dimension is itself used for other purposes. For example, the popularity of horror films as a dating activity among adolescents and young adults is partially the result of a boy's desire to impress his date by demonstrating his ability to withstand the shock and horror of the film. He has to assume that females are the weaker sex, and thus unable to cope with the grotesque and shocking horror of such movies (and perhaps then more likely to cuddle close to him for "protection"). Ien Ang (1985), a Dutch media researcher now working in Australia, performed a study of Dutch female viewers of *Dallas,* attempting to see how these viewers (economically and politically at odds with the characters of the TV show) made sense of and enjoyed the show. She coined the term *emotional realism* to explain the ways in which, even if audiences couldn't identify with either the material circumstances of the show (the wealthy) or the particulars of the plot (adultery, shady business dealings, and so on), they could identify with the emotions expressed (anger, sadness, desire, and so on). At the same time, Tamar Liebes and Elihu Katz (1990) found that *Dallas,* despite becoming the first global TV hit program, failed in Japan. It did so, they argued, because Japanese viewers could not identify emotionally with the main characters; the program was emotionally unrealistic to them, since, their Japanese informants argued, younger people could *never* treat their elders with such disrespect.

## Mood

The second affective state is mood. One of the most successful media products of the past couple of decades has been MTV. When Robert Pitman first conceived of a 24-hour music video channel, he described it as a "mood enhancer." What does this mean? What is a mood? Did you ever wake up on the wrong side of the bed? Conversely, have you ever awakened feeling wonderful? In both cases, the cause of your mood is likely to be entirely unknown, but what is clear is that your entire day, and everything that happens to you during the day, is colored by that state of feeling, that mood. Things that might have made you happy yesterday now only make you angry, or vice versa. Here, again, we can use music as an example, for as many critics have commented, music is one of the most powerful means of affecting people's moods. The omnipresence of background music testifies to the power of music. One psychologist described the affective dimension of music listening this way:

> Why, when I first saw the Grand Canyon and the Piazza San Marco and the Alps, did I feel that things had all been more moving in Cinerama? Why? Because both God and Man forgot to put in the music . . . in one sense, it's no surprise that music grabs us—it's supposed to. But once you look at the process, it seems quite miraculous that people can bowl one another over just by jiggling sound waves. (Rosenfeld, 1985, p. 48)

Think about the power of music in your life: Think about the lullabies that parents sing to their children or the ritual music that every society has (Elgar's *Pomp and Circumstance,* played at almost every graduation, or Mendelssohn's *Wedding March* or the hymns of religious services). Recall the enormous power that you feel in a rock club or concert. Think of how you sing to yourself in the shower, on the street, while you are working, when you feel lonely or happy or afraid. In fact, many writers on popular music would agree with Robert Pitman's assumptions about music use: Music fans are, in fact, highly sophisticated in their ability to choose different music in order to manipulate their moods. You can use music to get yourself out of a bad mood, to work off negative energy, or to wallow in your misery.

Music can construct socially shared moods that enhance people's commitment to action. The civil rights movement is perhaps the best-known instance of this use of music in recent generations. Protesters in the 1950s and early 1960s would sing songs, not only to gird themselves for protest marches and the upcoming battles, but also to cope with their fears and to spread an affective blanket over the group. In many cases, this intensity brought new recruits into the community of civil rights protesters. "We Shall Overcome" is emblematic of this movement, just as "Solidarity Forever" was emblematic of an early twentieth-century union movement. Of course, this has been true for ages and applied as well to war songs and to both the suffragette and the abolition movement.

## Pleasure

Finally, let us turn our attention to the question of pleasure. If you ask most people why they watch particular television programs, read particular novels, or listen to particular musical genres, they are likely to answer that they enjoy them, that they get some pleasure out of them. Pleasure is a deceptively simple notion; but it is, in fact, a very complex phenomenon, and we actually know very little about the mechanisms of the production of pleasure. The term *pleasure* covers a number of different relationships. The various ways in which pleasure is derived from media use signals the complexity of people's affective relationship to the media. Consider some of the different meanings of pleasure and the different ways pleasure is accomplished. There is, for example, the comfort of escaping from or forgetting negative situations, the sense of reinforcement that comes with identifying with a particular character, the thrill of sharing another person's emotional life, the stature of expertise and collecting, the euphoria of vegging out, the release that comes from relaxation and putting aside troubles and stress, the fun of breaking rules, the satisfaction of doing what you are supposed to, the fulfillment of desires and needs, the exhilaration of shocking others through "rebellion," and the relief of catharsis.

All of these are involved in the normal and common relationship to media products. People engage with specific products because, in some way and form, they are entertaining, they provide a certain measure of enjoyment, they are pleasurable. Think about your own pleasures in media use. Do you derive some pleasure out of every encounter with media? Are they always the same pleasures? Are there particular media products that regularly elicit the same kinds of pleasure?

One of the most heated debates about media today concerns the political implications of media pleasures. There are several positions on this issue. At one extreme are the critics who would morally police media use and excise pleasurable material they find objectionable. These people argue that particular pleasures are both evil and politically dangerous. These kinds of attacks have been made against popular culture throughout its history. The constant attacks on rock and roll since its inception—attacking the sexual energy of the music and often

identifying it as "Black" music—provides one of the clearest examples.
(See Box 9.2, "Attacks on Rock and Roll.")

---

**BOX 9.2**

**Attacks on Rock and Roll**

As soon as rock became a national hit in the mid-1950s, ministers, politicians, and educators launched campaigns to have it banned. Its sexuality, its association with Black music and culture, its supposed violence, its volume, its lack of quality, its appeal to youth, all became the subject of attacks. Many cities banned rock-and-roll concerts in the 1950s, and newspapers printed editorials attacking its lyrics, its sexual rhythms, and the violence it seemed to stimulate. Rock was blamed for juvenile delinquency, it was linked with the devil and the communist threat, and it was accused of trying to turn "America's children" into animals, which in the racist language of the time, often meant that it made White kids act like Black kids.

All of this came to a head in a series of congressional "payola" hearings held in 1958 and 1959 in front of the Special Committee on Legislative Oversight. The subtext of this hearing was a battle between ASCAP (American Society of Composers, Authors, and Publishers) and BMI (Broadcast Music Incorporated). These two organizations controlled music publishing and song licensing. ASCAP represented the traditional music publishing industry and had largely closed its doors to the new sounds of rhythm and blues and rock and roll, which BMI had welcomed. So, the hearings were, at one level, a battle between competing economic interests in the music industry. The explicit topic of the hearings was *payola:* a practice widely practiced (and still practiced) throughout the music and radio industries by which a record company or representative would pay a radio station or disc jockey to play its record on the air. Because radio exposure was quite important to the marketing of records—and had become even more important since the 1950s—and because there were more records than could be played, the practice was considered normal and acceptable. ASCAP accused BMI of subverting "good music" by using payola to promote the horrible sounds of rock and roll. The interesting thing about the hearings was that the vast majority of the testimony was given over to attacks on rock-and-roll music.

The result of the so-called payola hearings was not an end to the practice of payola but a large-scale dismantling of the radio system that

*(Continued)*

---

(Continued)

had grown up around rock and roll. Many of the best rock disc jockeys (Alan Freed was only the most famous) lost their jobs; many radio stations changed their format and either gave up rock and roll or started to separate the choice of music to be played (programming) from those who were playing it (and who knew and loved it).

The attacks on rock and roll all but disappeared in the 1960s and 1970s, surfacing as a major issue only occasionally, such as when then Vice President Spiro Agnew called upon radio stations to stop playing rock music as it advocated drugs and revolution. Some religious leaders continued to attack the music, and fundamentalist Christians accused rock and roll (as well as rock-and-roll musicians) of advocating and participating in Satan worship and using backmasking (the practice of recording a message backward on a record) and subliminal messages to influence listeners against their will.

However, in the mid-1980s, the attacks on rock took on a new seriousness and visibility, and legitimate spokespeople took up the cause. In 1986, Allan Bloom, a professor at the University of Chicago, published *The Closing of the American Mind,* a bestseller that seems to lay the blame for America's problems at the doorstep of rock music.

Also in 1985, four women who were married to key figures in the government, including Tipper Gore and Susan Baker, formed the Parents' Music Resource Center (PMRC), which advocated the voluntary labeling of records and videos. The PMRC did not attack all rock music, only music produced since 1970, and its leaders advocated giving parents more information and authority to decide what records their children could purchase and listen to. In September of that year, the Senate Commerce Committee held hearings on the problem of pornography in rock lyrics. Although no official consequences resulted, the music industry responded to the pressure by adopting a voluntary labeling program, which has not proven very successful.

At the same time, local and federal officials have been involved in a number of court cases that have charged rock groups (and record sellers) under obscenity laws. Local cities are increasingly trying to regulate the appearance of rock groups, and even the American Medical Association has recommended that doctors monitor children's tastes in music as a sign of psychological problems. For a fuller description of these attacks, see Martin and Segrave's *Anti-Rock* (1988) and *You Got a Right to Rock* (Rock and Roll Confidential, 1991).

Sources: Grossberg (1992), Martin and Segrave (1988), and Rock and Roll Confidential (1991).

At the other extreme, some critics argue that pleasure itself is a form of political resistance to the pressures of the dominant institutions and values of modern society. John Fiske (1989), a contemporary media critic, argues that the very fact that pleasure is derived from popular culture makes popular culture threatening to the status quo of the cultural mainstream. Fiske assumes that pleasure is always disruptive of social structures and cannot be controlled or regulated by them. Therefore, it is quite understandable why popular culture would always be the object of serious attack. And those attacks further prove that taking pleasure in popular culture is itself an act of resistance.

In between these two extremes are a number of positions that we need to briefly consider. Some people, especially feminist critics such as Janice Radway (1984), argue that women who consume serial narratives, such as soap operas and romance novels, are able to derive particular pleasures from texts that are in many ways oppressive to them. For example, the narrative of romance novels may reinforce images of weak women dominated by strong and powerful men. Radway's research demonstrates that pleasure goes beyond this dominating narrative. Radway found that regular readers of romance novels often interpret the narrative to give the woman more power in the relationship, and thus they construct a more pleasurable image for themselves of the role of women in contemporary life. She also found that for many of these women, the act of reading romance novels (sometimes more than a dozen novels a week) provided them with the only occasion for their own time, time when they were not responsible to other members of their family and to various domestic demands. In fact, Radway interprets this as a kind of resistance to the fact that women who do not work outside the home are constantly subject to the demands of others. By maintaining their right to enjoy romance reading, they refuse to define themselves as the object of other people's demands.

Another position argues that the political implications of pleasures can be understood only indirectly. Pleasure has to be judged in context. Consider Lawrence Grossberg's (1992, 1997) argument about the historical significance of the pleasures of rock-and-roll music. Grossberg argues that the pleasures of listening to rock-and-roll music are "empowering," that is, that they energize audience members and provide them with a sense that they can act in the world and accomplish something. To use a very specific example, Grossberg points to the apparent paradox of dancing to rock music. The more you dance, the more exhausted you become, the more you feel like dancing, and the more you can dance. The music actually generates an energy that keeps its audience going. These pleasures, this empowerment, however, have no direct political implications. What one does with the energy, with the feeling that some action is now possible, will be defined by the social context. Thus Grossberg argues that precisely because rock music is energizing, it can be used by conservative political forces as easily as by liberal political forces. Both Lee Atwater, head of the elder George Bush's first campaign for president and ex-chairman of the Republican National Party, and Bill Clinton, when he ran for president in 1992, mobilized the power of rock and roll to attempt to involve people in their political campaigns.[2]

## THE SOCIOLOGY OF CONSUMPTION

Consumption is a social activity; that is, it involves people doing a certain kind of work (buying and using media) in particular places, often with other people. Consequently, consumption is implicated in many different relations of power with others and with institutions. In this section, we will consider some of the contexts and consequences of the social nature of the activity of consuming media.

### The Geography of Media Consumption

Think of all the places you consume the media: in your room, in common spaces like a living room, in your car, in sports bars or music clubs, outdoors on the beach or by the pool or on the streets, in classrooms, as you walk through malls and department stores, at your workplace, in restaurants, in subways, trains, and buses, and in countless other places. Where you consume the media has an important influence on how you consume them, and it might also be said that the media themselves shape the geography of everyday life.

We can make some sense of this broad array of sites of consumption: Media are consumed in public spaces, private spaces, and transitional spaces. Another way of dividing these sites might be to differentiate between those places in which the media are the primary activity (movie theaters, for instance) and those places in which media are background

(Muzak and music videos in stores; see, for example, McCarthy, 2001, on television in public space).

A third aspect of the geography of consumption is whether the presence of a medium brings people together or sends them off into personal spaces. James Carey (1969) and Denis McQuail (2000) have called these differences *centripetal* and *centrifugal*. For example, movies can be thought of as having a centripetal force, because, in viewing a movie, the audience is brought together. The personal stereo has a more centrifugal impact, because it is used alone. The act of reading silently to oneself is always a solitary activity. Even if an entire class is told to read the same page in the textbook at the same time, they all do so individually. We should note that sometimes the force of a medium is largely the result of the technology itself (the personal stereo cannot easily be shared), whereas, at other times, the force is the result of how people use a particular technology (for example, when TV is viewed in a community center or when people read aloud to others).

The most important private space of media consumption is the home. It is in the home, for instance, that children first become introduced to media. Most people's first memories of the newspaper is seeing their parents read it. Television is in nearly every American home. Magazines and books for children are found in their homes. And video brings movies and special children's programs into the home.

The media technologies that first came into the home—the book, the phonograph, the radio, television—were thought to have a centripetal force within the private space of the home. That is, the family gathered around the medium; media use was a shared, communal activity. At one time, middle-class families read or made music together in their sitting room. Similarly, early phonographs and crystal set radios were found in American living rooms. Television, when it came along in the late 1940s and 1950s, replaced the radio as the central focus of family activities in living rooms. Today, "home theaters" are common. There are multiple reasons for these trends. First, the devices often were large and/or expensive, intended for such communal use. Second, such use legitimated the new technologies and helped to allay fears that their use would undercut traditional family relations. For instance, media historian Lynn Spigel (1992) has found the early advertising for television sets (on television and in magazines) often quite self-consciously created the image of the family gathered around the television set in the living room in order to encourage families to buy this new technology as a family activity.

In every case, as the technologies have become cheaper, smaller, more mobile, and more personal, their effects became more centrifugal. The transistor radio, for example, enabled teenagers in the 1950s to listen to their radio (and thus to rock and roll) in the privacy of their own bedrooms. And by the 1980s, more than three quarters of American households had more than one television set, so that children often had their own set to use.

It is also interesting to observe how over time, different media have become more or less appropriate to different spaces in the home. Increasingly, middle-class and upper-middle-class American families tend to locate the largest television set in a family room or playroom, which is differentiated from the living room where guests are entertained. But the main music system is likely to remain in the living room; there may be others in the playroom and in bedrooms. This distinction seems to be based on the assumption that music can serve as background, even for socializing, whereas television demands focused attention. As we shall see, this assumption is often false.

It is also important to recognize that the introduction of media technologies into the home has reshaped the geography of domestic space and life as well. Today, the use of large-screen televisions and sophisticated surround-sound stereo systems requires rooms typically larger than those designed for suburban homes. The proliferation of electronic media has resulted in new electrical codes and requirements for wiring houses. The introduction of a home computer usually requires power outlets and phone jacks (or cable connections) in close proximity, but it also raises questions of its proper space (in a quiet home office or bedroom or in a more open space where parents can monitor their children's use; see Cassidy, 2001). And some have speculated that putting small-screen televisions in the kitchen has led to the rebirth of "breakfast nooks" and "eat-in kitchens" in newer homes.[3] The availability of headphones for everything from televisions and stereos to electronic keyboards has made it less important to insulate the walls between rooms for sound.

It is surprising that when we think about the context of media consumption, we typically think about individuals consuming media in private places. Nonetheless, the fact of the matter is that an enormous part of actual media consumption takes place in public spaces. There are social rules regarding such consumption, which each of us has to learn about. (See Box 9.3, "TV in Public.") Have you ever taken a preschool child to a movie? They don't know the rules about keeping quiet, not standing up, not annoying the people around them. The ongoing debates about the noise levels of music played on car radios or boom boxes suggest that the rules of such public media consumption have not been socially agreed upon yet. Likewise, social rules are still being formed for cell phone use in public as well as public computer use. And now that TVs and DVD players are found in minivans and SUVs (sport utility vehicles), there are issues if content played on those TVs is visible outside the vehicle and if that content is inappropriate for the public context (for example, R-rated or pornographic content).

---

**BOX 9.3**

**TV in Public**

At some time, most of us have watched television in public spaces. Communication researcher Dafna Lemish (1982) conducted a participant observation study of the rules involved in watching television in public areas. She wanted to know what common knowledge people have about "how" to watch television in public: Should you talk to the person sitting next to you in the bar? Who has the right to change the channel? What are the guidelines or expectations about what can be done when watching television in public?

Lemish describes four rules of public viewing. She inferred such rules by observing hundreds of people viewing television in a variety of public places.

1. *A public viewer of television adjusts to the setting.* Clearly, shouting out advice to the football coach while watching a game in a bar was considered acceptable behavior, but it wouldn't be acceptable while watching the TV at a Sears store. Lemish noted that viewers adapted their behavior from public setting to public setting. This was the most obvious of all the rules she observed.

2. *A public viewer of television adjusts to other viewers.* Lemish observed television viewers trying to fit in to the social group watching television in any given setting. Fitting in involved being open for talking if other people in the group were talking about the

*(Continued)*

---

277

(Continued)

program; keeping a safe and civil distance from other viewers (not encroaching on other people's space); and giving angry looks or even a "shush" to people talking too loudly in a group when the rest of the group was trying to watch the set.

3. *A public viewer adjusts to the television set.* Lemish observed that people walking by the television set would nod toward it or comment on the program; she watched viewers act as though the TV set itself was what she called a "communicative partner and not merely a physical object":

> For example, viewers would rarely leave the viewing area in the middle of a segment. While it could be argued simply that viewers were involved in the program or that they were showing respect for other viewers, this observer could not avoid the impression that viewers acted as if leaving in the middle was rude and inconsiderate. (pp. 765–766)

4. *A public viewer of television is open for television-related social interaction.* In fact, the "most observable and consistent aspect of the public context for viewing was the role television served in the initiation and sustaining of social interactions among participants" (p. 767). Indeed, television in public places most often served the function of allowing strangers to find a common topic—the program—to talk about, to initiate conversations that might have seemed awkward or even impossible without the presence of the television. People seem to expect that when watching television in a public place, it is acceptable for other viewers to approach them and talk about the show. In short, the act of watching TV was a public activity.

We can distinguish several different forms of public spaces for media consumption. Some spaces or buildings are designed for media consumption or for activities in which media consumption is an integral part. The best examples are movie theaters, television and music bars, and concert venues. The activities that take place within such spaces often change with new technologies. Large-screen televisions and music videos have invaded bars and dance clubs and changed the ways people act in these spaces. Similarly, the invention of DiamondVision (those huge television screens used in arenas during concerts and sports events) has made possible larger audiences, and changed the ways people attend to concerts or games watching the screen and the field alternatively (Siegel, 2002).

In some spaces, the media are intentionally provided as background to another sort of activity. The use of Muzak in a variety of public spaces—including workplaces—is a good example. Or consider the multiple television sets in department stores; these are to market the sets themselves, to baby-sit the children of shopping parents, to distract bored shoppers, and to advertise new products or sales. Television has invaded professional spaces: Chris Whittle, the creator of Channel One (a commercial news program for schools), also created first magazines and then video channels for doctors' and dentists' offices; and CNN has a separate Airport News Network, with CNN programming but also with airtime sold to advertisers seeking the largely upscale air travel market. Televisions have also made appearances in McDonald's restaurants and in hotel elevators.

The media also exist in spaces that are between public and private: streets, transportation, parks, and so on. Our favorite: Using the digital readout on gasoline pumps to advertise hotdogs and soft drinks for sale inside the service station. In fact, the presence of the media in such transitional places fundamentally transforms the nature of these spaces. The existence of car radios and transistor radios in the 1940s and 1950s turned street corners and drive-ins into sites for a new type of youth culture that was organized around music. An even more striking example took place in the early 1990s in Eastern Europe, when radios were placed in apartment windows; people gathered in the streets to listen to the constant stream of revolutionary news. A different transformation has been achieved by the personal stereo, which has converted the public nature of transitional spaces into private, isolated bubbles of media consumption.

Indeed, every space and every place of everyday life is now a media space; no place is free of media messages and their complex patterns of consumption. The complexity of media consumption, however, owes much to the multiple forms of social relationships that define and shape media consumption.

## Media Consumption and Social Relations

One of the most common observations that people have made about the use of media in everyday life is that the media often function

279

in conjunction with other activities and social relationships. Consider what you do when you are consuming media products. Maybe the television is on and you are . . . eating, sleeping, talking, doing homework, reading, exercising, cooking, making out, writing letters, doing chores, or talking on the phone. Or music is playing and you are drinking, dancing, talking, or watching television. Clearly, what you are doing while consuming media products changes how you consume those products. The average viewer is unable to recall more than one or two stories from a newscast as little as a half hour after viewing; this finding is in part explained by the fact that TV watching is usually a secondary activity; that is, when we are watching TV, we are most often doing something else as well (see, for example, Robinson & Levy, 1986).

Our experience of consuming media products depends on whether that consumption is our primary activity or a secondary activity, and it depends as well on what other activities we are engaging in, how invested we are in the different activities, and how much the different activities compete with one another. For example, while we drive, we can pay attention to the music on the radio; while we read, we may not be listening carefully.

Sometimes producers of media products count on our doing several activities at once, and they may attempt to structure the media product in such a way as to enable us to do so. CD players that play multiple disks allow us to listen to music for hours at a time.

Equally important to the context of activities associated with media consumption are the social relationships that surround particular acts of media consumption. Sometimes, we do indeed consume media alone. But most of the time, there are other people present (if not involved) with us. Consider four sets of social relations: familial, peer group, anonymous, and institutional. The first two are easily pictured, although their relationships to media consumption are the most complex. So let's consider first anonymous and institutional social relations and media consumption.

### Anonymous Social Relations

As we consider media consumption in the context of anonymous social relations, we mean all of those occasions that involve the presence of strangers, such as viewing television in public places such as bars, going to concerts or dance clubs, or reading a newspaper on a bus or subway. Typically, there are social rules that govern how we interact with those around us and with the media product. For instance, it is considered rude in our culture, or at least aggressive, to read over another person's shoulder or to get up and change TV channels in a public setting. In some music clubs, the space of each dancing couple has to be respected; at others, that space is intentionally and violently violated. Any music fan knows what is appropriate at a particular kind of concert. The presence of other people is often crucial to defining the setting and hence the activity of media consumption, despite the fact that the relationships are totally impersonal. It's clear, too, that the response of others to the media message may have an impact on how we perceive the message: For example, a comedy movie may be funnier in a theater when everyone is laughing than if we watch it on the VCR at home. Likewise, the cult film *The Rocky Horror Picture Show* works much better in a theater with the audience acting out scenes and shouting at the screen than it does if one is alone in one's living room watching it.

## Institutional Relationships

Institutional relationships are the contexts of media consumption in which we are aware of the presence of other people who have power over us. Such hierarchical relations can be found at school with the teacher, at work with the boss, at church with the preacher, or in any organization with an official representative present. Such relationships are often quite constrained and uncomfortable: The social relationship makes us self-conscious. Do you giggle at the wrong places? Are you too exuberant in your enjoyment? Are you embarrassed by the sexuality of your own response? We see examples of this when we have occasions to play popular music in our classes. Students are often unsure how to respond. Many will sit through quite danceable tunes not even nodding a head or tapping a foot, looking much like they were trying to be serious and scholarly.

## Media in the Family

As we have said, the family is an important media context; it is within the family that tastes about media products and notions of appropriate behavior with media are formed. Researchers studying the socializing influences of the media find that adolescent children of parents who are well informed and interested in public affairs are themselves better informed and more interested in public affairs than others of their age (Morley, 1986). This finding should not come as a surprise: These young people have been raised in homes with information-rich media environments (those, for example, with daily newspapers, news magazines, and lots of books), and they likely have modeled their parents' attitudes, values (that keeping up with the world is important), and behaviors (reading and paying attention to news). Furthermore, and also not surprisingly, researchers observing families' use of media in the home, specifically television use, have found that the relationships of *power* within the family are reproduced and structure the social relationships of media consumption in the home. In many households, the father often controls the remote control device. The older siblings in the household probably control what the kids will watch. Typically, the male's choice of program will dominate. (See Box 9.4, "Gender and Power in TV Watching.")

---

**BOX 9.4**

**Gender and Power in TV Watching**

British communication researcher David Morley's (1986) observations of men and women watching television led him to note that *how* they watch says a great deal about power relations in families:

> Men and women offer clearly contrasting accounts of their viewing habits—in terms of their differential power to choose what they view, how much they view, their viewing styles, and their choice of particular viewing material. However, I am not suggesting that these empirical differences are attributes of their essential biological characteristics as men and women. Rather, I am trying to argue that these differences are the effects of the particular social roles that these men and women occupy within the home. Moreover, . . . this sample primarily consists of lower middle-class and working-class nuclear families (all of whom are white) and I am not suggesting that the particular pattern of gender relations within the home found here (with all the consequences which that pattern has for viewing behavior) would necessarily be replicated either in nuclear families from a different class or ethnic background, or in households of different types with the same class and ethnic

backgrounds. Rather it is always a case of how gender relations interact with, and are formed differently within, these different contexts.

However, aside from these qualifications, there is one fundamental point which needs to be made concerning the basically different positioning of men and women within the domestic sphere. . . . The essential point here is that the dominant model of gender relations within this society (and certainly within that sub-section of it represented in my sample) is one in which the home is primarily defined for men as a site of leisure—in distinction to the "industrial time" of their employment outside the home—while the home is primarily defined for women as a sphere of work (whether or not they also work outside the home). This simply means that in investigating television viewing in the home, one is by definition investigating something which men are better placed to do wholeheartedly, and which women seem only to be able to do distractedly and guiltily, because of their continuing sense of their domestic responsibilities. Moreover, this differential positioning is given a greater significance as the home becomes increasingly defined as the "proper" sphere of leisure, with the decline of public forms of entertainment and the growth of home-based leisure technologies such as video, etc. . . .

Masculine power is evident in a number of the families as the ultimate determinant on occasions of conflict over viewing choices. . . . More crudely, it is even more apparent in the case of those families who have an automatic control device. None of the women in any of the families use the automatic control device regularly. A number of them complain that their husbands use the control device obsessively, channel flicking across programs when their wives are trying to watch something else. Characteristically, the control device is the symbolic possession of the father (or of the son, in the father's absence) which sits "on the arm of Daddy's chair" and is used almost exclusively by him. It is a highly visible symbol of condensed power relations. (pp. 6–8)

Source: Copyright ©1986 from *Gender and Power in TV Watching* by David Morley. Reproduced by permission of Routledge/Taylor & Francis Books, Inc.

## Peers and Media Use

Even at home, you may be consuming media with people other than your family. Whether you go to a movie on a date or with friends, whether you watch *Gilmore Girls* with your roommate, whether you watch *American Idol* in a common lounge with fellow students, or whether you bring your best friend into your bedroom to hear the latest music and to learn the latest dance steps, peer relationships among children and young adults provide a major set of social relationships surrounding media consumption.

Research on adolescents (Morley, 1992; Press, 1991) has found that in questions of style—such as what to wear, how to style your hair, what media to watch, read, and listen to—peers are more important than family for most adolescents. In many cases, adolescents define their taste in relation to media, and, on the basis of media preferences, they distinguish their friends or peers from other peer groups. Think back to your high school. Can you remember the different cliques in your school? How did they dress? What music did they listen to? Did they ever socialize with one another? Numerous teenage movies, such as *Mean Girls, American Pie, Heathers,* or even *Clueless,* are based on these different peer group structures and the role that media consumption and style play in identifying adolescent subcultures.

These differences in social relationships and activities surrounding media consumption are not the same for all people. They vary along a number of dimensions: There are significant differences across the age span from childhood to senior citizenship. Clearly, peer groups are more important to children and adolescents; older people tend to spend more time with the media by themselves or with one other person. These relationships also vary by social class, gender, race, and nationality. According to research by David Morley (1992) in Great Britain and Andrea Press (1991) in the United States, working-class family TV viewing tends to be more hierarchically structured than does middle-class family viewing.

## Fans, Fashion, and Subcultures

When some individuals in the audience identify themselves with the media product, a particular media star, or a particular style depicted in the media, they can be thought of as fans or as followers of media fads or fashions. No one is a fan of all the media products they consume, for being a fan entails a different sort of commitment, a different degree of investment in the media product. Fans use particular media products or celebrities to define their own identity. Fandom is a matter of degree: For some, it just means buying every single live Pearl Jam album or buying an album from the Dave Matthews Band as soon it comes on the market, reading articles about these celebrities, and sharing the taste publicly. For others, fandom can become a matter of style, as they imitate the celebrity. For yet others, fandom defines a major part of their identity and a major activity of their life. The hip-hop subculture, focused on music and clothing style, is one example.

Fandom can bring members of the audience together to celebrate their interest in some media star or product; in this way, fandom relates to a peer group. A whole collection of activities can be involved in being a fan: fan clubs, fanzines, and conventions. Some fan clubs go on long past the death of their celebrity: consider, for example, Elvis Presley fans. Gilbert Rodman (1996) has pointed out that Elvis is far more popular, and is making much more money, dead than he ever did alive.

During the 1940s and 1950s, movie magazines were popular vehicles for indulging fans' interest in stars. Since the 1970s, mainstream magazines such as *People* and *Us* as well as television shows such as *Entertainment Tonight* and *Extra* have joined in. These media outlets offer opportunities for audiences to follow the lives of their favorite stars. The talk show circuit of morning news shows and the late night talk shows offer opportunities both to create fans for budding stars and to feed the frenzy of fans. In a slightly different way, music magazines are available for the different sorts of fans within popular music.

The growing importance of celebrity and fandom as a part of people's identity is very much the result of media since 1900. In fact, it is only in the twentieth century that people began to find their images of heroes in the media. According to Leo Lowenthal (1961), who studied biographies appearing in American magazines from the 1800s to the 1930s, there was a major shift in the kinds of idols or celebrities in American popular culture, from *idols of production* to *idols of consumption* during this period. In the 1800s and early 1900s, most magazine biographies celebrated famous men of business, such as John D. Rockefeller, the founder of Standard Oil Company, or Andrew Carnegie of U.S. Steel. By the 1930s, after the rise of the movie and radio industries and the development of public relations experts, there was a shift in the types of people who became celebrities and heroes in popular culture. These new idols of consumption were people involved in various aspects of American entertainment and sports: movie stars such as Charlie Chaplin and Mary Pickford, radio stars such as George Burns and Gracie Allen, bandleaders such as Jimmy and Tommy Dorsey, and baseball players such as Babe Ruth. Long before there was Jennifer Aniston and Brad Pitt, there was Mary Pickford and Douglas Fairbanks, whose marriage and divorce riveted the nation. Long before people mourned the deaths of John Lennon or

Kurt Cobain, Americans cried at the unexpected death of Rudolph Valentino.

The transformation of the hero figures in American culture was not accidental. It depended to a large extent on the development of an industry designed to promote the media and to create fans. The 1930s and 1940s were the heyday of the Hollywood studio system, where stars were under contract with a single studio, such as MGM or Warner Brothers. The studio "made" stars not only by featuring them in films but also by using the studio's publicity agents to assure that the stars appeared in newspaper gossip columns, in magazine feature articles, and on radio shows.

The Hollywood system of today is far different. Stars no longer are under contract with studios, and publicity is handled by stars' own agents. The process of producing the seemingly endless amount of information about media stars and the film and television industry requires an industry of its own; publicists, creative managers, public relations specialists, and a variety of tabloid and other magazines are required to feed fans' interests. Although media producers may not be able to create stars as successfully as they have in the past, they are quick to exploit them when they arise. Most major stars are handled by a small number of major firms, such as Creative Artists Agency (CAA), Music Corporation of America (MCA), and the William Morris Agency.

American presidential politics has followed a similar track in the same period. Until about 1960, the two major parties basically ran presidential campaigns. Since then, candidates have assembled their own campaign teams, complete with publicity agents, marketing and fund-raising experts, and pollsters, to compete in party primaries. Although they still need the party nomination, the campaigns are their own operation, not the party's.

Fans can also be fans of particular objects or styles. For example, over the years, the media promoted such unpredictable successes as coonskin caps, Hula Hoops, and pet rocks. Also, stars' "styles" of dressing and talking have started fashion trends. For example, hip-hop singer/producer/personality Sean "P. Diddy" Combs bootstrapped a music career into clothing design, and his Sean John fashion line now grosses several hundred million dollars a year worldwide.

Although almost all of us have been caught up in various popular fads and been fans of some popular culture, for most of us, that is as far as it goes. But sometimes groups of youths have taken their relationship to popular culture and style one step further: They use their taste to define and mark their primary and most visible identity. What does this mean? A member of a *subculture* visibly displays his or her identification with the icon of popular culture. This presentation of self defines the fan's identity. Such identities are often disapproved of by parents, teachers, the media, the government, and sometimes even other youth. The punk, skateboard, and biker subcultures are easy to identify because of their relationship to popular culture, for example. (Notice that the yuppies were never a subculture in this sense, because a yuppie is not an identity that people took on for themselves and visibly wore in the face of social ostracism. Similarly, Trekkers are not a subculture, although they may occasionally wear their identity visibly—such as when they dress up in costumes for conventions—because the identity of being a Trekker is not always present for its owner—Trekkers have other lives and take on other social identities.)

Society's response to youth subcultures—whenever they are perceived as a potential threat to mainstream middle-class youth—takes the form of a moral panic. The presence of the subculture becomes seen as a sign of moral decay and as a threat to the stability of the society itself. In the United States, teenage and motorcycle gangs since the 1950s have been the most frequent and troublesome subcultures. Even in the 1990s, the question of gangs, gang membership, and gang colors still evoked powerful and often violent reactions across the country, as movies such as *Colors* and *Boyz 'n the Hood* represent and in some cases provoke.

Presumably, anyone can become a member of a subculture: If you have the right taste, if you look right, if you talk and behave according to the right codes, you too can be a punk or a homeboy or a surfer. But, obviously, not everyone chooses to take on such a visible cultural identity, because it is usually seen not only as an act of rebellion but as an act of delinquency as well.

Sociologists argue that youth who participate in subcultures appropriate cultural products to construct an identity as an attempt to confront the contradictions they feel in their own lives. For example, poor kids might feel a real conflict between the optimistic promise of their youthfulness and the sense of hopelessness in which their economic position places them. Their style, then, becomes a sort of magical solution to the problem: The 1960s "mods" style (which copied Italian "modern" fashion) signaled British working-class youth's desire to be upwardly mobile when that was almost impossible. Similarly, according to British cultural critic Dick Hebdige (1980), the late 1970s punk style in Britain and the United States represented youthful attempts to break down the hypocrisy of contemporary society by attacking its cultural codes. (See Box 9.5, "Dick Hebdige on Punks.")

---

**BOX 9.5**

**Dick Hebdige on Punks**

British media sociologist Dick Hebdige (1980) wrote one of the classic interpretations of punk subculture. Here are a few excerpts:

The most unremarkable and inappropriate items—a pin, a plastic clothes peg, a television component, a razor blade, a tampon—could be brought within the province of punk (un)fashion. Anything within or without reason could be turned into part of what Vivien Westwood called "confrontation dressing" so long as the rupture between "natural" and constructed context was clearly visible.

Objects borrowed from the most sordid of contexts found a place in the punks' ensembles: lavatory chains were draped in graceful arcs across chests encased in plastic bin-liners [garbage bags]. Safety pins were taken out of their domestic "utility" context and worn as gruesome ornaments through the cheek, ear or lips . . . "Cheap" trashy fabrics (PVC, plastic, lurex, etc.) in vulgar designs (e.g., mock leopard skin) and "nasty" colours, long discarded by the quality end of the fashion industry as obsolete kitsch, were salvaged by the punks and turned into garments . . . which offered self-conscious commentaries of the notions of modernity and taste. Conventional ideas of prettiness were jettisoned along with traditional feminine lore of cosmetics. Contrary to the advice of every women's magazine, make-up for both boys and girls was worn to be seen. . . . The perverse and abnormal were valued intrinsically. In particular, the illicit iconography of sexual fetishism was used to predictable effect. . . .

Of course, punk did more than upset the wardrobe. It undermined every relevant discourse. Thus dancing, usually an involving and expressive medium in British rock and mainstream pop cultures, was turned into a dumb show of bland robotics. . . .

The music was similarly distinguished from mainstream rock and pop. It was uniformly basic and direct in its appeal, whether through intention or lack of expertise. . . . Johnny Rotten succinctly defined punk's position on harmonics: "We're into chaos, not music." (pp. 107–109)

The safety pins and bin liners signified a relative material poverty which was either directly experienced and exaggerated or sympathetically assumed, and which in turn was made to stand for the spiritual paucity of everyday

---

life. . . . We could go further and say that even if the poverty was being parodied, the wit was undeniably barbed; that beneath the clownish make-up there lurked the unaccepted and disfigured face of capitalism; that beyond the horror circus antics a divided and unequal society was being eloquently condemned. However, if we were to go further still and describe punk music as the "sound of the Westway," or the pogo as the "high rise leap," or to talk of bondage as reflecting the narrow options of working-class youth, we would be treading on less certain ground. Such readings are both too literal and too conjectural. They are extrapolations from the subculture's own prodigious rhetoric, and rhetoric is not self-explanatory; it may say what it means but it does not necessarily "mean" what it "says." . . .

The punk subculture, like every other youth culture, was constituted in a series of spectacular transformations of a whole range of commodities, values, common-sense attitudes, etc. It was through these adapted forms that certain sections of predominantly working-class youth were able to restate their opposition to dominant values and institutions. However, when we close in on specific items, we immediately encounter problems. What, for instance, was the swastika being used to signify? (pp. 115–116)

The punk ensembles . . . did not so much magically resolve experienced contradictions as *represent* the experience of contradiction itself in the form of visual puns (bondage, the ripped tee-shirt, etc.). (p. 121)

## The Availability of Media Consumption

It is a common myth in U.S. society that media consumption is equally available to all people: Because we have a "free marketplace" of media products, therefore everyone can consume—or so we like to think. This assumption underlies the media institutions' defense of the current system of media production ("We give the people what they want"); it also underlies the process that makes the act of consumption into a site of resistance. Some feminists have criticized the position that consumption always involves resistance because it ignores the fact that consumption itself is a form of labor; it is something that some people (namely, women) have to do for the family. Moreover, of course, not everyone can afford to consume the products they desire.

There are two ways in which this inequality is structured: by the distribution of economic power or capital and by the distribution of cultural capital. Media consumption takes money and time; leisure time is a luxury that is simply not available to the poor, the homeless, or people that have to work more than one job to subsist. In addition, some media are more expensive than others, and they are often outside the practical reach of some significant portions of the population. These sorts of considerations have given rise to policy discussions about the media rich and media poor, both in this country and around the world. These debates have been especially prominent around the Internet: Are we creating a digital divide? As the United States invests more money in ever more expensive media technologies, are we increasing the gap and condemning the media poor to an ever-downward spiraling social position? This gap in the media haves and have-nots often cuts according to economic status (rich, poor), race, and gender. Though by now roughly equal numbers of men and women use the Internet, African Americans are less likely to go online than Whites, even at equivalent income levels (Lenhart, 2003).

The second way in which the inequality of media consumption is structured is by what the French sociologist Pierre Bourdieu (1984) has called "the unequal distribution of cultural capital." *Cultural capital* refers to the knowledge and sensibility that enables one to comprehend and appreciate particular cultural products. For example, Bourdieu argues that people may not enjoy high art (such as classical music, art films, avant-garde writing) because they either do not have the knowledge necessary to understand what is going on or because they do not share the aesthetic outlook embodied in such cultural traditions. Even aside from considerations of art, many media products and technologies require specific knowledge or cultural capital. Take, for instance, computers. The computer revolution is occurring with a number of social inequalities that cannot be explained in purely economic terms; for example, women have generally been slower than men to adopt and become expert with computers. Partly this was due to the ways that computers were marketed. As they began to be seen as home appliances (as opposed to office machines), advertising for computers targeted women much more (Cassidy, 2001).

Critics have also pointed out differences in how different populations use the medium. For example, though women and men use the Internet in generally equal numbers, men focus on news and financial information while women tend to use the Internet for social contacts, health or religious information, or games. Leslie Regan Shade (2004) points out, "There are tensions in gender differences, whereby women are using the Internet to reinforce their private lives and men are using the Internet for engaging in the public sphere" (p. 63). Differences in use are also evident across racial categories, with certain groups more likely to engage in certain activities online than others. For example, African Americans are more likely to seek religious information online or download music than Whites, but less likely to purchase items online or seek financial information (Madden, 2003).

Sometimes cultural capital is not just a question of knowledge or expertise, but a matter of shared assumptions, shared values about the nature and function of cultural consumption. For example, Bourdieu (1984) argues that the middle class, with its formal educational training (in the United States, typically a college education), judges cultural products in terms of aesthetic values (such as enlightening the human condition), whereas the working class tends to demand that culture embody strong moral principles as well as provide entertainment. Responding to the above findings that minorities such as African Americans tend to engage in entertainment activities online rather than informational activities (such as stocks, weather, or retail information), Lisa Nakamura (2004) argues that such a distinction is a particular cultural valuing of these activities and that for minority populations so-called entertainment activities may provide more relevant cultural information for them than any stock report (p. 75).

It is not surprising to find that media consumption follows the patterns of the distribution of economic and cultural capital in the country. Public broadcasting tends to attract richer, more highly educated, and older audiences than do the commercial networks. This is not a judgment about the quality of public broadcasting products or commercial television products. It is a description of the fact that consumption itself is socially determined even as it helps to determine and shape everyday life and our place in the social structure.

This chapter has been a discussion of what we do with the media and theories of what the media do *for* us. Next, we turn to the controversial question of what media do *to* us.

## NOTES

1. Communication scholars John Stevens and William Porter (1973, p. 11) once quipped that audience research asking people what they liked to watch or read

was like asking Chinese villagers if they liked rice. They would of course like rice, since they ate it every day and had little awareness of what other options were available.

2. During the 1992 political campaign, too, many commentators noted that Clinton's appearances on MTV, both with and without his saxophone, were an indication of his sophistication with the media, because they allowed him access to an important bloc of potential voters, unmediated by the sharp questioners he faced on network newscast appearances.

3. Similarly, most college dormitories required rewiring in the 1980s because of increased student power consumption—for music systems, computers, and televisions, which earlier generations of students did not own in such numbers.

## SUGGESTED READINGS

Ang, I. (1985). *Watching* Dallas: *Soap opera and the melodramatic imagination* (D. Couling, Trans.). New York: Methuen.

Ang, I. (1991). *Desperately seeking the audience.* New York: Routledge.

Ang, I. (1995). *Living room wars: Rethinking media audiences for a postmodern world.* New York: Routledge.

Brunsdon, C., & Morley, D. (1978). *Everyday television: Nationwide.* London: British Film Institute.

Grossberg, L. (1992). *We gotta get out of this place: Popular conservatism and postmodern culture.* New York: Routledge.

Hay, J., Grossberg, L., & Wartella, E. (Eds.). (1996). *The audience and its landscapes.* Boulder, CO: Westview.

Hebdige, D. (1980). *Subculture: The meaning of style.* New York: Methuen.

Liebes, T., & Katz, E. (1990). *The export of meaning: Cross-cultural readings of* Dallas. New York: Oxford University Press.

McCarthy, A. (2001). *Ambient television: Visual culture and public space.* Durham, NC: Duke University Press.

McQuail, D. (2000). *Mass communication theory: An introduction* (4th ed.). Thousand Oaks, CA: Sage.

Radway, J. (1984). *Reading the romance: Women, patriarchy, and popular literature.* Chapel Hill: University of North Carolina Press.

Spigel, L. (1992). *Make room for TV: Television and the family idea in postwar America.* Chicago: University of Chicago Press.

# Media and Behavior | 10

W hat do mass media do to us? What effects do they have on how we act? In the spring of 2003, a group of overweight young people sued McDonald's; the company was accused of making the plaintiffs obese. A year later, the American Psychological Association (APA) issues a report saying that advertising and marketing of a variety of super-sized, heavily sugared, and fat-laden products was indeed contributing to an obesity "epidemic" in the United States. Do "the media" make us fat?

As media researcher Joseph Klapper argued as long ago as 1960, the effects of mass media are not so easily provable. Klapper's position, which is often called the *limited effects model* of media influence, suggests that when (and if) media affect behavior, they do so through a web of other influencing factors, such as personality characteristics, social situations, and general climates of opinion and culture. Untangling this web of influence has occupied many researchers for years.

Nowhere is there more debate than in the realm of behavior about the power of the media to influence their audience. Since the beginning of media studies, some analysts have held that media strongly and directly affect the audience's behavior; others have argued for the more limited influence of media on behavior.

In the 1992 presidential campaign, Vice President Dan Quayle attacked the TV program *Murphy Brown* because the title character had a child out of wedlock. Quayle assailed the program as an attack on "family values" and intimated that Murphy served as a role model encouraging unmarried women to have babies. Quayle assumed that viewers would model—imitate—what he saw as an undesirable behavior. Behavior—what people do—has always been the most important concern society has about mediamaking. Behavior *matters,* and it is concrete, observable, and measurable. For example, a television commercial may try to convince you that a Mercedes-Benz is a reliable, even loyal, automobile. But, in a very real sense, Mercedes-Benz and its ad agency really do not care whether you believe this or not. What they care about is that you buy *a Mercedes-Benz car*—that you, in other words, *behave* in a certain way. Likewise, a politician calculates the impact of a televised speech in terms of how it will affect people's vote, another important behavior. By far the most significant debates about media's behavioral effects are about the effects of violence and sexuality in the media, most pointedly the effects on children. In this chapter, we will first overview theories of media effects on behavior, and then, second, plunge into the debates over violence and sexuality.

As each electronic medium was developing over the past hundred years, virtually the first question the public asked about it—and the first source of controversy—was how the medium would influence behavior (Wartella & Reeves, 1985). For example, when movies developed as a mass medium in the 1920s, people feared that movies would lead youth to "lewd and licentious" behavior; did movies lead teenagers to engage in sexual conduct that earlier generations had not? When television came along a generation later, people wondered whether television turned adolescents into "juvenile delinquents." They asked what effect the violent television shows, movies, and comic books of the 1950s had on the rise of aggressive behavior in children.

And just as the public raised concerns about the behavioral influences of each new media technology, social scientists have been studying the effects of media on behavior throughout the twentieth century; behavior has been a very active area of communication research: It has attracted psychologists, sociologists, and other social scientists to the communications field. For instance, in the late 1920s, an eminent group of social scientists was commissioned, in what came to be known as the Payne Fund studies, to examine film's effects on youth. One of the most widely cited volumes in this research was Herbert Blumer's (1932) *Movies and Conduct.* The 12 Payne Fund volumes stand as a landmark in the research on the behavioral effects of media. (See Box 10.1, "The Payne Fund.")

---

**BOX 10.1**

**The Payne Fund**

A history of research on children and media (Wartella & Reeves, 1985) recalls the pioneering "Payne Fund" studies this way:

> The 1933 Payne Fund studies—twelve volumes of research conducted by the most prominent psychologists, sociologists, and educators of the time—represent a detailed look at the effects of film on such diverse topics as sleep patterns, knowledge about foreign cultures, attitudes about violence, and delinquent behavior. These studies have not been cited much in the last 25 years, despite the fact that they represent a research enterprise comparable to the 1972 Surgeon General's Committee on Television and Violence. But at the time the Payne studies generated significant press attention, academic review, and critical comment, and were the basis of recommendations for government action on what the authors believed were significant social problems.
>
> A major conclusion of the report was that the same film would affect children different depending on the child's age, sex, predispositions, perceptions, social environment, past experiences, and parental influences. In this sense, the report was similar to the most current summaries of research about children and television. Further, the effects were said to be conditional on whether the criterion concerns were behaviors, attitudes, emotions, or knowledge about people and events. For example, Blumer's study of *Movies, Delinquency and Crime* (1933) concluded that the effects of film on criminal behavior may be diametrically opposed, depending on the diversity of themes presented and the social milieu, attitudes, and interests of the observer.
>
> Although Blumer's contingencies were largely sociological, the conclusions of several other researchers involved affective and psychological differences. Dysinger and Ruckmick (*The Emotional Responses of Children to the Motion Picture Situation,* New York: Macmillan, 1933) studied emotional reactions and concluded, based on a physiologic measure, that children varied widely in emotional stimulation. They suggested that age differences in response were caused by varied abilities to comprehend information on the screen. For example, young children tended not to understand the romantic scenes to which adolescents responded enthusiastically. . . . [Also], the psychologists and educators on the Payne committee studied ideas and factual learning, social attitudes, emotions, sleep patterns, and moral development. (pp. 120–121)

---

Note: For an overview of the Payne Fund studies, see Charters (1933).

---

## BEHAVIORAL EFFECTS

Much of the research done on the behavioral effects of the media relies on the transmission model of communication that we outlined in Chapter 1. Harold Lasswell's (1948) question is exemplary here: *"Who says what to whom in what channel and with what effect?"* As we pointed out in Chapter 1, the ritual and transmission models each asks its own particular range of questions and has its own set of assumptions. Since we argue that it is fundamental to this book to hold both models in mind at once, it is necessary to recognize the different sorts of questions about behavioral effects that the cultural model would raise. Indeed, it is in the area of behavioral effects research that the two models have historically been most at odds. It could be argued that despite its long history and plethora of studies, the field of media effects research would be much richer if it did see the two models as complementary.

### Types of Effects

To understand how media make behaviors, we need to clarify a few things about behavioral effects, for effects may be of very different sorts. Effects are not just behavioral. For example, social psychologists studying persuasion usually divide attitudes into three components: the *cognitive* (the intellectual or knowledge) component, the *affective* (the emotional or evaluative) component, and the *conative* (intentional or behavioral) component. A media message may have an impact on one of these components but not on others. You might see, for example, a commercial for a deodorant that convinces you that it stops wetness (a cognitive effect), but you may not buy that deodorant. Nonetheless, the whole premise in persuasion is that usually our behaviors are consistent with our existing cognitions and attitudes. We behave in some way, in ways that are consistent with what we believe to be appropriate.

Usually, the consequences or effects of media messages can be fairly easily separated into *intended* or *unintended* consequences. That is, the message's sender wants and expects a message to have a particular effect that is transparent. For example, a commercial maker's primary intention, one we may call *manifest* (open, overt), is to encourage the audience to buy a product. However, there may be important *latent* (hidden, covert) intended consequences as well: Why would Lexus or Mercedes or BMW advertise on prime-time TV when it's clear that the large majority of the audience could not afford to buy these luxury cars? Because the secondary aim of the advertiser, the latent intention, is to convince those people who can afford them that everyone desires them.

Perhaps historically, the most famous incident involving unintended consequences of a mass-mediated message was the 1938 CBS radio broadcast of the American Mercury Theater's dramatization of H. G. Wells's novel *The War of the Worlds*. Producer and actor Orson Welles' intention was to entertain, and he never dreamed he would promote a mass panic. (Though he did intend his production to be a Halloween prank; see Box 10.2, "The War of the Worlds.") Nonetheless, the episode raises several important ideas for us to keep in mind:

1. Messages may have unintended, and unanticipated, consequences.

2. Even when the vast majority of an audience is presumably unaffected by a message, given the extent or size of an audience and the vast amplificative power of media, a message may have important social consequences if even a few audience members are affected.

3. The episode reminds us that media impact may be evaluated on multiple criteria: We may assess a situation on its effect, or, conversely, on its effectiveness. *Effect* relates to the general impact of a message or series of messages; *effectiveness* evaluates whether a message or series accomplished the goal its producers intended.

---

**BOX 10.2**

**The War of the Worlds**

These are the opening paragraphs of a remarkable little book, Hadley Cantril's *The Invasion from Mars* (1940/1966):

At eight P.M. eastern standard time on the evening of October 30, 1938, Orson Welles, with an innocent little group of actors took his place before the microphone in a New York studio of the Columbia Broadcasting System. He carried with him Howard Koch's freely adapted version of H. G. Wells's imaginative novel, *War of the Worlds*. He also brought to the scene his

*(Continued)*

---

(Continued)

unusual dramatic talent. With script and talent the actors hoped to entertain their listeners for an hour with an incredible, old-fashioned story appropriate for Halloween.

Much to their surprise the actor learned that the series of news bulletins they had issued describing an invasion from Mars had been believed by thousands of people throughout the country. For a few horrible hours people from Maine to California thought that hideous monsters armed with death rays were destroying all armed resistance against them; that there was simply no escape from disaster; that the end of the world was near. Newspapers the following morning spoke of the "tidal wave of terror that swept the nation." It was clear that a panic of national proportions had occurred. The chairman of the Federal Communications Commission called the program "regrettable." (p. 3)

An estimated six million people heard the broadcast; probably fortunately, CBS's main competitor, NBC, was running a far more popular comedy-and-variety program at the same time. As Cantril notes, "Had the program enjoyed greater popularity, the panic might have been more widespread" (p. 56). Survey evidence suggests that upwards of a million people were upset by the broadcast.

The format of the broadcast was a "pretend" radio variety program, interrupted periodically by news reports detailing first the sighting by scientists of an explosion on Mars, then the landing of a spacecraft in New Jersey, then a journalist's eyewitness account of the havoc wreaked by the invaders. According to a survey by the American Institute of Public Opinion at Princeton, some 28% of the survey respondents who heard the broadcast took the news accounts to be real.

In retrospect, anyone listening to that broadcast today, or reading a transcript of it, is astonished that people found it to be real—the news network, many of the places mentioned in the broadcast are fictitious (others, however, were real); there were disclaimers at the beginning and middle of the broadcast, and Welles himself closes with the following:

This is Orson Welles, ladies and gentlemen, out of character to assure you that the *War of the Worlds* has no further significance than as the holiday offering it was intended to be. The Mercury Theatre's own radio version of dressing up in a sheet and jumping out of a bush and saying 'Boo!' (Cantril, 1940/1966, p. 42)

Cantril's research team found not only survey evidence that people believed the broadcast; telephone calls went up in several parts of the country, and in northern New Jersey, where the cataclysm supposedly was occurring, phone traffic was up 39% over a normal Sunday evening.

First, let us note that the large majority—almost three quarters by the best estimate—were not taken in by the broadcast. But by the best estimate as well, perhaps a million people were. *Why* were people taken in, and *who* was most likely to be?

Cantril suggests that the nature of radio listening (and the same is true today of television drama) had something to do with it; much listening is inattentive, and only when listeners heard journalists and witnesses in the fictional account screaming and panicked did they pay close attention—thus missing the disclaimers. Moreover, we need to recall that the broadcast occurred in 1938, as the world was edgy about world events. War would break out in Europe less than a year later. Radio then, as TV now, was viewed as a credible medium for fast-breaking "hard" news.

Who was, and who was not, likely to be taken in? Those more likely to be upset were *proximate* to the purported event—those in northern New Jersey and New York (the creatures were advancing on Manhattan). And "social categories" were used to explain credulity as well: Those of lower socioeconomic status and education were more likely to be duped. Cantril suggests that such people were less able to do "reality checking" for the broadcast.

We would ask readers to bear a couple of points in mind: First is that the majority of listeners were *not* adversely affected by the broadcast. Second is that, because of the vast amplificative power of the mass media, even a small minority, in percentage terms, can translate into hundreds of thousands, even millions.

Could it happen again? A good question, perhaps, but one hard to answer. On the negative, we would note that virtually every mass communicator in the country knows some details of the *War of the Worlds* panic and virtually all would be wary of any attempt to repeat the experience; further, much of the public knows of it too and would be wary as well. But, on the other side, Abraham Lincoln had it right 130 years ago when he said that "you can fool some of the people all of the time, and all of the people some of the time. . . ."

As communication theorist Denis McQuail (2000) notes, media may lead to a number of different kinds of changes. They may

1. Cause *intended* change (conversion)

2. Cause *unintended* change

3. Cause *minor* change, of, for example, form or intensity of response

4. *Facilitate* change

5. *Reinforce* what exists (no change)

6. *Prevent* change (p. 425)

The first three of these are fairly self-explanatory, but the last three bear some comment. To say that media messages may *facilitate* change is to argue that although other social forces are the prime cause of a change, media messages make the changes easier or faster. For example, few would argue that media coverage of the civil rights movement in the South in the early 1960s caused the members of Congress to pass the 1964 Civil Rights Act, but many have argued that this coverage facilitated the passage of the act. At the beginning of this chapter, we noted Klapper's (1960) limited effects model of communication influence, which states that other factors also influence behavior in addition to media. Klapper argued that these other factors significantly limited the media's influence. He also pointed out that the media's greatest strength was not in causing changes in individuals or society but in reinforcing the status quo. In other words, effects are not always about changes, but can be about preventing change or strengthening the current social order. In some views, reinforcement of the status quo and/or the prevention of change can also be thought of as a profound—perhaps *the* most significant—effect of mass communication.

Also, in term of types of effects, we need to think about behavior making on several different time scales. The first time scale is the frequency of exposure to the message:

1. Short-term message exposure occurs when you are exposed to a message once, such as when you watch a TV show. You are amused while you watch it, but you neither think about it nor act on it later.

2. Intermediate-term message exposure is exposure to a series of related messages, such as a product campaign or "social marketing" of antidrug messages or the United Way.

3. Long-term media message exposure occurs after many cumulative exposures to related messages over time. For example, the argument that TV violence leads to aggressive behavior, or that pornography leads to violence against women, is asserting that these effects occur after repeated exposures to similar messages over time.

Moreover, the effects of media on behavior can themselves be either *transitory* (lasting a short time, such as only during or shortly after exposure, as when you buy a new brand of toothpaste after seeing an ad for the new product), or *persistent*, lasting a long time.

Returning to our example of juvenile obesity, the media effect on an *individual* might be that advertising makes consumption of junk foods desirable, while at the same time, TV messages rarely promote good nutrition. Moreover, watching TV is a largely sedentary activity, and watching lots of it usually means that the viewer is not getting much exercise. The effect on the individual, then, is a combination of both *intended* consequences (the advertiser does, indeed, want us to consume the products) and *unintended* consequences (no one particularly *wants* us to get fat). Clearly, too, these consequences are long term, rather than immediate. To the extent that a great many people are influenced this way, we can speak of this being a *social* or *aggregate* effect, and, indeed, some critics have described an "obesity epidemic." Here we have an example of an effect at two different levels of analysis.

## Levels of Analysis

Social acts can occur at different social levels or levels of analysis. Although we are most comfortable thinking of behavior as something *people* do—the individual level of analysis—behavior has meaning at higher levels of analysis as well. Organizations, institutions, and societies all act. When Congress passes a law, it has acted. Media may have impacts on how organizations, institutions, and societies behave. The problem, however, is that it is not always easy, concrete, and evident to observe and assess how each of these higher levels behaves. Therefore, we account for social behavior in terms of how individuals in the social unit have acted.

For a bill to become a federal law, a majority of the members of the Senate and the House of Representatives must vote in favor of it, and the president must sign it. If the president does not sign the bill, it can still become law if two thirds of the members of both houses again vote for it. To account for the behavior of Congress, then, we look at the behavior of its individual members, and when they formed a majority in voting the bill up or down. The majority is an *aggregated* measure. We think of, and use, aggregated social measures all the time, as when we think of "the average American" or suggest that television has "caused" a decline in achievement test scores. However, a complete account of the "behavior of Congress" must note the existence of a minority as well, for when we talk about social aggregates, the non-majority behavior may well be more significant than the behavior of the majority. For example, the vast majority of the *War of the Worlds* listeners did not take the broadcast as news of an invasion from Mars; but the minority who did were sufficient to cause a mass panic. To hold to a limited effects model of communication influence is not to suggest that the consequences of the behavioral effects of mass media are themselves necessarily limited. In an election campaign, the vast majority of voters are uninfluenced by any single media message—a commercial, a candidate speech, a debate, or a candidate endorsement. But if the election is a close one (let's say that 49% are predisposed to vote for Candidate A and 49% for Candidate B), what happens at the margins—the potential impact of media messages on the remaining 2%—looms large indeed.

## Models of Behavior Making

To understand how media affect behavior, too, requires that we specify the *mechanisms* by which media may have effects. For the individual, the minimal model for behavioral effects assumes a stimulus, a receiver, and a response. This is the familiar stimulus-response model of the psychologist:

Stimulus Message → Individual Receiver → Reaction

This model is the first and most enduring model of media effects considered by media scholars. It is often called either the *magic bullet*, *hypodermic needle* or *direct effects* theory of media influence. This unelaborated model of media effects argues essentially that media messages directly influence audiences' behavior. It is this model that represents the underlying fear of critics of mass media during the first third of the past century, that is, that media messages can have a direct, irresistible influence on the mass of the audience.

Over the years, much media research has gone into elaborating and correcting this model. First, it was noted that different people responded differently to the same messages. This phenomenon led to the development of theories about individual differences in media effects on behavior, and the assertion that some people may be more susceptible to the influence of media messages. As long ago as the 1950s, communication scholars Elihu Katz and Paul Lazarsfeld (1955) posited that there are individual differences in media effects because some audience members selectively attend to and remember media messages. It is in part because of our selective attention that Klapper claims the reinforcement effect of media: People usually only attend to media messages that they agree with and tune out the rest. Drawing on Katz and Lazarsfeld's study, sociologists Melvin DeFleur and Sandra Ball-Rokeach (1975) add the *social categories* perspective, which holds that there are groups in the social world who tend to react to any particular media message in similar ways. Such groups may be characterized by age, sex, income level, or religious affiliation. DeFleur and Ball-Rokeach also offer the *social relations* perspective as another type of individual difference in response to media: For some members of the audience, the influence of media messages is dependent on an opinion leader who tends to shape a group's opinion or reaction to the message.

Since these researchers are working within the transmission perspective, they are primarily concerned with what media do to various audiences. The cultural perspective might ask what various audiences do with the media and what meanings they make of it—in other words, recognize that the audience themselves have some control over their own behavior. For example, in comparison with DeFleur and Ball-Rokeach's work, there is that of David Morley (1980). Basing his work on Stuart Hall's (1980) encoding/decoding model of communication (see Chapter 6), Morley sought to determine if audiences in different social categories (particularly class) decoded texts in a similar fashion: they did (see also Brundt, 1992).

## Theories of Behavior Making

Various theories also have been developed of *how* media influence people's behavior, in other words, how these models of influence work. Among the theories we want to describe here are social learning theory, theories about imitation/contagion, and theories of social reality as a mediator of the effects of media messages on audiences' behavior.

## Social Learning

In 1941, two psychologists, N. E. Miller and John Dollard, proposed that people can learn new behaviors through their observation of others' behaviors. They called their theory *social learning theory.* They argued that imitative learning occurred when people are motivated to act like others, when people can observe others performing the behavior to be imitated, and when such imitative learning is somehow reinforced. In short, they offered a traditional stimulus-response learning model; that is, in the presence of a modeled behavior (or stimulus), an observer if motivated will make copied or patterned acts (imitation) of the model's behavior (a response), and such responses are more likely to be learned when they are reinforced.

Miller and Dollard's notion of social learning, however, wasn't terribly helpful in understanding media effects, because their model still relied on adequate reinforcement to ensure that media audiences could learn to imitate a media actor's behavior. What mattered, then, was whether or not an imitated behavior was reinforced and whether such reinforcement occurred in the everyday life of the audience member. Thus the ability of the media to influence audience behavior was still thought to be dependent on who the audience member was and the various social relationships in which that person was involved. That is, media effects depended on the various theories about the audience described above.

However, by the early 1960s, social psychologist Albert Bandura (1965) offered a revised social learning theory or observational modeling theory, which is a more powerful theory to account for imitative or observational learning. Bandura argued that actors in the mass media (and he and his colleagues studied primarily film and television programs) are so attractive that audience members want to be like the media actors. Therefore, media characters or models can influence the behavior of audience members simply by existing, because they are so attractive. Furthermore, Bandura argued that once an audience observer imitates or models the observed media behavior, the sheer act of acting like a media character reinforces the behavior. Indeed, Bandura believed that the best way to teach new behaviors, particularly to children, is to present the behavior you want the child to learn, and the child will imitate that behavior. In a series of early controlled laboratory experimental studies called the *Bobo doll studies*, Bandura and his colleagues demonstrated that children can and do learn new behaviors by observation.

Let's consider the classic Bobo doll experiment. Bandura wanted to study two different effects: first, whether observing a filmed behavior could teach children that behavior, and second, if such observation motivated the children to be like the film model. He showed nursery school children a film of a person hitting a Bobo doll, an inflated plastic clown doll with a sand base, which rocked back and forth when punched. According to Bandura (1965),

> The film began with a scene in which a model (an adult male) walked up to an adult-size plastic Bobo doll and ordered him to clear the way. After glaring for a moment at the noncompliant antagonist, the model exhibited four novel aggressive responses, each accompanied by a distinctive verbalization. First, the model laid the Bobo doll on its side, sat on it, and punched it in the nose while remarking, "Pow, right in the nose, boom, boom." The model then raised the doll and pummeled it on the head with a mallet. Each response was accompanied by the verbalization "Sockeroo . . . stay down." Following the mallet aggression, the model kicked the doll about the room, and these responses were interspersed with the comments, "Fly away." Finally, the model threw rubber balls at the Bobo doll, each strike punctuated with "Bang." This sequence of physically and verbally aggressive behavior was repeated twice.
>
> For one group of children, the film ended there. For another group, in the model-rewarded condition, the film went on to show a second adult appear and reward the adult who had been hitting the Bobo doll with soft drinks and candies and informing the model that he was a "strong champion." A third group of children in the "model-punished" condition saw a film which showed a second adult appearing on the scene, shaking his finger, and saying, "Hey there, you big bully. You quit picking on that clown. I won't tolerate it." (pp. 590–591)

Bandura wanted to see how much spontaneous imitation or copying of the filmed characters' actions toward the Bobo doll would occur. So, after each viewing condition, the children were taken into a room with various toys, including a Bobo doll like the one in the film, three balls, a mallet, a pegboard, plastic farm animals, and dolls with a doll house. Bandura argued that this set of toys allowed the children to either imitate the aggression on the film or engage in various nonimitative play behaviors. Each child was left alone in this playroom or laboratory for 10 minutes while experimenters observed through a two-way mirror.

Bandura found that the spontaneous modeling or imitation of the film actor's behavior toward the Bobo doll occurred in the playroom setting for those children who had seen the film with no consequence and those who had seen the model rewarded. Boys were more likely to imitate than girls. However, the children who had seen the adult punished were not likely to imitate the film character's actions toward the Bobo doll. But Bandura argued that these children had learned the behavior anyway. He went on to demonstrate this by having a second test. He had an experimenter enter the playroom after 10 minutes and offer the children fruit juice and stickers as treats if the children could reproduce what they had seen the film character do to the Bobo doll on the film. Even the children who had seen the model punished on the film were able to reproduce the film actor's behavior toward the Bobo doll. Thus Bandura concluded that filmed portrayals of new behaviors could be learned through observation of the behavior. However, seeing the model punished for a certain behavior decreases the likelihood of such imitative learning (this Bandura called an *inhibitory effect*), whereas seeing a model rewarded (or even not punished) for making an aggressive behavior increases the likelihood that the viewer will imitate the behavior (this Bandura called a *disinhibitory effect*). Moreover, Bandura used the term *vicarious reinforcement* to refer to the idea that audience members are reinforced in the viewing situation itself and that observation of a media behavior is sufficient for learning of the behavior to take place, provided that the audience member engages in the following four steps in the process of observing the model:

1. *Attentional processes:* The audience member must be able to attend to and understand the various parts of the behavior being modeled by the media character.

2. *Retention processes:* The audience member must be able to remember what he or she sees the model do and be able to recall it at the time of copying the behavior.

3. *Motoric reproduction processes:* The audience member must be able to physically reproduce the actions of the media model.

4. *Motivational and reinforcement processes:* The likelihood that an audience member will model what he or she observes a media character doing is dependent on the audience member's desire or motivation to act like the media character.

The social learning theory has been a powerful theory offered to account for children's learning from the mass media. It is important to know that social learning theory predicts that viewers can model media portrayals and that it has been the most widely used theoretical perspective in debates about the effects of television and film violence on children.

However, this theory has been subject to considerable criticism regarding the highly artificial nature of the initial laboratory studies. That is, the experiments significantly underplay the researcher's and the research setting's influence on the children (Fowles, 1999). The children may see the researcher as an authority figure and know that they are expected to behave in some way, and so, being socially sensitive, they behave in ways they observe in the film (unless that behavior is seen as being bad, and then they don't). Therefore, their behavior may not have been "spontaneous" but somewhat calculated. The Bobo doll used in the study is made to be punched and kicked around; that is its purpose as a toy. Is it any wonder that children are so ready to punch and kick it? Also, the experiments do not show that the children would "spontaneously" reproduce the same violent moves against another person (or even a different object), especially in an everyday context. As critic David Gauntlett (2001) has pointed out, these types of studies, in focusing solely on behavioral production, never ask the subjects what this all means to them. Though the children undoubtedly learned a behavior, these studies do not show that they become more aggressive individuals in everyday life as a result of their media exposure, though this is what these studies are often taken to imply. Experimental psychologists counter that while this may be true, experiments are in fact designed to show the operation of response factors under optimal conditions: If effects did not occur under optimal circumstances, then perhaps there would be nothing to worry about. That experiments, as all social scientists know, are characterized by low external validity is not a criticism of the method.

## Contagion

One of the most controversial "effects" of mass media are cases in which the media are presumed to have led to antisocial panic or "copycat" behaviors. For example, in the 1970s, the plot of a made-for-TV movie, *The Doomsday Flight*, had extortionists demanding ransom for a commercial jetliner on which they had placed an atmospherically controlled bomb that armed itself as the plane rose and would detonate when the plane descended below 5,000 feet. In the movie, the extortionists were foiled when the plane flew to Denver, the "Mile High City," but several copycat extortion attempts followed the film. Moreover, similar copycat crimes occurred in other nations when the film aired there.

Following the urban riots of the late 1960s and again after the 1992 Los Angeles riot, a chorus of critics charged that media depictions, especially television news, either led to or fanned the flames of subsequent disorders. Rock-and-roll lyrics have been blamed for suicides, news of suicides has been blamed for other suicides, reported terrorist and hijacking attempts have been blamed for subsequent ones, Halloween candy tainting has been blamed on news reports of similar tainting, and so on. These episodes are all terrifying, socially significant, and clear threats to social order.

The main problem with the contagion theory of effects is that the evidence is primarily anecdotal and that, though causation may seem obvious in a particular example, it cannot be proven. Also, many popular anecdotes are simply incorrect. For example, in the 1970s, NBC aired a TV movie, *Born Innocent*, which featured a depiction of the rape of a young girl. The parents of a young girl in San Francisco raped in similar fashion sued the network. The suit failed because the parents were unable to prove that the movie was the cause of the rape. Indeed, the main perpetrator had never seen the show.

Another well-publicized example is the *Beavis and Butthead* fire. In 1993, a 5-year-old child set fire to his house, killing his 2-year-old sister. His mother claimed that he was copying the antics of the irreverent cartoon duo, Beavis and Butthead, who often play with fire and show a fascination with fire. There was widespread popular criticism of MTV, which aired the show, and as a result, the network moved it to a late night slot and removed references to fire from subsequent episodes. However, later reports established that not only had the boy a history of pyromania, neither his house nor his neighborhood was wired for cable television—they could not even receive MTV (see Fowles, 1999, for these and other examples).

Despite the doubtful nature of the most prominent popular examples, there are such things as copycat crimes and it is not inconceivable that impressionable or foolish people might try to imitate dangerous stunts seen on TV. *In principle,* there is no reason to discount the ability of the media to cause such effects; they are quite consistent with the stimulus-response and social learning theories. Nonetheless, it is quite difficult to generalize about the way in which media can lead to such contagion, because so many other factors may be involved. As we noted earlier in this chapter, when messages are beamed to audiences in the millions, it cannot be surprising when a few—as few as one in a million—audience members mimic a behavior, no matter how antisocial that behavior might be, while 999,999 in a million do not.

In one sort of action, an individual—usually, we would suspect, a mentally unbalanced one—mimics a stimulus from a media message. The problem is that such individuals might be set off by any stimulus at any time, and so it is quite difficult to demonstrate that the media messages "caused" the behavior. Admittedly, in the case of copycat crime, it is abundantly clear that media reports are at least one among several contributing agents. Research studies by the sociologist David Phillips (Phillips, 1982; Phillips & Hensley, 1985) have purported to show that both news and soap opera portrayals of suicide lead to subsequent rises in suicide, vehicle fatalities, and airplane crashes (which Phillips asserts are copycat murder-suicides); his controversial research has been challenged by other researchers on both theoretical and methodological grounds.

The second class of examples—urban disorders and some terrorist attempts—involve collective or group behavior. Here, the best evidence again is that media depictions do not themselves cause subsequent rioting, although they may well influence the timing or form of rioting behaviors. The urban-disorder research suggests that personal and social contacts are far more influential in individuals' deciding to participate in riots. And, as Denis McQuail (2000) argues, in news coverage of riots and terrorism, consideration of the alternative course of action—that media should cover up such incidents—forces us to reflect on the possibility that such a cover-up would lead to rumor-generated mass hysteria among those able to observe disturbances in their own areas. However, McQuail does not consider that the events could be covered in a different way so as to mitigate these effects.

### "Social Reality" as Mediator of Behavior

*How* one perceives a media message—how one interprets a message as a statement about the world—has a profound impact on how one responds. When producer Norman Lear's *All in the Family* made its debut in 1971, the show became an immediate source of controversy. The main character, Archie Bunker, was an out-and-out bigot; and Lear's intention was clearly to ridicule him. But the critics suggested that, in fact, Archie would be seen by highly prejudiced people as a sympathetic character, thus reinforcing their prejudices. In other words, the critics were suggesting a process of *selective perception*. Several research studies, in fact, found this—racially prejudiced individuals saw Archie as sympathetic and were reinforced in their attitudes and values, whereas less prejudiced individuals saw just the reverse (Brigham & Giesbrecht, 1976; Vidmar & Rokeach, 1974). Moreover, one study of the program found that highly prejudiced individuals were more likely than others to avoid watching the program altogether (Wilhoit & deBock, 1976). Their choice is an example of *selective exposure.*

Selective perception speaks to the ability of individuals to mold their own view of reality from media content. Not all media portrayals, however, are equally subject to selective interpretation. Some are more concrete and unambiguous than others. But portrayals of reality do influence behavior. The simplest and most mundane example is that we listen to a weather forecast in the morning to decide how warmly to dress and whether to pack an umbrella.

Some commentators argue that the media's greatest impact is its influence on our pictures of the world. In other words, the behavioral effects of the media may indeed be quite limited, as Klapper suggests, under ordinary circumstances. But great media power may reside elsewhere—in media's ability to shape our cognitions and beliefs. Political scientist Bernard C. Cohen (1963) captured this idea in commenting on the power of the press: "It may not be successful much of the time in telling people what to think, but it is stunningly successful in telling its readers what to think *about*" (p. 13). This idea is central to the agenda-setting model of media effects discussed in Chapter 11.

In telling us about the world—what is true, what is important, what aspects of problems are critical, what positions various groups have on particular issues, what other people are thinking and doing, and what they think are appropriate ways of behaving—the media have the potential to exert enormous influence. The potential is great for an obvious reason: People have just three ways to learn. These are personal, direct experience; interpersonal interaction; and media. An overwhelming share of what we know of the world comes from media sources. If you've never been to Kenya (or Russia or France), virtually everything you know about the place comes from a media source.

Are beliefs and cognitions related to behavior? A particularly vivid example comes from research by Alexander Bloj, a Syracuse University graduate student (reported in McCombs & Shaw, 1974). His research topic was flying on commercial airliners. Bloj examined an airline's ticket sales records for five years and related these to news reports of commercial airplane crashes involving fatalities and skyjackings. When a skyjacking or crash occurred, ticket sales went down. Furthermore, during those same weeks, sales of flight insurance went up. Because we almost never learn of air crashes firsthand, the effect virtually certainly is media generated. In this example, the effect is concrete, in large part for two reasons. First, selective perception is unimportant: There's basically only one way to read the news that an airliner crashed and people were killed. Second, individuals' attitudes are likewise unimportant, because virtually everybody has the same strong belief that dying in an airplane crash is a lousy idea. Reports of crashes and skyjackings merely remind us that flying can be a risky business.

## PERSUASIVE COMMUNICATION RESEARCH

One major area of theorizing about media effects concerns advertising and its influence on buying. How does advertising work? What are the mechanisms involved in getting us to buy those jeans, that cola, the right face cream, which we see advertised on television, in magazines and newspapers, on billboards, and now even at movie theaters? Communications scholar Michael Schudson (1984) titled his book on advertising effectiveness *Advertising: The Uneasy Persuasion*. Schudson's argument is that advertisers are "uneasy" in the sense that the evidence on the "effectiveness" of advertising to actually get people to buy products is not at all clear; how precisely advertising works may be more art than science, may be more rules of thumb than clear knowledge. Theories have been developed that attempt to describe the process of persuasion. In fact, this literature is enormous; the social psychologist William McGuire (1989) found more than 7,000 published articles relevant to the study of persuasive communication. Let's consider some of the current well-regarded theories of how persuasion operates.

## The McGuire Process Model

McGuire has himself contributed a model of the persuasion process; he offers a general description of the different steps necessary for persuasion to take place:

1. *Presentation:* A persuasive message must be presented to the audience member.

2. *Attention:* The audience member must attend to the message.

3. *Comprehension:* He or she must understand the message.

4. *Yielding:* The person must yield to, accept, or agree with, the persuasive argument presented in the message.

5. *Retention:* After receiving the message and leaving the communicative situation, the audience member must remember the persuasive message.

6. *Overt Behavior:* The audience member needs to behave in the expected way.

For McGuire, each of these steps must be followed for an advertisement or any other message intended to persuade an audience to do something to be effective.

The effectiveness of this process is dependent, however, on the various components of the persuasion process—the source of the message, the manner in which the message itself is constructed, the channel through which the message is sent, and the receiver or audience for the message. This general model of the steps and components of the persuasion process is useful in describing the persuasion situation, but it does not show how to create the most persuasive message.

## The Theory of Reasoned Action

Other theoretical models have been advanced to address persuasion. One of the most widely known of these is Ajzen and Fishbein's (1980) *theory of reasoned action.*

According to this theory, the best predictor of behavior, such as buying a particular brand of car, is the person's *intention* to engage in the behavior. A person's intention is, in turn, determined by a person's *attitude toward the behavior* and by what Ajzen and Fishbein call a *subjective norm,* or the person's perceptions of how other people they value think he or she should behave. And underlying a person's own attitude about buying a new car and a person's subjective norms about car buying are a deeper set of beliefs about the sorts of cars that are appropriate for the person, beliefs perhaps about environmental pollution, beliefs about whether and how cars may express deeper personality characteristics, and a whole set of beliefs a person holds that underlie their particular attitude toward buying a particular car.

Because this theory assumes, then, that most behavior is ultimately determined by sets of underlying beliefs, it follows that to affect someone's behavior (such as persuading them to buy a certain brand of car) is accomplished by changing these underlying beliefs. Changes in underlying beliefs lead to changes in attitudes and norms, which in turn lead to changes in intentions to behave and ultimately to behavior. Thus a key tenet of the theory of reasoned action is that media messages intended to change behavior must be designed for and aimed at the underlying beliefs that are associated with behavioral intentions in the audience or population of interest.

## Information-Processing Approaches

Other theorists have focused on how the audience makes sense of the persuasive message—how they process the information. These theorists hope to gain insight into how to change the audience member's underlying beliefs about some object or behavior. According to this *information processing approach* to persuasion, it is necessary to determine how an individual processes a persuasive message, how that person's initial knowledge relevant to the message is represented or "remembered," how the message influences the person's selection of information from the message, and how the individual is transformed or changed in response to the message from an initial state of knowledge about the object of persuasion to final knowledge state. A number of what are called *cognitive response theories* have been developed, arguing that the best way to predict how a persuasive message will be understood by the recipient or audience member is to understand the thought that occurs to people when they are exposed to the message. That is, what are you thinking about when you watch a Britney Spears advertisement for Pepsi Cola? These thoughts (or cognitive responses) are assumed to be indicative of how you are interpreting the persuasive message.

One particular cognitive response theory is Petty and Cacciopo's (1986) extended work on responses to persuasive messages. They have found, for instance, that the degree to which an audience member perceives that a message is personally important and relevant (what's called *high involvement* with the message) determines how the person processes the persuasive message. An advertisement, for instance, in which an audience member is highly involved (such as seeing an ad for a new car just when you are thinking about buying a new car) leads the involved person to scrutinize the information and arguments of that persuasive message more than an uninvolved person. This is called the *central* route to information processing. For messages that are not personally involving, audience members will use simpler, less taxing strategies to make sense of and respond to the message, maybe just focusing on the source of the message or the expertise of the person making the claims; this is called *peripheral* processing. Cacciopo and Petty argue that both forms of processing may lead to attitude and behavior change. Attitude change through the central route, however, is more difficult to accomplish because the person to be persuaded is fully engaged in thinking about and even arguing with the persuasive message, because she or he cares about the attitude object. Attitude change through the peripheral route is usually easier, because the person is not really engaged. But attitudes changed through the central route are more persistent and harder to change subsequently than less involving ones.

These various theories of how to develop a persuasive message have become increasingly important in planned information campaigns, particularly in the rise of health information campaigns.

In this part of the chapter, we have tried to introduce you to some of the major theories of how media might influence individuals' behaviors.

You probably have noticed that some of these theories, such as Bandura's (1977) social learning theory or Petty and Cacciopo's (1986) cognitive response theory, have been developed to theorize about media influences in specific areas, such as effects of violence portrayals on aggressive behavior in the case of Bandura and advertising influences on product-purchasing behavior in the case of Petty and Cacciopo. Although we have reviewed various aspects of how to conceptualize media influences on behavior in general, it is the case that most theories of behavior influences of media have been developed to examine either a specific type of media content (for example, violence, pornography, political reporting, advertising) or a special domain of people's behaviors (for example, aggressive behavior, product purchasing, health behaviors, voting). Also, it is clear that much of the research on media influence on individuals has been directed over the years to studies of media content that is thought to be a social problem, such as pornographic films or magazines. We now turn to examine research on media influences in specific domains of behavior, and the ongoing debates over the extent and nature of that influence.

## DEBATE OVER MEDIA EFFECTS

Studies of media and behavior have been heavily tied to public fears about the effects of various media on their audiences. Indeed, the thousands of studies that have been conducted throughout the twentieth and into the twenty-first century to assess the power of media to influence behavior fall into categories that represent strong public concerns: Does viewing television violence cause viewers to be aggressive? What are the effects of pornographic images on their audiences? What influence does television have on the social behavior of children? How effective are advertising and other persuasive media messages? These questions have occupied much of the research on media and individual behavior.

### Violence in the Media and Aggressive Behavior

On April 20, 1999, two teenagers, Eric Harris and Dylan Klebold, walked into their high school in Littleton, Colorado, dressed in black trench coats and carrying semi-automatic weapons and explosives. By the time the two teens finally turned their guns on themselves, 12 students and a teacher were dead and another 25 people were injured. The tragic events at Columbine High School reignited a storm of debates about the effects of the media. As the news portrayed it, the killers lived within a violent world of media images: Fans of the stylistic but violent film *The Matrix* and the film *The Basketball Diaries,* about youth struggling with drugs and violence, the boys were also fans of shock-rock singer Marilyn Manson and played ultraviolent computer games like *Doom.* Documentary filmmaker Michael Moore's controversial 2002 film, *Bowling for Columbine,* uses these events and questions as the starting point of his investigation into the nature of violence in America. American society is reported to be one of the most violent in world. Moore's film goes beyond the issue of violent media to consider policies of gun control, aggressive American foreign policy, a history of violence toward indigenous peoples and slaves, and a culture of fear among other factors that may or may not have contributed to sparking these events. But, for the most part, the debate over the causes of this event is couched in the language of direct effect. These debates are not new.

In classical Greece, scholars argued that the violence depicted in plays was actually good for society and for individuals in the audience, because it gave them an outlet for their own aggression. This was called *catharsis.* The theory, then, was that viewing violence made one less violent. Scholars today generally dismiss the catharsis theory as unsubstantiated (indeed, attempts to prove a cathartic effect have been controversial at best), but it remains as the first foray into the issue of violent media effects.

At least since the early days of film at the beginning of the twentieth century, media violence has been an ongoing concern of the American public. It surfaced in the 1930s after the publication of the Payne Fund studies of film effects on youth and led to the creation in 1934 of the Hays Office, a self-regulation arm of the film industry. It surfaced in the 1950s in concerns over comic book violence and again led to self-censorship of violent comics by the comic book industry. And over the 50 years of American television, violence has been the most enduring concern of critics of television programming. That concern has translated into a lot of research attention: An estimated 3,500 research studies have examined the relationship between media and real-world violence (Whitney & Wartella, 2001).

Public debates around the issue of media violence have fueled a variety of government investigations into the topic. Since 1950, these debates have led to congressional investigations such as the Harris Subcommittee hearings of 1952, the Hendrickson-Kefauver Subcommittee hearings of 1954–1955, and the Dodd Senate Subcommittee hearings of 1961–1964. Major federal government commissions, including the National Commission on the Causes and Prevention of Violence (Baker & Ball, 1969), the Surgeon General's Scientific Advisory Committee on Television and Social Behavior (Rubinstein, Comstock, & Murray, 1972), and its 10-year follow-up (Pearl, Bouthilet, & Lazar, 1982), also issued reports. Senator Paul Simon of Illinois held hearings in Los Angeles in the summer of 1993 and in Washington in December of 1993 about the issue. The 1993 hearings led directly to two major research efforts and indirectly to inclusion of the requirement for V-chips in all American televisions in the 1996 Telecommunications Act. One of those research efforts, the National Television Violence Study (NTVS), included a three-year (1994–1997) content analysis of about 10,000 hours of network and cable programming; at the end, the NTVS concluded that more than half of TV programming contained at least some violence, much of it presented in a context that experimental research suggests is most likely to prompt aggressive behaviors—that is, TV programming in which the violence is "glamorized, sanitized, and trivialized" (NTVS, 1998, p. 26).

However, the causes of violence in American life are multiple. Most of us generally accept the notion that violent behavior is a complex problem formed of many influences. Racism, drug abuse, abusive family relationships, gangs, guns, mental illness, and the frustrations of poverty can all lead to violence and aggressive behavior. As psychologist Rowell Huesmann (1986) has argued, aggression is a syndrome, an enduring pattern of behavior that can persist from childhood through adulthood. Is media violence one of the contributory causes as well? What evidence is there for this position?

Clearly, a number of factors contribute to violence in American society; and although any one act of violence can be found to have a particular cause (let's say the aggressor was on drugs and incompetent to judge his actions), it is the persistent fact of violence throughout our society that has worried Americans. To ignore television, film, video games, gangsta rap, and other media violence would be a grave oversight.

For instance, violence tears across the television screen through many types of programs, from music videos and entertainment shows to reality programming and the evening news. By the time the average American child graduates from elementary school, he or she will have seen over 8,000 murders and more than 100,000 other assorted acts of violence (Huston et al., 1992). In 1985, the APA held that indeed television *can* cause viewers to act aggressively. In its overall review of television and behavior, the APA Task Force on Television and Society reaffirmed this view and asserted that media violence can contribute to two other outcomes: desensitization of viewers to violent actions and fear of being the victim of violence (Huston et al., 1992).

Strong evidence from survey research consistently shows that heavy viewers of violence on television are more likely to engage in aggressive behavior than are light viewers. Moreover, viewers of violent television express more willingness to use violence to resolve real interpersonal conflicts (Huston et al., 1992). However, these correlational studies simply say that television violence viewing is *associated with* holding favorable attitudes toward the use of violence and aggressive behavior. Such studies alone are not sufficient evidence that media violence *causes* aggression. However, correlational studies are common around social and public health concerns: Brad Bushman and Craig Anderson (2001) have noted in a review of the strength of relationships from correlational studies of smoking and lung cancer, media violence and aggression, condom use and avoiding sexually transmitted diseases, passive smoking and lung cancer, exposure to lead and lowered IQ scores, homework and academic achievement, and exposure to asbestos and contracting laryngeal cancer that the strength of the relationship between TV violence and aggression is the second strongest of all of these, second only to the smoking and lung cancer correlation.

The social learning studies with Bobo dolls (Bandura, 1965) described earlier in this chapter were designed laboratory experiments or field experimental studies. In experiments, the direction of causality can be demonstrated. When the hundreds of such laboratory studies are reviewed, in particular, those involving children and adolescents, there is support for the claim that viewing television violence "can lead to increases in aggressive attitudes, values, and behavior" (Huston et al., 1992, p. 55). The reason short-term experimental studies and correlational studies are used is that it is *unethical* to design long-term experimental studies with people for risky behavior: Just as we cannot force a random group of young people to smoke for years and a control group not to in order to find out whether the smokers are more likely to contract lung cancer, we can't force a group to watch high doses of violent TV if we believe that it's likely to make them more violent. It's true that neither short-term experimental studies nor correlational survey studies suggest that heavy doses of violent TV leads, for any individual, to aggression, to desensitization, or to fear of victimization—any more than going to a good university necessarily means that an individual will earn more money than another person who does not: That's the nature of correlational evidence.

Perhaps the most compelling evidence comes from longitudinal or panel studies, which study people repeatedly over time. One such longitudinal study examined children at age 8 and then restudied them again at ages 18 and 30. This study by Leonard Eron, L. Rowell Huesmann, and colleagues found a clear relationship between the amount of violence on television that children watched at age 8 with the aggressive behavior of these same youth at age 18, and the seriousness of criminal acts of these same people at age 30. According to the researcher, L. R. Huesmann (1986),

> Aggressive habits seem to be learned early in life, and once established, are resistant to change and predictive of serious adult antisocial behavior. If a child's observation of media violence promotes the learning of aggressive habits, it can have harmful lifelong consequences. Consistent with this theory, early television habits are in fact correlated with adult criminality. (pp. 129–130)

In addition, others have argued that viewing television violence may cultivate or shape positive attitudes toward violence and may activate other aggressive thoughts. Leonard Berkowitz and his colleagues assert that many media effects are immediate, transitory, and short-term (Berkowitz, 1984). When people watch television violence, it activates or *primes* other semantically related thoughts that may influence how the person responds to the violence on television. Viewers who identify with an actor on television may imagine themselves acting like that character, carrying out the character's aggressive actions. Research evidence suggests that exposure to media aggression does indeed prime other aggressive thoughts, evaluations, and behaviors, such that viewers of violence report a greater willingness to use violence in interpersonal situations. Furthermore, viewing television violence may lead to disinhibition of aggression—greater willingness to use violent means—among children and adults who are already predisposed to react to conflict in aggressive ways. In other words, viewing lots of violence leads people to ignore other factors in their everyday life that normally inhibit them from reacting violently. For example, the presence of adults in a room inhibits children from punching each other; the threat of having people catch you in the act—or criminal prosecution—keeps you from hitting your teacher or boss.

Media violence may also influence even those viewers who do not themselves behave violently or have positive attitudes toward using violence, and in two different ways: desensitization and fear, or "mean world" effects.

Research has demonstrated that prolonged viewing of media violence can lead to emotional desensitization toward real-world violence and the victims of violence, which in turn can lead to callous attitudes toward violence directed at others and a decreased likelihood to take action on behalf of the victim when violence occurs (Donnerstein, Slaby, & Eron, 1994).

Studies by George Gerbner and his colleagues (Gerbner, Gross, Morgan, & Signorielli, 1990) have demonstrated that heavy viewers of television violence become fearful of the world, afraid of becoming victims of violence, and, over time, they engage in more self-protective behaviors and show more mistrust of others, an outcome sometimes known as *the mean world syndrome*. It is not that heavy television viewers mistake the world of television for the world outside their doors; they know the difference. But still heavy viewers of television tend to see their world as more fearful and crime-ridden than those who watch comparatively less television. It is likely that both fictional and reality programs (including crime-saturated television news) contribute to this fear-inducing influence on viewers of television. So, it is that media violence begets not just violence, but also fear and other attitude changes.

Also at issue in the media violence debates is the nature of the violence depicted. What violence should we be concerned about? Is there any violence that could be positive? Gerbner et al. include cartoon violence and violent natural occurrences when they measure violence on television because such occurrences—even if random and "natural"—still portray the world as a violent place. As a 2003 review commissioned by the U.S. Surgeon General notes, not all depictions pose equal risks for all viewers for two main reasons—differences in the viewers and differences in the content (Anderson et al., 2003). Young viewers, particularly children who are not yet able to separate fantasy from reality, are more "at risk" from cartoon, slapstick, and fantasy violence than adults are, and the *context* of violence matters: Violence that is punished and violence shown to lead to long-term harm and pain or to pain to others (such as families of victims) has been shown experimentally to lead to less aggressive behavior than "glamorized, sanitized and trivialized" violence (NTVS, 1998).

Yet another issue that is raised about the nature of violence in the media is the gendered and racialized nature of the violence depicted in the media. Who is more likely to be the victim? Who is more likely to be the perpetrator?

Within the mainstream effects research community, there is strong agreement on these points, though there is not unanimity. Yet, over several decades, various research reviews have overwhelmingly concluded that television violence is *a* cause of real-world violence; almost no serious researcher believes it is *the* cause. And it cannot be dismissed as having no impact on the behavior of audiences. As we will highlight in Chapter 11, the evidence implicating media violence in the social problems associated with violence in the real world has led to the current television ratings system and the introduction of program-blocking devices for home television receivers.

As might be expected, in a research area that touches on vital questions of culture, policy, and, yes, ideology, the media-violence realm has prompted a great deal of controversy over appropriate methods, over the strength of conclusions that can be made, and even over the degree to which children and adults are able to contest and resist violent portrayals.

Research results are often misrepresented not only by the media itself but by research organizations, congressional committees, and others. For example, David Gauntlett (2001) shows how a research study that was not designed to analyze the effects of violent media on youth (though it was about the viewing habits of youth in prison) and that did not make any conclusions about the effects of violent media on youth nonetheless was trumpeted as proving just that by various newspapers and even one of the report's authors.

And there are criticisms of the landmark studies on media and aggression. The criticisms of Gerbner's work particularly have also been numerous and fundamentally question his conclusions. Attempts to reproduce his findings either in new studies or by re-analyzing the same data that Gerbner's team used have sometimes failed. Indeed, one study argued that there were crucial factors that Gerbner and his colleagues had ignored. For example, people who watch a lot of television tend to be uneducated, poor, and unemployed, and tend to live in neighborhoods with higher crime rates, so it is little wonder that they are more afraid of crime.

Regarding the work on desensitization, we could ask two questions: Could not the findings that after repeated exposure to violent media texts subjects had reduced arousal to the material mean that the subjects had become more familiar with, and therefore more comfortable with, the dimensions of the genre and began reading the texts as genre pieces rather than unexpected and undesired (assuming that the subjects were not fans of the genre) viewings? As a corollary question, could the results also indicate that the subjects were becoming more relaxed and accustomed to the research process and unfamiliar setting? The second question is, does desensitization to media violence lead to desensitization to real life violence? David Buckingham (1996), for one, in his study of children's emotional responses to television, concludes that it does not. Just because someone becomes desensitized to screen violence and can watch violent fare without blinking an eye doesn't mean that they would not be appropriately horrified if someone was gunned down on the street in front of them.

And this leads us to the second school of criticism of media effects research on violence, which are critiques of the whole research enterprise itself. Studies of viewers of media violence, even children, show that they tend to focus more on the plot and characters and do not simply focus on, or even isolate, violent acts by themselves. Context is all-important to how an audience understands and makes meaning of viewed violence. Studies of fans of violent fare, such as horror films and violent action films, also question assumptions that effects researchers make about the audience, such as their critical abilities or even their gender. Annette Hill's (1997) research on women fan's responses to violent films such as those by Quentin Tarantino has begun to undermine many of these assumptions. She found that both male and female fans often looked at the act of viewing a violent film as a challenge that they wanted to meet, a social event in which they enjoyed the audience reactions, and a testing of boundaries (for women, challenging the boundaries of gender role expectations). And David Buckingham's

(1993, 1996) work on children and the media questions researchers' tendency to treat children as passive victims of media violence.

As we mentioned earlier in the chapter, research into media effects tends to focus on content or behavior that is thought to be a social problem: We only study what we already consider to be a problem. Likewise, the act of studying something usually flags a concern about that object that even an inconclusive result cannot easily erase. For example, aggression is considered a social problem, so we research how media violence may cause aggression. But, by doing so, we may miss the point that other media content may produce aggression as well. Zillman (1982) pointed out some time ago that nonviolent but exciting content—car chases, for example—may produce aggression in the lab as well. This returns us to the point that context of content makes a difference: Not all TV content, even violent content, can be expected to produce uniform negative effects on a disparate set of viewers; some violent content is different from other kinds, and some kinds of nonviolent content arouses strong feelings. Effects research can be as much about the researcher's assumptions about the nature of the medium and the audience as the actual question of effects. Horace Newcomb (1978) has famously pointed out that Gerbner's work assumes from the start that television is "ruled with violence" rather than starting from the assumption that television is "ruled by the triumph of justice and order in the face of violence" (p. 268).

And, finally, critic David Gauntlett (2001) argues that the effects tradition has the entire question backward. Rather than starting from the assumption that the media is at fault and then studying the media (which is what he says they do), shouldn't they be studying the effects themselves? In other words, when studying media and violence, look at the real-world violence first rather than the media violence. He puts it succinctly: "To understand violent people, I recommend studying violent people" (p. 53). However, studying *only* violent people might tell us about violent people; without adequate comparisons with nonviolent people, we could not know whether their backgrounds, including the media they watch, differ.

## The Influence of Pornography

If one of the central questions of media violence is the definition of violence itself, and whether all violence is equally harmful, this is even more so with regards to pornography. As with violence, social concern with pornography is ancient: the Greek philosophers railed against it, and the social historian Robert Darnton (1995a, 1995b) argues that official crackdowns on printed pornography led to a reaction that hastened the French Revolution. Pornography, however, differs considerably from violence in that the *intended consequences* of violence rarely are to make people violent, while pornography and its cousin-in-law obscenity are usually intended to appeal to a prurient interest—that is, to stimulate sexual thoughts. Before we can even begin to discuss the literature on the effects of mediated pornography (or sexually explicit media), we have to consider the question of definition, and to discuss the question of definition is to take up the long debates about pornography, especially within feminism. We do so knowing that we cannot do justice to the nuances and specific positions within this debate. What follows is a general summary (drawing from the overviews of Cornell, 2000, and L. Williams, 1989).

Up until the 1970s, the debates over pornography had been subsumed under debates about obscenity.[1] Obscenity was, in many ways, a moral as well as a legal judgment as to whether the item in question had any redeeming social merit. The rise of what have been called the antipornography feminists changed the nature of the debate. Pornography was not about morality and aesthetics; pornography was about power, specifically the power wielded by men over women. This patriarchal power presented itself most boldly in the form of violence against women. Pornography, then, was about the submission, humiliation, and victimization of women by men. It was the systematic violation of a woman's human rights, which not only perpetuates patriarchal power in general but allows for if not encourages violence against women in real life. As feminist author Robin Morgan (1980) has put it, "Pornography is the theory, and rape the practice" (p. 139). A first step in the struggle against this abuse is to seek to stem the circulation of these texts: that is, censorship. Antipornography feminists argue that the pornography industry relies on the brutalization and coercion of women to participate in these films, which they liken to torture and sexual slavery.

The opposing group of feminists, called the anticensorship feminists, would agree that most mainstream, industry-produced pornography is misogynistic, that it overwhelmingly represents solely male desire and male fantasy, and they would acknowledge the brutality of some mainstream production practices. But they would argue that it doesn't have to be this way and that the practice of mainstream pornography is historically and culturally determined. To simply reject all pornography in principle is to assume that all pornography is (and always will be) in essence misogynistic and about male power and control. The elimination of all pornography would basically limit the range of sexual expression available to women (especially if a woman's desires are "nonnormative") by denying the possibility that women could be sexually dominant or diverse. Censorship would, moreover, only drive the industry further underground. Anticensorship feminists would seek to reform the pornography industry and point to examples of women producing nonstereotypical pornography, which is not about male violence and power and which focuses as much on the emotional aspect of the relationship as the physical intercourse. Such works are usually made outside of the mainstream industry. So, when considering the behavioral research into the effects of pornography on its audiences, the anticensorship feminists would caution that we consider what was actually being viewed: Not all pornography is the same.

The behavioral research on exposure to sexually explicit media can be contradictory at times, and inconclusive as well. But some general conclusions have been reached (see Gunter, 2002; Harris & Scott, 2002; Huston et al., 1992). These findings lead scholars to make a crucial distinction when it comes to possible effects between violent and nonviolent sexual depictions. Despite the attention given it, sexual violence is relatively rare in hardcore (or XXX) pornography (Gunter, 2002). Studies conclude that sexual violence on screen leads to antisocial effects such as desensitization toward rape victims or callousness toward women generally. These results hold whether the material is explicitly pornographic or not, meaning that R-rated films that combine sex and violence (such as popular slasher films) are a serious cause for concern because they circulate more widely than X-rated materials. In terms of the effects of violent materials, another crucial factor is whether the woman victim was portrayed as enjoying the rape or violent act. In some studies, men were more aroused if this was the case, and less so if the victim was portrayed as being terrorized (Harris & Scott, 2002). As Harris and Scott (2002), in an overview of the effects research on sex in the media, write, "There is nothing arousing or exciting about being raped in real life, and messages to the contrary do not help teenage boys understand the reality of how to relate to girls and women" (p. 325).

Nonviolent sexually explicit media (sometimes referred to as *erotica*) generally is not associated with antisocial effects (Huston et al., 1992). But this does not mean that nonviolent works cannot still be dehumanizing, dominating, and humiliating to women. It depends on what is actually depicted, how it is depicted, and how it is interpreted. In addition, nonviolent sexually explicit media texts may also have ideological effects by, for example, shifting what is perceived as "normal" attractiveness in a sexual partner or even what is considered normal sexual practice. Studies have shown that both men and women reported dissatisfaction with their sexual partners after viewing such materials and also tend to overestimate the frequency of sexual practices such as oral or anal sex (Harris & Scott, 2002).

As in the discussion of violence in the previous section, Harris and Scott emphasize that the context of these images and texts is important in considering their problematic effects (that is, whether or not the scene is gratuitous, as in a slasher film, or central to the plot, as in the film *The Accused*, or whether the text is meant to be a documentary or an entertainment program, and so on), as is the context of reception. They point out that though most material is produced by men and for men, "A few studies have shown women to have more positive reactions to sexual videos written and directed by women and for women" (p. 312).

However, some of the same caveats that applied to the behavioral research on violence also apply toward research on sex in the media. There is little consideration, for example, of how fans and regular viewers of such materials (from mainstream pornography to slasher films) make sense of them, what meanings they take from them, and how the viewing of such materials integrates with their everyday life.

These debates over the effects of pornography have grown more pressing in recent years as the availability of pornographic material has rapidly increased. First, this was through cable television and video rental in the 1970s and 1980s, but the rise of the Internet in the 1990s has reinvigorated these debates. Though the measurement of the presence of anything on the Internet, much less pornography, is notoriously unreliable, it has been argued that pornography was certainly the first industry that figured out how to make money online and has been very successful at doing so. Revenues for the porn industry in general in the United States is estimated at $10 billion per year (Kloer, 2003) and up to $56 billion globally (Harris & Scott, 2002). Bills to require software to block adult-oriented Web sites from children using public access terminals (for example, in libraries) have proved contentious. It is still too early, however, for any significant studies to have been done ascertaining whether the proliferation of sexually explicit material over the Internet has effects other than those attributed to the viewing of such materials in magazines, on television, or in theaters. But some speculate that the availability of pornography in the privacy of one's home via the Internet (or at least its sheer presence via e-mail spam) may make pornography more acceptable to the mainstream (Kloer, 2003). Also, it allows Internet users to produce and distribute their own pornography according to their own sensibilities from their own homes.

In addition, pornography has become more acceptable as a subject in mainstream discourse. Indeed, there seems to be a certain cultural "porno chic" (Kloer, 2003), with major films such as *Boogie Nights* or *Wonderland* depicting the porn industry or with pornography as a discussion topic on popular television shows such as *Friends* and *Six Feet Under*. A number of the mainstream media companies have major investments in the porn industry (especially through ownership of cable or satellite systems that offer adult channels or companies that provide pay-per-view pornography to hotels; see Egan, 2000; Kirk & Boyer, 2002).

One issue here is that young women are encouraged to take up this identity role of "porn star" through popular media such as MTV videos. Such identity roles are marketed as being empowering to young women, but do not lead them to question, or at least consider, issues of power and ideology that such roles raise (*Merchants of Cool*, 2001). That is, actively embracing stereotypical sexual identities may not necessarily be empowering, but may simply perpetuate the male domination of women.

## Media and Children

The violence controversies have focused heavily on children who view film and television violence, as well as on those who read violent comic books. More recently, attention has been paid to violent videogames. Additionally, concerns have been raised about the sexually explicit nature of programs, films, images, and music that children can access not only via television and video but now through the Internet. These concerns about children, who have historically been one of the earliest segments of the mass audience to adopt and use any new medium—from film to radio and television to video games, video-tapes, and the Internet—have led to ongoing studies of how media influence children's behavior.

Children are thought to be particularly susceptible to the power of the media. Why? Because of their naiveté and inexperience. Children are thought to have less information about the world and fewer defenses to resist the power of media images and persuasion. Indeed, the titles of books, especially about television and children, conjure up a fragile child, gullible, with eyes glued to the television screen and easily overwhelmed by the powerful mass medium.

Children's abilities to make sense of the world around them develop from birth through early adolescence. Because children have less information about the world, their interpretations of media mes-sages vary with age and experience. This is what is meant by the idea that children develop increasing sophistication with media as they get older. For instance, a 4-year-old may think that television characters live inside the TV set, while a 9-year-old may have difficulty connect-ing a character's actions with the consequences of those actions when a villain is caught at the end of a show—may not be able to relate that to the crime he committed earlier in the program. Over the course of childhood, children come to understand the nature of narratives, the difference between programs and commercials, and the ways in which television's audiovisual conventions (such as zooms, cuts, and slow motion) shape the message (Singer & Singer, 2001).

Children are not born with the inherent abilities to make sense of the sorts of codes and genres, the messages, of most of the mass media, including television. Even though children are introduced as babies to television, other videos, recordings, and books, their abilities to interpret those messages change steadily over the course of child-hood. Not until the early teenage years do children's understandings of a given television message resemble adult interpretations. In short, children have to learn to make sense of television's codes and content (see the discussion in Chapter 5). For example, they have to learn to make distinctions between modes of fantasy and reality, distinctions that become more sophisticated over time. Furthermore, children can and do learn social behaviors from media.

So, what has research shown about what children can learn from the media? First, we know that children can learn a whole range of planned education content from TV programs such as *Sesame Street* and *Dora the Explorer*. Letters, numbers, words, and math concepts have all been taught successfully to children via media (Singer & Singer, 2001). This has been demonstrated across a wide range of behaviors, both violent and more positive or prosocial behaviors (such as altruism, learning to share or help others, and self-control). Bandura's (1965) Bobo doll experiments, which we described earlier, are the classic example of such studies. We will consider children's learning in these domains: the effects of planned educational programming on children's learning of school-related knowledge and behaviors, children's learning about people and how they should behave, and children's learning about consumption. (See Box 10.3,"Television's Forms.")

---

**BOX 10.3**

**Television's Forms**

Television as a communicative medium has certain characteristic visual and auditory production and editing techniques. In a series of experimental studies, Rice, Huston, and Wright (1982) and their colleagues have examined the impact of the forms of television on children's attention to and learning from television.

The use of slow motion, cuts, pans, zooms, pacing, dialogue, auditory distortion, and animation are production techniques used in television, and researchers describe these as forms or formal features. These forms influence both what is communicated and how child viewers interpret messages communicated.

Two kinds of forms can be distinguished: *perceptually salient forms* and *reflective forms*. Perceptually salient forms are those that have their greatest impact in drawing children's attention to the television set when they are not watching but *are* in the room with a set on. Perceptually salient forms include such television production techniques as fast pacing, strange voices, and high levels of visual and auditory special effects—such as distortions of visuals or voices. Reflective forms, on the other hand, include such production techniques as zooms, singing, and moderate levels of action. They are called reflective forms because they are thought to encourage repetition and elaboration of the program content.

*(Continued)*

---

(Continued)

According to this research, perceptually salient and reflective forms are associated with different kinds of programs on television. Moreover, they influence children's learning from the programs in different ways. For instance, researchers found that many of the perceptually salient forms, in particular the fast pacing, high-action formal features, are associated with many of the Saturday morning children's cartoon shows. In contrast, educational television shows such as *Mister Rogers' Neighborhood* and *Sesame Street* are more likely to use a lot of reflective forms. They have also found that the more reflective forms—in particular, high amounts of dialogue and slower pacing—are associated with children's learning from the content. Perceptually salient production techniques seem to be good at bringing children's attention to the set when they aren't watching, as both educational programmers and advertisers have learned.

The 1969 development of *Sesame Street* marks the standard of educational programming for children that incorporates a planned curriculum (teaching preschoolers about their numbers, letters, grammar) and is entertaining. The popularity of Jim Henson's Muppets, along with the quickly paced and cleverly written magazine format of this program, was immediate. *Sesame Street* is now available in at least 67 countries in the world; it has affiliated magazine and book series featuring the Muppets and live characters, and it has won every U.S. and international award for children's television. Over the years, *Sesame Street* has been shown to teach children of different social classes and both sexes the planned curriculum, such as their letters and numbers (Ball & Bogatz, 1970; Bogatz & Ball, 1972). Another study demonstrates that regular viewers of *Sesame Street* learn new words and improve their vocabulary from such viewing (Rice, Huston, Truglio, & Wright, 1990; Wright & Huston, 1995).

Since the success of *Sesame Street*, other planned educational programs, such as *Where in the World Is Carmen Sandiego, Bill Nye the Science Guy, Square One Television, Reading Rainbow, Gullah Gullah Island, Blue's Clues,* and *The Magic School Bus,* have been found both to increase children's interest in the educational content of programs and to teach some of the planned curriculum. In addition, other children's shows that focus less on teaching cognitive skills but more on such positive behaviors as helping others and sharing toys can be successful. The most important evidence here comes from a study of preschool children's effective learning of such helping or prosocial behaviors from watching *Mister Rogers' Neighborhood*. Furthermore, recent evidence is that preschool viewing of planned educational shows has a long-term positive influence on children's overall educational attainment at least through third grade. However, the entire nature of the relationship between television and school performance is not wholly clear (see Huston et al., 1992).

Does watching television throughout the grade school years help children in school? Does it depend on both the type of programs the children view and the amount of time they spend watching? The evidence is mixed. There is no clear relationship between amount of television viewed during the grade school years and such school achievement measures as reading ability, scores on achievement tests, and so on (Huston et al., 1992). A major national study of the effects of Channel One's 10-minute daily news broadcast demonstrated relatively little student learning about public affairs. The argument the researchers made was that Whittle's program may be high on entertainment values (fast pace, short segments) but not attentive enough to those production characteristics that aid the student's learning from the programs (Johnston, 1995). In fact, it is probably not reasonable to expect a strong relationship between television viewing overall and children's school performance. The relationship depends on which programs children watch and what other activities in their life reinforce television and other media use.

But children do learn other sorts of information and expectations about people and places from watching television and using other media. Many have described television for young children as "a magic window" on the world, which brings into the child's home an array of people and places not part of the child's everyday experience. Children learn about how fathers, mothers, and families are to behave from watching television; they also build up expectation of African Americans and other races and ethnic groups, as well as information about the world outside of their experience. Television can be a powerful teacher (Liebert & Sprafkin, 1988).

One part of everyday life children learn about from TV is the world of advertised products, for television aggressively advertises to children. Kids are an attractive audience, because, according to a recent Harris poll, preteens (ages 8 to 12) spend $19.1 billion per year and teens spend $94.7 billion ("Generation Y," 2003). Since the 1970s, analyses of the products advertised to children on television have shown that the majority of advertising during children's programs is for food products (one half of all these ads are for cereals, candy, snack food, and fast-food restaurants—that is, mostly for products high in sugar and fat). After food products, toys make up the second largest category. And these commercials tend to rely on animation, fast pace, and repetition of the product's name. According to the APA report (Huston et al., 1992),

> Objective information about the product is scarce in advertisements. Instead, commercials rely on verbal assertions about the subjective qualities of the product (e.g., "it's delicious") and descriptions of the physical components of the product (8% by weight). Advertisements to children stress such food qualities as taste, texture, appearance, fun associations, and accompanying prizes as reasons for choosing foods. Nutritional information is usually brief or nonexistent. Products are sometimes lauded for making the consumer strong, but "being good for you" is rarely stressed. In fact, advertisements often imply that a healthy food is unpalatable by saying it tastes great despite the fact that it is healthy. (p. 72)

In fact, there is concern that the types of foods marketed to children may be implicated in the rise of childhood obesity in the past 20 years. Both the United Kingdom and Australia are moving more quickly than the United States to reform food advertising directed toward children.

And what do we know about the effects of such advertising? First, children only gradually come to understand that commercials are trying to sell something (Ward, Wackman, & Wartella, 1977). That is, below the age of about 5 or 6, the majority of children do not understand the *persuasive intent* of advertisements and hence cannot criticize the advertiser's motives. Even older children, those under the age of 12, have not yet mastered a full and wary understanding of advertising and the nature of persuasive appeals. However, advertising's appeal to children declines as they grow older and become more mature, wary, and experienced viewers of such advertising, having bought products advertised and been disappointed with them.

Advertising does influence children's requests to parents for advertised products, and the more advertising children watch, the more they tend to request such products. There is some evidence that such product requests can lead to parent-child conflict. There is, however, little evidence that watching lots of advertising teaches children generally about the world of the consumer (what's known as *consumer socialization*), saving as well as spending, or a range of what are considered useful consumer practices such as comparison shopping. In summary, advertising can be successful with children, and its success is higher with younger rather than older children.

Evidence of advertising's influence on young children, coupled with a belief that young children are not an appropriate audience for advertising messages, led to passage of the 1990 Children's Television Education Act. One part of this federal law limits the amount of advertising during children's programs to 10 minutes per hour on weekends and 12 minutes per hour on weekdays.

Television is still the medium that most children spend the most time with. Considerable evidence indicates that television can teach a wide range of information, attitudes, expectations, and behaviors to child viewers. The concern is not whether television *can* teach children things, but rather what it *is* teaching them.

## THE EFFECTS OF MEDIA EFFECTS

The nature and types of impact that the media have are an immensely important policy question. We care about what the media may do to people because public behavior is a significant policy question: None of us wishes to live in a cruel, violent, or lawless society. To argue that a television depiction is corrosive of public values, to suggest that media portrayals promote violence or that listening to pop music can sanction suicide, is an opening argument for regulating or suppressing of media content: It suggests that we can solve the problem by rooting out the offending material. To this, we would offer several observations.

Our review should suggest that the media may have many different impacts on public behavior. At the same time, several generations of research on the impact of the media suggest that it is quite difficult to be specific about the effect of any content, indeed any class of content, on its audience. The same content, indeed, may have different effects on different segments of the audience. Moreover, by its very nature, most social science research must be highly qualified about its findings: It is very difficult to speak definitively about media impact.

Our discussion of causation has, we hope, made it clear that most behaviors have multiple causes; television alone, or recorded music, or movies, or newspapers, or all the media together, are rarely if ever a necessary and sufficient cause of public behavior; they operate in a larger social system that itself mediates most social behavior. Thus the argument for media regulation usually ignores covariates that should not be ignored. In other words, it is likely that regulation of content would not alleviate most social problems. On the other hand, media factors may be the contributors that are the easiest to alleviate—certainly easier than eliminating poverty or abusive family relationships—and therefore cannot be ignored.

At the same time, the media are easily made the scapegoats of those who do not wish to address the more difficult sources of social problems. Speaking specifically to his area of research, David Buckingham (2001) makes an argument that is more generally applicable:

> The debate about children and media violence is really a debate about other things, many of which have very little to do with the media. It is a debate that invokes deep-seated moral and political convictions, and it is rooted in people's unsettling experiences of social change and their genuine fears for the future. The issue of "violence" serves as a cipher for some very diverse, but none the less fundamental, anxieties—about the decline of the family and of organized religion, about the changing nature of literacy and contemporary culture, or, indeed, about the shortcomings of capitalism. (pp. 75–76)

If these debates are really about other things, we need to ask what the effects of the effects debates themselves are. That is, what are the political, social, and cultural ramifications of how these debates have been carried out? Many of the debates are concerned about the effects of the media on others, either societal "others" like children, or simply other people (we are often less concerned about the media's effects on ourselves and our own families than we are about their effects on other people and their families; see the discussion of "Third-Person" Effects in the next chapter). Some have argued that this concern for the protection of the supposedly needy is part of a desire for the upper classes to control the lower classes (the "unruly masses" have been viewed as the easy victims of media influence since the mass society debates of the nineteenth and early twentieth century; Petley, 2001). Some have seen the touting of images of women and children as helpless victims to be protected by society to be an excuse for regulation and a continuance of "the most conventional and pernicious gender stereotypes" (L. Miller, 1995, p. 57). Others see it as the attempt of moralists to simply try to get rid of material that they do not agree with. And still others see the focus on children as underplaying effects on adolescents and adults in general (Potter, 2003).

We are not saying, however, that society is helpless to make arguments about the impact of mass media, either pro or con. What we are saying is that the research record indicates caution. Arguments about media impact should be made, but we must recognize that the moral and cultural content of such arguments—what is good, desirable, and appropriate—should predominate. The effects research carries us only part of the way to their answers. Chapter 12 returns to the moral, ethical, and cultural context, or normative theory and media regulation.

## NOTE

1. *Obscenity* is material with sexual content that is legally prohibited, whereas pornography is a broader category, including legal and illegal material. What is obscene is decided by courts, whereas what is pornographic is open to public debate.

## SUGGESTED READINGS

Anderson, C. A., Berkowitz, L., Donnerstein, E., Huesmann, L. R., Johnson, J. D., Linz, D., Malamuth, N. M., & Wartella, E. (2003). The influence of media violence on youth. *Psychological Science in the Public Interest, 4*(3), 81–110.

Bandura, A. (1977). *Social learning theory.* Englewood Cliffs, NJ: Prentice-Hall.

Barker, M., & Petley, J. (Eds.). (2001). *Ill effects: The media/violence debate* (2nd ed.). New York: Routledge.

Bryant, J., & Zillman, D. (Eds.). (2002). *Media effects: Advances in theory and research* (2nd ed.). Mahwah, NJ: Lawrence Erlbaum.

Huston, A. C., Donnerstein, E., Fairchild, H., Feshbach, N. D., Katz, P. A., Murray, J. P., Rubinstein, E. A., Wilcox, B. L., & Zuckerman, D. M. (1992). *Big world, small screen: The role of television in American society.* Lincoln: University of Nebraska Press.

Potter, W. J. (2003). *The 11 myths of media violence.* Thousand Oaks, CA: Sage.

Shanahan, J., & Morgan, M. (1999). *Television and its viewers: Cultivation theory and research.* New York: Cambridge University Press.

# PART IV

# Media and Public Life

# Media and Politics

Our next two chapters discuss the media and public life. There are big issues here: How do the media represent public life—how do they cover it as news and what views of political reality predominate in such coverage? What role do the media have in political behavior and how can we best describe the relationships between the public and media? In dealing with these, we will try to connect the answers to perspectives we have introduced earlier: seeing media and politics, media and public life, is best accomplished through multiple lenses, those of historical narrative, ideological frame, and studies of behavior.

A beginning point in this discussion must be a distinction: In the explicitly political realm, we will concern ourselves largely with media representations of reality. As we explain below, the principal influence of the media on public life is through the ways media present information and the contexts within which they present it—how, in short, they treat the "real world" and how we, in turn, react to those presentations.

There are significant differences between the ways various media sectors approach reality: The news and information media attempt to represent it. Advertising and public relations practitioners try to focus attention on those aspects of reality that further their clients' interests. And producers of entertainment may use the "real world" as a source of raw material for fictional content and, as we noted in Chapter 6, are usually bound by requirements of verisimilitude.

## NEWS AND REALITY

From a contemporary vantage point, we couple the goal and purpose of journalism—the news and information function—with an attempt to represent political reality. Thus we begin there, approaching news in three ways: through a quick history of the evolution of news as an idea, through a discussion of how news might be defined, and by returning to the question of how news gets made.

### A Thumbnail History of News

Journalism historian Mitchell Stephens (1988) argues that it is impossible to find any society, past or present, without a "thirst for news." The members of all human societies in any historical epoch are marked by a "need to know" what is going on around them. But as Stephens, and virtually any other media historian will also tell us, how each society satisfies this need varies drastically. In "primitive" societies, everyone is a journalist, keeping up on what's happening through oral communication. Stephens observes that news in preliterate cultures could travel over great distances with breathtaking speed, as gossip can even today. In such cultures, however, it is not wholly correct that everyone is his or her own journalist, for virtually every known culture has evolved "news specialists"—criers, drummers, messengers, and minstrels. Interestingly, these bearers of news are almost always adjuncts of commercial or political power: They carry news along trade routes or are the servants of the king or chief.

Over time and across cultures, societies vary in how they conceive of, gather, and disseminate news, and, as we note below, how news is gathered and disseminated is deeply related to how it is defined.

From the American colonial period through the first third of the twentieth century, newspapers were the principal means of news delivery for the nation. The newspapers of the early period in American history were quite different from today. Access to information was limited in two pivotal ways: The audience had limited access to newspapers and newspapers had limited access to information. Early newspapers were expensive, beyond the reach of the average American. In the late 1700s, too, literacy rates were low, and much of the population lived on farms or in small towns. Because long-distance communication was slow, costly, and hazardous, news in early newspapers consisted of local stories, most usually written by the editor (who frequently doubled as the newspaper's publisher); texts of political addresses, proclamations, and laws; clippings of stories from papers in other cities with whom the editor exchanged papers; and commercial notices. The most important—the most timely—of these were notices of the availability of goods on ships docking in the harbor or river. The bulk of the news in each paper concerned commerce, trade, and politics—the important concerns of the elites that read the newspapers. Each important town had multiple newspapers, and newspapers differentiated themselves mostly in terms of the faction or political party they represented. As the discussion "Old News, New News" (Box 11.1) suggests, the division that we now take for granted between news and opinion— news on the front pages, opinion on editorial pages—was then non-existent. News *was* opinion, with facts selected to buttress the point of view of the editor and his political and commercial benefactors. Moreover, papers were small in size (typically four to eight pages), circulation (in the hundreds of copies, except in the largest cities), and staff: A "typical" newspaper in about 1800 might have an editor-publisher-printer and one or two other employees to help him print and distribute copies of the paper; distribution was largely local.[1]

---

**BOX 11.1**

**Old News, New News**

Below are the first few paragraphs from two New York newspaper stories, one a front-page story from 1734 (we have modernized the orthography and spelling) and the other from the front page of *The New York Times'* Web site in early 2005.

*The New York Weekly Journal*

*New Brunswick* (NJ), March 27, 1734. (By) Mr. (John Peter) Zenger—I was at a public house some days since in company with some persons that came from New York; most of them complained of the deadness of trade. Some of them laid it to the account of the repeal of the Tonnage Act, which they said was done to gratify the resentment of some in New York in order to distress Governor Burnet, but which has been almost the ruin of that town, by paying

*(Continued)*

---

(Continued)

the Bermudians about 12,000 pounds a year to export their commodities which might be carried in their own bottoms, and the money arising by the freight spent in New York.

They said that the Bermudians were an industrious frugal people, who bought no one thing in New York, but lodged the whole freight money in their own island, by which means, since the repeal of that Act, there has been taken from New York above 90,000 pounds and all this to gratify pique and resentment.

But this is not all; this money being carried away, which would otherwise have circulated in this province and city, and have been paid to the baker, the brewer, the smith, the carpenter, the shipwright, the boatman, the farmer, the shopkeeper, etc., has deadened our trade in all its branches and forced our industrious poor to seek other habitations, so that within these three years there has been above 300 persons have left New York; the houses stand empty, and there is as many houses as would make one whole street with bills upon their doors. And this has been as great a hurt as the carrying away the money and is occasioned by it, and all degrees of men feel it, from the merchant down to the carman. . . .

*The New York Times*

"Bush Praises Modest Pledge From NATO on Training Iraqi Forces," By Elaine Sciolino and Elisabeth Bumiller

BRUSSELS, Feb. 22 - The North Atlantic Treaty Organization announced agreement today on a modest plan to train and equip Iraq's new army and police force. The agreement is an important display of unity, but whether it can be translated into a dramatic change in the situation on the ground in Iraq remains to be seen.

The agreement by the 26 countries of the alliance came after France quietly dropped its refusal to participate under a NATO umbrella, pledging a modest $500,000 to a fund for training and equipping Iraqi forces and assigning one French officer to the Iraq mission at NATO headquarters near Brussels.

The United States is eager to get Iraq's security forces in fighting form both to restore stability to the country and allow the eventual withdrawal of the 150,000 American service men and women there.

But the training mission is going much more slowly that was hoped for. In Congressional testimony early this month, two senior Pentagon officials acknowledged that less than a third of the Iraqi security forces that the Pentagon claims have been trained are capable of tackling the most dangerous missions in the country.

In addition, the officials said, Iraqi Army units are suffering severe troops shortages, and absenteeism and even corruption in the security forces is a problem.

The French about face has enormous symbolic importance because France, which fiercely opposed opposed [*sic*] the American-led war in Iraq, has succumbed to American pressure and has agreed to work on the Iraq project through NATO.

But the mission is hampered by the fact that six NATO countries—France, Germany, Belgium, Luxembourg, Greece and Spain—have refused American and Iraqi requests to help train military forces and police inside Iraq, preferring to do training outside the country or to help pay for the mission.

If you find the 1734 story hard to follow, what *we* take it to say is that the correspondent is complaining that Governor Burnet's repeal of a trade act has led the city into a recession. This story was one of two that prompted the colonial government to bring seditious libel charges against Zenger (see Chapter 3).

The similarities and differences in these stories are worth comment. Both are political stories. Both rely on unnamed sources (Zenger appears to use anonymous sources to protect them from retribution; Sciolino and Bumiller, because the names of the sources are incidental—although on other occasions the *New York Times* and most other contemporary newspapers *do* use anonymous sources for the same reason Zenger did).

The dissimilarities, however, are more striking. Note first that the 2005 *New York Times* story reports events that occurred that same day. The 1734 *Journal* article report was written almost two weeks before it was published. The delay in publication reflects the time it took to get the report back to New York and the fact that the newspaper appeared but weekly. An important stylistic difference is that the *Journal* article is written in the first person ("*I* was at a public house . . ."), whereas the *New York Times* article is in the third person. Moreover, the 1734 article is discursive, with its information in no apparent particular order, whereas the 2005 article is in the inverted pyramid news form, with the most important information first, and information later presented in decreasing order of importance. But probably the most significant difference is in *point of view:* Zenger clearly is offering his own opinions, whereas Sciolino and Bumiller write a descriptive account, and the first few paragraphs offer virtually no opinions (later in the story, there were statements of opinion, but they were offered by government sources, not by the writer).

Source: Copyright © *New York Times*. "Bush praises modest pledge from NATO on training Iraqi forces" By Elaine Sciolino and Elisabeth Bumiller BRUSSELS, Feb. 22.

## The Newspaper as Mass Medium

As we noted in Chapter 4, a variety of factors in the middle half of the nineteenth century transformed the newspaper from a "class" to a "mass" medium: increasing literacy of the population, a technological revolution that enabled the rapid and cheap production of thousands of copies of papers, the emergence of mass advertising to supplement the economic support of the medium, and increasingly rapid modes of transportation that enlarged the potential distribution area of newspapers.[2] Transformation to a mass medium was also accompanied by a gradual evolution in what news was—what was considered to be news and how news was gathered and produced. From the 1820s onward the content of American newspapers slowly became "democratic," popular, fast, and "objective" (see Emery & Emery, 1984; Nerone, 1987; Schudson, 1978).[3]

*More Democratic:* To say that the press became more democratic is to say that, for both ideological and commercial reasons, the press first geared itself toward producing news that attracted and represented the tastes and interests of a wider, generally less elite audience, and, second, actively promoted a post-Revolutionary ideology of democracy and interest of the common people over those of wealth and privilege. Sociologist Herbert Gans (1979) has noted that the press even today promotes a value he calls *altruistic democracy:* Briefly, that popular democracy is *the* valued form of government, and individuals (and the press) have responsibilities for, and the right to, preserve and extend it.

*More Oriented Toward the Popular:* We've noted that newspapers evolved from a *class* to a *mass* medium. This evolution was in both audience and content. The content became less focused on politics and more on crime, human interest, and sensational content. This is not to say that sensationalism in the press was new; Stephens (1988) finds it in the ancient Greek, Roman, and Chinese precursors to newspapers. The important point, however, is that newspapers began to compete for a mass audience on the basis of the popularity and attractiveness of their content.

*More Event Centered and Timely:* News becomes more timely as newsgathering technologies allow for this to happen. We noted above that a

1734 newspaper features a "lead story" by John Peter Zenger that is more than a week old, whereas modern newspapers tell what happened yesterday. Two years stand out as pivotal in accelerating the speed at which news is delivered: the first American telegraphed news item (announcing the Whig presidential ticket) in 1844 and the 1963 launch of the Telstar communications satellite. As we noted in Chapter 2, the telegraph for the first time separated time from space, information from transportation. News could be known virtually instantaneously anywhere there were telegraph wires. Communications satellites allow for instantaneous transmission of visual images anywhere on earth.[4] In part, the technologies help account for why news becomes event centered rather than discursive: A reporter on the scene of an event "covers" that event and transmits a report to a newsroom rather than digesting it and other events for later writing. And media compete with each other to bring the latest news to audiences first. (See Box 11.2, "Coming Into Their Own.")

---

**BOX 11.2**

**Coming Into Their Own**

*The New York Times* has described "defining moments" for various news media, times when a medium "came into its own" as a purveyor of news. Their defining moments include the following:

*Newspapers:* April 13, 1861
   Newspaper circulation shoots up during the Civil War, beginning with the siege of Fort Sumter in Charleston Harbor. The *New York Herald's* readership grows from 77,000 in 1860 to 107,520 the day after Fort Sumter is attacked.

*Radio:* December 8, 1941
   Sixty million people tune into President Franklin D. Roosevelt's address asking Congress to declare war on Japan the day after the bombing of Pearl Harbor.

*Network Television:* November 22, 1963
   CBS, NBC, and ABC drop regular programming to broadcast news the day President John F. Kennedy is assassinated. From 4 p.m. until 11 p.m., more than half of America's 51.6 million homes with television tune into these broadcasts.

*(Continued)*

---

---

(Continued)

*Cable Television:* January 17, 1991
  When the United States and its allies bomb Baghdad in the Persian Gulf War, CNN, with Peter Arnett filing reports from the Iraqi capital, reaches a record audience for a cable network, with 12.9 million households (a 22.7 Neilsen rating) tuning into the network.

*The Internet:* July 4, 1997
  The National Aeronautics and Space Administration (NASA) reports 45 million "hits" on its Web site and mirror sites in the week following the landing of its Mars Pathfinder robot explorer.

---

Source: *New York Times,* July 14, 1997 (national edition), pp. C1, C5, citing Frank Luther Mott's (1941/1962) *American Journalism,* NASA, CNN, and the A. C. Neilsen Co.

---

*More "Objective" and Less Partisan:* Whereas early American big-city newspapers were largely the creatures of parties and interest groups bent on promoting their own point of view, modern mass news purveyors— newspapers, television networks, and news radio—largely deal in "objective" news. By objective, we mean two things: First, that media become more neutral, less likely to take overt political positions on their own, and, second, that *news* itself becomes less politically colored. In other words, news becomes facts, whereas opinions and values, when expressed in media, are labeled and compartmentalized as commentary, editorials, and news analyses.

Media historian Donald L. Shaw (1967) has written that the development of the first great American telegraph wire service, the Associated Press (AP), is in large part responsible for news's becoming less partisan and more objective after 1848. Serving varied newspapers with varied political allegiances required the AP to develop a news style that would be acceptable to all, and this led to an objective, "just the facts ma'am"[5] AP news style that in time came to be imitated by newspapers and, later, other news media.[6] The notion of objectivity was important not just to the development of journalism, but also to other professions and especially to science (Schudson, 1978). The early twentieth century saw what historians call the Progressive Era, an era of popular reform in which many writers and thinkers popularized and glorified science, *scientific management* (the rise of efficiency experts), and the importance of the expert.

346

## News Today

To describe what news is today requires us to do two things. First is, finally, to *define* what we mean by news, anyway. Second is to describe how news is made. Both aspects are important, because both how we define news and how we make news shape the types of stories or information presented in the media as being important or the truthful version of events.

### *Defining News*

The *Webster's New World Dictionary* defines news as "1. New information about anything; information previously unknown. 2. Recent happenings, especially those broadcast over the radio, printed in a newspaper, etc. 3. reports of such events, collectively." A widely used news reporting textbook adds two other definitions: "News is information about a break from the normal flow of events, an interruption in the expected," and, "News is information people need in order to make rational decisions about their lives" (Mencher, 1984, p. 72).

Defining news is also asking what makes something newsworthy or worth reporting to audiences. Following a reporting textbook tradition, author Melvin Mencher (1984), a former reporter and longtime professor at the Columbia University Graduate School of Journalism, lists seven factors that determine the newsworthiness of a potential story:

1. *Impact:* The significance, importance, or consequence of an event or trend.

2. *Timeliness:* The more recent, the more newsworthy. In some cases, timeliness is relative. An event may have occurred in the past but only have been learned about recently.

3. *Prominence:* Occurrences featuring well-known individuals or institutions are newsworthy. Well-knownness may spring either from the power the person or institution possesses (the president, the speaker of the House of Representatives) or from celebrity (the late Princess Diana or Paris Hilton).

4. *Proximity:* Closeness of the occurrence to the audience may be gauged either geographically (close by events, all other things

being equal, are more important than distant ones) or in terms of the assumed values, interests, and expectations of the news audience.

5. *The Bizarre:* The unusual, unorthodox, or unexpected attracts attention. Boxer Mike Tyson's 1997 disqualification for biting off a piece of Evander Holyfield's ear moves the story from the sports pages and the end of a newscast to the front pages and the top of the newscast.

6. *Conflict:* Controversy and open clashes are newsworthy, inviting attention on their own, almost regardless of what the conflict is over. Conflict reveals underlying causes of disagreement between individuals and institutions in a society.

7. *Currency:* Occasionally something becomes an idea whose time has come. For example, national news attention in the summer of 2002 focused on the abduction of children. The matter assumes a life of its own, and for a time assumes momentum in news reportage. What had been local news stories became national for a time.

Other textbooks add *human interest* as another dimension, although one can argue that it figures in Mencher's *proximity, prominence, the bizarre,* and *currency* categories. The more cynical phrase, "If it bleeds, it leads," is also used in considering the newsworthiness of events.

Presumably, the more categories or dimensions any potential news story fits into, the more newsworthy it is. Years ago, journalism folklore suggests, a British journalist was asked for a definition of news, and he replied using a similar categories approach. News, he said, is anything with mystery or sex or religion or the Royal Family. "I guess that would mean," he quipped, "that the most newsworthy story in the world would begin, 'Oh my God, the Queen's pregnant. I wonder who did it?'"

### Making News

A *second* approach to defining news begins by noting that many journalists and communication researchers have discovered that reporters and editors have a hard time defining news for themselves: News is just something "they know when they see it." A reporter might say, "I can't really define it, but tell me a story, and I'll tell you if it's news." Communication researcher John Dimmick (1974) once performed a very elaborate experiment, asking working reporters and editors to tell him how newsworthy a group of stories—ones he had constructed using categories or dimensions of news like the one above, and then statistically analyzed the journalists' answers. What he found, using the powerful statistical approach of factor analysis, was that no categories really explained how the journalists selected the stories they did. "A possible interpretation, of course," he wrote, "is that for the newsmen-subjects, the single dimension is 'news'" (p. 35).

So perhaps the way to figure out what news is is to describe what journalists *do* to make news. In other words, we describe the structure and process by which news gets made. Sociologist Gaye Tuchman (1973) began doing research in newsrooms by asking journalists to define news. She got puzzled "I don't know" looks from reporters and editors. And so she took a slightly different approach, which was to ask how reporters worked on stories. When she did so, she found that journalists tended to classify stories into a relatively small number of categories—"hard" and "soft" news: that is, "breaking" stories about current events and feature stories that were less time-bound. Moreover, hard-news stories were further subdivided into *spot* stories, news that develops unexpectedly and quickly (a fire or a plane crash); *developing* stories, or spot-news stories that continue to develop over time, requiring follow-up stories; and *continuing* stories, or stories known about in advance, which, like developing stories, require a news organization to devote a reporter to the story for an extended period (a trial, a presidential candidate's campaign tour). An interesting feature of this classification system is that not only does it describe the way journalists think about their work, it also describes the way the news organization itself can organize reporters to cover the news: Some reporters can be assigned in advance to cover developing and continuing stories; others can be shifted around to cover the spot stories that develop without warning; and when there's time, the news organization can have reporters spend time on soft news or feature stories. Tuchman calls this "routinizing the unexpected."

Because news is "new information," it very much is, as Tuchman and many, many others note, "unexpected." But as Tuchman notes, journalists' conceptions of what news is and how it's covered also clue us in to the way news becomes routinized or made predictable (sort of).

Only a fraction of the news stories in any newspaper and in any newscast are unanticipated events that break without warning. The rest can be predicted in advance. News is made predictable by several structures and processes; together, they help answer the question, *Where does news come from and who gets to make it?*

First, consider individual news stories and who gets to make them. There are essentially three origins for stories:

1. Naturally occurring events such as disasters, floods, earthquakes, fires, and airline crashes are inherently unpredictable, and journalists must respond after the fact. News stories about disasters follow a predictable pattern: Early reports, which frequently overestimate the severity of the disaster, rely on everyday people, because they're frequently the only witnesses; later stories, assuming the story is newsworthy enough to become developing news over several days, tend to rely on officials—mayors and governors, insurance company representatives, disaster relief agency officials, and the like—another way that news becomes routinized.[7]

2. Created and "subsidized" news is more frequent than unpredicted news. It occurs because a person, group, or organization does something public and newsworthy (for example, files an important lawsuit, passes a law, breaks a law, opens or closes a plant) and/or seeks and gets press attention. We will discuss both of these in a bit more detail below.

3. So-called enterprise news is made when journalists act rather than react, as they do to accidents and disasters. In enterprise news, an editor or reporter takes the initiative on a story. There are two main cases: beat coverage and investigative journalism. We will discuss both in a bit more detail below.

In two of our three types, news doesn't "just happen" but rather is made. Billions of events occur daily, and only a tiny fraction of them can become news. Tuchman (1978) uses the metaphor of a "news net." Not knowing in advance exactly where news might come from, journalists strategically organize themselves to be in places where news is most likely to happen, hoping to catch news in their net. Coping with too much potential news is too costly, not only in terms of money but in psychic costs as well. Walter Lippmann (1922) observed long ago that, "Without standardization, without stereotypes, without routine judgments, without a fairly ruthless disregard of subtlety, the editor would die of excitement" (p. 222). Much journalistic work, particularly on newspapers, magazines, and network television, is organized around a beat system; that is, reporters are assigned to a particular topic or specialty—city government, the police and courts, the White House. Most beats are *geographic*—reporters cover places and the people who occupy them and make news there (science, environment, medicine, the arts are exceptions)—and most of these places are official. In fact, several content analyses of the news show that two thirds to three quarters of all sources quoted in the news are public officials (Brown, Bybee, Wearden, & Straughan, 1987; Gans, 1979; Whitney, Fritzler, Jones, Mazzarella, & Rakow, 1989). In part, officials make news because they do newsworthy things, and, in part, they make news simply because journalists are known, familiar, and accessible to them, and vice versa (see also Chapter 3). By extension, nonofficials are relatively *dis*advantaged in their ability to make news: They have to work harder to capture journalists' attention or they fall between the holes in the news net. Furthermore, official news, because of its familiarity to reporters and editors, starts off with a presumption that it is legitimate—it's news because that's the way news is.

There is one major potential problem for journalists who spend much of their time covering public officials. Journalists fear "going native": That is, there's a risk of journalists adopting the goals and values of the people they cover rather than keeping an objective distance. Sociologist Mark Fishman (1980) noted that journalists who cover officials virtually inevitably also frame their news stories according to what he calls the "bureaucratic phase structures" of the organizations they cover. That is, the organization's routine decides for them when something is news. Think, for example, about crime stories: When do we get news about crime, and where does information in the story really come from? Virtually all crime stories are about the commission of a crime (police report) and when a person is arrested (arrest report), charged with the crime (arraignment), brought to trial, convicted or acquitted, and, if convicted, sentenced. In other words, news is organized in exactly the same way as the criminal justice system organizes crime. And because it is organized that way and follows the same routines, the coverage tends to assume or take for granted the official organizational ideology.

It is, however, possible that anyone can make news. As we noted above, public officials are relatively advantaged in making news, and others are less so. Recall our discussion of resource dependence in Chapter 3: Journalists want access to news and can offer publicity; potential news sources often have information that, if known, would be newsworthy, and they may want several different things. Public officials may want to inform the public about new programs. They may be engaged in conflict with other officials (a Republican president versus a Democratic congress, a state senator who wants to increase the income tax versus a governor who does not) or others in the public and may want publicity for their side of the issue. Social action groups likewise want to promote their side of an issue and seek press attention as well.

In a classic study of *The New York Times* and *Washington Post*, researcher Leon Sigal (1973) discovered that about two thirds of stories in those papers originated from news releases, handouts, and documents provided by news sources to reporters; in other words, the initiative for the story was with the *source*, rather than the reporter. Potential sources who go to the trouble of providing information to journalists in a form they can use with relatively little reportorial "legwork" or in-house editing work of their own will have greater success in making news than others. The past few years have seen the development by large corporations and public relations agencies of video news releases, DVDs, and satellite links provided directly to stations; particularly in smaller TV markets, stations have frequently aired such news releases without acknowledging their sources. Now the Internet is being used to distribute such "news" (see, for example, the Web site www.prnewswire.com). Communication researcher Oscar Gandy (1982) refers to such tactics as *information subsidies*. Clearly, the ability to shape news this way favors groups that are already advantaged—companies and organizations able to do skilled public relations or to hire others to do it for them.

But anyone who has ever visited any newsroom knows that, for every news release used, dozens of others end up in the wastebasket. What makes the difference? Several things do, and each of them also applies to making news more generally.

Timing is important. It's better to have information arriving in newsrooms at slack times—at the beginning of the cycle (as editors get started on the day) and especially on weekends; on weekends, there's less official news to cover. It's also better to focus on topics of current interest (recall that Mencher, 1984, mentioned currency as a news value).

Those who angle news toward satisfying one or more of those values are more successful at making news than are others. Gans (1979) has argued that for ordinary people to attract the attention of the news media, they frequently have either to demonstrate or resort to violence (the conflict value) or engage in odd or unusual activities (the bizarre value). And media scholar Todd Gitlin (1980) has suggested that this can have the impact of altering a social movement that is trying to attract the public's attention through the media. Gitlin argues that the Students for Democratic Society (SDS) evolved in the 1960s from being a left-liberal mainstream social action group to a radical and violent one because media accounts of its activities focused on one aspect of its work—demonstrations against the Vietnam War—rather than its full agenda of civil rights and antipoverty work. Media coverage attracted to the SDS antiwar activists willing to be violent, people far less interested in peaceful action. Finally, prominence as a value is attractive to journalists. The already famous and powerful again are advantaged in making news.

Another powerful resource is expertise. To help them make news, journalists often turn to sources who are in a position either to know what's going on (present or former public officials, topic specialists in universities, interest groups, and think tanks) or who are believed to have valuable insights into current events. The key characteristics of a media expert are not only expertise but also accessibility and reliability. The accessibility factor favors experts in places where journalists are concentrated, especially in the key news centers of New York and Washington. The reliability factor favors people who have already been in the news, whose information has been solid, and who can deliver a quick, understandable sound bite. Because journalists are always in a hurry, they tend to rely on sources who appear in what researchers Mark Cooper and Lawrence Soley (1990) refer to as the "Golden Rolodex," the list of sources already known about.

What may become news also depends on the news cycle—what's news for a particular day, for a newspaper or TV evening newscast, or a particular week or month for a magazine. Again, the potential number of stories is mammoth. Perhaps 20% of the news stories that the typical daily newspaper has in hand during a day will appear in the paper; at major dailies such as *The New York Times, Los Angeles*

*Times,* or *Washington Post,* perhaps 5% will; and at the network evening newscasts, perhaps 1% will (Whitney & Becker, 1982). Where do these stories come from and how do editors decide which ones to use?

*Where do stories come from?* At large newspapers, the networks, and newsmagazines, many stories come from the organization's news staff. Each has several hundred reporters, most of them covering specific beats. But at both large and small news operations, the large majorities of stories come from wire services such as the AP; supplementary news services, most of them organized by newspapers (*The New York Times,* the Gannett news service); and, in the case of broadcasting, from the parent network for each station as well. These are supplied to newsrooms either by high-speed computer links or satellite feeds.

*What becomes news?* Much of this news is redundant: A paper or station may have several stories about the same news event, in which case it will most likely use the version prepared by its own staff member. If there is no in-house version of the story, an editor making selection decisions relies on several determinants to decide what's news. First is to follow cues provided by news suppliers: At the beginning of each news cycle, for example, the AP runs a "menu" alerting editors to the most important stories it will transmit. It may follow cues from opinion leaders within the news media themselves, especially *The New York Times, Washington Post,* the major newsmagazines, and the networks; these processes are sometimes called *intermedia agenda setting.* (See the discussion of agenda setting later in this chapter.)

These and other forces lead to a great deal of *standardization* of news. You have no doubt noticed that the front page of your daily newspaper is not terribly different from the news you see on television or hear on the radio, particularly in terms of what stories you see in a given day. There are several reasons for this: First, newsmen and women are constrained by the values they share for what news is. Second, each works for an organization with routines that constrain what news is. Third, each organization operates in a larger news environment in which other organizations are influencing their own news decisions (competition, we have noted, often leads to standardization rather than to differentiation);[8] moreover, in that environment, each relies on other, common suppliers of news such as the wire services. Fourth, given the number of media mergers, many of the different news outlets might be owned by the same company. Finally, each lives in a social and cultural environment that exercises its own influences on reporters, editors, and the organizations for which they work.

*News as Report.* The dictionary definition notes that news is not the event itself, but the *report* of an event. Not only is news made by newsmakers, but "raw" occurrences must be made into stories. Each medium imposes its own demands on what a story is. TV stories, for example, demand a visual element; print media stories frequently are structured (and have been for more than a century) in inverted pyramid style, with the most essential information at the beginning of the story and less essential detail and explanatory information further down. A useful exercise, always, is to compare across different media to see how they have structured their stories.

At another level, stories must be structured in terms of their content. We have noted that many news stories feature conflict. Conflict is important and frequently interesting; moreover, conflict serves journalistic interests. Because what's news in an event or issue is frequently unknown and ambiguous, journalists can employ conflict in the interests of their value of objectivity; an objective story is one that covers "both sides" (or "all sides") of an issue. Gaye Tuchman (1972) has pointed to objectivity as a "strategic ritual" for journalists: By quoting both sides in a story, the journalist can remain detached and nonpartisan. But, as Tuchman further notes, the routine practices of journalists usually mean that the sides quoted tend to be the usual, and usually powerful, sources of news. Journalistic objectivity, then, meets the standards suggested in Chapter 7 to describe an ideology (see also Glasser, 1985; Hackett, 1984).

## News and Reality, Today and Tomorrow

News is supposed to be a representation of reality, something even some of its most vocal critics suggest. (Note that "representation of reality" is a pretty good definition of ideology.) For example, critical scholar Todd Gitlin (1979) admits that journalists seek "truth—partial, superficial, occasion- and celebrity-centered truth, but truth nevertheless" (p. 263). But what can a 10-second sound bite capture the truth of? How we interpret how well journalism succeeds in truth seeking is a matter of perspective. Recall the three theories of reality set out in Chapter 7. Those of us who adhere to the first (reality as a collection of facts) or second (reality as differing from appearances) views of reality tend to believe that the relationship between news and reality is fairly close. Faced with information that news tends to advantage the already powerful and advantaged, those holding one of these two views might well answer, "Well, yes; journalists are doing no more than reflecting the world in which they, and we, live." Faced with the same set of circumstances, those who hold the third view (reality as socially constructed and its ideology-and-hegemony cousins) would conclude something slightly different: that journalists reflect, uphold, and support the existing power relationships of the society.

The summer 1997 movie hit *Men in Black* had a running joke that the most reliable source of news and information about human contact with space aliens was the supermarket tabloid newspapers. The joke is funny because the movie—based on a comic book—is a sheer fantasy, but within the parameters of the fantasy, supermarket tabloids could be a reliable source of information. We note this because the lines between reality and unreality are far less clearly drawn than the preceding pages might suggest. During the 1990s, on television, in motion pictures, in magazines, and in a variety of ways, the genres of the real and unreal have blurred.

All media bear some relationship to reality, but not all do so as directly as do news media. Most fictional programming is, of course, fantasy; but as we noted early on, entertainment producers must aim for the appearance of reality, so that the audience will willfully suspend its disbelief and thus be entertained.

Advertising presents a separate set of concerns. In the first place, advertisers are watched over by the Federal Trade Commission, the Food and Drug Administration, and the National Advertising Review Board of the self-regulatory Council of Better Business Bureaus. All prohibit outright lying and deception. But the reality of much advertising, especially for many consumer products, is that the products within a particular category are far more similar than they are different. Still, none of us expects to hear any time soon a commercial that says, "Our pain reliever works just as well as half a dozen others, and it might cost a little more because we advertise." Rather, when the products in a category are not very different, the creative genius of the advertiser is either to find what advertiser Ted Bates called a "unique selling proposition" for the product, some characteristic that differentiates that product from others, or else to create an image for the product that associates the product with an emotion or image that the audience-market desires. Is this reality? It is not deceptive; it is in the interstices.[9]

By the same token, ethical public relations practitioners—those who, for example, belong to the Public Relations Society of America and adhere to its code of ethics—will not purposefully lie to the public or the media. At the same time, they are obligated to present clients in the best possible light, to advance the client's goals. Is this reality, deception, or something in between? (See Box 12.4, "Codes of Ethics," in the next chapter.)

In the last decade, the ability to digitally manipulate images increased as desktop computers became more powerful. The ethics of the practice (manipulating images for compositional, aesthetic, or political reasons) became the subject of debate in the 1980s and 1990s as such notable examples came to light as *National Geographic* moving one of the pyramids in a cover photo or *Time* magazine darkening O.J. Simpson's mug shot so that he looked more menacing.

## MEDIA AND POLITICS

We have spent as much time as we have on the relationships between news, information, and reality because they are so important to the sort of society we have. As we further detail in the next chapter, reliable information is the cornerstone of a civil, public society, something the framers of the U.S. Constitution clearly understood. For a citizenry to make intelligent choices, it must have access to the day's intelligence before it can act. The next few pages outline the influences that media have on how we make up our minds and then act politically.

Media clearly perform important functions in politics. First, by the time we are teenagers, media are our most important source of political information (Atkin, 1981). Second, media serve as potential sources of persuasion and decision making, both directly, through endorsements and editorials, and indirectly, as a vehicle for candidates' and parties' speeches, platforms, and advertisements. Finally, information and persuasion may lead to behavior or political activity.

## Political Behavior

Media effects on politics have been studied extensively, not only because they are socially important, but also because they're easy to study: Political campaigns have a reasonably definite beginning and a very definite end—election day—and that end is a concrete, measurable behavior: People either do or do not vote, and if they do, they vote for a named candidate. There are, of course, other forms of political behavior: volunteering time to campaigns, contributing money, trying to persuade others. And there are likewise strong individual differences in how much the American public actually engages in each of them: On average, about half of Americans vote in presidential elections, fewer than a quarter in presidential primaries; one in five wear campaign buttons or display posters, and only about one person in nine has worked in a political campaign or given money to one.[10]

Why is there so much variation in how people do—and do not—behave politically? There are a number of causes: level of political interest, strength of political attitudes and opinions, amount of political information, degree of attention to politics (largely through the media), and strength of partisanship. Moreover, these are deeply interrelated—mutually causal—so that a person high on one of these variables (a strong partisan) is likely to be high on others as well (politically well-informed), and those low on any one variable are likely to be low on others as well.

## Information

We've noted before that the media serve as the principal source of political information, determining how well we are informed about politics (or most other matters). The average American, it is safe to say, is *not* well informed about politics: At the height of the fall electoral campaigns, for example, fewer than half can name any candidate for U.S. House of Representatives from their district or both candidates for U.S. Senate from their state (Neuman, 1986). But, as with political behavior, there are profound individual differences in what, and how much, we know about politics.

Communication researcher Philip J. Tichenor and his colleagues (Tichenor, Donohue, & Olien, 1970) have postulated, and they and many others have found a great deal of evidence to support, what they call the *knowledge gap hypothesis* (see also Gaziano, 1983). It suggests that, in the development of any social or political issue, the more highly educated segments of the population know more about the issue early on and, moreover, acquire information at a faster rate than the less well educated. In other words, the information-rich get richer, and the gap between them and the information-poor widens over time. Why should this occur? Just as the causes of variation in political behavior are multiple, the causes of knowledge acquisition are, too. Level of education predicts not only what and how much we're likely to know on a given topic at any given time, but also how interested in and motivated we are to learn about that topic. It also predicts the quality and quantity of media attention we pay to it, and how able we are to learn new information about that topic, a notion that E. D. Hirsch (1987) has labeled *cultural literacy*. Tichenor and other scholars, however, point out that whereas knowledge gaps are widespread, they are not inevitable: Gaps can close. They do so particularly when issues "heat up" to an extent that all segments of the public are likely to learn about them—when, in other words, issues become so important that they generate interpersonal discussion and saturation media coverage, motivating people usually not interested in the topic to pay attention and to learn. Extensive research on how people learn about timely events supports this: We're more likely to learn about the most intensely newsworthy events—a presidential assassination attempt, the crash of a spacecraft—from other people rather than from the media. We learn about the most newsworthy events from other people because those people want to talk about what they know. To the extent that we're likely to hear about unimportant things at all, we learn them from other people, simply because the media do not report on them. We're more likely to get intermediately important news from the media because the media do report on them but people aren't likely to focus conversations on them.

## Persuasion and Decision Making

How persuasive are the media in political questions? Much of the communication research literature suggests that the effects are quite limited, for it is often difficult to separate the effects of media—the messengers—from the messages and their initial sources—candidates, parties, and interest groups. At the same time, a half-century of research does help us understand the process of political communication effects.

Fifty years ago, the first large-scale studies of the impact of media on politics were conducted by the legendary Paul F. Lazarsfeld and his Columbia University colleagues (Berelson, Lazarsfeld, & McPhee, 1954; Lazarsfeld, Berelson, & Gaudet, 1948). In two communities in two presidential elections, they conducted panel studies or repeated surveys of the same samples to ascertain when potential voters made up their minds for whom they would vote. The panel design allowed them to speculate on what led these potential voters to the decisions they made. They initially suspected that mass media messages would be enormously important in vote decisions, but they found in each study that this was simply not so. In each, as a matter of fact, solid majorities of voters had made up their minds for whom they would vote *even before the candidates were officially nominated.* Their explanation for this was simple and straightforward—a social categories one: Blue-collar families said they would support the Democrat, white-collar ones the Republican. Moreover, they found two other important things: First, among those who had not made up their minds at the beginning of the campaign, relatively few cited any media source as the determining influence on their vote. Far more cited the influence of other people. Second, voters who make up their minds early in a campaign are different in several respects from those who make up their minds later on.

## The Opinion-Leader Concept

Surprised by their failure to find large-scale media effects, Lazarsfeld and his fellow researchers followed up on those who had identified "other people" as their sources of a vote decision. They found that these other people were not a random assortment, but the same names cropped up as sources. In their voting studies and subsequent research, they did find a media effect of a sort: These other people, whom they dubbed *opinion leaders* or *influentials*, were not remarkably different demographically (or in social categories terms) from the people they influenced, but they were different. As Elihu Katz and Lazarsfeld (1955) explain it,

partisan: They are more likely to be political independents but are somewhat less interested in politics than early deciders; they pay lower routine attention to political content in the media but are somewhat more likely to follow political news during the campaigns (motivated, we would guess, by a desire for information on which to base a vote choice); and they are intermediate in the amount of political discussion in which they engage and in their ultimate likelihood of voting. *Late* or *last-minute deciders* are lowest on all these measures: They are the least partisan and the least likely to follow politics in general or the campaign in particular, to discuss politics, and, for that matter, to vote.

What does this typology tell us about media impact? Something subtle. Early deciders pay close attention to media, and so we might guess that the potential effect of media on them would be great. But because they've already made up their minds, media messages have little impact on their political decisions. Because they make up their minds during the campaign, campaign deciders, on the other hand, are open to influence by media because they lack the strong partisan ties early deciders have and because they pay closer attention to media (and especially candidate debates) during the campaign. But because they discuss the campaign with others, they're likewise open to interpersonal influence. The last-minute deciders are the most perplexing and, at the same time, most interesting of all: Because they don't discuss the campaign or follow it closely in the media, are unlikely to watch televised debates, and lack the political party ties that tell them how to choose, it's not clear what leads them to a choice. (In fact, fewer of them vote than in the other categories; some of them flip coins; still others resort to *latent partisanship,* voting for candidates of parties with which they very weakly identify.) But political scientist Philip Converse (1962) has suggested a paradox: Even though late deciders pay the least attention to media politics, they are the *most* susceptible to media influence, for they have so little else on which to base vote decisions. For this reason, last-minute saturation advertising, particularly on television (and during or between entertainment programs) may be very effective.

## Endorsements and Advertising

Media messages make evaluative statements in efforts to persuade and to influence behavior, most usually in two ways: through endorsements, in which a medium urges voters to support a particular candidate or referendum position, and through *political advertising,* in which third parties—the candidates, political parties, or others—urge a course of behavior.

Over the years, the U.S. print press has become decidedly less partisan, and declining numbers of newspapers endorse candidates for office, particularly for the office of president. However, many papers, including most of the largest ones, do endorse candidates, and whether endorsements have an impact is an important question. The answer is yes, they do have an effect, but the effect is modest in size, particularly at the presidential level. The most careful statistical study of the effects of newspaper endorsements on presidential voting, conducted by John Robinson (1976a, 1976b) over five presidential elections (1956–1972), indicated that the presence of an endorsement made an average three percentage point difference in the vote for endorsed candidates. Although that's not a large difference, we've previously noted that, in close elections, a small difference can have a large effect. However, Robinson (1976b) found the largest endorsement effects (an endorsement persuading voters to vote for a supported candidate) in the two landslide elections (Lyndon Johnson's 1964 victory over Goldwater, Richard Nixon's 1972 win over George McGovern) among the five he studied; in short, he found the largest effects when it made no political difference. It is generally suspected, however, that in lower-level races—for city and county offices and judicial seats—where voters tend not to be well informed about candidates, the effects of endorsements may be somewhat greater, simply because the fact that a newspaper endorsed a candidate may be one of the only things that a voter may know about the candidate.

We earlier cited Michael Schudson's (1984) book, *Advertising, the Uneasy Persuasion,* noting that when Schudson interviewed advertising researchers, they were unable to give him any clear idea of how much impact advertising has. That applies to political advertising as well as to consumer products. At the aggregate level, there is scanty evidence that the amount of money spent on candidate advertising is itself directly related to whether candidates win or lose, once incumbency is accounted for (that is, incumbents tend to be reelected, and they also tend to be able to raise a lot more money).[11] Nonetheless, there is evidence that some advertising, in some contexts, can be effective, and so we will take a brief closer look.

One perhaps unanticipated impact advertising has on elections is information. Political scientists Thomas Patterson and Robert McClure (1976) found in a study of one presidential election that advertising, in fact, contributed more to the public's knowledge of candidates and issues than even the news did, and although subsequent studies have generally found that news is more informative than advertising, the fact remains that advertising's contribution to knowledge is impressive, particularly among less active voters. Political candidate advertising, however, differs from most consumer-product advertising in several respects. What we're being sold is a candidate and/or his or her ideas and promises about what public policy should be, rather than some product we will use and later discard. Moreover, the behavior sought is a vote, not a sale. Finally, political advertising, unlike consumer-product advertising, tends to be *comparative* and frequently *negative:* The candidate tries to persuade people to vote for her or him by finding something to criticize in an opponent's past or record. (When was the last time you saw a product ad that tried to sell you something by pointing out how awful the competition was?)

Despite the fact that polls show large majorities of the public find negative political ads distasteful, politicians use them frequently because they think they work, and historians often point to ads that appear to have had profound impacts on campaigns, such as the "Daisy" ad in the 1964 Goldwater-Johnson election and the Willie Horton commercial in Bush's 1988 victory over Michael Dukakis. (See Box 11.3, "Negative Political Ads.") But negative ads may have several different impacts on individual voters. A voter may believe the ad and form a negative impression of the candidate, which is the ad's intent; at the same time, however, it may also translate into a negative impression of the sponsoring candidate, although usually the negative belief about the target candidate is somewhat more important (which is why negative ads appear to work better in two-candidate general elections than in multicandidate ones; in multicandidate races, if Candidate A attacks Candidate B, they may both "lose" while Candidate C emerges unharmed). In general, however, we can never be quite sure how successful negative advertising really is with individual voters. A secondary effect of negative ads is more easily documentable: They tend to focus political debate, particularly in the news media, on the issues the negative ads have raised.

365

---

**BOX 11.3**

**Negative Political Ads**

Perhaps the most famous television political commercial of all time was the 1964 "Daisy" commercial, created by political consultant Tony Schwartz. Showing a little girl plucking the petals off a daisy and moving to a close-up of her pupils, a voice-over counts down ("10 . . . 9 . . . 8 . . .") followed by a quick cut to a view of a nuclear explosion. Then, on a black background, came an appeal to vote for Lyndon Johnson. The ad never even mentioned Johnson's opponent, Senator Barry Goldwater, but the "message" was unambiguous, suggesting that Goldwater was a dangerous warmonger who might lead the country into a nuclear holocaust.

First runner-up would be the 1988 "Willie Horton" commercial, in which the campaign for George H. W. Bush showed a still picture of an African American man who raped a woman while he was on furlough from a Massachusetts prison, during the time Bush's Democratic opponent, Michael Dukakis, was governor of Massachusetts. The voice-over blamed the act on Dukakis, although, in fact, the furlough program had become law while Dukakis's predecessor—a Republican—was governor.

Both ads became controversial—and newsworthy: The ads were replayed many times, not as paid advertising, but in news programs (the "Daisy" commercial, in fact, aired only *once* as a paid commercial on the NBC *Movie of the Week*). Each ad thus helped form the political debate of the respective campaigns.

But can we be sure of the commercial's impact? No. In the first place, it becomes impossible to separate the impact of the commercial as a commercial from the impact of the news coverage of the political issue. In each case, only minorities of the electorate ever saw the commercials as commercials. Moreover, at a very aggregate level, poll data tend to discount the effect: In both of these cases, the percentages of likely voters expressing a preference for the eventual winners *at the time the commercial first aired* were virtually identical to the fraction of the popular vote the winner received two months later in the presidential election.

---

We now turn to several related models of communication influence that bear some similarities. Each suggests that major impacts from the media may flow not from intentional efforts to persuade (what we think), but by changing our cognitions (what we think about). These are the ideas of *agenda setting, priming, third-person effects,* and the *spiral of silence.*

## The Agenda-Setting Model

The news media, by and large, do not set out to persuade, but rather to inform. We are first of all suggesting that the media, in telling us what to think about, *set the public agenda;* that is, they tell us what issues are important for public debate. The idea behind agenda setting is quite simple: The media, over time, by featuring some issues prominently, some issues less prominently, and still other issues not at all, give us a sense of what issues are important or, in the research literature, a sense of the issue's *salience.* By salience, we mean the amount of public or political importance an issue possesses—the "light and heat" it generates.

Media cue us as to the importance of issues in different ways: First, we get a sense of the importance of an issue in media by its prominence: Is it at the top of the front page, or buried somewhere inside? Is it the first item in the evening news, or near the end? Second, media importance is conveyed by both the extensiveness of stories in a given day and the duration of coverage over time: Is there one story, or is there a main story and one or more related *sidebar* stories? How long and detailed are the stories? Does artwork—photos, charts, or graphs—accompany the story? Does the issue receive treatment over many days, weeks, months?

Communication researchers test for agenda-setting impact by obtaining measures of the media agenda and the public agenda and then comparing the two. For example, we might content-analyze a sample of news media to see which issues received how much coverage and then rank-order those issues. The economy might rank first, crime second, drugs and drug abuse third, and so on. We would then look at survey or polling data on what Americans described as important problems. If the two lists looked similar, we might conclude that the media set the agenda for the public, and when researchers have done such analyses, they usually conclude this. (For good reviews, see McCombs & Gilbert, 1986; McCombs & Reynolds, 2002; Rogers & Dearing, 1988).

However, we should ask, Who's to say that it doesn't work the other way around—that the *public* sets the *media* agenda? And isn't it also quite possible that something else—for example, what's happening in the real world—sets *both*?

We can design studies that elaborate both questions. To test the relative strength of the public and media agendas on each other, researchers rely on a technique called *cross-lagged correlation:* Measures of the public and media agenda are taken at two points in time, and the impact of the media agenda at the first time point is correlated with the public agenda at the second time point, whereas the impact of the public agenda at the first time point is compared with the media agenda at the second. Researchers have found that the impact of the media on the public agenda is virtually always greater than the opposite: In other words, the media do more to set the public agenda than the public do to set the media agenda (although there is a noticeable effect of the public on the media). Answering the second question—Does something else, the "real world," set both agendas?—requires a different research strategy. Researchers use not only measures of the media and public agendas, but also some real-world indicators as well, such as unemployment and inflation rates, crime rates, wartime casualty rates, and so on. A number of analyses have found that the closest correlations are between the media and public agendas—closer than between the real-world and media agendas or between the real-world and public agendas, although, as before, each does of course somewhat influence the other (Rogers & Dearing, 1988).

But the relationships between the media and public agendas in research studies are never perfect: The lists are never identically ranked. In other words, the power of the media to set the public agenda is somewhat constrained or limited, and in ways—and by things—that are instructive. Among the limitations are the following:

1. *Individual Differences:* The strongest agenda-setting effects have been found in experimental research studies, which suggests that a major condition for obtaining the effect is attention; that is, in experiments, subjects are expected to pay attention, but under naturalistic conditions, some people do and others don't (Iyengar & Kinder, 1987). And, as we noted in discussing knowledge effects more generally, the sorts of things that lead one to attend to the news are related to levels of education, interest, and the like. Indeed, in the experimental studies, the strongest agenda-setting effects generally were among people who did not usually follow news closely. Moreover, David Weaver (1980)

and others have noted that an individual's "need for orientation" on an issue—one's recognition that an issue may be important, coupled with a belief that one doesn't know enough about it—is a strong predictor of agenda-setting effects.

2. *Media Differences:* It should be fairly obvious that not all media present precisely the same agendas at the same time, and logically people's agendas should correspond to the media to which they do pay attention. On average, however, most major national media do present very similar news and hence news agendas, as we argued earlier in the chapter.

3. *Issue Differences:* Issues differ in two principal ways. The first is content; some issues concern problems facing a society or group, whereas other issues more specifically focus on policy proposals (legislation or executive orders) or solutions to problems. Second is the kind of impact issues may have on the public or society. Some issues are obtrusive ones, affecting nearly everyone and affecting them in pretty much the same way (inflation, when it is high; gasoline shortages); others are selective, affecting some people deeply, while affecting others far less so (noise pollution); still others are remote, directly affecting small numbers of people (U.S. foreign policy toward Malawi; Lang & Lang, 1983). In general, agenda-setting effects are greatest on remote issues and smallest on obtrusive ones.

4. *Salience Differences:* There are different kinds of salience. Social salience is our sense of an issue's impact on the larger society. Interpersonal salience is what we think is important to the people with whom we're in regular contact—what we talk about with others. Individual salience is what we personally think is important. In general, agenda-setting effects are greatest on social salience and least evident on individual salience.

## Priming

The *priming* effect is a close cousin of agenda setting, and, in fact, it was described by researchers conducting agenda-setting studies. Like agenda setting, priming is a metaphor. Here, the metaphor is of priming a pump—adding enough liquid to the pump to get it started working on its own. It is described by political psychologist Shanto Iyengar (1991) this way:

The so-called "priming effect" refers to the ability of news programs to affect the criteria by which individuals judge their political leaders. Specifically, researchers have found that the more prominent an issue is in the national information stream, the greater will be the weight accorded it in making political judgments. While agenda-setting reflects the impact of news coverage on the perceived importance of national issues, priming refers to the impact of news coverage on the weight assigned to specific issues on making political judgments. For instance, after watching news stories on the increased budgetary outlays for the Pentagon under the Reagan administration, viewers were not only more likely to cite the arms race as an important national issue, but were also likely to give more weight to their evaluations of President Reagan's performance on arms control when rating his performance overall. (p. 133)

Thus priming blurs the line between "what to think" and "what to think about." In recent years, McCombs and his colleagues (e.g. McCombs & Reynolds, 2002) have come to describe cases in which media emphases on attributes, descriptions, and "frames" of issues and political candidates are transferred to public sentiment as "second-level" agenda setting.

Agenda setting, framing, and priming are largely inside-the-head psychological models; they affect how we behave only to the extent that we *act on what we "know" or believe*. We'll now turn to two other models that have a bit more to say about behavior.

## Third-Person Effects

Public opinion researcher W. Phillips Davison (1983) coined the term *third-person effect* to try to describe how, in some cases, media messages may have an impact on our behavior but little or no impact on our attitudes. He began his classic article on the effect with a historical anecdote about the World War II battle of Iwo Jima in the Pacific. A historian friend of Davison's had asked him if he could give a good explanation for the fact that Black soldiers did not fight in that battle because they were kept from the battle by superiors who had heard a Japanese propaganda radio broadcast urging them not to fight. Why, the historian asked, did the commanders withdraw the Black troops, when they had no evidence that the Black soldiers had been persuaded by the broadcast? Davison responded by formulating his third-person model.

All of us, Davison suggests, go through a little mental calculation when we see or hear media messages. First, we calculate whether we personally believe or are affected by them (first-person effects). We then calculate whether our friends—people like us—are affected (second-person effects). Finally, we calculate whether "other people"— those about whom we are likely to know little or nothing (third persons)—are affected. A usual response, he says, is to believe that we, and others like us, will not be affected, but that other people will be. A simple example: How much does advertising affect *you*? How much does it affect other people? Reams of survey data tell us that most people believe that advertising messages generally don't have much impact on them, but the same people believe that other people are more affected than they are. As Davison points out, it's possible that we either underestimate effects on ourselves or overestimate impacts on others, or both, but he and we believe that, more often than not, we overestimate effects on others. We see something of the third-person effect in debates over media effects discussed in the last chapter. It is always the behavior of others we are worried about.

There is likely a fair degree of generality to the third-person model. Each of us finds ourselves in situations in which, before doing or saying something—that is, before we behave—we calculate what others think or believe. Indeed, this is a component—subjective social norms—in the Ajzen and Fishbein (1980) attitude-and-behavior-change model presented in the last chapter. Reporters, for example, in writing a second-day story on new developments in a story since the day before, have to calculate how much the audience is likely to remember (they usually calculate, based on experience, that it won't remember much). Political operatives must calculate how much impact the speeches and ads of opponents have had on voters and respond accordingly. What the third-person model suggests is that when we must behave, and when that behavior depends on our estimate of how others have been influenced by a message, and lacking information (usually we are) about how much these others have been affected, we are likely to overestimate the influence of media messages.

## The Spiral of Silence

The *spiral-of-silence* model introduced by the German social scientist Elisabeth Noelle-Neumann (1974, 1984) is similar to Davison's third-person model. It, too, argues that media messages alter people's, and society's, behavior. But the behavior that interests Noelle-Neumann is how and when people are willing to express their opinions.

She argues that a "fear of isolation" is very important in motivating people; that we dread putting ourselves in a position where other people will shun or make fun of us. So, before we are willing to let other people know what we think on some issue, we perform a mental calculation quite similar to the one Davison suggests; that is, we try to assess what other people think on a topic before we let them know what we think. If we think that they are likely to agree with us, or if we think that more and more people feel the same way, then we go ahead and speak out. If we think, however, that they disagree with us or that the opinion is becoming unpopular, we do not speak out. Moreover, Noelle-Neumann suggests that we are each endowed with a *quasi-statistical* sense that allows us to intuit "public opinion," or the predominant opinion of others. The spiral-of-silence model is a media model only because the media serve as the primary sources of our information about the distribution of public opinion and about trends in that opinion.

As outlined above, the model is an individual-level model, describing what goes on in our heads. But the model is also a social-level model, describing the dynamics of public expression and opinion. If, as Noelle-Neumann suggests, people *do* decide whether to express themselves based on their view of predominant opinion or trends in opinion, then, *over time,* those favoring the majority opinion should express it willingly and those favoring the minority position should prefer to remain quiet. If this occurs, the majority opinion will be expressed loudly and frequently, whereas the minority position will "spiral into silence."

Although there is both historical and research support for the spiral of silence, it, too, does not always occur, which is a good thing, or we would eventually devolve into a society in which there was never any expressed difference of opinion. Why does it sometimes work, and sometimes not?

1. *Individual Differences:* "Willingness to express" is an attribute on which people differ, regardless of topic or predominant opinion; some people are simply more outspoken than others. Willingness to express an opinion is also a function of opinion intensity—how strongly someone

holds an opinion: People who hold strong opinions may well express them regardless of their perceptions of how others feel.

2. *Perception of Predominant Opinion (and Future Trends):* The model's assumption that people are able to figure out what others think on all issues is almost certainly not always correct. Social psychologists have written extensively on pluralistic ignorance, or uncertainty about the distribution of opinions of others. If we are uncertain about the opinions of others, the model may not apply. If we are uncertain, the theorists say, we generally react in one of two ways: In general, we may have "looking-glass perceptions," believing that others feel the same way we do, or, if we believe the topic to be touchy or controversial, we may exercise a conservative bias, thinking that others are more conservative or restrictive than in fact they are (Taylor, 1982).

3. *Perceptions of "Others'" Opinions.* The model assumes that, in our mental calculation, we have some generalized other or (in Davison's terms) third person, in mind. In fact, most of most people's public or political talk is not to a generalized mass audience. Before a more specialized audience, someone might believe that the opinion expressed will be a majority one, even if it's not a majority opinion in the mass audience. In other words, most of our discussion is among friends or people whose views we think we know pretty well and whom we think are likely to agree with us. When we don't think this, however, the model is more likely to apply.


## CHALLENGING THE AGENDA

When people want to challenge the political agenda, to put forth a view not congruent with the norms of mainstream media, it is often difficult to get onto the media's agenda. However, a variety of other media are continually made and remade as ad hoc networks of newsletters, e-mail, videotapes, and Web sites produce alternative messages. We have discussed the notion of radical media earlier in this book (see Chapter 4). Here, we would briefly like to introduce Clemencia Rodriguez's (2001) notion of *citizens' media*. Rodriguez points out that most theories of radical media (or alternative media) are simply oppositional in the political positions espoused by their texts. Or they define their object of study as everything mainstream, corporate-owned media is not (in terms of scale, budget, financial backing, distribution, and so on). As a corrective to this work, Rodriguez coins the term *citizens' media*. Citizenship is a form of political identity, something constructed:

> "Citizens' media" implies first that a collectivity is *enacting* its citizenship by actively intervening and transforming the established mediascape; second, that these media are contesting social codes, legitimized identities, and institutionalized social relations; and third, that these communication practices are empowering the community involved, to the point where these transformations and changes are possible. (p. 20)

This sort of media is made not simply by people picking up video cameras or logging on to the Web to represent their opinions; it implies a more active personal investment. She writes,

> I could see how producing alternative media messages implies much more than simply challenging the mainstream media with *campesino* correspondents as new communication and information sources. It implies having the opportunity to create one's own images of self and environment; it implies being able to recodify one's own identity with the signs and codes that one chooses, thereby disrupting the traditional acceptance of those imposed by outside sources; it implies becoming one's own storyteller, regaining one's own voice; it implies reconstructing the self-portrait of one's own community and one's own culture; it implies exploring the infinite possibilities of one's own body, one's own face, to create facial expressions (a new codification of the face) and nonverbal languages (a new codification of the body) never seen before; it implies taking one's own languages out of their usual hiding places and throwing them out there, into the public sphere, and seeing how they do, how they defeat other languages, or how they are defeated by other languages. . . . What matters is that, for the first time, one's shy languages, languages used to remain within the familiar and the private, take part in the public arena of languages and discourse. (p. 3)

As you can see from the extract, this type of mediamaking is political in a way seldom considered by most media theories in this chapter. We are not discussing the political as the government's and citizens' abilities to shape governance, but as the relations of power between individuals and groups; the power to create oneself, to make meaning, and to influence others. This also serves to bring into question the nature of the public, the topic to which we turn in the next chapter.

## CONCLUSION

The social reality models we have discussed—agenda setting, priming, third-person effects, and the spiral of silence—have several aspects in common: All of them suggest that behavioral impacts such as how we vote or whether we give money or speak aloud may result from media-induced changes in beliefs or cognitions. Each also suggests that media impact does not result from a single message, but from the cumulative impact of media messages over time. And whereas research to date has confirmed each model, one cannot argue that any one of them works equally effectively all of the time, even at the individual or personal level.

This chapter has focused on two aspects of politics and the news media: how media cover news and how they affect people. We turn next to two other aspects of people and the media: the media and the people as a public, and public considerations of how the media ought to behave—or normative theories of the media.

## NOTES

1. Our characterizations here are necessarily general and overly simple; for a more complete characterization of early newspapers, see Nerone (1987). Nerone in particular notes that the degree to which newspapers were partisan before 1840 was highly variable; many papers, particularly in larger cities, were highly partisan, but others were more objective by present-day standards. He also notes that changes in the newspaper were evolutionary, occurring slowly and undramatically, rather than revolutionary.

2. In the United States, however, unlike Europe, the newspaper has remained largely a local phenomenon almost to the present. Among American newspapers, only a handful—the *Wall Street Journal, USA Today,* and *The New York Times*—have an appreciable circulation outside the cities in which they are produced. In Europe, however, the principal newspapers are national—produced in the capital and distributed throughout the nation. The "mass" newspaper evolved in Europe at the same time as the national railroad system, enabling

metropolitan newspapers to be on breakfast tables the next morning throughout the country. The size of the United States, however, did not allow this, and what "national" newspapers we do have emerged as national only in the 1970s and 1980s, when communications satellites and commercial jet aviation made it economically feasible to print national papers in satellite printing facilities across the country.

3. It might be noted that historians disagree over the pace at which, and reasons why, these changes occur, but they tend to concur that they did.

4. Although Telstar was used to televise the funeral of President John Kennedy in 1963, routine TV news usage of satellites did not come into being until the 1970s. The Vietnam War is often called "the first televised war," and writer Michael Arlen (1969) dubbed it "the living-room war." But, for most of that war (from 1960 to 1969), the TV images were on film flown from Vietnam to California and aired two days after the events were filmed.

5. This slogan was a favorite of Lieutenant Joe Friday (Jack Webb, also the show's producer) on the 1950s and 1960s TV show *Dragnet*. The *message* was that if the witnesses he and his partner were interviewing would stick to the facts, the police could interpret them and more quickly and efficiently catch the criminals.

6. One aspect of news style that is indisputably an AP legacy is the inverted pyramid style of constructing news stories, with the most important facts first and less central ones later in the story—the "who, what, when, where followed by why and how" or "5 Ws and H" formula.

7. Tuchman (1973) has noted that even unpredicted stories, especially when they are obviously big news, are quickly covered in ways that allow reporters and editors to apply routines to them.

8. In their memoirs, many journalists have commented on the second-guessing that their own editors do when the staff journalist's story is different from the other versions: That is, the staff journalist is asked to account for "why your story is different from what the AP [or *The New York Times* or ABC] says." And reporters agree that, over time, this serves as a powerful standardizing influence—not to be too different from what other journalists are writing.

9. Sisella Bok (1978) is the standard work on truth and deception and gray areas in between, and is highly recommended to anyone who is considering any media career.

10. The Gallup Poll, May 1988 and November 1986. The *Gallup Opinion Index* is published monthly and available in most research libraries. See, also, Robert Putnam's (2000) book, *Bowling Alone.*

11. A study of the 1988 elections by political communication researcher Michael Robinson found that in 60 primaries that year, the biggest spender won the primary only 40% of the time (cited in Kolbert, 1992).

## SUGGESTED READINGS

Barnhurst, K. G., & Nerone, J. (2001). *The form of news: A history.* New York: Guilford.

Jamieson, K. H. (2000). *Everything you think you know about politics . . . And why you're wrong.* New York: Basic Books.

Katz, E., & Lazarsfeld, P. (1955). *Personal influence.* Glencoe, IL: Free Press.

Meikle, G. (2002). *Future active: Media activism and the Internet.* New York: Routledge.

Rodriguez, C. (2001). *Fissures in the mediascape: An international study of citizens' media.* Cresskill, NJ: Hampton.

# The Media, the Public, and Normative Theories | 12

W e talk about "the public" throughout this book, for no term in understanding mass media is more vital. This chapter focuses on the public. We will try to delineate what we mean by the public, talk a bit about where contemporary ideas of the public come from, show how different notions of the public lead us to different questions, and raise issues of how the media *ought* to operate.

## DEFINING THE PUBLIC

In ordinary language, we think of *public* in a variety of ways. Among the most common are the following:

▮ Public as the not-private, that which goes on in the open, observable by and accessible to others, as in "open to the public"
▮ Public as general, pertaining to or emanating from all citizens, as in *public interest* or *public opinion*
▮ Public as communal, or governmentally owned or regulated, as in *public television* or *public utilities*

⌐ublic implies openness, community, citizenship, discussion, debate.
⌐e relationship between media and public can be discussed on
⌐els by reference to these terms.

The media clearly serve public functions in two essential ways. First, the media have become the key instrument of publicness in our first sense: That is, they bring information and issues out into the open; they constitute *publicity*. When the news media argue that trials (the Kobe Bryant trial, the Oklahoma City bombing trials) and military operations (the Gulf Wars) should be open to media access, they assert "the people's right to know." They argue that the public can hold its own institutions accountable only to the degree that public (or governmental—our third sense of *public*) business is conducted "in public" (our first sense). Second, media constitute a key portion of what we sometimes call the *public sphere*, the multiple forums in which issues and controversies can be debated (our first and second senses of *public*), something essential in a democracy, if what we mean by *democracy* is the manifestation of the public will.

For the *public will* to have much meaning, we have to have some sense of how we might know what that will is—what the public wants and needs—and how we might find that out. For now, we will note that the public can be thought of in a variety of ways, ways that are related to how the public is *represented*—as individuals (or as aggregations of individuals), as groups or publics, or through the usual political form of representation, the government ("We, the people . . ." are the opening words of the U.S. Constitution).[1] The very idea of a public is intertwined with the idea of a democracy.

## CREATING THE PUBLIC

The first thing we need to say is that there is no such thing as "the public." It is not a natural category somehow discovered by the Greeks. It is an idea, a concept, about how people act together as a whole. Publics have to be created, they do not just arise, and what it means to be a public will change as historical circumstances change. In addition, we always need to ask, Who speaks on behalf of the public?

The notion of democracy is an ancient one, dating from the golden age of Greece; its modern manifestation, however, dates from the Enlightenment, roughly dating from the 1700s, and especially in Britain and Holland, and slightly later in France.[2] Prior to this period, the notion of the public—in the sense of a body of citizens capable of expressing public opinion—is virtually absent, and for good reason: As we discuss later in this chapter, Europe was ruled by coalitions of kings, feudal lords, and the hierarchy of the church. Real power and authority rested in very few hands, and the opinions of anyone else (if they had them and dared express them) mattered for little. Such dissent as existed was usually ruthlessly suppressed.

## The Rise of the Public

From the mid-1700s to the present, there has been a gradual shift toward greater democracy. It arises first with the gradual empowerment of the bourgeoisie, an urban upper-middle class whose claim to political voice and power was based on its accumulating wealth and knowledge, not on the traditional claims to power of title and land held by the nobility. As the bourgeoisie gradually gained political stature, they begin the development and transformation of the public sphere. Public debates over justice, equality, and a hundred other questions spring up in the coffeehouses of London and Amsterdam, and in the salons of Paris, meetings of intellectuals in the mansions of the recently rich. And even at this early juncture, the media—newspapers, journals, and books—are important carriers of the information and opinion that formed the bases of debate.

We must emphasize, however, that in the middle to late 1700s, the public was still a rather small segment of the whole population. If we take citizenship—the right to vote—as a rough indicator of membership in the public, as an index of publicness, we may remind ourselves that at the founding of the United States, the first modern republican democracy, its 1789 Constitution extended the right to vote only to property-owning (and, in most states, White) males. In the United States, as in Europe, the next 150 years would see the expansion of the voting franchise to include almost everyone as a citizen—as part of the public. Sometimes, this extension was accomplished peacefully, sometimes only after bloody conflict.

## The Decline of the Public

As this story is frequently told, especially by those familiar with the important work of Jürgen Habermas (1962/1989), a scholar of the German critical theory Frankfurt School, the "transformation of the public sphere" divides roughly into a classical and a modern period.

In the classical period, the expansion of the public sphere was an ideal time, when public debate was robust, eloquent, well reasoned, and vigorous: Competing viewpoints found public forums—the pulpits, stump-speaking political debates such as the classic Lincoln-Douglas debates of 1858, well-attended town meetings, a flourishing newspaper press. Recall from the previous chapter that newspapers were individually partisan and partial but, in the larger cities at least, collectively represented wide ranges of viewpoints (Habermas, 1962/1989; Postman, 1985). In this formulation, however, there is what media scholar Peter Dahlgren (1995) calls a "second act," a modern period characterized by decline:

> The second act traces the decline of the bourgeois public sphere in the context of advanced industrial capitalism and the social welfare state of advanced democracy. With mass democracy, the public loses its exclusivity; its socio-discursive coherence comes apart as many less educated citizens enter the scene. The state, to handle the growing contradictions of capitalism, becomes more interventionist; the boundaries between public and private, both in political economic terms and in cultural terms, begin to dissipate. Large organizations and interest groups become key political partners with the state, resulting in a "refeudalization" of politics which greatly displaces the role of the public. The increasing prevalence of the mass media, especially where the commercial logic transforms much of public communication into PR, advertising and entertainment, erodes the critical functions of the public. The public becomes fragmented, losing its social coherence. It becomes reduced to a group of spectators whose acclaim is to be periodically mobilized, but whose intrusion in fundamental political questions is to be minimized. (p. 8)

In other words, this criticism suggests that, in the present day, the public itself has become disenfranchised: Although citizens may still vote, fewer see a reason to do so, and fewer actually do so. Christopher Lasch laments "the transformation of politics from a central component of popular culture into a spectator sport" (cited in Schudson, 1995, p. 189)—and at that, a spectator sport with declining attendance, as networks prune their coverage of the presidential nominating conventions further and further back and as news media rely on "lite" coverage and attention-grabbing graphics rather than substantial political coverage. The American political system, suggest distinguished journalists Haynes Johnson and David Broder (1996), echoing an argument made by Walter Lippmann (1922) almost 75 years earlier, has gotten so large, cumbersome, and dominated by organized special interests that it is unable to come to terms with fundamental social problems, such as health care, and its journalism is unable to explain those problems and policy questions to citizens. Television coverage of politics devolves into 10- to 15-second sound bites, and pundits trying harder to score points on each other than to broaden public debate. At the same time, Harvard political scientist Robert Putnam (2000) strikes a responsive chord with an argument that America's "social capital" is eroding, largely because people are staying home to watch TV, rather than joining organizations, talking with each other, and participating in politics.

Such scholars argue that the classical unity of *audience* and *public* has dissolved. Whereas once the public constituted the audience for serious political media, today, the public is eroding, as audiences have become no more than markets, commodities, "eyeballs" to be bought and sold and traded. Some argue that publics now act more like audiences (more passive observers seeking entertainment than active participants in civic affairs) and that while broadcasters and politicians may refer to "the public," they actually mean "the audience."

## Is There a Problem of the Public?

The story told by Habermas, Dahlgren, Lasch, Putnam, and many others has not gone unchallenged. There are two strong arguments against it. First is that the classical public sphere cannot be painted in such rosy hues as its proponents suggest. Second is that the public is a flexible concept, one that is constantly being reinvented.

Media scholar Michael Schudson (1995) points out that the American public of the 1800s may have turned out for political debates and lengthy speeches, but we have scant evidence that the majority of attendees spent all that time carefully weighing the speakers' arguments.

The longing of contemporary critics of our political culture to stand in the sun for three hours to listen to political speeches is selective. If there is nostalgia for the Lincoln-Douglas debates (not that they left any words, phrases, or ideas that anyone can recall), there is no hankering for dramatic readings of Edward Everett's hours-long address at

Gettysburg. Instead, it is Abraham Lincoln's sound bite–length address that has left a lasting impression. As it happens, not long ago, people did listen to literally hours of political addresses, interspersed with music, at antiwar rallies in the 1960s. If it is any measure, we can say from personal experience that there is a big difference between attending a rally and actually listening to the speeches.

Schudson (1995) notes further that the percentage of eligible voters who actually vote is an unreliable index of public participation. Across the course of American history, voter turnout has cycled up and down, with downward cycles occurring regularly when different groups are newly enfranchised—immigrants before World War I, women between the world wars, African Americans in the South, and 18- to 21-year-olds since the 1960s. As he notes, if one's standard for a democratic public is that it incorporates all individuals, then contemporary America is far more "democratic" than at any other period (see also Calhoun, 1992). Finally, he notes, critics who argue that the level and quality of public and political discourse was higher at some past point are likewise being selective: As many critics have pointed out, political discourse in the preceding two centuries, although it indeed featured strong and well-crafted arguments, also contained slanders, mudslinging, and sloganeering that we would find familiar today. Moreover, critics have seen the public in decline for a long time. Walter Lippmann, for example, in *Public Opinion* in 1922 and in *The Phantom Public* in 1925, French sociologists Gustav LeBon (1977) and Gabriel Tarde (1901/1969) in books at the turn of the century, and Alexis de Tocqueville (1835, 1840) in *Democracy in America* in 1835 all expressed reservations about the ability of mass or general publics to govern themselves rationally (see also Peters, 1995).[3]

A second challenge suggests that classical understandings of the public must change with the times; that traditional ways—both structures and narrative forms—of political expression are changing. This is especially true in online environments such as the Internet. In the 1990s, the Internet was hailed as creating cybercitizens who could participate more directly in matters of government and society. Online, it was argued, one could participate in "town hall" discussions, which could include thousands of people scattered across the country or world. More recently, the Internet has been used for political organization in new ways. MoveOn.org, an online group set up in 1998, maintains an e-mail list of over two million persons to whom they will send petitions and campaign information. List members can then donate to particular campaigns (for example, contributing to particular television ads) or sign particular petitions depending on their political preferences. And by collecting small donations (made online) from thousands of people, MoveOn.org has been able to rapidly collect large sums of money for these causes. MoveOn.org refers to these as *electronic advocacy groups*. This aspect of the Internet was not lost on the 2003–2004 presidential campaign of Dr. Howard Dean, whose organization used the Internet to collect small donations from thousands of supporters. His campaign also used a particular software program, which allowed Dean supporters to locate and communicate with other Dean supporters in their town or neighborhood, allowing them to coordinate meetings (called *meetups*) and rallies more efficiently.

Arguments about the decline of the public are inherently moral and political. As such, they are contests over readings of history and weighing of evidence and thus incapable of settlement (see, for example, Whitney & Wartella, 1988). There is no denying, however, that in these times, the very notion of publicness is strongly tied to the mass media, and the public has a strong stake in what the media say and do. We now explore two further issues: the relationship of the contemporary public to the media and the question of how the media should relate to the public.

## REPRESENTING THE PUBLIC

In understanding the ways the media and the public interact, we return to our levels-of-analysis argument. We are the public, and we have relationships with the media, in four ways: as individuals, as aggregates, as members of organized groups, and as citizens ("We, the people"). For each level, we will discuss not only what constitutes that level of the public but how each level judges or responds to the mass media.

### The Public as Individuals

We relate to the mass media as individuals every time we make a choice about what to watch, which magazines or audio tapes or books we buy, which movies we pay to go to, and so on. In this, we either are or are not the audience. But audience and public are distinct concepts: The *audience* is a market or commodity, but as part of the public, our range of concerns is wider. When we're part of the *public*, we put on a different hat: We think not only of ourselves and our own interests, but of a public interest—what we think is good and right and fair not just for ourselves but for our fellows. In other words, our public selves are social selves, and our public opinions are expressions of what content and conduct we think is good or bad, moral or immoral, ethical or unethical, tolerable or intolerable.

Clearly, most of our judgments about media are private or shared only among close friends ("Did you see *Six Feet Under* last night?" "What do you think of the new U2?"). But, occasionally, we may be moved by a social judgment to want to weigh in using some more public form—a fan letter or call, a congratulatory letter, or complaining call. The best estimates are that fewer than one in five Americans have ever written or called any mass medium to express an opinion (about one in four have communicated to an elected official). Moreover, workers in the news media inherently distrust the feedback they get from individuals, especially if it's critical—and most of it is (Gans, 1979). Why? First, they believe that such feedback is unrepresentative—that people who react strongly are somewhat different from those who do not (and, after a while, they begin to recognize "repeat offenders," people who repeatedly write and call in). Second, most know from experience that many calls and letters arise not spontaneously from individual sentiment but from organized campaigns by interest groups. Their judgments about "what the public thinks" are in most cases much more shaped by organized *aggregate* measures of feedback—polls, surveys, ratings, and sales data—which rarely show the same patterns of public reaction as do individual responses.

## The Public as Aggregate

When a producer or editor responds that a letter writer is "not representative," essentially he or she is arguing that an individual's expressed opinion is different from what the editor takes public opinion to be. More often than not, that judgment of public opinion is based on some *aggregated* or accumulated evidence: *How many* individuals have responded or behaved in a countable way—how many have bought a magazine? News magazine editors usually judge the popularity of an individual issue as some mixture of the newsworthiness of the news in a given week and the presumed appeal of the cover subject and cover story. How many calls or letters, pro or con, does an issue generate? (We'll give an example in a moment.) Most especially, what do polls, surveys, ratings, and other interview-based research tell them? There's a subtle but essential difference between the individual response (what one letter writer says, specifically) and aggregated individual responses (how many individuals, counted up, respond in roughly the same way), and that difference is that the individual voice and inflection is lost, while some sense of representativeness is gained. "What the public thinks," then, is based on the judgment of some people and the measures of others (surveys and polls). "What the public thinks" is also shaped by what individual survey participants are actually asked (phrasing questions differently can result in different answers) and by the particular media texts they consume.

Furthermore, as previously noted, different modes of aggregation may produce different representations of public opinion. One such example comes from the October 1983 invasion of Grenada, when President Reagan decided that the news media would not be present when U.S. troops landed on the island. The press raised a furor, citing the people's right to know, but as *Time* magazine reported, the news media found their calls and mail running from 3 to 1, up to 99 to 1, in favor of the Reagan administration, against the news media (Henry, 1993). "It may well be," *Time* quotes former *Washington Post* ombudsman Robert McClosky, "that the public reacted cumulatively with a judgment that the press had it coming" (p. 76). Over the next 18 months, however, a number of polls and surveys, many of them commissioned by the media, found that, in fact, the public, at least as measured by polls and surveys, was reasonably supportive of the news media (Whitney, 1987).

So, what *do* polls and surveys, as measures of aggregate public opinion, tell us about what and how the public thinks about the media? There's no quick and easy answer to that question, but several dimensions of public attitudes and beliefs are notable.[4] (See Box 12.1, "Public Opinion About the Media.")

**BOX 12.1**

**Public Opinion About the Media**

The following are selected results from opinion surveys about the news media. All results are from national polls of Americans age 18 and older, with sample sizes of 1,000 or greater and sampling errors of ± 3% or less.

1. From 1939: *Do you feel that the news story (in newspapers) itself is almost always accurate as to its facts, is usually accurate as to its facts, or is not accurate in most instances?*[a]

| | |
|---|---|
| Always accurate: | 23.3% |
| Usually accurate: | 45.1% |
| Not accurate: | 24.7% |
| No opinion: | 6.9% |

2. From 1985: *In general, do you think news organizations get the facts straight, or do you think that they are often inaccurate?*[b]

| | |
|---|---|
| Accurate: | 55% |
| Inaccurate: | 34% |
| No opinion: | 11% |

3. From 1991: *How would you rate the honesty and ethical standards of people in these different fields—very high, high, average, low, or very low?* (percentage saying *high* or *very high*)[c]

| | | | |
|---|---|---|---|
| Pharmacists | 60 | Business executives | 21 |
| Medical doctors | 54 | Building contractors | 20 |
| Dentists | 50 | Senators | 19 |
| College teachers | 45 | Local political officeholders | 19 |
| Engineers | 45 | Congressmen | 19 |
| Police officers | 43 | Real estate agents | 17 |
| Funeral directors | 35 | State political officeholders | 14 |
| Bankers | 30 | Stockbrokers | 14 |
| TV reporters, commentators | 29 | Insurance salesmen | 14 |
| Journalists | 26 | Labor union leaders | 13 |
| Newspaper reporters | 24 | Advertising practitioners | 12 |
| Lawyers | 22 | Car salesmen | 8 |

*(Continued)*

(Continued)

4. From 2003: [d] (Note how attitudes shifted briefly in November of 2001, the month after the events of September 11.)

**Press Ratings Consistently Negative**

| | Feb 1999 | Early September 2001 | November 2001 | July 2002 | July 2003 |
|---|---|---|---|---|---|
| *News organizations . . .* | % | % | % | % | % |
| Usually get facts straight | 37 | 35 | 46 | 35 | 36 |
| Often report inaccurately | 58 | 57 | 45 | 56 | 56 |
| Don't know | 5 | 8 | 9 | 9 | 8 |
| | 100 | 100 | 100 | 100 | 100 |
| Willing to admit mistakes | 26 | 24 | 35 | 23 | 27 |
| Try to cover up mistakes | 66 | 67 | 52 | 67 | 62 |
| Neither/Don't know | 8 | 9 | 13 | 10 | 11 |
| | 100 | 100 | 100 | 100 | 100 |
| Are politically biased | 56 | 59 | 47 | 59 | 53 |
| Are careful to not be biased | 31 | 26 | 35 | 26 | 29 |
| Neither/Don't know | 13 | 15 | 18 | 15 | 18 |
| | 100 | 100 | 100 | 100 | 100 |

**Press Professionalism and Patriotism**

| *News organizations . . .* | % | % | % | % | % |
|---|---|---|---|---|---|
| Are highly professional | 52 | 54 | 73 | 49 | 62 |
| Are not professional | 32 | 27 | 12 | 31 | 24 |
| Neither/Don't know | 16 | 19 | 15 | 20 | 14 |
| | 100 | 100 | 100 | 100 | 100 |
| Care about how good a job they do | 69 | 69 | 78 | 65 | 68 |
| Don't care about the job | 22 | 22 | 14 | 23 | 22 |
| Neither/Don't know | 9 | 9 | 8 | 12 | 10 |
| | 100 | 100 | 100 | 100 | 100 |
| Stand up for America | 41 | 43 | 69 | 49 | 51 |
| Too critical of America | 42 | 36 | 17 | 35 | 33 |
| Neither/Don't know | 17 | 21 | 14 | 16 | 16 |
| | 100 | 100 | 100 | 100 | 100 |
| Protect democracy | 45 | 46 | 60 | 50 | 52 |
| Hurt democracy | 38 | 32 | 19 | 29 | 28 |
| Neither/Don't know | 17 | 22 | 21 | 21 | 20 |
| | 100 | 100 | 100 | 100 | 100 |

**Perceptions of Press Bias Go Beyond Ideology**

|  | July 1985 | Jan 1988 | Jan 1992 | Jan 1994 | Feb 1997 | Early Sept 2001 | July 2003 |
|---|---|---|---|---|---|---|---|
|  | % | % | % | % | % | % | % |
| Deal fairly with all sides | 34 | 30 | 31 | — | 27 | 26 | 26 |
| Tend to favor one side | 53 | 59 | 63 | — | 67 | 67 | 66 |
| Don't know | 13 | 11 | 6 | — | 6 | 7 | 8 |
|  | 100 | 100 | 100 |  | 100 | 100 | 100 |
| Pretty independent | 37 | 40 | 35 | 28 | — | 23 | 23 |
| Influenced by the powerful | 53 | 49 | 58 | 63 | — | 71 | 70 |
| Don't know | 10 | 11 | 7 | 9 | — | 6 | 7 |
|  | 100 | 100 | 100 | 100 |  | 100 | 100 |

Notes:

a. A *Fortune* magazine poll reported in Erskine (1970, p. 641)

b. A Gallup poll reported in Times-Mirror Center for the People and the Press (1985, p. 20)

c. *The Gallup Poll* (1988, p. 115)

d. The Pew Research Center for the People and the Press (2003, pp. 5–7).

In general, the public is inclined to be favorable toward the media; a variety of opinion polls have found that, on average, a majority of the public finds the media reasonably fair, reasonably accurate, and reasonably believable. When it comes to the news media, people to a great extent value the press's performing a "watchdog" function, scrutinizing the performance of other institutions, especially government.

When it comes to specifics, however, the public is critical of the media. Majorities fault the media for invading people's privacy, believe the media should not report the results of election-day exit polls before polling places close, find the media sensationalistic, believe that the news media focus too heavily on bad news, and find the media *biased*. Extensive research on how people think the media are biased shows, however, that somewhat fewer than half of them see this bias in political or ideological terms (among those who do, two thirds are likely to say the media have a liberal bias, but a third see them as conservatively biased). *More* people say that the bias is toward special interests, big business, government, and especially advertisers. And when people are questioned about the accuracy of stories they say they know something about firsthand, they give the media lower marks than they do in general.

The public both does and does not make distinctions between and among media; their expectations of how media *should* perform, that they should be truthful and impartial, are similar, but they do not believe all media meet these standards equally well. The public has a slightly higher opinion of their own media (the newspapers they usually read and local TV and radio) than of national media or "the media" in general and a slightly higher opinion of television and radio than of print media. Abundant survey evidence suggests that most do not find either supermarket tabloids or "tabloid TV" credible—at least this is what they tell pollsters.

Public assessment of the relationship between media and government shows some paradoxes. Although the public usually finds the media more believable than government officials and has a slightly higher general opinion of the media than of government, at the same time, a majority always sides with the government on questions of executive secrecy and particularly national security matters.

The public makes distinctions between kinds of media it would restrict, giving widest leeway to news and political content (except for national security matters) and least to entertainment content, particularly that which offends some people's sensibilities—materials containing profanity, sexual themes, and the like. In almost all cases, however, a significant fraction of the public would allow more censorship than the law currently allows, making the media less free to say and print what they now can.

## The Public as "Publics"

John Dewey (1927) has argued that to think of *the public* as some mass or aggregate—as everybody—is not useful in understanding how a society works; he preferred to think of *publics* of like-minded individuals, concerned with and communicating with each other about a common interest or problem. Looking at the contemporary media landscape, we can say that these publics come in many forms. The most prominent are special interest groups like voluntary organizations. A more recent form is that of the virtual community. We will consider these in turn.

## Special Interest Groups

As early as 1835, Tocqueville was able to note in his classic *Democracy in America* that Americans were, far more than contemporary Europeans, joiners of voluntary associations to promote all manner of interests. Tocqueville also took note of the fact that newspapers furnished the means of communication between members of such groups, that "hardly any association can do without newspapers" (1981, p. 69). The newspapers of that day were less mass media and were more specialized publications issued by what were then called *factions* to allow publics both to speak among themselves and to recruit others to their point of view. Today in the United States, there are an estimated 35,000 voluntary associations, from the National Rifle Association (NRA) to almost every school's Parent-Teacher Association, and 40,000 private charitable foundations giving up to $30 billion per year.[5] Most of the time, these voluntary groups go their own way, doing their own business. But, at every level, from the local to the national, public associations interact with the media, either to further their own ends, as when the NRA and Handgun Control, Inc., purchase ads to further their conflicting positions on gun control, or when they attempt to influence the media and the government to take positions consistent with their own. This influence can take several forms.

First, mentioned earlier, is what communications researcher Oscar Gandy (1982) calls *information subsidy*, as groups (interest groups, businesses, and the government itself) feed information via news releases, videotapes, reports, and press conferences to the news media and to talk shows, information supporting that group's point of view.

Second is *lobbying and persuasion*, both directly to the media and indirectly, through attempts to influence public policy. A variety of civil rights groups, for example, successfully lobbied the federal Equal Employment Opportunity Commission and especially the FCC to insist that they provide better employment opportunities to ethnic minorities in the 1960s and 1970s. And the efforts of Action for Children's Television, a social action group active in the 1970s and 1980s, were instrumental in the 1990 Children's Television Act, which restricted the amount of commercial time broadcasters could air during children's programs. Recently, interest groups have employed the Internet and e-mail with organized campaigns to reach political leaders so successfully that some complain that "Astroturf" lobbying has replaced traditional grassroots lobbying.

Third is *confrontation* with the media to influence their content, as when the National Council of Catholic Bishops and other Catholic groups vehemently protested TV producer Norman Lear's 1972 script for the CBS program *Maude*, in which the 47-year-old character accidentally became pregnant and had an abortion. That protest eventually led virtually all the program's sponsors to pull their advertising and 21 of 198 local affiliates to drop the program for the episodes dealing with the abortion.[6] On the other hand, the 1997 Southern Baptist Convention boycott of Disney appeared to have few immediate consequences for the company. Whether one views such efforts as good—democratic free expression aimed at winning the hearts and minds of the wider public—or bad—blue-nosed attempts at censorship of ideas—usually depends on where one stands on the issue at hand.

Three points stand out in this quintessentially American exercise: First, social action, through protest, boycotts, and lobbying, can have profound consequences; it is almost indisputable that interest groups have been instrumental, particularly since the 1960s, in toning down if not eliminating stereotypical portrayals, especially on television, of African Americans, women, gays, and other social groups. One consequence, however, is that television executives, as we noted in Chapter 4, have increasingly followed the LOP—least objectionable programming—dictate, preferring bland content to controversy.[7] Second, however, the elevating of offensive depictions to the status of controversy not infrequently leads to *celebrity* for the offenders: It's likely that attempts to stifle the Martin Scorsese film *The Last Temptation of Christ* and 2 Live Crew's recording "As Nasty as I Wanna Be" in fact increased interest in and sales of these media products. Third, it's easy to argue that suffering the discomfort of having to defend oneself from would-be censors is a fair price for media to pay for their freedom of speech and press.

### Virtual Communities

The second form of public utilizes the Internet to bring people with similar interests but in diverse locales together to interact in a virtual environment (Jones, 1998; Rheingold, 1993). These groups may end up acting much like the other public interest groups discussed above.

But new forms of publicness are forming through technologies such as text-pagers and cell phones. Loosely affiliated groups of individuals, which Howard Rheingold (2002) refers to as *smart mobs,* can keep in almost constant contact throughout the day by sending each other short text messages. This technology tends to be especially popular with youth in places such as Finland and Japan where friends keep in contact throughout their day. But this same technology can also be used to quickly organize rallies and protests. For example, in 2001 in the Philippines, opposition groups used text messaging to gather massive crowds hoping to bring about the resignation of their president. Such publics do not have rigid hierarchies and are decentered. A simple text message (for example, what to wear and when and where to gather) is sent to a small group and each member sends it off to others that they know and so on.

This technique has more recently been used as a form of performance art (or prank, depending on whom you ask) called *flash mobs,* where the message disseminated isn't political in nature, but almost random ("7th Avenue and Pine; 3:00 pm; wear roller skates"). As a result, groups of hundreds if not thousands suddenly appear in urban centers, perform some random act, and then disperse. Flash mobs have appeared in the United States, Europe, India, and elsewhere. Such networks of affiliation revealed by both the political and nonpolitical uses of the smart mob highlight the ways that we are interconnected with others into aggregates which are a new form of the public.

## The Public as Citizens

We've noted that democratic theory presupposes that government is the creature of the public. In essence, this means that majority public opinion *should* translate into public policy and law, including policy and law about the media. However, a recurrent theme in recent political campaigns is that government, especially in league with other powerful institutions, frustrates rather than enacts the public will. This assertion requires several qualifications. First, there is in fact some empirical evidence that much more often than not—although clearly not always—policy changes *can* be attributed to changes in public opinion, at least as measured by opinion polls.[8] Second, the Constitution provides the government, the media, and the public some insulation from the whims of the public. On the government side, the

393

Constitution requires extraordinary majorities for amending the Constitution itself and makes the election of the president indirect, through the Electoral College, rather than direct, through popular election. Also, the Bill of Rights, the first 10 amendments to the Constitution, enumerates the rights of the people that are to be off limits to government.

Sometimes, the public needs protection from public opinion, especially to protect the rights of minorities, be they racial, ethnic, or opinion minorities. U.S. history, unfortunately, is replete with examples of violence against the media, much of it waged by opinion majorities and aimed at suppressing unpopular minority sentiments (Nerone, 1990). Although not all violence against the press is conducted by local majorities, and although not all opinion majorities resort to violence to suppress unpopular opinion, the government, largely through the courts, has the obligation to protect individuals' (and the media's) First Amendment rights. However, when majority opinion becomes strongly dominant and deeply held—as occurred in the 1798 Alien and Sedition Acts, in "Red scares" in the 1920s, 1930s, and 1950s, and during most U.S. wars including, most recently, the so-called War on Terrorism—the courts have on occasion yielded to the dominant opinion and curtailed freedom of expression.

Episodes of violence are extreme forms of the urge to censor. We are all free to choose what we will read and listen to, and we all have the right to attempt to persuade others of the correctness of our own opinions and taste. The trick is to balance our rights, whether we are in the majority or minority, against the rights of others.

## Media Response to the Public

We've seen how the public respond to the media, but we also have to consider how the media respond to the public. The media respond to pressure from a number of groups. Always present is the possibility of government regulation, so media companies try to voluntarily respond to public criticism so as to avoid more regulations. So, in responding to periodic outcries about media violence, the industry self-regulates by rating television programs, films, and videogames, and labeling music CDs for adult content. Pressure is often brought to bear on media industries through the advertisers that support them, and so special interest groups may threaten to boycott a sponsor's products if they continue to advertise during a controversial program (such as the episode of Ellen DeGeneres's 1990s television program when she came out as a lesbian); the sponsors do not wish to lose customers and so pull their ads. In the fall of 2003, politically conservative interest groups protested against a television dramatization of the life of President Ronald Reagan; bowing to the controversy, CBS ended up not airing it (it aired later on the pay cable television channel Showtime).

The examples of all media types responding to public pressure are numerous. But what these examples bring up is that the relation of media and public depends upon how we conceive of the role of each of these; that is, how we feel the media and the public *ought* to be and act. "The public" has a variety of meanings, meanings that have evolved over time, and meanings that have real-world consequences for the way that media operate. The public view of the media as reflected by public opinion and public action suggests a recognition both of the power and importance of the media and of their shortcomings, and recent events suggest some media recognition of the need to address these shortcomings. The public view of the media also reveals our assumptions as a society about how the media ought to act. Though we may take for granted that the way the media are is the only way they could be, there are alternative norms; that is, alternative ways of conceiving of the public, the media, and the relation between them. For example, the media can be conceived as the means for educating, shaping, and controlling the public. In the most extreme version of this, the media simply acts as an instrument of the state. Or the media can be conceived as the means for the public to better itself, to become part of a community and not simply a force upon it. We see this notion in social responsibility theories of the media, especially around what is called *public journalism* or *civic journalism*. We discuss these different models of how the media *ought* to perform, called *normative theories* in the next half of the chapter.

## NORMATIVE THEORIES OF THE MEDIA

Discussions of normative theories of the media usually focus on a small handful of models: authoritarian, libertarian, social responsibility, and what was the Soviet communist model (see Siebert, Peterson, & Schramm, 1956). These theories are usually described from the perspective of Western scholars working within the assumptions of the libertarian viewpoint (Nerone, 1995). In doing so, they often over-emphasize the problems of more authoritarian systems (like limiting the range of opinions and ideas) and underemphasize the problems of more libertarian systems (like private monopolies, which can also limit the range of opinions and ideas). These theories also are usually constructed around the media's relation with the state (Are media state or privately owned? Is state regulation heavy or light?), which tends to ignore variations in cultural value that can also sit at the heart of a media system. For example, regardless of who owns it, do the media have a greater responsibility to better the public and society, to better particular groups within a society, or to return a profit? Some cultures may place the needs of the community, nation, or state above those of any individual, and so would favor a media system more focused on the former than the latter. In our discussion below, we do not try to list or map out every variation on how the media should operate (that is, we won't list every norm). Instead, our purpose here is to sketch out the principles of what is arguably the dominant model of media, especially in the West, libertarianism, and the particular responses, critiques, and alternatives that have been made to that model.

## Classical Liberalism

The media, beginning with the printing press, were born into Western society in a system we have earlier described and that we can characterize as an authoritarian normative approach. But for most of their existence, questions about how they ought to perform have been answered by resort to other, newer, theories, first the libertarian, and later the social responsibility, development communication, and materialist models.

The beginnings of the modern Western press, and later all Western mass media, are tied to the political ferment of the late 1700s and the philosophy of the Enlightenment—and the foundations of the American Revolution. The Enlightenment brought forth a view of human freedom and human nature that characterizes modern Western history, including key concepts that relate directly to how media should operate.

First and foremost is the assumption that humans are rational creatures, capable of setting aside base emotions and choosing between right and wrong, between what is false and what is true.

Second is the concept of liberty, reflected in the first few words of the American Declaration of Independence—"All men are created equal and endowed by their Creator with certain unalienable rights," including liberty. *Liberty* in this context is freedom *from* intrusion by government.

Third, that there is such a thing as truth, that it *is* discoverable by people through a process of reasoning, rather than being handed down by God. English poet and philosopher John Milton put it this way in a 1644 essay called *Areopagitica:* "Let [Truth] and Falsehood grapple. Whoever knew Truth put to the worse in a free and open encounter?" In more modern terms, truth emerges from the competition between ideas. Rational people will be able to discriminate between the true and the false.

This overall philosophy of society comes to be called *classical liberalism* in economics or *libertarianism* in theories of freedom of expression. One should not, however, confuse this form of liberalism with its current everyday usage: A classical liberal philosophy is closer to modern conservatism or libertarianism, which emphasizes individualism and minimal government roles in society. Classical liberalism was, however, quite consistent with the then-developing theory and practice of economics we know today as capitalism (epitomized by the 1776 publication in England of Adam Smith's *The Wealth of Nations*). We see the two merge in a familiar metaphor, "the free marketplace of ideas."

The idea of a free marketplace of ideas assumes equivalence between the world of commerce and the world of ideas: As products compete, ideas do, too. In free competition, it is assumed that the good and useful drive out the bad and worthless. Thus the driving spirit of liberal capitalism suggests that free people, left to their own initiative, will make economically and intellectually profitable choices. And "left to their own" largely means that the state, the government, will not interfere. In the realm of expression, this idea is embodied in the First Amendment to the U.S. Constitution: "Congress shall make no law abridging freedom of speech, or of the press. . . ." If the government does not interfere in expression, the free marketplace will assure that good ideas will drive out bad ones, and truth will prevail.

According to common wisdom, this philosophy has prevailed, at least in England and the United States, from the late 1700s to today. The history of *formal* or *government* control of media (remember that, until the twentieth century, mass media were exclusively print media) is largely one of decreasing state or government control. Moreover, media became more abundant in the same period, with rising literacy, rising wealth, and increasing technological sophistication. In 1900, there were 2,226 daily newspapers in America, with every major city having more than one and the largest cities having half a dozen or more. And these newspapers competed with each other not only for news, but also in the realm of ideas, staking out different positions on the political spectrum. Although we have substantially fewer (about 1,500 daily newspapers) today, we also have other kinds of news media: radio, television, and online news services such as MSNBC (Microsoft Network with the National Broadcasting Corporation), CNN, and so forth.

Nonetheless, between the 1880s and 1940s, cracks began to appear in the conceptual foundation of classical liberal capitalism, both in its notions of rationalism and in the assumption that the marketplace is free.

The popularization of Darwinian theories of evolution and Freudian ideas in psychology and psychoanalysis gradually led to a widespread questioning of the nature of human nature. If the theory of evolution is substantially correct, humans are animals, not, as biblical authority would have it, direct descendants from God. Freudian psychoanalysis emphasizes the degree to which human behavior is motivated not by rational but by irrational impulses. The work of Karl Marx similarly challenged the concept that human thought is rational and logical. For Marx, human thought is determined by the material and economic relations of social life.

Events of the first half of the twentieth century seemed to validate this revised, negative view of human rationality. The incredible carnage of World War I (in which more soldiers died than in World War II, Korea, Vietnam, and the Persian Gulf War combined) seemed wholly senseless. Fifteen years later, there seemed no accounting for how a cultivated and civilized nation such as Germany could democratically vote into power an Adolf Hitler. And another 10 years later, the world was staggered by the horror of the Holocaust.

Substantial cracks also appeared in the idea of a free marketplace. In the commercial and industrial arena, the same time period, roughly the 1880s to 1930, saw not a free marketplace but its opposite—the formation of trusts, combines, and cartels. Oil, railroads, meatpacking, and steel were consolidated into *monopolies,* in which one firm controls all or almost all of the trade, or *oligopolies,* in which a small number of firms control a commercial sector. A monopoly becomes almost wholly free to charge what it will and to treat workers as it will. There is no competition, and any effort by outsiders to establish competition can be suppressed by the monopoly, which can control necessary resources and make the cost of attempting to compete prohibitively expensive.

An oligopoly can operate in much the same way if the companies agree to charge the same prices and otherwise limit competition. And, as noted, oligopoly characterized a number of key American industries until the government began to intervene with antitrust legislation in the first two decades of the twentieth century. For such legislation to pass, however, required a widespread public recognition that in the commercial arena, the possibility of competition did not guarantee a free marketplace. It also required a recognition that the government might have to intervene to promote competition in some instances, whereas in others, the government might actually promote monopoly, as in the telephone industry and other utilities. Government grants of monopoly, however, were always accompanied by government regulation of the prices such monopolies could charge.

Changes in the media landscape also challenged the idea of a free marketplace of ideas. The early part of the century saw the development of motion pictures and radio. Movies were virtually born as a monopoly, or rather as a cartel. A small number of people, of whom the inventor Thomas Edison is the most notable, held the patents on motion picture cameras and projectors and thus could control who could make motion pictures. (A major reason Hollywood became the American movie industry center was that "outlaw" moviemakers moved there to be beyond the reach of the agents of the New York–based movie trust. When the trust was broken up, Hollywood remained the center because the weather and scenery were more conducive to outdoor filming year-round.)

Radio was different. Even in the 1910s and 1920s, the technology for rudimentary radio transmission and reception was fairly widely available, so much so that hundreds of radio stations began operating.[9] But radio transmission (and the same, later, is true of television) relied on peculiarities of the electromagnetic spectrum: Only on a finite number of spaces on this spectrum can clear signals be transmitted and received. As more stations came on the air in the 1920s, their signals began to interfere with each other, and reception became difficult—the airwaves became the biblical Tower of Babel. The solution for individual radio operators was either to increase the power of the transmission, to tell listeners that a station was moving its broadcast to a different place on the dial, or to go off the air. But this was only a temporary solution for any one operator, and these strategies compounded the problem for the operators and the audience. By the mid-1920s, radio operators appealed to the federal government to clean up the mess—to regulate the airwaves so that some voices, at least, could be heard. In 1927, Congress passed the Federal Radio Act to regulate radio broadcasting, and it was refined with further regulation in 1934 as the Federal Communications Act. This regulation (remember that classical liberal capitalism presupposes little or no government interference) assigned particular frequencies and power levels to individual license holders and, significantly, *limited* the number of stations on the air. This control of broadcasting was additionally justified by the idea that the airwaves were public property.

Thus the regulation explicitly—and for the first time with regard to a U.S. medium—recognized limits on numbers of voices. In theory, then and now, anyone can publish a newspaper, a magazine, or a book. But in regulating broadcast media, the government was left with the question of who should be allowed to have a broadcast license and who should not. The early Federal Radio Commission emphasized three criteria: adequate financial means to put and keep a station on the air, the technical ability to reproduce an adequate broadcast signal, and operation of the station in the "public interest, convenience, and necessity." This last criterion was meant to assure that, because not everyone could have a station, those who did would operate for the public benefit. To assure that, once on the air, broadcasters would continue to serve the public interest, licenses were to be renewed every six years. Renewal required demonstrating that the licensee had lived up to his or her public interest obligations. Thus, for the first time, the government found itself—and at the invitation of those to be regulated—applying a very different formula for how media ought to operate. Classical liberalism urges a negative conception of regulation—that the government should take no role, make no law: Broadcasting requires a positive or affirmative role—that the government must intervene, as a referee to decide who can use a medium.

In Britain, this positive role is described as a public service imperative. This imperative informs the content broadcast as well as the model of ownership. The BBC is an independent body funded by the British government from annual license fees on television sets.

The excerpt from the most recent Royal Charter (Box 12.2) states the programming mission of the BBC. The tone of program content was set by its first Director, Sir John Reith, in 1927, who saw broadcasting's purpose not to cater to the lowest common denominator but to program things that would enrich society (as he saw it). Reith saw broadcasting as a democratic medium in that it could help inform all parts of society; potentially no one was out of the reach of the signal. This approach has been criticized for being paternalistic; that is, for giving the audience not what they wanted but what he felt they needed. This philosophy of public service underlies all aspects of broadcasting in Britain, whether they are publicly or privately owned. The commercial television and radio stations are heavily regulated in keeping with this philosophy. Within the last decade, the rise in the number and availability of cable television and satellite channels has fueled arguments against the heavy regulation on broadcasting in Britain (Sparks, 1995). It was argued that, with potentially hundreds of channels available, all constituencies would be catered to; the BBC would no longer have to program for all interests. However, the Royal Charter was renewed in 1996 and the system will continue at least until it is up for renewal in 2006. (See Box 12.2, "The Royal Charter.")

---

**BOX 12.2**

**The Royal Charter**

The following is an excerpt from the current Royal Charter, which delineates the mission of the BBC. "Home Services" refers to broadcasting within Britain itself, in distinction with the BBC's "World Service."

Copy of Agreement

DEPARTMENT OF NATIONAL HERITAGE BROADCASTING
    Copy of the Agreement Dated the 25th Day of January 1996 Between Her Majesty's Secretary of State for National Heritage and the British Broadcasting Corporation

TREASURY MINUTE DATED THE 25th January 1996

[. . .]

*(Continued)*

---

(Continued)

## 3. PROGRAMME CONTENT

3.1 Without prejudice to the generality of clause 5, the Corporation undertakes to provide and keep under review the Home Services with a view to the maintenance of high general standards in all respects (and in particular in respect of their content, quality and editorial integrity) and to their offering a wide range of subject matter (having regard both to the programmes as a whole and also to the days of the week on which, and the times of the day at which, the programmes are shown) meeting the needs and interests of audiences, in accordance with the requirements specified in subclause 3.2.

3.2 The requirements referred to in subclause 3.1 are that the Home Services—

(a) are provided as a public service for disseminating information, education and entertainment;

(b) stimulate, support and reflect, in drama, comedy, music and the visual and performing arts, the diversity of cultural activity in the United Kingdom;

(c) contain comprehensive, authoritative and impartial coverage of news and current affairs in the United Kingdom and throughout the world to support fair and informed debate at local, regional and national levels;

(d) provide wide-ranging coverage of sporting and other leisure interests;

(e) contain programmes of an educational nature (including specialist factual, religious and social issues programmes as well as formal education and vocational training programmes);

(f) include a high standard of original programmes for children and young people;

(g) contain programmes which reflect the lives and concerns of both local and national audiences;

(h) contain a reasonable proportion and range of programmes for national audiences made in Northern Ireland, Scotland, Wales and in the English regions outside London and the South East.

At the same time as broadcasting was changing in the United States, the print media were changing too. Improved technology had led to lower production costs and a special postage rate available since 1879 for mailing periodicals helped increase distribution. Two phenomena served to nationalize media: the rise of modern marketing and advertising of national brands and the development of transcontinental communication systems, first the telegraph, later the telephone.

The telegraph gave rise to national news or wire (as in telegraph wire) services, of which the largest and most important is the AP. The AP is a cooperative service owned by newspaper publishers, which gave a local monopoly to its members: Only one daily newspaper in a city could belong to it, and thus one newspaper would have a substantial advantage over its competitors in the gathering of national and international news. The one-paper-per-city rule ended in the 1940s after the Supreme Court ruled that it violated antitrust law.

Advertising had come to play a more important role in newspapers and magazines, and circulation—the price the customer pays for the product—a less important one. As this happened, the advertiser became a more important influence on what appeared in the newspaper and the reader or subscriber became less important. Newspapers had to pay more attention to the demands of advertisers.

All together, the strategies publishers learned from their counterparts in other industries, and technological and economic changes within the publishing industry, created an important trend that continues to this day: the consolidation and concentration of print media into smaller numbers of companies, with, in newspapers particularly, smaller numbers of newspapers. We earlier noted that in 1900, there were 2,226 daily newspapers. By 1950, U.S. population had doubled, but the number of daily papers had shrunk to 1,900; by 1990, population had gone up another 30%, but the number of daily newspapers declined to under 1,750 (Bogart, 1989), and today there are 1,500 daily newspapers (U.S. Census, 2004). In other words, whereas broadcasting has a physical limit on the number of operators or possible channels, economic and technological constraints began in the early decades of the twentieth century to limit the number of voices the public could hear, especially in the print media.

By the mid 1990s, the case of online communication via the Internet and World Wide Web and the spectacular growth of this form of communication raised anew questions of media regulation. Anyone can set up a Web page, anyone can use (for minimal cost) electronic mail, and anyone can access information that may or may not be appropriate to all users, especially children. This new form of communication, without national boundaries, clear ownership, or standards for conduct, has posed a challenge regarding how to think about a free marketplace of ideas. This medium offers an unprecedented opportunity to increase the number of voices in the marketplace. Indeed, the libertarian nature of the Internet is often asserted in that anyone (given access, money, and know-how) can set up a Web page and have his or her voice heard. But, at the same time, Internet users tend to access a smaller range of well-known Web sites rather than availing themselves of every Web page on offer, leading to concentration rather than diversification, a trend many experts believe will continue and perhaps accelerate (Bagdikian, 2004; McChesney, 1999). In a key ruling—*Reno v. ACLU,* which struck down the Communication Decency Act—the U.S. Supreme Court decided that the Internet was to be regulated like a print medium (such as a newspaper) rather than as a broadcast medium, meaning that the Internet would be less regulated.

What does this media history and media economics have to do with normative theories of media performance? Everything. The historical challenge makes us question how the media are organized economically as well as what they say to us. The basic argument between supporters and challengers of classical liberalism's conception of media performance has to do with how well the media serve the public. Liberalism as a theory of media performance is predicated upon classical liberal economic theory. Does a capitalist system of media organization allow for the widest variety and diversity of viewpoints, or does it limit cultural and informational products along particular lines?

This thinking suggests several subquestions, as well: First, as consumers of media, do we have access to the widest possible variety of ideas and to truthful, intelligent, and comprehensive accounts of society? Second, to what extent do we and others have access to media to express our own ideas, to promote points of view about which we may care deeply? In other words, are we free and able to be producers of ideas as well as consumers? These questions of consumption and production are pivotal in a debate about how well a liberal capitalist system performs.

The strongest argument on the liberal side is the sheer volume of the media. In the United States, there are 1,500 daily newspapers, 7,400 weekly newspapers, 13,800 magazines, almost 6,900 radio stations, almost 1,900 television stations, 2,600 book publishers annually issuing almost 120,000 book titles and selling 2.43 billion books per year (U.S. Census, 2003b, 2004), and seven major motion picture studios. There are four major broadcast television networks (and two smaller networks, UPN and the WB), two major U.S. news wire services, and dozens of other newspaper-affiliated news services, five major recording companies (and numerous independent companies), and countless other media and ancillary services—newsletters, film processors, shoppers (free circulation newspapers), computer networks, syndication services, cable television systems in virtually every community, and on and on. The output of this system—millions of words, sounds, and images every day—is literally incalculable.

This media system, by accident or design, produces an astounding variety of material. On the consumption side, its beauty, the libertarian argument goes, is that of the free marketplace of ideas. These media compete with one another in a very direct sort of way. As consumers, we are wholly free to buy what we want, not to buy what we don't want; to "vote" with our TV remote controls and our radio dials, with the videocassettes or DVDs we choose to rent; to buy products and vote for politicians if we like their ads or to boycott them if we do not. Moreover, the system is democratic and, even better, pluralistic—if you or I don't like and don't buy something like the *National Enquirer,* that's fine. If the product can't find a market, can't find an audience, it will cease to exist. But if other people do like it and buy it, then they're free to do so, and if enough others do so, then it will remain available.

On the production side, the argument for the libertarian model is that the producer is remarkably free to produce whatever he, she, or it wants. If a media product can find an audience, the product will be produced. To be profitable, the producer must "give the audience what it wants," and if he, she, or it does so, then all obligations have been met, save one: As with any other product, no media producer may knowingly produce anything that is dangerous to the audience. On the production as well as on the consumption side, this process is viewed as both democratic and pluralistic. If there is too much competition in some media sector, the producer is free to shift to another one, to try to find an audience. If the producer fails, it is only because the audience won't buy—the audience is supreme.

However, we have already suggested that as an overall theoretical model and for practical and economic reasons, this rosy picture cannot go unanswered.

## Challenges to Classical Liberalism

### Social Responsibility Theory

A social responsibility position is the mainstream counterpoint to the liberal capitalism viewpoint. Shortly after World War II, a blue-ribbon Commission on the Freedom of the Press (1947), largely funded by *Time* magazine publisher Henry Luce and chaired by the very respected president of the University of Chicago, Robert Maynard Hutchins, was convened to discuss the state of American media. The panel was frankly worried that economic, cultural, and technological trends, and particularly the decreasing number of editorial voices in the nation's press, were leaving the nation less well served by its media than it should be. In its 1947 report, the Commission observed, among other things, that the media spent too much effort on the trivial and sensational, that the press was not meeting its responsibility to provide "a truthful, comprehensive, and intelligent account of the day's events in a context which gives them meaning" (p. 20). The press should be providing a forum for the exchange of ideas, presenting the widest variety of views. The press should avoid stereotyping and provide a representative view of the society. This could be accomplished, the Commission said, if the press were more responsible, if its practitioners were better trained, and if it effectively regulated itself. If it could not, the Commission suggested, then the government might have to establish its own media and more directly intervene to assure that the press was responsible—a departure from the libertarian notion.

In another departure from libertarianism, the Commission suggested that the media should be a "common carrier" of ideas. The press had obligations to present different ideas. This departed significantly from the libertarian idea that the media are wholly free—free, if they wish, to promote only those ideas of their own choosing.

Note that the intellectual seeds for such a social responsibility position are planted by the case of broadcasting, where government intervention was necessary to allocate channels. The very idea that government had a role in assuring a free and responsible press—at least in the United States—was born of the necessity of assuring an open marketplace.[10]

As might be expected, the print press greeted the Commission report with hostility and derision, but its ideas over time have gained ground. Since 1947, the American press has professionalized itself considerably, with far larger proportions of media producers having received university and college training in communications or journalism and more of them subscribing to some social responsibility notions, especially that they have obligations to be fair, truthful, and objective and to provide balanced representations of the society and its varying opinions. (See Box 12.3, "The Fairness Doctrine," and Box 12.4,

"Codes of Ethics.") At the same time, virtually none of them would subscribe to a notion that government control or ownership of media would enhance free expression.

---

**BOX 12.3**

**The Fairness Doctrine**

As we noted in earlier chapters, the histories of the print media and of the broadcast media travel along different tracks, and the regulatory environment of each differs. At about the same time as the Hutchins-led Freedom of the Press Commission was writing its report, the FCC, which regulates broadcasting and telecommunications, was writing a policy that came to be known as the Fairness Doctrine. When the FCC issued it in 1949 as an advisory to broadcasters, the set of regulations was to guide radio and television station operators in dealing with issues of controversy: After all, the "scarce-channel" logic goes, if not everyone can have a radio or TV station of their own, then broadcasters have an affirmative obligation to see that all views are represented. This is a prototypical example of social responsibility theory in action.

Basically, the Fairness Doctrine required some degree of balance in the presentation of controversial issues. If a broadcaster supported one side in a controversial issue (say, in a prolife editorial during a newscast, or in giving or selling air time to a group), then the broadcaster was obligated to make time available to others to present other sides of the issue. Later, the FCC extended the doctrine to require that if a personal attack were made on an individual, a station was required to inform the individual and offer air time for a reply.

From its earliest days, the Fairness Doctrine was vigorously criticized by the broadcast industry. The argument was the libertarian one, that as far as possible, government should keep its hands off the free marketplace: Let the broadcasters, in a competitive environment, be the ones to decide what should be seen and heard. The effect of government regulation in this area would be, they argued, not that "all sides" would be heard on controversial matters, but that broadcasters would be discouraged from allowing *any* sides to be heard, that broadcasting would steer away from any matters of controversy. Moreover, they argued, channels are not that scarce, and new technologies are making more and more channels available to the audience.

*(Continued)*

---

(Continued)

In the deregulatory political climate of the 1980s, the anti–Fairness Doctrine arguments won out at the FCC. In August 1987, the FCC voted unanimously to suspend—but not repeal—the Fairness Doctrine, effectively relieving broadcasters of direct legal requirements to be fair, although they are still bound, broadcasters argue, by moral and ethical social responsibility requirements to be so. (It should be noted, too, that the *equal time* rule, requiring broadcasters to provide equal amounts of time in comparable parts of the day to all legally qualified candidates for political office, remains in effect.)

---

## BOX 12.4

## Codes of Ethics

A number of media organizations have adopted codes of professional ethics. Below is a list of links to a sampling of these.

| | |
|---|---|
| Society of Professional Journalists | spj.org/ethics/ |
| Associated Press Managing Editors | www.apme/com/about/code_ethics.shtml |
| American Society of Newspaper Editors | www.asne.org/kiosk/archive/principl.htm |
| Radio-Television News Directors Association | www.rtnda.org/ethics/coe.shtml |
| National Press Photographer's Association | www.asne.org/ideas/codes/nppa.htm |
| Public Relations Society of America | prsa.org/profstd.html |

---

In fact, the social responsibility school of thought is not that far from libertarianism. The two viewpoints share, to some degree, two key assumptions that more radical critics will question: the general rationality of the audience, its ability to separate truth from falsehood, and the assumption underlying *this* assumption, that of an independent, discoverable truth in the first place. The main point of divergence is over the matter of the role of government, with libertarians insistent that the government have no role and social responsibility advocates maintaining that government should remain in the background, prodding media to be responsible through self-regulation.

There are two variations on social responsibility that we need to consider briefly here: *public* (or *civic*) *journalism* and *development journalism.* The 1990s saw the beginning of a more grassroots movement dubbed civic or public journalism, which, through a variety of approaches, is attempting to reconnect media to the communities that they serve (see Glasser, 1999). It varies from the social responsibility school by advocating that journalists become active in their communities and their issues (Shafer, 1998). The Pew Center for Public Journalism, a major supporter of this movement, describes the development of public journalism as first being interested in election issues (that is, how the press can be more responsive to local constituents and their issues during an election) but then broadening to include other issues of concern to a community, including diversity issues (Friedland & Nichols, 2002). In one experiment, the Columbus, Georgia, *Ledger-Enquirer* organized community discussion groups that led to a civic association; in others, newspapers have used focus groups and surveys to determine what issues local citizens think are most important and have then crafted their election coverage around those issues rather than the more traditional approaches of deciding for themselves or focusing on issues nominated by the candidates themselves. Still others have formed community boards to discuss newspaper play and coverage with editors (Charity, 1995; Merritt, 1995). Some view public journalism as a return to the spirit of muckraking (in which journalism's role was to "comfort the afflicted and afflict the comfortable"). What the movement does represent is one effort to recognize— and to remind their publics—that the media do have a stake in public life.

The second variation is something more of a departure from social responsibility theory. Development journalism was a form of journalism initially created in Southeast Asia in the 1960s. The idea was that the press should be a positive advocate for the development of a society, especially if the country was economically less developed. One of the pioneers of development journalism, Nora Quebral, defines it as follows:

> Development communication is the art and science of human communication applied to the speedy transformation of a country and the mass of its people from poverty to a dynamic state of economic growth that makes possible greater social equality and the larger fulfillment of human potential. (quoted in Shafer, 1998, p. 42)

Like public journalism, development journalism promotes an active, social advocate role for the press. But unlike the more recent model, development journalism seeks change on the scale of the nation and not the local community (Shafer, 1998).

These two variations share similar problems. First, neither is clearly defined at all, so there is no consistency or even core set of criteria for either. Second, both are theories of journalism that tend not to work as well in practice. Though the Pew Center report concludes that "civic journalism has been a success in the communities where it has been practiced with any consistency, even over relatively short periods of time" (Friedland & Nichols, 2002, p. 20), it has also been accused of being a marketing gimmick and can become simply another way of targeting news coverage to issues relevant to prominent (and wealthy) demographics. Development journalism, on the other hand, is too easily turned into an instrument for state propaganda (see, for example, Kariithi, 1994). Third, neither is much liked by journalists, who see them either as unduly restrictive on journalistic practice (as they understand it) or antithetical to the classical liberal idea of journalistic objectivity (Shafer, 1998). In the face of these criticisms, one might point out that there does not have to be only one model of the press working in any single nation or community, and that a nation or community might be better off with both an objective and an interventionist press.

There are other approaches to the question of how media should operate, however, that diverge more fundamentally from the liberal tradition than the social responsibility doctrine does.

### Marxist Critique

In 1846, Karl Marx and Friedrich Engels wrote, in *The German Ideology* (Marx & Engels, 1970), that "in every epoch, the ruling ideas are the ideas of the ruling class" (p. 64). In this century, much of the criticism of the media economy has been shaped to some degree by Marx and his followers. On examination, the Marx quotation goes to the heart of the assumption of the discoverability of truth by asking the degree to which, as both consumers or producers, the average person has a chance to see the truth.

Marxism is based on two major sets of arguments. First, Marxism offers an interpretation of the principles of the capitalist economy.

Second, it emphasizes the relations between the economy, politics, and the various forms of communication and culture.

According to contemporary Marxists, it is important to recognize that the mass media are implicated in the various structures of capitalism at a number of different levels. The media involve the production of goods, hardware as well as programming. The media are a major source of advertising and the promotion of other goods. Moreover, we have to remember that the media play a very central role in contemporary society: They shape our desires for goods, they control the information we receive around the world, they organize our leisure activities, and they provide many of the interpretations of reality we use in our everyday lives.

The nub of the critical argument is that some sectors of the society and economy have so much access to the resources to put forward their ideas that others essentially have none. On the production side, the critical argument is that those who have access to the means of production will use those means to promote points of view that either forward their own interests or at least bolster the status quo. Moreover, the critical counterpoint argues that, on the consumption side, we are thwarted from receiving ideas that seriously challenge the existing order. Although the libertarians, this argument goes, may be quite right that we have available a great *variety* of media fare, there's not much diversity there (Glasser, 1985). (See Box 12.5, "Variety and Diversity in Children's Television.") What's the difference?

---

**BOX 12.5**

**Variety and Diversity in Children's Television**

How much variety and diversity of programming is there in the media? This question was addressed in a study of children's programming in a Midwestern community (Wartella, Heintz, Aidman, & Mazzarella, 1990). The study was prompted by arguments made at the FCC throughout the 1980s: that the growth of new technologies, such as cable television, video, pay television, and satellites was increasing the diversity of programming available to children and therefore no single broadcaster in a community had a responsibility to program for child audiences. The study asked,

*(Continued)*

---

411

(Continued)

*Beyond over-the-air broadcast television, what sorts of programming are available for children in one media marketplace, Champaign-Urbana, Illinois?* A survey of all audio-video programming available to children in this one community was conducted to test the proposition that there indeed is both variety and diversity.

Program variety in children's programming refers to the amount of broadcast, cable, and videocassette rentals of children's product in this one community. Program diversity, on the other hand, is measured by the number of different genres or types of programs that could be delivered through any of the different media delivery systems, such as over-the-air broadcast television stations, cable channels, or videocassette rentals. In particular, two genres of program have been the focus of much public debate about children's television: animated, toy-related programs (such as *Teenage Mutant Ninja Turtles* or *Ghostbusters*) and educational/ informational programming, or those programs designed to educate children and provide them with information about science, history, culture, and so on (the best example here is *Sesame Street*).

So, how much variety did the researchers find in this one community? First, children's programming was available on all television, cable, and pay cable services during weekdays and weekends, and in fairly large amounts. On broadcast television, researchers found 52 hours on weekdays and 21 hours on weekends (even though Saturday morning is thought to be children's time). And basic cable services in the community aired 149 hours of children's shows during weekdays and 36 hours on weekends (thanks to the inclusion of Nickelodeon, the children's channel on cable). However, there were relatively few children's videos available for rental: Only 9% of all videotapes available in the community's 17 video rental stores could be classified as children's video.

Aside from variety, which the children do seem to have, do they have diversity of programming? Only if their families could afford cable ($18 a month—$216 a year—at the time):

> The most striking characteristic of these data is their clear indication that there is no diversity of children's programming on commercial television. All the weekday commercial children's programs are cartoons; two thirds of these are toy related. Public television provides the only alternative genres: educational and variety children's programming such as *Sesame Street* and *Captain Kangaroo.* Weekend commercial television provides minimal diversity: Only 3 of the 28 commercial children's programs over the weekend are not cartoons. A very different picture emerges, however, in the analysis of children's

program offerings on cable television. Although cartoon programming still predominates, composing more than one half of all basic cable children's offerings, there is much more diversity. Nearly all of the seven categories of genres (including: animated toy, animated non-toy, live action comedy or drama, quiz, variety, exercise, instructional, or other) are represented on cable services. It appears that Champaign-Urbana children with access to basic cable and pay cable services are able to receive both a variety and a diversity of children's programming that far exceed that provided by the broadcast television stations in the community. . . . And unlike adult tapes, which tend to represent Hollywood film product, children's video tapes (with the exception of Disney movies and old cartoons) represent television-originated product. . . . Dominating this television product on videotape is toy-related programming. . . . Videotape rentals in Champaign-Urbana simply provide more of what is available on television and cable. Little educational programming is available for rent or purchase, and few stores carry a majority of non-toy related animated tapes. (pp. 51–54)

This study confirms what critics of children's television argued throughout the 1980s: that there was too little diversity in children's television provided by the traditional broadcasters. Such evidence helped to bring about the passage of the Children's Television Act of 1990, which, among other provisions, requires all broadcasters to identify their information/educational children's programming and which establishes a National Endowment for Children's Television to encourage and fund the production of more educational television. As of fall 1997, it is too early to tell whether, in this one community or nationwide, the act's requirement that broadcasters air and label educational and informational programming for children has had much of an impact on variety and diversity.

Source: From Wartella, E., Heintz, K., Aidman, A., & Mazzarella, S. (1990). Television and beyond: Children's video in one community. *Communication Research, 17*(1), 45–64. Reprinted with permission of Sage Publications, Inc.

Variety suggests lots of material that is superficially, but not basically, different. Suppose all car manufacturers built basically the same car—say a four-door, five-passenger, four-cylinder, automatic transmission model—but allowed us to choose among 500 different colors of paint. That would be a lot of variety. Diversity suggests fundamental difference. Diversity in motor vehicles would include motorcycles, minivans, vans, pickups, two-door sports models, convertibles, sedans, station wagons, and so on. And real diversity would not only offer us private transportation but comfortable and efficient public transportation. So what if we have 75 channels on our cable television if all we can see during prime time are situation comedies, cop shows, and bland old movies? So what if we have competing television news, but we can't tell the difference between one station or network and another? So what if we have competing newspapers if all the competitors ignore or trivialize the same groups—African Americans, women, the young—and keep their politics close to the political center?

The critical counterpoint argues that economic structures foreclose true diversity of ideas. The critical argument comes in two main forms, the political economic and the cultural. Political economic criticism focuses on the ownership of the means of production as the mode of control of the social order. "Freedom of the press belongs to those who own one" is a quotation variously attributed to Mohandas Gandhi and to the American press critic A. J. Liebling. Cultural criticism focuses on the processes by which dominant forms of thought—ideologies— support the existing social order and suppress social change.

## *The Political Economic Argument*

We have noted the great number of different media in the United States. Press critic Ben Bagdikian (1997) has pointed out that if American daily newspapers, magazines, radio and television stations, and book publishers were owned by separate individuals, there would be 25,000 different owners (a large number, yes, but still only one out of every 10,000 Americans). But there are not 25,000 different owners. Today, Bagdikian (2004) says, just five corporations dominate the output of daily newspapers and most of the sales and audience in magazines, broadcasting and cable, books, and movies (see our discussion in Chapter 4). Bagdikian (2000) notes that,

> as the United States enters the twenty-first century, power over the American mass media is flowing to the top with such devouring speed that it exceeds even the accelerated consolidations of the last twenty years. . . . Even with the dramatic entry of the Internet and the cyber world with their uncounted hundreds of new firms, the controlling handful of American and foreign corporations now exceed in their size and communication power anything the world has seen before. Their intricate global interlocks create the force of an international cartel. (p. vii)

Not only do a relatively small number of people head these corporations, a very small number effectively control them. Although the directors of these corporations constitute a larger number than the chief officers of the companies, there are interlocks between these boards; that is, the same people tend to sit on boards of a number of corporations, both within media and in other pivotal sectors of the economy, and they are the same *types* of people, drawn from a very small upper stratum of the society.

Many of the dominant media firms are not *just* media firms but part of larger multinational corporations with diverse interests. To what extent can the media perform other functions—information and entertainment—adequately if their major role is to make money? A corollary question is the extent to which a media enterprise will be subject to the corporate goals and interests of a parent company. For example, questions have been raised about whether network news programs adequately cover stories that negatively portray their corporate owners, and there have been numerous suggestions of the possibility of both corporate and self-censorship. Can NBC and CBS, whose parent companies have strong financial interests in power generation, including nuclear power, be counted on to report fairly and in depth about utilities and their regulation? Can a news unit whose parent company has extensive contracts to manufacture military hardware fairly report on a war in which such equipment is in use?[11] Perhaps the news divisions are sufficiently insulated from corporate influence, but the appearance of a conflict of interest may erode the confidence of the public in their credibility.

Media economics in general, the political economic argument goes, are driven by a *logic of capitalism,* a pursuit of maximal profit, in which advertising plays a primary role. We noted in Chapter 4 that the *Saturday Evening Post* was driven out of business, not because it failed to attract readers, but because it was deserted by advertisers. The liberal point argued for the supremacy and democracy of the audience as voter. The death of mass magazines, entertaining and informing large audiences, is a counterpoint. But, you may argue, the vitality of specialized magazines supports the libertarian argument. Yes, but only to a point, that point being where some profit exists. It is worth observing that, among the thousands of magazines in this nation, there is none called *Old and Poor* or *South Central Los Angeles.*[12]

And it is worth remembering that there are millions of people, even in America, who simply cannot afford to purchase any media products. If a medium cannot attract advertisers, and its potential audience cannot afford to buy it, it probably does not exist. As the short essay "Variety and Diversity in Children's Television" (Box 12.5) points out, variety and diversity exists only for kids whose parents can afford cable TV, premium cable channels, VCRs, and DVD rentals.

Thus the political economic argument against liberal capitalism focuses on ownership of media production and the power that ownership and control exercises over both individuals' ability to produce messages they would like others to see and hear and individuals' abilities to receive or consume messages as well. Where the liberal point emphasizes openness and variety, the political economic counterpoint answers, "Only if there's a profit in it." And, increasingly, the number of independent voices through which ideas can be expressed with any real hope of reaching more than a few eyes and ears is declining.

### The Cultural Argument

The cultural argument points to the logic-of-capitalism argument, as well. But, instead of focusing on the ownership of the means of production, it looks at the programs—the messages—that are produced. The cultural response builds on our discussions in Chapter 5 on the cultural approach to meaning. The cultural argument suggests that a media system such as America's is a site of ideological struggle.

Ideologies are not merely particular systems of representation or ways of seeing. They are also ways of excluding and limiting, for they set the boundaries on what we are able to understand and accept into the realm of the possible. Finally, ideologies are not neutral. Obviously, they are connected to the struggle of one group or another to maintain or challenge particular social organizations, particular relations of power. On this view, culture involves constant struggles between competing ideological codes, each attempting to gain the upper hand, to somehow win people into seeing the world in terms of its particular meanings, to experience the world on its terms. Obviously, although some ideological codes are explicitly linked to political positions and philosophies (we can think of the ideologies of communism and capitalism, or of the Democrats and the Republicans), the cultural argument makes ideology into a much more pervasive and common feature of our lives.

This cultural or ideological argument does not suggest that no space is left for alternative views. What it does suggest is that, when they appear in the mainstream media, such views are likely to be clearly identified as "controversial," and hence suspect; moreover, consistent with the more materialist critics' thinking, the view argues that they likely will be crowded out by profit-seeking producers who would rather avoid controversy in the first place. Another common strategy is to rewrite controversial events or positions so that their content is transformed from a challenge to the dominant values into a reaffirmation. For example, during the protests of the 1960s, news media reporting on demonstrations would often emphasize that the very fact of such protests confirmed that our society was free and equal (in Chapter 7, we referred to this process as *recuperation*). In the process, the actual object of the protest—for example, the war in Vietnam or the disproportionate number of Blacks serving in the armed forces—was forgotten or ignored (Gitlin, 1980).

Thus our ability to produce messages is constrained by the taken-for-granted assumptions of normality by those who operate the media system, at the same time that the fare we have available to consume is caught up in the same assumptions. The job of cultural critics is to unmask the ideologies inherent in various media products: the news, advertising, films, the Internet, and so forth.

## Normative Solutions: What Should Be Done?

What do such normative theories ultimately have to say about the context in which media should operate?

A strict, radical libertarian would argue that the media should be free to publish and broadcast what they wish, that sovereign, rational consumers should determine their fate. The government should have no role in the media, except perhaps to foster and encourage their economic success and to referee frequency allocations, as it does in broadcasting and cellular communications.

A strict, radical Marxist, either of a cultural or a political-economic stripe, would argue the opposite: that media should be created by and owned by the public, with the state or government serving the necessary function of allocating the means to produce media to the people.

There is, however, a lot of territory in between. Social responsibility theorists argue for a tripartite division of responsibility for media performance. Ownership of media would remain private, with both owners and the professionals who actually create and distribute media messages invested in a set of values emphasizing their responsibility for fair, accurate, and complete presentations to and about all constituent groups of a society. The role of the state and the government is in three areas: It should prevent flagrant abuses by the media—in false advertising, libel, and profoundly harmful communications; it should correct the marketplace's tendency toward ownership concentration and foster competition; and it should assure that where the marketplace cannot adequately serve underrepresented groups and points of view, publicly owned media will do so. Furthermore, the position usually argues that educational institutions have an obligation at all levels, and particularly in primary and secondary education, to teach media literacy. The social responsibility position emphasizes, too, that the public has a role, through citizens' groups and through personal feedback to media outlets, to assure that the media know what the public thinks of them and the jobs they are doing.

## NOTES

1. A good general discussion of how public opinion is represented is in Herbst (1993).

2. Important sources for this historical discussion are Eisenstein (1978), Ginsberg (1986), Calhoun (1992), and especially Habermas (1962/1989).

3. It might be noted that Tocqueville and Lippmann were both writing in periods in which the composition and definition of the public was being transformed—in Tocqueville's case, by the opening of what was then the West (west of the Atlantic states but east of the Mississippi) and the increasing political empowerment of tradesmen, small merchants, and yeoman farmers, and in Lippmann's case, by immigrants from central and southern Europe.

4. The discussion that follows draws from the following: Alter (1984); Erskine (1970); *Gallup Poll* (1988); Times-Mirror Center for the People and the Press

(1985); and Wyatt (1991). A very valuable (and constantly updated) source of information on public attitudes about the media is the Web site of the Pew Research Center on the People and the Press (people-press.org).

5. Foundation estimate from National Public Radio's *Morning Edition*, July 28, 1997. We should note that total charitable contributions from all sources in the United States, including individuals and corporations as well as foundations, is just over $240 billion (Brunner, 2003, p. 174).

6. Montgomery (1989) has a good account of the *Maude* controversy and other episodes of protests against television through the 1980s.

7. The coming out of Ellen DeGeneres on ABC's *Ellen* is an exception, but it ignited its own controversy when the network inserted, in the fall 1997 premiere episode, a parental advisory. DeGeneres protested the advisory and the TV-14 rating as evidence of the network's acquiescence to a view of homosexuality as a deviant lifestyle.

8. See Page and Shapiro (1983, 1992). In the earlier work, the authors argue that, in two thirds to three quarters of all cases they examined from the 1930s to the 1970s, changes in public opinion led to changes in public policy; such changes were most likely on large-scale domestic issues and most likely in the later time periods (i.e., the 1960s and 1970s) and least likely for low-salience issues—ones less likely to get extensive media coverage. On such issues, they argue, special interests rather than the mass public probably dominate policy.

9. A "patents trust" involving the British Marconi Company, GE, the Radio Corporation of America, American Telephone and Telegraph (AT&T), Westinghouse, and others, also operated, allowing for these companies to gain an upper hand both in making radios and in radio broadcasting, once the commercial potential of the medium was assured by the late 1920s.

10. In almost all of the rest of the industrialized world, radio broadcasting began as a public—that is, government-owned—monopoly system and would remain so until well after the institution of television, which likewise emerged as a public system.

11. Media critic Doug Kellner (1992) cites the following quotation that, during the first Iraq war, "when correspondents and paid consultants on NBC television praised the performance of U.S. weapons, they were extolling equipment made by GE, the corporation that pays their salary" (Lee & Solomon, quoted in Kellner, 1992, pp. 59–60).

12. Our thanks to Professor Robert Reid of the University of Illinois for this example.

## SUGGESTED READINGS

Glasser, T. L. (Ed.). (1999). *The idea of public journalism.* New York: Guilford.

Habermas, J. (1989). *The structural transformation of the public sphere: An inquiry into a category of bourgeois society* (T. Burger, Trans.). Cambridge, MA: MIT Press. (Original work published 1962.)

McChesney, R. W. (1999). *Rich media, poor democracy: Communication politics in dubious times.* Urbana: University of Illinois Press.

Nerone, J. (Ed.). (1995). *Last rights: Revisiting four theories of the press.* Urbana: University of Illinois Press.

Putnam, R. D. (2000). *Bowling alone: The collapse and revival of American community.* New York: Simon & Schuster.

Schudson, M. (Ed.). (1995). *The power of news.* Cambridge, MA: Harvard University Press.

Siebert, F. S., Peterson, T., & Schramm, W. (1956). *Four theories of the press: The authoritarian, libertarian, social responsibility, and Soviet communist concepts of what the press should be and do.* Urbana: University of Illinois Press.

# Media Globalization

13

O ne of the strangest stories of media globalization occurred in the wake of the September 11, 2001, attacks. News reports of a pro–Osama bin Laden protest in Bangladesh showed a protestor holding a large sign with many pictures of bin Laden. One of these pictures showed bin Laden apparently standing next to the Muppet Bert of the U.S. children's television program *Sesame Street*. The juxtaposition came as a shock to many (and Children's Television Workshop, the producers of *Sesame Street*, were understandably upset). The tale of that image is one of mediamaking in a global age.

It began with an award-winning Web site by San Francisco student Dino Ignacio. The Web site was www.bertisevil.com and the high concept behind it was that the Muppet Bert was evil; this site was a forum for its creator to show his skill at digital image manipulation by inserting Bert into various photos with infamous evil people (standing with Hitler, for example). The site, an attempt at ironic, postmodern humor, became popular, and others began establishing their own "tribute" Web sites showing even more images of Bert with evil people. The image of bin Laden and Bert came from a Dutch tribute site and not from Ignacio's site (though it was mistakenly attributed to him). When the story broke, Ignacio took down the Bert is Evil site, arguing that he had never wished to harm children's views of the Muppet, that the site was meant for a relatively limited group of people, and that all the news coverage made it too likely that children would see the site and its images. So, what had happened? An image from a children's television program produced in New York was manipulated by a Web programmer in the Netherlands, influenced by another Web programmer in California. Someone in Bangladesh was searching the Web for images of bin Laden for a poster and found one on the Dutch site. News photos of the poster from the march were then distributed to the global media. We may never know if those who downloaded the image and created the poster even knew who Bert was or what meaning they made of the strange, angry-looking puppet.

If we think of global media as media ranging over vast areas, the roots of global media are deep in the origins of writing. The history of the medium of written language spans the globe. A number of writing systems (or *scripts*) arose autonomously across the world—in Egypt and Babylon, Crete, the Indus Valley, Turkey, the Americas, China, and Korea—but they didn't always remain local. Let us give you a brief example. The explorer Ferdinand Magellan was Portuguese. The script he wrote in derived originally (through Roman, Etruscan, and Greek) from a Phoenician alphabet, which had traveled west through the Mediterranean shipping lanes. When Magellan made his ill-fated landing on the Philippine Islands in 1521 as he attempted to circumnavigate the globe, the people of the islands already had in place their own script systems quite different from Portuguese. However, that script system derived from a Javanese system from Indonesia, which was itself derived from a script brought to the area by Buddhist monks from South India. The South Indian script, the Brahmic, was derived from an Aramaic variation on the Phoenician alphabet (see Diringer, 1968). Small world.

Recall our discussion of media history from Chapter 2. Oral cultures were predominantly local in nature. With the advent not just of writing but of relatively light and portable writing materials, it became possible for centralized authorities to exert control over larger and larger areas. Harold Innis (1950) refers to this as the start of *empire.* The origins of empire included media systems of increasingly rapid and far-reaching communication and information, including networks of roads, postal systems, and organized news gathering and dissemination.

However, despite the extended reach of these media, they are not *global* media, because the term *global media* implies a sense of the globe as an interconnected whole. Globalization is more than simply the circulation of things (films, cars, t-shirts, guns) around the world through

422

networks of communication or trade. Globalization is about an *awareness* of the world as a whole and one's place within it, an awareness intimately connected with global processes of economics, politics, and culture. As sociologist Ronald Robertson (1992) has defined it, "Globalization as a concept refers both to the compression of the world and the intensification of consciousness of the world as a whole" (p. 8). Globalization is about the awareness of the changing nature and influence of geography: Not only do far off places seem closer, there is an awareness that decisions, events, and activities occurring in far off places could have a profound impact on one's own way of life and that decisions made locally could have impacts far away (see Giddens, 1990). For example, a financial decision made by a bank in London to sell its gold and invest in other ways could shut down gold mines in South Africa, throwing hundreds if not thousands of people out of work. Deforestation in the South American rainforest affects the climate of the rest of the globe. Robertson points out that globalization entails a sense of relativism, that is one's own culture, values, and way of life are no longer considered absolute but rather relative to other cultures, values, and ways of living (though one may still assume that one's own is true or better).

For a working definition of globalization, we'll turn to Australian sociologist Malcolm Waters (2001):

> [Globalization is] a social process in which the constraints of geography on economic, political, social and cultural arrangements recede, in which people become increasingly aware that they are receding and in which people act accordingly. (p. 5)

To "act accordingly" tends to take one of two directions: The first is to connect globally into personal networks that span the globe and to become global in a sense, and the second is to retreat from the intrusion of the global into reactionary ethnic, political, and cultural enclaves (Castells, 1997; see also the discussion of Barber, 1996, below). Some people have no choice as to whether to be connected or not, and to "act accordingly" could be to react against this involuntary global connection or disconnection.

Globalization is, in a way, a continuation of the processes of modernization. Recall from our discussion of modernization and postmodernization in Chapter 2 that modernization has to do with the profound economic, social, and cultural changes in Europe and America since the dawn of capitalism. These changes include new forms of mass

423

production, new social relations (including urbanization), new political relations (the state becomes active in regulating public affairs and the economy), and new cultural relations (especially the sense of continual revolution). *Postmodernization* refers to the acceleration and transformation of modernization. The postmodern is about the flexibility and mobility of production and marketing and the complete immersion of the population within worlds of media images, commodification, and consumption. Postmodernization is not the same as globalization, though the processes they describe overlap. A village in Vietnam may be quite intimately connected with globalization through factory work for transnational corporations, but that doesn't necessarily make life there postmodern.

Globalization is a recent phenomenon with a long history. As a critical term, it has only come into wide use since the early to mid-1980s. And globalization has only really come into its own in terms of the intensity of its interconnections and the breadth of the global consciousness in the last 50 years. It's best to think of globalization as an ongoing process, but one of "profound unevenness" (Hall, 1991, p. 33). In a fully globalized world, economics, politics, and culture would be indifferent to location. The economic, political, and cultural processes of globalization have deep roots; scholars trace globalization back to the early days of colonialism and empire, if not earlier. Cultural studies scholar Stuart Hall (1991) describes two general eras of globalization. The first, stretching roughly from the eighteenth century to the mid- to late twentieth century, was "that era when the formation of the world market was dominated by the economies and cultures of powerful nation-states" (p. 20). The second, current era of globalization "has to do with a new form of global mass culture. . . . Global mass culture is dominated by the modern means of cultural production, dominated by the image which crosses and re-crosses linguistic frontiers much more rapidly and more easily, and which speaks across languages in a much more immediate way" (p. 27).

This chapter is structured around these two eras of globalization. The first part describes the era of the nation-state and the media-related issues that arose from it. This era has provided the context for much of the scholarship on international communication. Within the problematic of this era, we situate a discussion of a key idea of international communication, cultural imperialism, not as a theory of globalization but of relations between states. Cultural imperialism in the notion that a nation can dominate another country or people by dominating that country's communication and culture. For example, if most of the TV shows broadcast, films screened, and music purchased in a country are American, cultural imperialism scholars argue that America has in essence colonized that country.

The second part of the chapter describes the shift to contemporary globalization, tracking the recent changes in economics, politics, and culture which shape global media. Economic forces of finance and production are disconnected from locality, and global cultural flows create new channels for creative exchange as well as domination. In this section, we will overview George Ritzer's (1993) argument that the world is becoming McDonaldized and Benjamin Barber's (1992, 1996) argument that the globalized world is characterized by two opposing tendencies: what he calls McWorld and jihad. We will consider these arguments in the context of a theory of cultural hybridity, concluding that contemporary globalization is more characterized by difference than homogeneity. Finally, we will discuss global media itself within Arjun Appadurai's (1996) model of global flows of finance, technology, people, ideology, and media.


## GLOBALIZATION, THE NATION-STATE, AND CULTURAL IMPERIALISM

Karl Marx wrote, "The need of a constantly expanding market for its products, chases the bourgeoisie over the whole surface of the globe. It must nestle everywhere, settle everywhere, establish connections everywhere" (quoted in Waters, 2001, p. 9). The expansion of capitalism in the eighteenth and nineteenth centuries pushed global trade (and colonialism) to new levels as the need for new resources, pools of labor, and markets increased. This same period saw the rise of a powerful form of political organization: the nation-state. The *nation-state*, as Waters (2001) puts it, "becomes the principal vehicle for the establishment of collective social goals and their attainment" (p. 13). The nation-state provides a means of economic, social, and physical security for its people. Nation-states are considered sovereign, meaning that they are not under the control of external forces and that states have control of their own territories and peoples. But no nation-state can be entirely self-sufficient and autonomous: "The attainment of national goals obliged the states to establish relations with other states and there emerged a system of international relations" through "war, alliance, diplomacy and colonialism" (Waters, 2001, p. 13). Globalization in this era is marked by the positioning for power between global empires and alliances. It becomes a time of international relations, the relations between nations. In the twentieth century, the nation-state becomes more actively involved in managing its own economy (rather than the *laissez-faire* approach of the previous century).

After World War II, global trade becomes dominated by trade negotiations between states and often within the context of international organizations. Scholars often point to the Bretton Woods agreement of 1944 as characteristic of this stage of globalization. The Bretton Woods agreement was an attempt to create global institutions that would manage the global economy to stave off another economic depression partly by stabilizing monetary exchange and trade around a fixed standard of U.S. dollars and gold. It also created the International Monetary Fund (IMF) and the World Bank, as well as the General Agreement on Tariffs and Trade (GATT), a relatively loose treaty that in 1994 was made into a global institution in its own right—the World Trade Organization (WTO; Ellwood, 2001).

World War II and the decades immediately following saw the dissolution of the old empires as colony after colony achieved independence (establishing new, independent nation-states). But what was soon realized was that, though the old empires no longer held direct political power over the newly independent countries, they still held them in a position of dependence. This *neocolonialism* meant that European and North American nations maintained control through economic power (a colony's primary trading partner will be the imperial home country, and these relations of the export of raw materials to the empire and import of manufactured goods from the empire continued after independence; in addition, the Bretton Woods institutions were seen to be dominated by Western industrialized countries, especially the United States) and through maintaining control of international communication and culture.

## Cultural Imperialism

It is within the context of this era of globalization—the ascendancy of the nation-state as the default political form globally and the creation of international institutions to regulate global economics—and especially in the dual moment of decolonization and neocolonialism, that we wish to discuss the idea of cultural imperialism. *Cultural imperialism* is the idea that empires could be maintained, if not created, by means other than military conquest and occupation. It is the idea that if one could control the culture of another people—their ideologies, values, styles, and meanings—then one could more easily control the people themselves. Note that cultural imperialism is not a theory of globalization; it is a theory of relations between states. But it prefigures important debates around global media which we will discuss in the second half of this chapter.

Cultural imperialism is an old practice: For example, empires would often impose the language of the imperial homeland as the official language of their colonies, in the process enforcing their own cultural values. Media play a particular role within cultural imperialism, because they are the means of disseminating cultural texts. Control of the media becomes an important strategy of cultural imperialism (though not the only one; control of education would be another). For example, let's look at the wire-based news agencies of the nineteenth century. The telegraph allowed for the more rapid transmission of news and information across the Atlantic. Indeed, a telegraph cable connected the United States with Europe long before one connected the east and west coasts of the United States. The first wire services were international in character. Through a formal agreement, the French agency Havas (founded in 1835) covered the countries of the French Empire, the Mediterranean, and South America; the German agency Wolff (founded in 1849) covered Central and Northern Europe; and the British agency Reuters (founded in 1851) covered the British Empire (which, at this point, covered much of Asia) and North America (Herman & McChesney, 1997; Mattelart, 1994). The first American press agency, the AP, though founded in 1848 did not expand significantly overseas for almost 50 years.

One lesson that was learned early was that those who owned the means of distribution of news and information could shape that information in different ways. And if one did not control the international wires (and wire services) leading in and out of one's country, then one couldn't control how one was portrayed to the rest of the world (or what information one received from the rest of the world). This issue continues to haunt international communication. At the time, when international telegraph lines were controlled by others, Americans complained that they were never portrayed favorably in the international news, that the news agencies tended to bring up issues of the treatment of Native Americans and the slavery of Africans, while Europe was portrayed much more glowingly (Frederick, 1993). A second lesson is that routes of international communication follow the geography of political and economic power. The telegraph lines that crisscrossed the world in the latter part of the nineteenth century were connecting imperial centers such as London and Paris with their colonies in India, Africa, or Indochina. In some cases, countries are still struggling with this colonial legacy. In Africa, for example, telephone calls between African nations often have to be routed through the colonial capitals in Europe.

The control of international communications by a handful of nations can lead to an imbalanced and biased portrayal of world events. A number of studies performed in the 1960s and 1970s showed that a great imbalance in the flow of news and information still existed at that time.[1] Most of the news was about the industrialized Western nations (who overwhelmingly controlled the international wire services and the radio spectrum), and relatively little pertained to what were called the developing (or Third World) countries, despite the fact that the latter account for three quarters of the world's population. What little was reported of the developing world was distorted to make it fit with the expectations of Western news media. For example, it seemed (and arguably still seems) that the only time Bangladesh is mentioned in the Western press is if there has been disastrous flooding. Those who get their news from the Western press (that is, almost everyone, since the non-Western press obtained at least some if not much of its news from the Western press) then get a quite distorted view of what life in Bangladesh must be like. The developing world worried that issues of importance to them were treated unsympathetically in the press and that they were misrepresented generally. This is similar to the situation that the United States found itself in a hundred years earlier, when it did not have a voice among the international wire services.

In addition to the direction of the flow of information and the bias of that information, these studies found that much of the world's population simply had inadequate access to information, a factor of special concern to those who conducted these studies. This work had been carried out under the auspices of the United Nations Educational, Scientific, and Cultural Organization (UNESCO), founded on the principles of the free flow of information and the human right to communicate. The former principle is based on the classical liberal view of news and information covered in the last chapter; the latter, on a clause of the United Nations' *Universal Declaration of Human Rights* (1948), which states that

> Everyone has the right to freedom of opinion and expression; this right includes freedom to hold opinions without interference and to seek, receive, and impart information and ideas through any media and regardless of frontiers.

What makes this declaration different from the ideas of freedom of speech and freedom of the press contained in the U.S. Constitution is that it includes the right to *obtain* information in addition to the right to express one's self. The extreme imbalance in the flow and accessibility of information globally was therefore considered a violation of human rights. Note that this declaration also challenges the sovereignty of nation-states by asserting common rights "regardless of frontiers."

We should point out that it was not just the developing countries that were concerned with the flow of information; many countries (Australia, Canada, and France, to name just three) were concerned with the amount of foreign content in their media—not just the domination of news by Western wire services but also the domination of the film and television industries by the United States.

In the 1960s, as neocolonialism and the imbalance of global power, economics, and information were making themselves felt, many countries in the developing world also realized that if they worked collectively they might be able to address this imbalance in ways that would be impossible individually. One such collective organization was a group of countries calling themselves the Non-Aligned Movement (NAM), ostensibly because they did not consider themselves aligned with either side of the cold war (the United States or the USSR). Members of the NAM were from nations and liberation movements in Asia, Africa, and Latin America and represented about two thirds of the world population. The NAM put forward two proposals. One was for a *new international economic order* (NIEO) and the other for a *new world information and communication order* (NWICO). The NIEO was to be based on equity, interdependence, an orientation toward people instead of just capital or technology, environmental harmony, respect for human rights, and satisfaction of basic human needs. The NIEO was not a direct challenge to capitalism; the NAM simply wanted better terms of trade for its members and more local control of capital, labor, and technology as well as greater representation and voice in the world economic institutions. The NWICO was similar in some respects: It called for an increased two-way flow of information and communication, more news about developing countries, assistance with media production, greater control for countries over their own media industries, and greater representation and voice in the institutions that regulated world communication. The NAM even created its own news agency, the Non-Aligned News Agencies Pool.

The NAM was successful in that its proposals for the NIEO and NWICO were taken up and debated by UN agencies: the UN Commission for Trade and Development (UNCTAD) for the former and UNESCO for the latter. The problems that subsequently arose around the NWICO within UNESCO were based on a fundamental contradiction. UNESCO was founded on the principle of the free flow of information, but it was also designed to promote peace and understanding and to prevent war, propaganda, and racism. The problem is this: To insure a free flow of information, one does not have to look at content, just at whether the information is flowing freely. But to promote peace and so on meant that UNESCO was concerned with the content of the communication and that it was in the business to somehow stop, prevent, or speak out about information that advocated war, propaganda, and racism. The problems really began in the mid-1970s when UNESCO began work drafting what was to become its Mass Media Declaration. In early drafts, any language used to indicate the forbidding of information or communication (even forbidding racism and propaganda) met with stern resistance from the West. Thus any attempts to require the press to fulfill any particular role was seen as being against the free flow of information (recall the debate on development journalism in the previous chapter).

In true bureaucratic fashion, in 1976 UNESCO postponed a decision by setting up a committee to study the situation. This committee was headed by Seán MacBride (a founding member and Chairman of Amnesty International and the only person to have been awarded both the Lenin and Nobel Peace Prizes) and was given the task of studying "the totality of communication problems in modern societies" (MacBride et al., 1980, p. xvii). The MacBride Commission didn't finish its report until 1980, by which time UNESCO had finally passed its

Mass Media Declaration, which called for "a wider and more balanced dissemination of information" but avoided the key issues by not including concrete measures to balance the flow and not calling for any form of international code of journalistic ethics. (See Box 13.1, "UNESCO's Mass Media Declaration.") The MacBride Report, entitled *Many Voices, One World: Towards a New, More Just, and More Efficient World Information and Communication Order*, consisted of over 100 individual studies and papers and made 82 recommendations. Among its main points, it condemned censorship, emphasized that the right of access to information applied to both public and private sectors, rejected any move to license journalists, condemned the use of journalists for national security intelligence, and stated that information and communication were vital social resources. The report was a compromise document between competing ideological positions; the fact that a report was produced at all, and that it was approved by all UNESCO members, is amazing. It was praised for its scope and compromise, but criticized for not having a coherent overarching theoretical framework.

---

## BOX 13.1

### UNESCO's Mass Media Declaration

The following statements about the roles and responsibilities of mass media are excerpted from UNESCO's *Declaration on Fundamental Principles Concerning the Contribution of the Mass Media to Strengthening Peace and International Understanding, to the Promotion of Human Rights and to Countering Racialism, Apartheid and Incitement to War* (1978):

#### Article II

1. The exercise of freedom of opinion, expression and information, recognized as an integral part of human rights and fundamental freedoms, is a vital factor in the strengthening of peace and international understanding.

2. Access by the public to information should be guaranteed by the diversity of the sources and means of information available to it, thus enabling each individual to check the accuracy of facts and to appraise events objectively. To this end, journalists must have freedom to report and the fullest possible facilities of access to information. Similarly, it is important that the mass media be responsive to concerns of peoples and individuals, thus promoting the participation of the public in the elaboration of information.

*(Continued)*

(Continued)

3. With a view to the strengthening of peace and international under-standing, to promoting human rights and to countering racialism, apartheid and incitement to war, the mass media throughout the world, by reason of their role, contribute to promoting human rights, in particular by giving expression to oppressed peoples who struggle against colonialism, neo-colonialism, foreign occupation and all forms of racial discrimination and oppression and who are unable to make their voices heard within their own territories.

4. If the mass media are to be in a position to promote the principles of this Declaration in their activities, it is essential that journalists and other agents of the mass media, in their own country or abroad, be assured of protection guaranteeing them the best conditions for the exercise of their profession. (p. 102)

**Article X**

1. With due respect for constitutional provisions designed to guarantee freedom of information and for the applicable international instruments and agreements, it is indispensable to create and maintain throughout the world the conditions which make it possible for the organizations and persons profes-sionally involved in the dissemination of information to achieve the objectives of this Declaration.

2. It is important that a free flow and wider and better balanced dissem-ination of information be encouraged.

3. To this end, it is necessary that States facilitate the procurement by the mass media in the developing countries of adequate conditions and resources enabling them to gain strength and expand, and that they support co-operation by the latter both among themselves and with the mass media in developed countries.

4. Similarly, on a basis of equality of rights, mutual advantage and respect for the diversity of the cultures which go to make up the common her-itage of mankind, it is essential that bilateral and multilateral exchanges of information among all States, and in particular between those which have different economic and social systems, be encouraged and developed. (pp. 103–104)

Despite the passage of the MacBride Report by UNESCO, the West, especially the United States, had been increasingly concerned with the idea of the free and balanced flow of information from the Mass Media Declaration, feeling that it went against the principle of freedom of the press. The same year that the MacBride Report was presented to UNESCO, Ronald Reagan became President of the United States.

A conservative Republican, Reagan was much more suspicious of UNESCO and less willing to compromise on these issues than his predecessor, President Jimmy Carter, had been. Much of the U.S. press at the time spoke up against the idea of a NWICO, claiming that it would lead to a government-sponsored press and that it advocated censorship and the licensing of journalists. Conservative think tanks such as the Heritage Foundation furthered the interpretation that UNESCO and the NWICO were anticapitalist, anti-U.S., Soviet-controlled, and procensorship.[2] The United States withdrew from UNESCO in 1984 citing the mismanagement and politicization of the organization as well as threats to press freedom. The United States only rejoined UNESCO in 2003 after the organization "reformed" itself sufficiently. Since 1984 UNESCO has dropped any mention of the NWICO and has let the MacBride Report go out of print.

We have spent so much time on this discussion of the NWICO because it represented a sustained challenge to both the philosophy of classical liberalism, discussed in the last chapter and the dominance of international communication by Western industrialized countries. We should not overly idealize the NAM, UNESCO in the 1970s, or the NWICO debates, however. There were significant problems with these, especially around the idea of elites and popular representation. That is, many of those actually debating these issues represented governments and urban elites and not necessarily the majority of people in their countries. Also, a number of countries did use this forum to openly attack the United States and the West, while failing to follow through on NWICO principles at home. For example, in the 1970s, India, a proponent of the NWICO, declared martial law and imprisoned journalists. Authoritarian countries did not wish to cede their own sovereignty and apply these principles of human rights to their own situations, but were interested in using these principles to challenge the power of the United States and Western Europe.

The principles of the NWICO have continued to be discussed in NAM-sponsored MacBride Roundtables in Communication and in such organizations as the World Association for Christian Communication. The current discussions around the issues raised by the NWICO tend to come from nongovernmental organizations and from grassroots movements rather than from urban elites. Indeed, they seek the implementation of ideas such as the right to communicate on the local level rather than at the international level. This shift of strategies to what is called "globalization from below" is characteristic of the shift of globalization to its contemporary form, which we will discuss in the second half of the chapter.

One of the early criticisms of cultural imperialism is the book *How to Read Donald Duck* by Ariel Dorfman and Armand Mattelart (1991). This book was written in Chile in 1971 during the presidency of Salvador Allende. Allende, a Marxist, had been elected President in 1970 and, as part of his policies, tried to nationalize much of the industry and mining of Chile (which had been controlled by Western corporations that retained most profits). The United States, clearly not happy with the election of a Marxist in their backyard or with his socialist policies, which undermined U.S. business interests, staged an unofficial boycott of Chile, and the CIA, in 1973, helped support a military coup in which Allende was assassinated and General August Pinoche was installed as a dictator. Some of the few American products that were allowed to enter Chile during Allende's rule were Disney comic books. This was the context in which Dorfman and Mattelart wrote their book.

They argued that the Disney comics, being written and produced in the United States, make a number of ideological assumptions about the values of society: the value of competition; the origins of wealth; the value of work; and so on. These assumptions are simply a part of the world of the comics, where characters never have steady jobs yet lead middle-class lives, where characters go on adventures to exotic lands in search of treasure and are showered with wealth by grateful simple peasants (who seem better off without it), where criminality is innate in certain persons, and where the rich really are much more unhappy than the poor. These comics also included caricatures of Third World peoples, including those from Latin America, and were being sold to those very people as entertainment. Dorfman and Mattelart write,

> These clichés are also used by the mass culture media to dilute the realities common to these people. The only means that the Mexican has of knowing Peru is through caricature, which also implies that Peru is incapable of being anything else, and is unable to rise above this prototypical situation, imprisoned as it is made to seem, within its own exoticism. (p. 54)

Despite the fact that these children's comics are popularly considered pure entertainment and fantasy, far removed from the politics and economics of the real world, Dorfman and Mattelart show how the comics often make fairly specific arguments about current social, environmental, and political affairs. In the end, they argue that Chilean children are influenced by the ideology of the comics to see the world in capitalist terms, to take on their values and ways of seeing the world: "a permanent compulsion to buy objects they don't need" (p. 66); valuing "individual goals at the expense of collective needs" (p. 98); being grateful for foreign invasion; and so on. They assert that this ideology was at odds with the social values and economic situation of Chile at the time. Even when all other influences were missing, the United States was extending its influence through the culture that the children consumed.

There have been significant challenges to the cultural imperialism thesis that are important to note. One challenge is to its model of media effects. For the most part, cultural imperialist scholars tend to assume a fairly direct model of media effects. For example, Dorfman and Mattelart analyze the content of the Disney comics and pay no attention to what meaning is made of the comics by the children (and adults) reading them. They seem to assume that the ideology of the comics is somehow implanted in the children. By not considering the audience as active interpreters who use comics in different ways, critics of cultural imperialism seem to argue that the mere presence of U.S. programming on global television and film screens (and on radios, stereos, and bookshelves) in other parts of the world is sufficient to conclude cultural imperialism (see Tomlinson, 1991). One cannot read the effects of cultural imperialism directly off content or authorship of media texts. While studies of international media did show the dominance of, for example, American programming on televisions and in movie theaters worldwide, little attention was paid to how this programming was interpreted.

A second challenge to the cultural imperialism thesis was that the picture of information and cultural flow looked very different at the regional level, where one saw quite different flows of information and programming (Sinclair, Jacka, & Cunningham, 1996). For example, looking at Spanish-speaking Central and South America, one sees the dominance not of the United States but of Televisa of Mexico. Similarly, Globo in Brazil, programming in Portuguese, produced not only a new and popular form of television (the *telenovela*) but also exported programming to its neighbors in Central and South America and even to

Europe. Scholars point to other regional centers of media production as well: India and Hong Kong for films, for example.

A third challenge was that language and culture could act as limits on foreign cultural imperialism (Sinclair, Jacka, & Cunningham, 1996; Straubhaar, 2000). That is, local audiences would prefer local media content over foreign fare, if the quality was equal (though this applies more for television than film; Silj, 1988). The linguistic and cultural proximity of a program to one's own language and culture is a factor in the popularity and interpretation of foreign media. Koichi Iwabuchi (2005) argues that cultural proximity can be created not only through common languages and common cultural traditions, but also through comparable experiences of modernization, globalization, and cultural imperialism. For example, the countries of East Asia are culturally diverse but they share a common history of imperialism (Japanese and Western) and experienced a common pressure to modernize and globalize. Iwabuchi contends that it is this common experience that allows for recent regional flows of popular culture in East Asia.

Much of the foundational writing on cultural imperialism took place when local television and film production in many parts of the world was still quite primitive; therefore, it was much cheaper to import foreign programs (indeed, U.S. media companies could sell their programs overseas quite cheaply since they had already made a profit at home) and they would be of higher quality than what could be produced locally. This became less the case as local industries matured (see Wang, Ku, & Liu, 2000).[3] In addition, even though a country's television schedule might seem to be dominated by foreign programs, many of these were used to fill in the schedule and aired at less-than-prime-time slots.

Finally, one could consider the reasons for the movement of cultural products. For example, in the late 1990s, Japanese television dramas (known as *J-Dramas*) became quite popular in Hong Kong and China without even being officially exported by Japan (Nakano, 2002). Television production houses in Japan, one of the regional centers for television and music production in Asia, did not even consider exporting their programs because they did not assume that there was going to be a market. Instead, pirated copies on video CDs (VCDs, digital video on a CD that can be played on a computer's CD-drive or on a stand-alone VCD player) circulated widely and were, in fact, the trendy shows to watch. Is this a case of Japanese cultural imperialism if the products are being pulled into rather than pushed on other countries?

The cultural imperialism thesis was quite influential and fueled not only the NWICO debates but also debates within nations about whether to put a limit or quota on foreign cultural imports (or, conversely, arguing for a minimum percentage of local content on television, movie theaters, and so on). The thesis has been modified somewhat by those who argue that it is no longer particular nations that are behind cultural imperialism, but capitalist corporations beholden to no one except profit (see Schiller, 1992) spreading what sociologist Leslie Sklair (1995) has called the *culture-ideology of consumerism* (persuading people to buy more than they need, to focus on private profit, and that happiness and meaning lie in things).

The revision of the cultural imperialism thesis to focus on the work of multinational corporations rather than nation-states is an indication of a change to a new form of globalization. It is our contention that the ways in which communication research has tried to understand global media, especially through the relatively narrow and reductive theory of cultural imperialism, is inadequate to fully understand the complexities of mediamaking today. A more nuanced and perhaps more accurate view of global media must take into account the form of contemporary globalization and from there look in particular at the media's role. It is to delineating the current formation of globalization that we now turn.

## GLOBALIZATION, CULTURE, AND MEDIA

In the years since the Bretton Woods agreement, there have been a significant number of changes in the global economy. Rather than the mass production of the previous era, manufacturing has become flexible in that factories retool themselves quickly in order to produce a variety of items sensitive to niche markets and rapidly changing consumer tastes. A growing deregulatory movement seeks to remove government regulation from industries and trade and to privatize government and national services, empowering the private sector. Multinational corporations have the ability to move across nations or locales, to where regulations are less strict or taxes are lower, which gives them leverage to affect government policies regarding the economy (though corporations are perhaps less footloose in practice than in theory). Production then becomes mobile as well as flexible, with factories moving to the Third World to take advantage of cheaper labor, taxes, or regulation. Production, consumption, and distribution are all intimately coordinated so that one day's sales in one country can alter what and how much is produced in factories the next day on the other side of the world. With production moved overseas, most workers in industrialized nations labor in service fields rather than production. Another significant shift is that in 1973, President Richard Nixon dissolved the stable link between the U.S. dollar and the gold standard established at Bretton Woods allowing for more dynamic, independent, and speculative global financial markets generating profits without having to produce goods or services (Harvey, 1989).

Let us give you a quick example of the economic landscape and its consequences in contemporary globalization. The IMF and the World Bank emphasize a strategy referred to as the *Washington Consensus* in which they recommend that if a country wants to develop, it needs to deregulate to spur foreign investment (which means liberalizing trade, being open to direct foreign investment, privatizing state institutions, reforming tax codes, and emphasizing property rights, among other things; Ellwood, 2001). The countries of Southeast Asia had been traditionally economically conservative, protecting and nurturing local industries. However, in the early 1990s, following the advice of the Washington Consensus, Thailand, Malaysia, Indonesia, and the Philippines opened their countries to direct foreign investment. And investment poured in to the tune of tens of billions of dollars. But this was not long-term infrastructural investment that could aid development, but speculative short-term investment—for example, in stock markets and real estate—looking for quick profits. This speculation inflated prices far above their worth and greatly increased state debt. Foreign investors finally realized that this was a bad situation in 1997 and got out of the Southeast Asian market. Over $100 billion was withdrawn from that region in 1997 alone. The bubble burst, banks defaulted, industries collapsed, Asian currencies plummeted in value, and hundreds of millions of Asians fell into poverty (Ellwood, 2001). The crash also subsequently adversely affected the economies of Russia and Latin America, especially Brazil. Malcolm Waters (2001) points out that the Asian crash of 1997 illustrates four features of contemporary economic globalization:

▋ It is truly global in scope, interconnecting the planet's economies.

▋ It "demonstrates the connection of the global to the local" (p. 89); global financial decisions affect people in many locales.

▋ "It illustrates the impact of fluid movements of credit and capital that compressed time into an intensive flash of a crisis" (p. 89).

▋ It showed that globalization is unfinished.

All this goes to show that the character of economic exchange in the current deregulated environment is substantially different from that of earlier eras of globalization. The global market is even more integrated and unified—to the extent that it emphasizes further deregulation globally—and yet even more uncontrollable (Harvey, 1989). At the same time, current levels of trade are not much higher than those around World War I (Hirst & Thompson, 1996).[4] What makes this era more globalized, however, is not just the disorganized state of capitalism but the increased importance of what Waters calls *symbolic exchanges* over material exchanges (meaning trade and exchanges of labor) and power exchanges (meaning political control, influence, leadership), which dominated earlier eras of globalization. Symbolic exchanges disconnect or abstract ideas and images from local contexts. Waters writes,

> Symbolic exchanges release social arrangements from spatial referents. Symbols can be proliferated rapidly and in any locality. It is much more difficult to monopolize the resources (human ingenuity) required to produce signs than it is to monopolize the resources (capital) involved in producing material objects or those involved in the exercise of power (coercion) and therefore much more difficult to concentrate them in space. Moreover, they are easily transportable and communicable. Importantly, because symbols frequently seek to appeal to human fundamentals they can also claim universal significance. (pp. 19–20)

This makes culture the most important dimension of globalization today. Globalization has created a means for global cultural exchange. Marshall McLuhan (McLuhan & Fiore, 1967) pioneered this idea in the 1960s with the suggestion that media (in particular) were creating a "global village" of mutual understanding: "Ours is a brand-new world of allatonceness. 'Time' has ceased, 'space' has vanished. We now live in a *global* village . . . a simultaneous happening" (p. 63). Since we are now in each others' backyards, McLuhan argued, we are now responsible for one another. Summarizing some of the primary dimensions of this idea of cultural globalization, James Curran and Myung-Jin Park (2000) write that "globalization is opening up new lines of communication between different groups, and constructing new spaces for the building of mutuality, without suggesting that the world is shrinking into a single, harmonious village" (p. 7). They also point out that these networks of cultural exchange provide people with information that local authorities might not have wanted them to have. They also allow cultural groups not only to remain in contact with home cultures (for example, Iranians in Los Angeles watching Iranian TV; Naficy, 1993), but to communicate with other minority groups forming global communities and markets.

What Waters calls *cultural action* has challenged global capitalism through such things as environmental activism, activism for fair trade and labor practices, activism against genetically modified foods, and other movements that often get labeled as antiglobalization movements. At the same time, the cultural action of ethnic and other groups is challenging political structures (even dissolving states into ethnic homelands).

If contemporary globalization concerns global cultural flows, what are the nature of these flows? Is globalization simply a newer form of cultural imperialism? Two recent theories address some of the issues raised by the contemporary form of globalization. One is George Ritzer's (1993) theory of McDonaldization and the second is Benjamin Barber's (1992, 1996) argument that a globalized world is the stage for two competing forces: McWorld and jihad.

Ritzer argues that contemporary cultural globalization is an extension of the process of rationalization identified by Max Weber in the early twentieth century. *Rationalization* is the advancement of the criteria of efficiency as the dominant measure of any social relationship (economic, political, or cultural). Rationalization works as a solvent of sorts, in that potentially any economic, political, or cultural difference gets translated into its terms (Waters, 2001). What is more efficient or rational becomes more important than what is morally or culturally correct. Rationalization is a fundamental component of modernization with its emphasis on mass production. Ritzer identifies four dimensions of rationalization that underlie how the fast food industry operates, with McDonald's serving as an ideal case. *McDonaldization* is, then, "the process by which the principles of the fast food restaurant are coming to dominate more and more sectors of American society as well as the rest of the world" (p. 1). The four principles are: efficiency, calculability, predictability, and control.

The principle of *efficiency* is the idea of finding the optimum means to an end; that is, of getting to a desired state in less time and with less expenditure of energy. Fast food is efficient in that it gets us from being hungry to being full in the least amount of time and with the least amount of effort on the part of the customer (you don't even have to get out of your car) or the employee (machines pour drinks for you). It is more efficient for McDonald's to put the customer to work as well as the employee: Customers fill their own drinks, carry food to the table, and even clean up.

*Calculability* is the principle that reduces all decisions to those involving numbers. The desirability of a fast food meal is measured in terms of amount of food (large, extra-large, super-size, or "biggie") and cost ("super value meals"). One measures efficiency in terms of calculability, and it is much easier to measure success in terms of the amount of profit than unquantifiable notions such as quality or satisfaction.

*Predictability* is the principle by which a set menu is more efficient for both the customer and the restaurant. Customers know exactly what they're getting and can order faster; the restaurant can have meals pre-prepared or ready to be prepared quickly. Also, if all McDonald's restaurants serve the same food, there is predictable demand, and so supply can be better managed.

*Control* is the principle of careful management of all tasks; this usually entails careful training of personnel as well as the assistance of technology, if not the wholesale replacement of unpredictable humans with predictable, controllable machines. Control refers not only to the control of the production and service of the product, but the consumption of it as well. Customers have to be trained to order in a certain way, to line up, and so on. In addition, the movement of customers through the restaurant is carefully controlled; the seats inside are hard and plastic for a reason: So that customers don't linger too long but eat quickly and leave, freeing up the seat for someone else.

Ritzer argues that these principles can be found in other industries as well and in many aspects of life: hotels, clothing stores, motion pictures, oil change shops, sellers of eyeglasses, and so on. For example, education has become McDonaldized by attempts to make education more efficient (machine-readable, multiple-choice tests rather than essay exams), calculable (students are judged based on their grade point average and test scores), predictable (slick mass-produced textbooks and prepackaged course materials ensure that different classes of Mass Communication 101 look a lot alike despite the institution), and controlled (statewide high school exit exams often determine the content of courses throughout the previous years, with little room for individual variation). Ritzer argues that the problem with McDonaldization is that it only provides the illusion of choice and is ultimately dehumanizing, creating a homogeneous world. We find McDonald's, Starbucks, the Gap, and a Marriott hotel everywhere we go. As these companies (and local versions of these companies based on their principles) open up around the world, the ideology of consumerist rationality follows; the world becomes a shopping mall with the same outlets selling the same thing over and over to consumers who expect nothing else. Cultural diversity and any sense of local tradition or culture are lost.

Political scientist Benjamin Barber's (1992, 1996) view of globalization is more complex. He sees two forces at odds with one another in the world today: the forces of what he calls McWorld (which are similar to what Ritzer has called McDonaldization) and jihad. On the one hand, the world is shaped by forces of capitalist rationalization, which are integrating and homogenizing daily life for everyone. Barber points to four factors driving this global uniformity: the expansion of capitalism in its quest for markets, the dependency of countries on other countries for vital resources, the flow of information and communication, and the awareness of the balance and interconnection of the global environment. But Barber notes a force explicitly opposing McWorld: jihad, or the struggle against globalization and interdependence by groups retreating into ethnic and cultural enclaves. It is important to clarify Barber's use of the term *jihad*. He is not using the term literally to refer to Muslim struggle or holy war, but as a general metaphor for struggle against those who impose on one's group, territory, or beliefs. The forces of jihad that Barber identifies include a number of ethnicities and faiths. As Barber (1992) puts it in his original article (subsequently expanded into a book), "The planet is falling precipitantly apart and coming reluctantly together at the very same moment" (p. 53). A central theme of

Barber's argument is this: Jihad and McWorld "have one thing in common: neither offers much hope to citizens looking for practical ways to govern themselves democratically" (p. 53). Whereas McWorld presents the illusion of democracy in a consumer's choice of product, jihad often offers no choice at all. "Neither McWorld nor Jihad is remotely democratic in impulse. Neither needs democracy; neither promotes democracy" (p. 63).

Let us say a couple of things in response to Ritzer and Barber before we return to our discussion of global media proper. First, Waters (2001) points out that jihad and McWorld are not "contradictions but aspects of a single globalization-localization process in which local sensibilities are aroused and exacerbated in fundamentalist forms by such modernizing flows as McDonaldization" (p. 230). Second, many companies don't simply present the same product everywhere, but tailor their offerings to local tastes and cultures. McDonald's has vegetarian offerings in some places, mutton in others; Revlon presents its products in different color ranges depending on local skin tones; and so on (Zwingle, 1999). Third, it could be argued that the forces of McDonaldization and globalization could diversify the commodities and choices available. As anthropologist Richard Wilk (1995) asks, *Why must we assume that the importation of foreign goods necessarily replaces local goods; could they not simply be available in addition to local options?* Could they be an expansion of local culture rather than a substitution for it? It is also argued that, in a McDonaldized world, the lack of choice drives middle-class consumers to seek out both the authentic and the diverse or exotic, and can actually promote a revival of local customs, cultures, and tastes.

Stuart Hall (1991) points out that globalization homogenizes the world in an interesting way, through difference. On the one hand, he writes that global mass culture is a form of American culture; on the other hand, that global culture becomes local as well. An example he uses is that the language of globalization is English, but the English around the world is made into local hybrids (Singlish in Singapore, Taglish in the Philippines, Hinglish in India, and so on). Globalization recognizes and absorbs cultural differences within a global framework of capitalism. Wilk (1995) refers to this as a *structure of common difference.* Global capitalism creates a framework for exchange in which places are encouraged to be different but only in specific ways. One is encouraged to have different food, dress, crafts, and music (because these sell on the global market), but discouraged from having different beliefs or politics that challenge the global structure (especially global trade).

However, one of the consequences of this situation is that it allows for the creation of new identities, ones marked by hybridity and difference (one is Jamaican and English, Iranian and American). But this situation also allows marginalized groups the opportunity to speak, using the global capitalist network to connect with others and to represent their own situation. Hall writes, "The most profound cultural revolution has come about as a consequence of the margins coming into representation—in art, in painting, in film, in music, in literature, in the modern arts everywhere, in politics, and in social life generally" (p. 34). For Hall, globalization involves the transformation of every local culture into a hybrid that already includes elements from many different cultures. Globalization does not pit a dominant global culture against a local traditional culture. Rather, for Hall, the commonality of globalization is that every culture is a hybrid—though each culture is hybrid in a different way, as the result of different power struggles and historical circumstances. Every culture remains different insofar as it is a variant of a common global culture. Globalization is a force of hybridization; our commonality is that we are different. This new global postmodern culture does not speak a single language or ideology. Thus, for Hall, both international capitalism and fundamentalism are forces working against globalization and toward domination.

The truth of this theory is apparent to anyone who travels. Entering any big city around the world at first offers a common visual experience: skyscrapers, Coca-Cola signs, Benetton shops, McDonald's restaurants, and CNN on cable. Many of the pieces that make up the kaleidoscope that is a city are universal. But each city is configured differently, and each city offers itself as a unique experience. Different languages, ethnicities, and religions will dominate any given city, but virtually every major city will have other minority languages, ethnicities, and religions reflected and refracted through their food, their videos, and their music.

## GLOBAL MEDIA

Most of the theories of international media discussed in the first part of this chapter, not to mention much of the body of research in international communications, assume that global forces are still mediated through and by the nation-state; that is, they focus on media in terms of political and economic power. The nation-state remains the main actor on the global stage and culture is subordinated to economics and politics. For example, most textbooks on international media survey mass communication systems on a country-by-country basis (see Gross, 1995; Head, 1985) or by the political systems dominating the regulation of the media (Curran & Park, 2000). Issues usually addressed in debates over international media include such things as transborder broadcasting (from state to state across national borders) and local media regulations (from the banning of satellite dishes to prevent reception of foreign content to limiting nonlocal content on the airwaves). And even the NWICO was a transnational negotiation by representatives of nation-states.

To more fully understand the global media today, however, we must take into account the complex terrain of cultural globalization. To address the landscape of global media, we wish to set out one further model of globalization. Anthropologist Arjun Appadurai (1996), in an attempt to model the complexity of globalization, proposed what has become a quite generative heuristic (or means of gaining knowledge): the notion of the global as a set of interlinked yet contradictory landscapes. He proposed five such landscapes: ethnoscapes, mediascapes, technoscapes, finanscapes, and ideoscapes. Each landscape has its own particular features, but importantly these landscapes are in constant motion. Appadurai argues that these separate landscapes do not work together, but can be at odds. It is because of the disjunctures between these landscapes that Appadurai dismisses concerns about globalization as a homogenizing process. We will briefly describe each scape and then address mediascape more fully.

*Ethnoscape*, according to Appadurai, is "the landscape of persons who constitute the shifting world in which we live: tourists, immigrants, refugees, exiles, guest workers, and other moving groups and individuals constitute an essential feature of the world" (p. 33). *Technoscape* is "the global configuration, also ever fluid, of technology and the fact that technology, both high and low, both mechanical and informational, now moves at high speeds across various kinds of previously impervious boundaries" (p. 34). *Finanscape* refers to the landscape of investment, speculation, and the transfer of currency. It is the flow of finances through global stock markets and direct investment. *Ideoscape* refers to the landscape of more expressly political or ideological ideas, images, and concepts. For example, it would map the movement of the idea of democracy (or rights or terrorism) as it moved from country to country, being taken up and reinterpreted in different ways as it moves. Finally, *mediascape* refers "both to the distribution of the electronic capabilities to produce and disseminate information (newspapers, magazines, television stations, and film-production studios), which are now available to a growing number of private and public interests throughout the world, and to the images of the world created by those media" (p. 35).

It is obviously mediascape with which we are most concerned here in this book, but the concerns of mediascape are inseparable from those of the other scapes as well. At first scan, the contemporary mediascape is marked by familiar brands (CNN, MTV), corporations (Sony, News Corporation, TimeWarner), and content (*Spiderman 2*). But such a vision of global media as uniform and primarily Western (if not American) does not hold up to scrutiny. For example, it does not explain the recent trend in Hollywood films of remaking relatively obscure Japanese horror films (*The Ring, The Grudge,* and so on) or the fact that within just a few minutes one can find shops selling recent DVDs, videotapes, and CDs from Korea, China, India, the Philippines, Mexico, and other places. It also does not explain the case of *bhangra*, the music of Punjabi harvest festivals. It was brought from India to Britain by Punjabi immigrants and performed on special occasions, but it soon became a more generalized dance music for Indian expatriates in the United Kingdom. The *bhangra* style merged with other dance and musical styles, including Reggae and Rap, and became a prominent form of British popular music in the 1990s. It was then exported back to India where it influenced the form of popular music there. It was also exported to the United States, where second-generation immigrant Indian youth took it up as a form of return to their roots (Maira, 2002).

There are a shrinking number of global corporations that dominate the global mediascape and they originate in a handful of places: the United States, Europe, Japan, and Australia. But, by and large, they do not advance nationalist agendas: Sony didn't start making Japanese films when it purchased Columbia pictures; the French firm Vivendi doesn't produce only French music (it owns the Universal Music Group, which has a 24% share of the world market in recorded music); the German corporation Bertelsmann is the world's largest publisher of

English language books; Rupert Murdoch's News Corporation, originally based in Australia, publishes racy tabloids in England, broadcasts sensationalist reality programs in the United States (on the Fox Network), and owns the largest publisher of Bibles in the United States (Bagdikian, 2004). Rather than a nationalist agenda, what they do advance is a *capitalist-consumerist agenda;* they are interested in promoting consumption to increase their profit (for example, convincing people that identity is based on the things you own so that people buy more), and they do have tremendous influence on determining what gets played on the radio or shown on film screens around the world. But it would be a mistake to assume that their influence is universal and without contradictions. That is, it would be a mistake to see the mediascape as a smooth, unbroken landscape of homogenized culture.

Let's take two examples of global media channels most often accused of promoting McWorld: CNN and MTV. CNN changed television news: Its 24-hour format created pressure for instant news and constant updates from around the globe. It is also one of the few news organizations that still retain a number of foreign bureaus and correspondents able to gather news quickly, and it is one of the few news channels to broadcast globally. Critics worry that live, 24/7 reporting from around the world (especially behind the front lines in wars) adversely affects any government's foreign policy or diplomacy initiatives (this has been dubbed the *CNN effect*). Governments must now react quickly to events reported, without the careful consideration and deliberation characteristic of the diplomatic process. Governments must also respond quickly to the public's reaction to vivid images of war, disaster, scandal, and so on. Often, CNN can provide reports of events faster than the government's own sources. Thus world leaders watch CNN, especially in times of crisis. What does and does not get reported on CNN can shape foreign policy, it is argued—an extension of the theory of agenda setting.

However, this is quite different from saying that CNN is a global news channel. It is a channel available globally to select audiences. World leaders may watch it, and it is certainly available in most high priced hotels catering to tourists and business leaders and on many satellite systems and cable TV systems (almost ubiquitously in the United States). Though CNN might reach over 150 countries, it reaches very few people in those countries (Wang & Servaes, 2000). Let's provide a quick example. It is widely reported as a mark of

CNN's influence that, during the Persian Gulf War of 1991, leaders on both sides of the conflict were watching the progress of the war on CNN. However, few others in Iraq were watching CNN. Indeed, many in Iraq were without electricity after the bombing began and pulled out battery-operated shortwave radios, following the progress of war on local radio or the BBC and other world radio services.

A second example is MTV, the music television network. Broadcasting globally to 139 countries, MTV is often cited as an example of cultural homogenization and American cultural imperialism, shaping the musical tastes of youth worldwide and promoting consumerism (McPhail, 2002). However, MTV does not broadcast the same programming everywhere, having almost 30 separate channels (not including VH1 and its spinoffs) targeted regionally, including MTV Asia, MTV Southeast Asia, MTV China, MTV Philippines, MTV Brazil, and so on. Also, over 90% of MTV's programming is locally produced in those regions (McPhail, 2002) and it is MTV's policy that over 70% of its content be local as well (S. Jones, 2005). But the localization of the sound and look of MTV has its limits. A quick trip to MTV Asia's Web site reveals coverage of a lot of Western artists, including Jennifer Lopez as Artist of the Month for March 2005, and none of the top 20 artists on MTV Asia's top hit list are Asian. This holds less true for other more specifically targeted channels such as MTV China or MTV India, though a significant presence of Western artists can be seen.

Let's look at MTV India. The cultural imperialist perspective would argue that MTV India and its main competitor, Channel V, globalize Indian youth, shape their tastes so that they consume more Western products, and shape their self-concept to become more American and less Indian. But studies of Indian audiences for music television in India reveal more complexities (to the cultural imperialism viewpoint, these would be contradictions):

▋ Music television in India is strongly localized. An early version of MTV with primarily Western programming did not succeed. Current music video channels in India have an Indian look, use Indian on-air personalities (or those of Indian descent), play Indian music, and engage Indian popular culture (Cullity, 2002; Juluri, 2003). However, MTV India is owned by Viacom and its primary competitor, Channel V, is owned by News Corporation (another competitor, Music Asia, is owned by the Indian media company Zee TV and markets itself as a real Indian music channel). Music video channels are still dependent on the form of the music video itself: Local music must be slickly produced with vibrant visuals (effectively marginalizing from the popular music scene those acts which cannot afford to produce videos). Given the fact that Indian popular music is dominated by songs from Indian musical films, this form is less a stretch than in other countries. Program formats also remain similar to MTV in the United States, and so is its focus on youth culture and consumerism (Cullity, 2002).

▐ Indian youth culture was constructed by MTV as family friendly and cross-generational rather than as a form of generational rebellion, as youth culture is marketed elsewhere (Juluri, 2003). At the same time, youth culture sees itself as part of a modern India (watching MTV) rather than strictly traditional. We should point out that the youth targeted by the music video channels are a small, privileged percentage of all the youth in India.

▐ Rather than promoting a global popular culture, music videos have been involved in highly nationalistic campaigns to reaffirm an Indian cultural identity. Ironically, such campaigns tend to use blatantly orientalist images of India, including snake charmers and elephants, which fit with Western stereotypes of the country and its people. By borrowing such stereotypes in fashioning its own national self-image, it could be said that Indian music videos have globalized after all (Juluri, 2003). This example also shows that the processes of McWorld and Jihad are not always opposed.

What this example of MTV in India does is raise the question of what counts as cultural influence. Let us clarify through another example. Rap as a musical style and hip-hop as a cultural form have become a prominent fixture in global popular culture. Rap groups have formed in Japan, Korea, Brazil, Colombia, and across Europe and elsewhere. But though this phenomenon can simply be explained as popular artists using the latest Western cultural fashion to get a hit, it is also more than that. Tony Mitchell (2001), in his survey of hip-hop worldwide notes that hip-hop scenes "all tend to seek out local roots" (p. 32). Hip-hop has become a means of "reconstructing the 'roots' of local histories, as in the use of local dialects in Italy and the Basque Country and indigenous rhetorical and linguistic practices in Aotearoa-New Zealand" (p. 32). Not only does the localization of hip-hop make the music's message more credible to the listeners (Straw, 2000, cited in Mitchell, 2001), but hip-hop become a means of cultural and political expression for non-Western nations, ethnic minorities, and immigrant groups (Turkish rappers in Germany, for example). Hip-hop becomes the means of describing and commenting on daily experience for marginalized groups not just in the United States but worldwide. This is an example of what Stuart Hall (1991) meant when he said that, through recent forms of globalization, the margins come into representation. The form of hip-hop and the circulation of rap music both unofficially through informal channels of music distribution and exchange and officially through the circulation of commercially produced recordings becomes a means of cross-cultural communication and collaboration. As music scholar George Lipsitz (1994) writes,

> In an era when every continent seems convulsed by ethnic, religious, and racial violence, examples of cross-national and multi-racial music offer hope for a better future. . . . But while very much a product of the ever expanding reach and scope of capital, these cultural creations also testify to the ways in which artists from aggrieved communities can use the very instruments of their displacement and dispossession to forge a new public sphere with emancipatory potential. (p. 14)

Hopefully, it is clear by now that, to account for global media, one must carefully consider the particularities of the landscapes and movements of people, technologies, finances, and ideologies. For example, the ethnoscape affects media in a number of ways. Most prominent is the fact that people tend to bring their media texts, cultural forms, and media themselves with them when they move. This can influence the culture of the country to which they move. For example, black slaves brought with them from Africa their own music, which profoundly influenced the popular music of the Americas. Also, European brass military bands, part of a colonial occupying force in the eighteenth and nineteenth centuries, brought new instruments, rhythms, and sounds into African popular music (Stapleton & May, 1990). These, in turn, produced some of the music styles assumed characteristic of African popular music.

The diaspora of various ethnic populations creates global markets for cultural products from the originary culture. Indian film and popular music circulates through populations of Indian guest workers in the

Middle East and North America and immigrants of Indian descent throughout the old British Empire and other countries. Each of these populations will have a different set of attitudes toward, uses for, and relations with Indian popular culture. Indian immigrants in the United States and their children, for example, often view Indian popular culture through the framework of nostalgia for some and as performances of authenticity for others (Maira, 2002). Media products themselves change as diasporic audiences become more important. A locally produced television program might play well for a Chinese audience in Hong Kong, but what of Beijing, Taiwan, Singapore, Los Angeles, or other places with significant diasporic Chinese populations? Joseph Man Chan (1996) writes that "Chinese people all over the world constitute a potential market for television programmes that are made in any of the constituent nations of Greater China [China, Hong Kong, and Taiwan]" (p. 137), but at the same time there are significant cultural, linguistic, and political differences between Chinese populations that must be overcome. Locally produced cultural texts begin to reflect the tastes and desires of these other audiences as well. Hybrid cultural forms, like the example of *bhangra* music discussed earlier, are developed that combine elements of local place with diverse cultural traditions.

In another example, karaoke as a cultural practice—singing along in public to a prerecorded backing track while the lyrics display on a screen—spread from Japan throughout Asia, Europe, North America, and elsewhere following the movements of Japanese businessmen (see Mitsui & Hosokawa, 1998). The earliest karaoke spaces outside of Japan were often set up in bars and restaurants catering to that expatriate clientele. Karaoke then caught on (or didn't catch on) with local populations based on a number of factors, including the presence of a local culture of people singing in public as a form of entertainment and socialization, the structure of the local recording industry in that country, that country's historical relationship with Japan, and so on (Ōtake & Hosokawa, 1998). In many places, karaoke is no longer even seen as a Japanese practice or technology at all, but a local one.

Karaoke is also an example of a technoscape, the movement of technologies. As Ōtake and Hosokawa (1998) note, "None of the basic parts of the karaoke apparatus—microphone, magnetic tape, video, laser disc, PA system—is a Japanese invention: what Japan created is a new combination and style of use in a certain spatial setting" (p. 196). Once the karaoke apparatus was created from these disparate parts and practices, it was then exported from Japan to other countries. But the technoscape of karaoke also involves local versions of these technologies. For example, Korea forbade the importation of Japanese technology and so created its own technology for singing in public to a prerecorded track (and the practice was referred to by the Korean term *norae bang* and only rarely as *karaoke*).

Technoscape also includes consideration of the global communication infrastructure. This infrastructure includes the systems of communication satellites 26,000 miles above the Earth that can rapidly beam sounds and images from one side of the globe to the other. It also includes networks of terrestrial communications such as cables crossing continents and oceans, microwave relay stations, and so on. Internet communication rides on both satellite and cable. Satellite broadcasting raises the issue of a satellite's "footprint," the geographic area to which it can beam a signal. Since satellite signals do not stop at national borders, signal spillover is one way in which media texts cross cultures. Many countries ban or heavily regulate the ownership of satellite dishes for just this reason. Traditional broadcast signals can also spill across borders. For example, most of the population of Canada can receive television signals from U.S. stations, and citizens in Guangzhou, China, can receive programming from Hong Kong.

Technoscape is also the varied landscape of technologies and technical broadcasting standards—such as NTSC (National Television Standards Committee), PAL (phase alternation line, a European TV standard), SECAM (sequential color and movement, the French TV standard), and HDTV (high-definition TV). For example, across much of Asia, the VCD has been the preferred digital video technology over the DVD. DVDs are more expensive, more high tech, and more tightly controlled by regional encoding and antipiracy measures. The VCD is much cheaper, easier to copy, and less regulated (thus more anarchic) in many ways. VCDs also tend to be considered as a more Asian technology than the more Western-seeming DVD (Hu, 2005). And technoscape also includes unofficial and ad hoc media systems such as pirated cable television systems in India, pirated VCDs in Hong Kong, the global Internet newsgathering of Indymedia, the distribution of video cameras by Project Witness to aggrieved populations to document human rights violations, and so on.

The Internet is the latest factor in global media. International in scope, media content online crosses borders regularly, evading local regulations and standards. The early critiques of the Internet note that it was dominated by U.S. and European users and that the default language of the Internet was English (indeed, the basic character set of the Internet was ASCII, the American Standard for Information Interchange). As more countries go online, this is less the case (though English remains prominent; Chen, Boase, & Wellman, 2002). In terms of sheer numbers, the United States no longer dominates Internet use. Indeed, the U.S. and European markets are reaching saturation, as over 60% to 70% of their populations are online. China has the second highest number of Internet users (behind the United States), but this number represents only a very small percentage of the total Chinese population. For example, about 63% of the U.S. population of 294 million is online (186 million Internet users), but only 6% of China's 1.3 billion people are online (for 80 million Internet users). A similar case can be made for India: only 1.5% of their 1.1 billion people are online, for a total of 16 million users (www.internetworldstats.com).

By numbers alone, the future Internet may be predominantly Chinese. However, linguistic and cultural proximity applies to the Internet as well as broadcast media. Though technically the whole world is open to be surfed, most may prefer Web pages in their own languages that address issues specific to their nation and culture. For example, "to the majority of people in China, Korea, Taiwan, Hong Kong and Japan, the Internet is more domestic and regional than global. The Internet offers these large non–English speaking countries enough space and attractions for them to hook up even though their personal use of the Internet is much less global in nature" (Hao & Chow, 2004). The issue, then, is what is to become of the large numbers of countries and nonurban areas that do not have the infrastructure and population to support their own local networks. Though the growth of Internet use globally is staggering at times (between 2000 and 2004, the number of users in the Middle East grew by 174%, in Latin America the rate was almost 140%, and in Africa 123%), these numbers represent relatively small percentages of the global population. Only 11% of the world's population is online so far.

Among the population that is online (primarily in urban centers), many use the technology to maintain kinship ties with far-off relatives (Chen, Boase, & Wellman, 2002). The speed of e-mail and the range of the World Wide Web seems to put the world at our fingertips, allowing diasporic populations the ability to maintain close personal and cultural ties with home cultures. Internet access changes the experience of immigration. For example, Madhavi Mallapragada (2000) argues "that the Internet, especially the Web, is being utilized by the Indian diaspora (and arguably, by a host of other 'marginal' cultures) to meet important social and cultural needs" (p. 179; see also Mitra, 1997). These populations use the Web to construct and maintain notions of cultural identity: for example, negotiating the transition from Indian to the hybrid Indian-American. Mallapragada concludes, "The Web offers the immigrant populace a space where, unlike in a more traditional medium, such as mainstream television, the immigrant can feel at home" (p. 185).

## CONCLUSION

As we stated at the beginning of this book, the idea of mediamaking is that media are both made within a complex context that is at the same time institutional, economic, social, cultural, historical, and global, and the media help make that context as well. Many people will have been surprised in reading this book at the extent to which we have written about things other than media, things that on the surface would seem to have little to do with the media. Yet that is just the point. If we are to understand society and our lives, we have to look at how media make our lives. If we are to understand the media, we have to understand how the context of our lives makes the media.

It is a mistake to think that global media only exist elsewhere, that it is the study of others' media or others' consumption of "our" media. As Hall (1991) argued, all cultures are hybrid. All media participate in and respond to the global as well as the local. This is not to say that there are not severe imbalances in power, control, or access to information and representation. Barber (1992, 1996) is correct that the dominant processes of globalization are not democratic. But, at the same time, we need to recognize the creativity and ingenuity of people to find means of communication and representation both inside and outside of the institutions of global media. Mediamaking in a global context is the most ordinary and extraordinary aspect of everyday life.

The questions surrounding the media are, paradoxically, too important to be left to the media themselves. These are questions that are central to our lives and our future, and we need to find ways to integrate our understanding of mediamaking into everyday life. The challenge for all of us is to take the growing importance of the media and the knowledge we have of how they work and turn them into a force that we can use to realize a world of our own making.

## NOTES

1. The following discussion draws on Frederick (1993).

2. On the relation of the U.S. Press and UNESCO, see Preston, Herman, and Schiller (1989).

3. The maturation of local media industries has not led to a decrease in U.S. exports at all. In fact, cable and satellite systems with dozens of channels have a voracious appetite for programs. U.S. exports were 40% of the total TV exports globally in 1974, and are 75% of the total TV exports in 1995 (Wang, Ku, & Liu, 2000).

4. Global trade in the nineteenth century was high as the result of colonization: Raw materials and manufactured goods were being exchanged between Europe and the colonies. "Such was the extent of globalization a century ago that capital transfers from North to South were actually greater at the end of the 1890s than at the end of the 1990s" (Ellwood, 2001, p. 14).

## SUGGESTED READINGS

Curran, J., & Park, M.-J. (Eds.). (2000). *De-westernizing media studies*. New York: Routledge.

Dorfman, A., & Mattelart, A. (1991). *How to read Donald Duck: Imperialist ideology in the Disney comic* (D. Kunzle, Trans.). New York: International General.

Erni, J. N., & Chua, S. K. (Eds.). (2005). *Asian media studies*. Malden, MA: Blackwell.

Parks, L., & Kumar, S. (Eds.). (2003). *Planet TV: A global television reader*. New York: New York University Press.

Sinclair, J., Jacka, E., & Cunningham, S. (Eds.). (1996). *New patterns in global television: Peripheral vision*. New York: Oxford University Press.

Wang, G., Servaes, J., & Goonasekera, A. (Eds.). (2000). *The new communications landscape: Demystifying media globalization*. New York: Routledge.

Waters, M. (2001). *Globalization* (2nd ed.). New York: Routledge.

# References

AdAge.com. (n.d.). *Coen's spending totals for 2002*. Retrieved June 5, 2005, from www.adage.com/page.cms?pageId=1010.

Ajzen, I., & Fishbein, M. (1980). *Understanding attitudes and predicting social behavior*. Englewood Cliffs, NJ: Prentice Hall.

Allen, R. (1992a). Audience-oriented criticism and television. In R. Allen (Ed.), *Channels of discourse, reassembled: Television and contemporary criticism* (2nd ed., pp. 101–137). Chapel Hill: University of North Carolina Press.

Allen, R. (Ed.). (1992b). *Channels of discourse, reassembled: Television and contemporary criticism* (2nd ed.). Chapel Hill: University of North Carolina Press.

Alter, J. (1984, October 22). The media in the dock. *Newsweek*, pp. 66–68, 70, 72.

Althusser, L. (1970). *For Marx* (B. Brewster, Trans.). New York: Vintage.

American Society of Newspaper Editors. (2005). Newsroom employment census. Retrieved May 3, 2005, from www.asne.org/index.cfm?id=1138.

Anderson, C. A., Berkowitz, L., Donnerstein, E., Huesmann, L. R., Johnson, J., Linz, D., Malamuth, N. M., & Wartella, E. (2003). The influence of media violence on youth. *Psychological Science in the Public Interest, 4*(3), 81–110.

Ang, I. (1985). *Watching* Dallas: *Soap opera and the melodramatic imagination* (D. Couling, Trans.). New York: Methuen.

Appadurai, A. (1996). *Modernity at large: Cultural dimensions of globalization*. Minneapolis: University of Minnesota Press.

Arlen, M. J. (1969). *Living-room war*. New York: Viking.

Arnold, M. (1960). *Culture and anarchy.* Cambridge, UK: Cambridge University Press. (Original work published 1869.)

Atkin, C. K. (1981). Mass communication and political socialization. In D. D. Nimmo & K. R. Sanders (Eds.), *Handbook of political communication* (pp. 288–328). Beverly Hills, CA: Sage.

Baby boomers go Hollywood. (2003, February 19). CBSNews.com. Retrieved July 7, 2004, from www.cbsnews.com/stories/2003/02/19/entertainment/printable541222.shtml.

Bagdikian, B. H. (1997). *The media monopoly* (5th ed.). Boston: Beacon.

Bagdikian, B. H. (2000). *The media monopoly* (6th ed.). Boston: Beacon.

Bagdikian, B. H. (2004). *The new media monopoly.* Boston: Beacon.

Baker, R. K., & Ball, S. J. (1969). *Violence and the media: A report to the National Commission on the Causes and Prevention of Violence.* Washington, DC: U.S. Government Printing Office.

Ball, S., & Bogatz, G. A. (1970). *The first year of* Sesame Street: *An evaluation.* Princeton, NJ: Educational Testing Service.

Bandura, A. (1965). Influence of models' reinforcement contingencies on the acquisition of imitative responses. *Journal of Personality & Social Psychology, 63*(3), 590–591.

Bandura, A. (1977). *Social learning theory.* Englewood Cliffs, NJ: Prentice Hall.

Barber, B. (1992, March). Jihad v. McWorld. *The Atlantic Monthly, 269,* 53–65.

Barber, B. (1996). *Jihad v. McWorld: How globalism and tribalism are reshaping the world.* New York: Ballantine.

Barnhurst, K., & Wartella, E. (1992). Newspapers and citizenship: Young adults' subjective experience of newspapers. *Critical Studies in Mass Communication, 8,* 195–209.

Barthes, R. (1974). *S/Z: An essay* (R. Miller, Trans.). New York: Hill & Wang. (Original work published 1970.)

Baudrillard, J. (1983a). *In the shadow of the silent majorities.* New York: Semiotexte.

Baudrillard, J. (1983b). *Simulations* (P. Foss, P. Patton, & P. Beitchman, Trans.). New York: Semiotexte.

Baudrillard, J. (1988). *The ecstasy of communication* (B. Schutze & C. Schutze, Trans.). New York: Semiotexte.

Baym, N. (2000). *Tune in, log on: Soaps, fandom and online community.* Thousand Oaks, CA: Sage.

Benjamin, W. (1969). *Illuminations.* New York: Harcourt Brace.

Berelson, B., Lazarsfeld, P., & McPhee, W. (1954). *Voting.* Chicago: University of Chicago Press.

Berger, J. (1972). *Ways of seeing.* London: Penguin.

Berkowitz, L. (1984). Some effects of thoughts on anti- and prosocial influence of media events: A cognitive neoassociationistic analysis. *Psychological Bulletin, 95*(3), 410–427.

Berman, M. (1982). *All that is solid melts into air*. New York: Simon & Schuster.

Blondheim, M., & Liebes, T. (2002). Live television's disaster marathon of September 11th and its subversive potential. *Prometheus, 20*(3), 271–276.

Blumer, H. (1932). *Movies and conduct*. New York: Macmillan.

Bogart, L. (1989). *Press and public* (2nd ed.). Hillsdale, NJ: Lawrence Erlbaum.

Bogatz, G. A., & Ball, S. (1972). *The second year of* Sesame Street: *A continuing evaluation*. Princeton, NJ: Educational Testing Service.

Bohannon, L. (1967). Miching Malecho: That means witchcraft. In J. Middleton (Ed.), *Magic, witchcraft, and curing* (pp. 43–54). Garden City, NY: The Natural History Press.

Bok, S. (1978). *Lying: Moral choices in public and private behavior*. New York: Pantheon.

Bourdieu, P. (1984). *Distinction: A social critique of the judgment of taste* (R. Nice, Trans.). Cambridge, MA: Harvard University Press.

Braudel, F. (1972). *The Mediterranean world in the age of Philip II* (Vol. 1; S. Reynolds, Trans.). New York: Harper & Row.

Brigham, J. C., & Giesbrecht, L. W. (1976). *All in the Family:* Racial attitudes. *Journal of Communication, 26*(4), 69–74.

Brown, J. D., Bybee, C. R., Wearden, S. T., & Straughan, D. M. (1987). Invisible power: News sources and the limits of diversity. *Journalism Quarterly, 64*(1), 45–54.

Brundt, R. (1992). Engaging with the popular: Audiences for mass culture and what to say about them. In L. Grossberg, C. Nelson, & P. Treichler (Eds.), *Cultural studies* (pp. 69–76). New York: Routledge.

Brunner, B. (Ed.). (2003). *Time almanac 2004: With information please*. Needham, MA: Pearson Education.

Buckingham, D. (1993). *Children talking television: The making of television literacy*. London: Falmer.

Buckingham, D. (1996). *Moving images: Understanding children's emotional response to television*. New York: Manchester University Press.

Buckingham, D. (2001). Electronic child abuse? Rethinking the media's effects on children. In M. Barker & J. Petley (Eds.), *Ill effects: The media/violence debate* (2nd ed. pp. 63–77). New York: Routledge.

Budget for One-Hour TV pilot. (2003). *Plunkett's entertainment & media industry almanac*. Houston, TX: Plunkett Research.

Bureau of Labor Statistics. (2003). Occupational employment and wages, May 2003. Washington, DC: Bureau of Labor Statistics, U.S. Department of Labor. Retrieved May 3, 2005, from www.bls.gov/news.release/archives/ocwage_04302004.pdf.

Bureau of Labor Statistics. (2004). Consumer expenditures in 2002 [Report 974]. Washington, DC: Bureau of Labor Statistics, U.S. Department of Labor. Retrieved May 5, 2005, from www.bls.gov/cex/csxann02.pdf.

Bushman, B., & Anderson, C. (2001). Media violence and the American public. *American Psychologist, 56*(6/7), 477–489.

Calhoun, C. (Ed.). (1992). *Habermas and the public sphere.* Cambridge, MA: MIT Press.

Cantril, H. (with Gaudet, H., & Herzog, H.). (1966). *The invasion from Mars: A study in the psychology of panic.* New York: Harper & Row. (Original work published 1940.)

Carey, J. (2002). Media use during a crisis. *Prometheus, 20*(3), 201–207.

Carey, J. W. (1969). The communications revolution and the professional communicator. In P. Halmos (Ed.), *The sociology of mass-media communicators* (pp. 23–38). Keele, UK: University of Keele.

Carey, J. W. (1989). *Communication as culture: Essays on media and society.* Boston: Unwin Hyman.

Cassidy, M. (2001). Cyberspace meets domestic space: Personal computers, women's work, and the gendered territories of the family home. *Critical Studies in Media Communication, 18*(1), 44–65.

Castells, M. (1997). *The information age: Economy, society, and culture. Volume II: The power of identity.* Malden, MA: Blackwell.

Chaffee, S. H., & Choe, S. Y. (1980). Time of decision and media use during the Ford-Carter campaign. *Public Opinion Quarterly, 44,* 53–69.

Chan, J. M. (1996). Television in greater China: Structure, exports, and market formation. In J. Sinclair, E. Jacka, & S. Cunningham (Eds)., *New patterns in global television: Peripheral vision* (pp. 126–160). New York: Oxford University Press.

Charity, A. (1995). *Doing public journalism.* New York: Guilford.

Charters, W. W. (1933). *Motion pictures and youth.* New York: Macmillan.

Chen, W., Boase, J., & Wellman, B. (2002). The global villagers: Comparing Internet users and uses around the world. In B. Wellman & C. Haythornthwaite (Eds.), *The Internet in everyday life* (pp. 74–113). Malden, MA: Blackwell.

Cinema concessions, an essential luxury: Evaluating popcorn for the big screen. (2002, July). *Screen Digest, 213.* Retrieved May 9, 2005 from TableBase.

Clark, D. G., & Blankenburg, W. B. (1973). *You & media.* San Francisco: Canfield.

Cohen, B. C. (1963). *The press and foreign policy.* Princeton, NJ: Princeton University Press.

Commission on the Freedom of the Press. (1947). *A free and responsible press: A general report on mass communication.* Chicago: University of Chicago Press.

Comstock, G., & Paik, H. (1991). *Television and the American child.* New York: Academic Press.

Converse, P. (1962). Information flow and the stability of partisan attitudes. *Public Opinion Quarterly, 26,* 578–600.

Cooper, M., & Soley, L. (1990, February–March). All the right sources. *Mother Jones, 15,* 20–27, 45–48.

Cornell, D. (2000). Introduction. In D. Cornell (Ed.), *Feminism and pornography* (pp. 1–15). New York: Oxford University Press.

Cornfield, M. (1988). The Watergate audience: Parsing the powers of the press. In J. W. Carey (Ed.), *Media, myths, and narratives* (pp. 180–204). Thousand Oaks, CA: Sage.

Cullity, J. (2002). The global *Desi*: Cultural nationalism on MTV India. *Journal of Communication Inquiry, 26*(4), 408–425.

Curran, J., & Park, M.-J. (2000). Beyond globalization theory. In J. Curran & M.-J. Park (Eds.), *De-westernizing media studies* (pp. 3–18). New York: Routledge.

Dahlgren, P. (1995). *Television and the public sphere.* Thousand Oaks, CA: Sage.

Darnton, R. (1995a). *The corpus of clandestine literature in France, 1769–1789.* New York: Norton.

Darnton, R. (1995b). *The forbidden best-sellers of pre-revolutionary France.* New York: Norton.

Dávila, A. (2001). *Latinos, Inc: The marketing and making of a people.* Berkeley: University of California Press.

Dávila, A. (2002). Talking back: Spanish media and U.S. Latinidad. In M. Habell-Pallán & M. Romero (Eds.), *Latino/a popular culture* (pp. 25–37). New York: New York University Press.

Davison, W. P. (1983). The third-person effect in communication. *Public Opinion Quarterly, 47*, 1–15.

DeFleur, M. L., & Ball-Rokeach, W. (1975). *Theories of mass communication.* New York: David McKay.

Derrida, J. (1981). *Dissemination.* (B. Johnson, Trans.). Chicago: University of Chicago Press.

Dewey, J. (1925). *Experience and nature.* LaSalle, IL: Open Court.

Dewey, J. (1927). *The public and its problems.* New York: Holt & Rinehart.

Dewey, J. (1939). *Intelligence in the modern world.* New York: Modern Library.

DiMaggio, P., Hargittai, W., Neuman, W. R., & Robinson, J. (2001). Social implications of the Internet. *Annual Reviews of Sociology, 27*, 307–336.

Dimmick, J. (1974, November). The gate-keeper: An uncertainty theory. *Journalism Monographs, 37.*

Diringer, D. (1968). *The alphabet: A key to the history of mankind. Vol. I.* (3rd ed.). New York: Funk & Wagnalls.

Dominick, J., & Pearce, M. C. (1976). Trends in network prime time programming, 1953–1974. *Journal of Communication, 26*, 70–80.

Donnerstein, E., Slaby, R., & Eron, L. (1994). The mass media and youth violence. In J. Murray, E. Rubinstein, & G. Comstock (Eds.), *Violence and youth: Psychology's response* (Vol. 2, pp. 219–250). Washington, DC: American Psychological Association.

Dorfman, A., & Mattelart, A. (1991). *How to read Donald Duck: Imperialist ideology in the Disney comic* (D. Kunzle, Trans.). New York: International General.

461

Dysinger. W. S., & Ruckmick, C. A. (1933). *The emotional responses of children to the motion picture situation.* New York: Macmillan.

Eastman, K., & Laird, P. (n.d.). Teenage Mutant Ninja Turtles. Retrieved May 5, 2005, from www.ninjaturtles.com.

Edelman, M. (1964). *The symbolic uses of politics.* Urbana: University of Illinois Press.

Egan, T. (2000, October 23). Wall Street meets pornography. *The New York Times on the Web.* Retrieved January 10, 2005 from www.nytimes.com/2000/10/23/technology/23porn.html.

Eisenstein, E. (1978). *The printing press as an agent of change* (2 Vols.). New York: Cambridge University Press.

Elkin, T. (2002, January 7). Interactive. *Advertising Age, 73,* 16.

Ellwood, W. (2001). *The no-nonsense guide to globalization.* London: Verso.

Emery, E., & Emery, M. (1984). *The press and America* (5th ed.). Englewood Cliffs, NJ: Prentice Hall.

Erskine, H. (1970). The polls: Opinion of the news media. *Public Opinion Quarterly, 34,* 630–643.

Ettema, J. S. (1982). The organizational context of creativity: A case study from public television. In J. Ettema & D. C. Whitney (Eds.), *Individuals in mass media organizations: Creativity and constraint* (pp. 91–106). Beverly Hills, CA: Sage.

Ewen, S. (1976). *Captains of consciousness.* New York: McGraw-Hill.

Fishman, M. (1980). *Manufacturing the news.* Austin: University of Texas Press.

Fiske, J. (1989). *Reading the popular.* Boston: Unwin Hyman.

Foucault, M. (1970). *The order of things: An archaeology of the human sciences.* New York: Pantheon.

Foucault, M. (1973). *The birth of the clinic: An archaeology of medical perception* (A. M. Sheridan Smith, Trans.). New York: Pantheon.

Foucault, M. (1977). *Discipline and punish: The birth of the prison* (A. Sheridan, Trans.). New York: Pantheon.

Fowles, J. (1999). *The case for television violence.* Thousand Oaks, CA: Sage.

Frederick, H. H. (1993). *Global communication and international relations.* Belmont, CA: Wadsworth.

Friedland, L. A., & Nichols, S. (2002). *Measuring civic journalism's progress: A report across a decade of availability.* College Park, MD: The Pew Center for Public Journalism. Retrieved April 28, 2005, from www.pewcenter.org/doingcj/research/measuringcj.pdf.

Frith, S. (1981). *Sound effects: Youth leisure and the politics of rock 'n' roll.* New York: Pantheon.

Gabler, N. (1988). *A world of their own: How the Jews invented Hollywood.* New York: Crown.

*The Gallup Poll: Public opinion 1991.* (1988). Wilmington, DE: Scholarly Resources.

Gandy, O. H., Jr. (1982). *Beyond agenda-setting: Information subsidies and public policy.* Norwood, NJ: Ablex.

Gans, H. J. (1979). *Deciding what's news.* New York: Pantheon.

Gardner, H., Csikszentmihalyi, M., & Damon, W. (2001). *Good work: When excellence and ethics meet.* New York: Basic Books.

Gauntlett, D. (2001). The worrying influence of 'media effects' studies. In M. Barker & J. Petley (Eds.), *Ill Effects: The media/violence debate* (2nd ed., pp. 47–62). New York: Routledge.

Gaziano, C. (1983). The knowledge gap: An analytical review of media effects. *Communication Research, 10*(4), 447–486.

Generation Y earns $211 billion and spends $172 billion annually. (2003). Harris Interactive. Retrieved September 9, 2003, from www.harris interactive.com.

Gerbner, G., Gross, L., Jackson-Beeck, M., Jeffries-Fox, S., & Signorielli, N. (1978). Cultural indicators: Violence profile No. 9. *Journal of Communication, 28*(3), 176–207.

Gerbner, G., Gross, L., Morgan, M., & Signorielli, N. (1990). Living with television: The dynamics of the cultivation process. In J. Bryant & D. Zillman (Eds.), *Media effects: Advances in theory and research* (pp. 17–41). Hillsdale, NJ: Lawrence Erlbaum.

Giddens, A. (1990). *The consequences of modernity.* Stanford, CA: Stanford University Press.

Ginsberg, B. (1986). *The captive public: How mass opinion promotes state power.* New York: Basic Books.

Gitlin, T. (1979). Prime time ideology: The hegemonic process in television entertainment. *Social Problems, 26,* 251–266.

Gitlin, T. (1980). *The whole world is watching: Mass media in making and unmaking the New Left.* Berkeley: University of California Press.

Glasser, T. L. (1985). Competition and diversity among radio formats. In M. Gurevitch & M. R. Levy (Eds.), *Mass communication review yearbook* (Vol. 5, pp. 537–562). Beverly Hills, CA: Sage.

Glasser, T. L. (Ed.). (1999). *The idea of public journalism.* New York: Guilford.

Goldman, N., & Hall, S. (1987). *Pictures of everyday life: The people, places, and cultures of the commonwealth.* London: Comedia.

Gramsci, A. (1971). *Selections from* The prison notebooks (Q. Hoare & G. Nowell-Smith, Trans.). New York: International Publishers.

Gross, L. S. (Ed.). (1995). *The international world of electronic media.* New York: McGraw-Hill.

Grossberg, L. (1992). *We gotta get out of this place: Popular conservatism and postmodern culture.* New York: Routledge.

Grossberg, L. (1997). *Dancing in spite of myself: Essays on popular culture.* Durham, NC: Duke University Press.

Gunter, B. (2002). *Media sex: What are the issues?* Mahwah, NJ: Lawrence Erlbaum.

Habermas, J. (1989). *The structural transformation of the public sphere: An inquiry into a category of bourgeois society* (T. Burger, Trans.). Cambridge, MA: MIT Press. (Original work published 1962.)

Hackett, R. (1984). Decline of a paradigm: Bias and ideology in news media studies. *Critical Studies in Mass Communication, 1,* 229–254.

Hall, S. (1980). Encoding and decoding in the television discourse. In S. Hall, D. Hobson, A. Lowe, & P. Willis (Eds.), *Culture, media, language* (pp. 128–139). London: Hutchinson.

Hall, S. (1985). Signification, representation, ideology: Althusser and the post-structuralist debates. *Critical Studies in Mass Communication, 2*(2), 91–114.

Hall, S. (1991). The local and the global: Globalization and ethnicity. In A. King (Ed.), *Culture, globalization and the world-system* (pp. 19–39). London: Macmillan.

Hallin, D., & Mancini, P. (1985). Speaking of the president: Political structure and representational form in U.S. and Italian television news. In M. Levy & M. Gurevitch (Eds.), *Mass communication review yearbook* (Vol. 5, pp. 205–224). Beverly Hills, CA: Sage.

Hao, X., & Chow, S. K. (2004). Factors affecting Internet development: An Asian survey. *First Monday.* Retrieved February 10, 2004, from www.firstmonday.org/issues/issue9_2/hao/index.html.

Harmon, A. (1997, July 14). Mars landing signals defining moment for web use. *New York Times*, pp. C1, C5.

Harris, R. J., & Scott, C. L. (2002). Effects of sex in the media. In J. Bryant & D. Zillman (Eds.), *Media effects: Advances in theory and research* (2nd ed., pp. 307–331). Mahwah, NJ: Lawrence Erlbaum.

Harvey, D. (1989). *The condition of postmodernity.* Cambridge, MA: Blackwell.

Havelock, E. (1982). *The literate revolution in Greece and its cultural consequences.* Princeton, NJ: Princeton University Press.

Head, S. W. (1985). *World broadcasting systems: A comparative analysis.* Belmont, CA: Wadsworth.

Hebdige, D. (1980). *Subculture: The meaning of style.* London: Methuen.

Henry, W. A. (1993, December 12). Journalism under fire: A growing perception of arrogance threatens the American press. *Time*, pp. 76–77, 79, 82–86, 91, 93.

Herbst, S. (1993). *Numbered voices: How opinion polling has shaped American politics.* Chicago: University of Chicago Press.

Herman, E. S., & McChesney, R. (1997). *The global media: The new missionaries of corporate capitalism.* London: Cassell.

Hertzog, H. (1944). What do we really know about daytime serial listeners? In P. F. Lazarsfeld & F. N. Stanton (Eds.), *Radio research 1942–1943* (pp. 2–23). New York: Duell, Sloan & Pearce.

Hill, A. (1997). *Shocking entertainment: Viewer response to violent movies.* Luton, UK: John Libbey Media.

Hirsch, E. D. (1987). *Cultural literacy: What every American needs to know.* Boston: Houghton Mifflin.

Hirst, P., & Thompson, G. (1996). *Globalisation in question.* Cambridge, UK: Polity.

Hodge, B., & Tripp, D. (1986). *Children and television: A semiotic approach.* Cambridge, UK: Polity.

Howard, P. N., & Jones, S. (Eds.). (2004). *Society online: The Internet in context.* Thousand Oaks, CA: Sage.

Hu, K. (2005). Techno-orientalization: The Asian VCD experience. In J. N. Erni & S. K. Chua (Eds.), *Asian media studies: Politics of subjectivities* (pp. 55–71). Malden, MA: Blackwell.

Huesmann, L. R. (1986). Psychological processes promoting the relation between exposure to media violence and aggressive behavior by the viewer. *Journal of Social Issues, 42*(3), 125–139.

Huston, A. C., Donnerstein, E., Fairchild, H., Feshbach, N. D., Katz, P. A., Murray, J. P., Rubinstein, E. A., Wilcox, B. L., & Zuckerman, D. M. (1992). *Big world small screen: The role of television in American society.* Lincoln: University of Nebraska Press.

Innis, H. A. (1950). *Empire and communications.* New York: Oxford University Press.

Innis, H. A. (1951). *The bias of communication.* Toronto: University of Toronto Press.

Iwabuchi, K. (2005). Discrepant intimacy: Popular culture flows in East Asia. In J. Erni & S. K. Chua (Eds.), *Asian media studies: Politics of subjectivities* (pp. 19–36). Malden, MA: Blackwell.

Iyengar, S. (1991). *Is anyone responsible? How television frames political issues.* Chicago: University of Chicago Press.

Iyengar, S., & Kinder, D. (1987). *News that matters.* Chicago: University of Chicago Press.

Jameson, F. (1991). *Postmodernism or the cultural logic of late capitalism.* Durham, NC: Duke University Press.

Jameson, F. (1992). *Signatures of the visible.* New York: Routledge.

Johnson, H., & Broder, D. (1996). *The system: The American way of politics at the breaking point.* Boston: Little, Brown.

Johnston, J. (1995). Channel One: The dilemma of teaching and selling. *Phi Delta Kappan, 76*(6), 436–443.

Jones, S. (1998). *CyberSociety 2.0: Revisiting computer-mediated communication and community.* Thousand Oaks, CA: Sage.

Jones, S. (2005). MTV: The medium was the message. *Critical Studies in Media Communication, 22*(1), 83–88.

Juluri, V. (2003). *Becoming a global audience: Longing and belonging in Indian Music Television*. New York: Peter Lang.

Kariithi, N. K. (1994). The crisis facing development journalism in Africa. *Media Development, 4*, 28–30.

Katz, E., Blumler, J., & Gurevitch, M. (1974). Utilization of mass communication by the individual. In J. Blumler & E. Katz (Eds.), *The uses of mass communications* (pp. 19–32). Beverly Hills, CA: Sage.

Katz, E., & Lazarsfeld, P. (1955). *Personal influence*. New York: Free Press.

Kellner, D. (1992). *The Persian Gulf TV war*. Boulder, CO: Westview.

Kidd, D. (2003). Indymedia.org: A new communication commons. In M. McCaughey & M. D. Ayers (Eds.), *Cyberactivism: Online activism in theory and practice* (pp. 47–69). New York: Routledge.

Kirk, M. (Writer, Director), & Boyer, P. J. (Writer). (2002). American porn [Television series episode]. In M. Kirk (Producer), *Frontline*. Boston: WGBH. Additional information available from www.pbs.org/wgbh/pages/frontline/shows/porn.

Klapper, J. (1960). *The effects of mass communication*. New York: Free Press.

Klein, N. (1999). *No logo: Taking aim at the brand bullies*. New York: Picador.

Kloer, P. (2003, August 17). Upscale vendors cash in on porn. *Atlanta Journal Constitution*. p. A1.

Kolbert, E. (1992, March 22). Political ads may wound, but not win races. *New York Times*, p. E4.

Kosinski, J. (1970). *Being there*. New York: Harcourt Brace.

Kovach, B., & Rosenstiel, T. (1999). *Warp speed*. New York: Century Foundation Press.

Kozloff, S. (1992). Narrative theory and television. In R. Allen (Ed.), *Channels of discourse, reassembled: Television and contemporary criticism* (2nd ed., pp. 67–100). Chapel Hill: University of North Carolina Press.

Kraut, R., Patterson, M., Lundmark, V., Kiesler, S., Muckophadhyay, T., & Sherlis, W. (1998). Internet paradox: A social technology that reduces social involvement and psychological well-being? *American Psychologist, 53*, 1011–1031.

Lang, G. E., & Lang, K. (1983). *The battle for public opinion: The president, the press, and the polls during Watergate*. New York: Columbia University Press.

Lasswell, H. (1948). The structure and function of communication in society. In L. Bryson (Ed.), *The communication of ideas* (pp. 32–51). New York: Harper.

Lazarsfeld, P. F., Berelson, B., & Gaudet, H. (1948). *The people's choice*. New York: Columbia University Press.

LeBon, G. (1977). *The crowd: A study of the popular mind*. New York: Penguin.

Lemish, D. (1982). The rules of viewing television in public places. *Journal of Broadcasting, 26*(4), 757–781.

Lenhart, A. (2003). *The ever-shifting Internet population: A new look at Internet access and the digital divide.* Washington, DC: The Pew Internet and American Life Project.

Lesser, G. S. (1974). *Children and television: Lessons from* Sesame Street. New York: Vintage.

Lichter, R., Rothman, S., & Lichter, L. (1986). *The media elite.* Baltimore: Adler & Adler.

Liebert, R. M., & Sprafkin, J. (1988). *The early window: Effects of television on children and youth* (3rd ed.). New York: Pergamon.

Liebes, T., & Katz, E. (1990). *The export of meaning: Cross-cultural readings of* Dallas. New York: Oxford University Press.

Lippmann, W. (1922). *Public opinion.* New York: Macmillan.

Lipsitz, G. (1994). *Dangerous crossroads: Popular music, postmodernism, and the poetics of place.* New York: Verso.

Littlefield, H. M. (1964). *The Wizard of Oz*: Parable on populism. *American Quarterly, 16*(1), 47–58.

Lopiano-Misdom, J., & De Luca, J. (1997). *Street trends: How today's alternative youth cultures are creating tomorrow's mainstream markets.* New York: HarperCollins.

Lowenthal, L. (1961). *Literature, popular culture, and society.* Palo Alto, CA: Pacific.

Lynd, R. S., & Lynd, H. M. (1929). *Middletown: A study in modern American culture.* New York: Harcourt, Brace & World.

MacBride, S., et al (1980). *Many voices, one world: Communication and society, today and tomorrow.* New York: Unipub.

Madden, M. (2003). *America's online pursuits: The changing picture of who's online and what they do.* Washington, DC: The Pew Internet and American Life Project.

*Magazine Industry Market Place.* (1996). New York: Bowker.

Mailer, N. (1974, May). The faith of graffiti. *Esquire.* pp. 77–158.

Maira, S. M. (2002). *Desis in the house: Indian American youth culture in New York City.* Philadelphia: Temple University Press.

Mallapragada, M. (2000). The Indian diaspora in the USA and around the Web. In D. Gauntlett (Ed.), *Web.studies: Rewiring media studies for the digital age* (pp. 179–185). London: Arnold.

Martin, L., & Segrave, K. (1988). *Anti-rock: The opposition to rock 'n' roll.* Hamden, CT: Anchor.

Marx, K. (1975). *Early writings.* (Q. Hoare, Ed.). New York: Vintage.

Marx, K. (1977). *Capital, Volume 1.* (B. Fowles, Trans.). New York: Vintage.

Marx, K., & Engels, F. (1967). *The communist manifesto* (S. Moore, Trans.). Harmondsworth, UK: Penguin.

Marx, K., & Engels, F. (1970). *The German ideology.* New York: International Publishers.

Mattelart, A. (1994). *Mapping world communication: War, progress, culture* (S. Emanuel & J. A. Cohen, Trans.). Minneapolis: University of Minnesota Press.

McCarthy, A. (2001). *Ambient television: Visual culture and public space.* Durham, NC: Duke University Press.

McChesney, R. W. (1999). *Rich media, poor democracy: Communication politics in dubious times.* Urbana: University of Illinois Press.

McClintick, D. (1998, November). Town crier for the new age. *Brill's Content,* pp. 112–127.

McCombs, M., & Gilbert, S. (1986). News influence on our pictures of the world. In J. Bryant & D. Zillman (Eds.), *Perspectives on media effects* (pp. 13–27). Hillsdale, NJ: Lawrence Erlbaum.

McCombs, M., & Reynolds, A. (2002). News influence on our pictures of the world. In J. Bryant & D. Zillman (Eds.), *Media effects: Advances in theory and research* (2nd ed., pp. 1–18). Mahwah, NJ: Lawrence Erlbaum.

McCombs, M., & Shaw, D. L. (1974, August). *A progress report on agenda-setting research.* Paper presented to the Association for Education in Journalism, San Diego, CA.

McGuire, W. J. (1989). Theoretical foundations of campaigns. In R. Rice & C. Atkin (Eds.), *Public communication campaigns* (2nd ed., pp. 43–65). Thousand Oaks, CA: Sage.

McLuhan, M. (1964). *Understanding media: The extensions of man.* New York: McGraw-Hill.

McLuhan, M., & Fiore, Q. (1967). *The medium is the massage: An inventory of effects.* New York: Bantam Books.

McLuhan, M., & Fiore, Q. (1968). *The medium is the massage* [LP record (CS 9501, CL2701)]. New York: Columbia.

McPhail, T. L. (2002). *Global communication: Theories, stakeholders, and trends.* Boston: Allyn & Bacon.

McQuail, D. (1987). *Mass communication theory: An introduction* (2nd ed.). Thousand Oaks, CA: Sage.

McQuail, D. (2000). *Mass communication theory: An introduction* (4th ed.). Thousand Oaks, CA: Sage.

Meikle, L. (2002). *Future active: Media actions and the Internet.* New York: Routledge.

Mencher, M. (1984). *News reporting and writing* (3rd ed.). Dubuque, IA: Wm. C. Brown.

The merchants of cool [Television series episode]. (2001). In B. Goodman & R. Dretzin (Producers), *Frontline.* Boston: WGBH.

Merritt, D. W. (1995). *Public journalism and public life: Why telling the news is not enough.* Hillsdale, NJ: Lawrence Erlbaum.

Miller, L. (1995). Women and children first: Gender and the settling of the electronic frontier. In J. Brook & I. A. Boal (Eds.), *Resisting the virtual life: The culture and politics of information* (pp. 49–57). San Francisco: City Lights.

Miller, M. C. (1997, March 17). The crushing power of big publishing. *The Nation,* pp. 11–18.

Miller, N. E., & Dollard, J. (1941). *Social learning theory and imitation.* New Haven, CT: Yale University Press.

Mitchell, T. (2001). Introduction. Another root—Hip-hop outside the USA. In T. Mitchell (Ed.), *Global noise: Rap and hip-hop outside the USA* (pp. 1–38). Middletown, CT: Wesleyan University Press.

Mitra, A. (1997). Virtual commonality: Looking for India on the Internet. In S. Jones (Ed.), *Virtual culture* (pp. 55–79). Thousand Oaks, CA: Sage.

Mitsui, T., & Hosokawa, S. (Eds.). (1998). *Karaoke around the world: Global technology, local singing.* London: Routledge.

Montgomery, K. C. (1989). *Target: Prime time, advocacy groups, and the struggle over entertainment television.* New York: Oxford University Press.

Morgan, R. (1980). Theory and practice: Pornography and rape. In L. Lederer (Ed.), *Take back the night: Women on pornography* (pp. 134–140). New York: William Morrow.

Morley, D. (1980). *The "nationwide" audience.* London: British Film Institute.

Morley, D. (1986). *Family television: Cultural power and domestic leisure.* London: Comedia.

Morley, D. (1992). *Television, audiences, and cultural studies.* New York: Routledge.

Naficy, H. (1993). *The making of exile cultures: Iranian television in Los Angeles.* Minneapolis: University of Minnesota Press.

Nakamura, L. (2004). Interrogating the digital divide: The political economy of race and commerce in new media. In P. N. Howard & S. Jones (Eds.), *Society online: The Internet in context* (pp. 71–83). Thousand Oaks, CA: Sage.

Nakano, Y. (2002). Who initiates the global flow? Japanese popular culture in Asia. *Visual Communication, 1*(2), 229–253.

*National television violence study: Vol. 1.* (1997). Thousand Oaks, CA: Sage.

*National television violence study: Vol. 3. Executive summary.* (1998). Santa Barbara, CA: University of California Santa Barbara, Center for Communication and Social Policy.

Nerone, J. (1987). The mythology of the penny press. *Critical Studies in Mass Communication, 4*(4), 376–404.

Nerone, J. (1990). Violence against the press in U.S. history. *Journal of Communication, 40*(3), 6–33.

Nerone, J. (Ed.). (1995). *Last rights: Revisiting four theories of the press.* Urbana: University of Illinois Press.

Neuman, W. R. (1986). *The paradox of mass politics.* Cambridge, MA: Harvard University Press.

Newcomb, H. (1978). Assessing the violence profile studies of Gerbner and Gross: A humanistic critique and suggestion. *Communication Research, 5*(3), 264–282.

Noelle-Neumann, E. (1974). The spiral of silence: A theory of public opinion. *Journal of Communication, 24*(2), 43–51.

Noelle-Neumann, E. (1984). *The spiral of silence: Public opinion—our social skin.* Chicago: University of Chicago Press.

Nucifora, A. (2003, February 3). Hispanic market no longer a sleeping giant. *Atlanta Business Chronicle,* Retrieved March 21, 2003, from www.atlanta .bizjournals.com/atlanta/stories/2003/02/03/smallb2/html

Ong, W. (1982). *Orality and literacy: The technologizing of the word.* New York: Methuen.

Ōtake, A., & Hosokawa, S. (1998). Karaoke in East Asia: Modernization, Japanization or Asianization? In T. Mitsui & S. Hosokawa (Eds.), *Karaoke around the world: Global technology, local singing* (pp. 178–201). London: Routledge.

Page, B., & Shapiro, R. Y. (1983). Effects of public opinion on public policy. *American Political Science Review, 77,* 175–190.

Page, B., & Shapiro, R. Y. (1992). *The rational public.* Chicago: University of Chicago Press.

Paton, D. (1999, December 3). *War of the worlds: Virtual media versus Manchester Press.* Retrieved April 27, 2005, from www.csmonitor.com.

Patterson, T., & McClure, R. (1976). *The unseeing eye.* New York: Putnam.

Pearl, D., Bouthilet, L., & Lazar, J. (Eds.). (1982). *Television and behavior: Ten years of scientific progress and implications for the eighties.* Washington, DC: U.S. Government Printing Office.

Peirce, C. S. (1958). *Selected writings.* New York: Dover.

Peters, J. D. (1995). Historical tensions in the concept of public opinion. In T. Glasser & C. T. Salmon (Eds.), *Public opinion and the communication of consent* (pp. 3–32). New York: Guilford.

Petley, J. (2001). Us and them. In M. Barker & J. Petley (Eds.), *Ill effects: The media/violence debate* (2nd ed., pp. 170–185). New York: Routledge.

Petty, R. E., & Cacciopo, J. T. (1986). *Communication and persuasion: Central and peripheral routes to attitude change.* New York: Springer-Verlag.

Pew Research Center for the People and the Press. (2003). *Public wants neutrality and pro-American point of view: Strong opposition to media cross-ownership emerges.* Washington, DC: Pew Research Center for the People and the Press.

Phillips, D. P. (1982). Airplane accidents, murder, and the mass media: Toward a theory of imitation and suggestion. In D. C. Whitney & E. Wartella (Eds.), *Mass communication review yearbook* (Vol. 3, pp. 97–120). Beverly Hills, CA: Sage.

Phillips, D. P., & Hensley, J. E. (1985). When violence is rewarded or punished: The impact of mass media stories on homicide. In M. Gurevitch & M. Levy (Eds.), *Mass communication review yearbook* (Vol. 5). Beverly Hills, CA: Sage.

Pollak, A. W. (1991, July 23). Computer images are staking out star roles in movies. *New York Times*, pp. B1–2.

Postman, N. (1985). *Amusing ourselves to death*. New York: Viking.

Potter, W. J. (2003). *The 11 myths of media violence*. Thousand Oaks, CA: Sage.

Press, A. (1991). *Women watching television*. Philadelphia: University of Pennsylvania Press.

Preston, W., Jr., Herman, E. S., & Schiller, H. I. (1989). *Hope and folly: The United States and UNESCO 1945–1985*. Minneapolis: University of Minnesota Press.

Putnam, R. D. (2000). *Bowling alone: The collapse and revival of American community*. New York: Simon & Schuster.

Radway, J. (1984). *Reading the romance: Women, patriarchy, and popular literature*. Chapel Hill: University of North Carolina Press.

Rainie, L., Fox, S., & Fallows, D. (2003). *The Internet and the Iraq War: How online Americans have used the Internet to learn war news, understand events, and promote their views*. Washington, DC: Pew Internet and American Life Project.

Rappaport, P. (2002). The Internet and the demand for news. *Prometheus, 20*(3), 255–263.

Rheingold, H. (1993). *The virtual community: Homesteading on the electronic frontier*. New York: Harper.

Rheingold, H. (2002). *Smart mobs: The next social revolution*. Cambridge, MA: Basic Books.

Rice, M. L., Huston, A. C., Truglio, R., & Wright, J. C. (1990). Words from *Sesame Street*: Learning vocabulary while viewing. *Developmental Psychology, 26*, 421–428.

Rice, M. L., Huston, A. C., & Wright, J. C. (1982). The forms of television: Effects on children's attention, comprehension, and social behavior. In National Institute of Mental Health, *Television and behavior: Ten years of scientific progress and implications for the eighties: Vol. 2. Technical Reviews* (pp. 24–38). Rockville, MD: National Institute of Mental Health.

Ritzer, G. (1993). *The McDonaldization of society*. Thousand Oaks, CA: Sage.

Rivers, W., Peterson, T., & Jensen, J. W. (1971). *The mass media and modern society* (2nd ed.). San Francisco: Rinehart.

Robertson, R. (1992). *Globalization: Social theory and global culture*. Thousand Oaks, CA: Sage.

Robinson, J. P. (1976a). Interpersonal influence in election campaigns: Two step-flow hypotheses. *Public Opinion Quarterly, 40*, 315–325.

Robinson, J. P. (1976b). The press as king-maker. *Journalism Quarterly, 51*(4), 587–594, 606.

Robinson, J. P. (1996, November). Remarks at the Speech Communication Association, San Diego, CA.

Robinson, J., & Levy, M. (1986). *The main source.* Thousand Oaks, CA: Sage.

Robinson, M. J. (1976). Public affairs television and the growth of political malaise. *American Political Science Review, 70,* 409–432.

Rock and Roll Confidential (Eds.). (1991). *You gotta right to rock* (3rd ed.). Los Angeles: Author.

Rodman, G. B. (1996). *Elvis after Elvis: The posthumous career of a living legend.* New York: Routledge.

Rodriguez, C. (2001). *Fissures in the Mediascape: An international study of citizens' media.* Cresskill, NJ: Hampton.

Rogers, E. M., & Dearing, J. (1988). Agenda-setting research: Where has it been, where is it going? In J. Anderson (Ed.), *Communication yearbook* (Vol. 11, pp. 555–594). Thousand Oaks, CA: Sage.

Rosenfeld, A. H. (1985, December). Music, the beautiful disturber. *Psychology Today,* p. 48.

Rubinstein, E., Comstock, G., & Murray, J. (Eds.). (1972). *Television and social behavior: Report on the U.S. Surgeon General's Scientific Advisory Commission on Television and Social Behavior.* Washington, DC: U.S. Government Printing Office.

Sapir, E. (1921). *Language.* New York: Harcourt, Brace & World.

Saussure, F. de (1983). *Course in general linguistics* (C. Bally & A. Sechehaye, Eds., R. Harris, Trans.). La Salle, IL: Open Court.

Schiller, H. I. (1992). *Mass communications and American empire* (2nd ed.). Boulder, CO: Westview.

Schudson, M. (1978). *Discovering the news.* New York: Basic Books.

Schudson, M. (1984). *Advertising, the uneasy persuasion: Its dubious impact on American society.* New York: Basic Books.

Schudson, M. (1995). Was there ever a public sphere? In M. Schudson (Ed.), *The power of news* (pp. 189–203). Cambridge, MA: Harvard University Press.

Shade, L. R. (2004). Bending gender into the Net: Feminizing content, corporate interests, and research strategy. In P. N. Howard & S. Jones (Eds.), *Society online: The Internet in context* (pp. 57–70). Thousand Oaks, CA: Sage.

Shafer, R. (1998). Comparing development journalism and public journalism as interventionist press models. *Asian Journal of Communication. 8*(1), 31–52.

Shaw, D. L. (1967). News bias and the telegraph: A study of historical change. *Journalism Quarterly, 44*(1), 3–12, 31.

Shoemaker, P., & Reese, S. (1991). *Mediating the message: Theories of influence on mass media content.* White Plains, NY: Longman.

Shoemaker, P., & Reese, S. (1996). *Mediating the message: Theories of influence on mass media content* (2nd ed.). White Plains, NY: Longman.

Siebert, F. S., Peterson, T., & Schramm, W. (1956). *Four theories of the press: The authoritarian, libertarian, social responsibility, and Soviet communist concepts of what the press should be and do.* Urbana: University of Illinois Press.

Siegel, G. (2002). Double vision: Large-screen video display and live sports spectacle. *Television and New Media, 3*(1), 49–73.

Sigal, L. V. (1973). *Reporters and officials.* Lexington, MA: D. C. Heath.

Silj, A. (1988). *East of Dallas: The European challenge to American television.* London: British Film Institute.

Sinclair, J., Jacka, E., & Cunningham, S. (Eds.). (1996). *New patterns in global television: Peripheral vision.* New York: Oxford University Press.

Singer, D., & Singer, J. (Eds.). (2001). *Handbook of children and the media.* Thousand Oaks, CA: Sage.

Sklair, L. (1995). *Sociology of the global system* (2nd ed.). Baltimore: Johns Hopkins University Press.

Snyder, D. (2000). Webcam women: Life on your screen. In D. Gauntlett (Ed.), *Web.studies: Rewiring media studies for the digital age* (pp. 70–73). London: Arnold.

Sousa, J. P. (1906, September). The menace of mechanical music. *Appleton's Magazine, 8,* 278–284.

Sparks, C. (1995). The future of public service broadcasting in Britain. *Critical Studies in Mass Communication, 12*(3), 325–341.

Spigel, L. (1992). *Make room for TV: Television and the family ideal in postwar America.* Chicago: University of Chicago Press.

Stapleton, C., & May, C. (1990). *African rock: The pop music of a continent.* New York: Dutton.

Stark, R. W. (1962). Policy and the pros: An organizational analysis of a metropolitan newspaper. *Berkeley Journal of Sociology, 7*(2), 11–31.

Stein, B. (1979). *The view from Sunset Boulevard: America as brought to you by the people who make television.* New York: Basic Books.

Steinberg, J. (2004, June 7). Move to stiffen decency rules is losing steam in Washington. *New York Times,* p. C1.

Stephens, M. (1988). *A history of news.* New York: Penguin.

Sterngold, J. (1997, October 7). Networks' lineups reflect their stakes in shows they offer. *New York Times,* pp. A1, C2.

Stevens, J., & Porter, W. (1973). *The rest of the elephant.* New York: Harper & Row.

Straubhaar, J. (2000). Culture, language and social class in the globalization of television. In G. Wang, J. Servaes, & A. Goonasekera (Eds.), *The new communications landscape: Demystifying media globalization* (pp. 199–224). New York: Routledge.

Straw, W. (2000). The political economy of credibility. In T. Mitchell & P. Doyle (Eds.), *Changing sounds: New directions and configurations in popular music* (pp. 260–262). Sydney: University of Technology.

Sullivan, R. (1997, November). Style stalker. *Vogue*, pp. 182, 187–188.

Tarde, G. (1969). The public and the crowd. In T. Clark (Ed.), *On communication and social influence* (pp. 277–294). Chicago: University of Chicago Press. (Original work published 1901.)

Tarleton, J. (2000, Winter). Protesters develop their own global internet news service. *Mark Newman Reports, 54*(4), 53–55.

Taylor, D. G. (1982). Pluralistic ignorance and the spiral of silence: A formal analysis. *Public Opinion Quarterly, 46,* 311–335.

Tichenor, P. J., Donohue, G. A., & Olien, C. N. (1970). Mass media flow and differential growth in knowledge. *Public Opinion Quarterly, 34,* 159–170.

Times-Mirror Center for the People and the Press. (1985, June–July). *The people and the press.* Los Angeles: Author.

Tocqueville, A. de. (1835, 1840). *Democracy in America* (2 Vols., G. Lawrence, Trans., J. P. Mayer, Ed.). Garden City, NY: Anchor.

Tocqueville, A. de. (1981). Newspapers and public associations in the United States. In M. Janowitz & P. Hirsch (Eds.), *Reader in public opinion and mass communication* (2nd ed., pp. 68–73). New York: Free Press.

Tomlinson, J. (1991). *Cultural imperialism: A critical introduction.* London: Pinter.

Tuchman, G. (1972). Objectivity as strategic ritual. *American Journal of Sociology, 77,* 660–679.

Tuchman, G. (1973). Making news by doing work: Routinizing the unexpected. *American Journal of Sociology, 79,* 110–131.

Tuchman, G. (1974). Assembling a network talk-show. In G. Tuchman (Ed.), *The TV establishment* (pp. 119–135). Englewood Cliffs, NJ: Prentice Hall.

Tuchman, G. (1978). *Making news: A study in the construction of reality.* New York: Free Press.

Turner, G. (1993). *Film as social practice* (2nd ed.). New York: Routledge.

Turow, J. (1982). Unconventional programs on television: An organizational perspective. In J. S. Ettema & D. C. Whitney (Eds.), *Individuals in mass media organizations: Creativity and constraint* (pp. 107–129). Beverly Hills, CA: Sage.

Turow, J. (1984). *Media industries: The production of news and entertainment.* White Plains, NY: Longman.

Turow, J. (1991). *Playing doctor.* New York: Oxford University Press.

Turow, J. (1997). *Breaking up America: Advertisers and the new media world.* Chicago: University of Chicago Press.

United Nations. (1948). *Universal declaration of human rights.* Retrieved May 31, 2005, from www.un.org/Overview/rights.html.

United Nations Educational, Scientific and Cultural Organization. (1978). *Declaration on Fundamental Principles Concerning the Contribution of the Mass Media to Strengthening Peace and International Understanding, to the Promotion of Human*

*Rights and to Countering Racialism, Apartheid and Incitement to War.* In *Records of the general conference, twentieth session, Paris, 24 October to 28 November 1978. Volume I: Resolutions.* Retrieved May 31, 2005, from unesdoc.unesco.org/images/0011/001140/114032e.pdf.

U.S. Census Bureau. (2003a). *Census projection of U.S. population 2003.* Washington, DC: Author. Retrieved May 16, 2005, from www.census.gov/population/projections/nation/summary/np-t1.txt.

U.S. Census Bureau. (2003b). *Statistical abstract of the United States: 2003.* Washington, DC: Author. Retrieved June 5, 2005, from www.census.gov/prod/2004pubs/03statab/inforcomm.pdf.

U.S. Census Bureau. (2004). *Statistical abstract of the United States: 2004–2005.* Washington, DC: Author. Retrieved May 5, 2005, from www.census.gov/prod/2004pubs/04statab/infocomm.pdf.

Vidmar, N., & Rokeach, M. (1974). Archie Bunker's bigotry: A study in selective perception and exposure. *Journal of Communication, 24*(1), 36–47.

Wang, G., Ku, L.-L., & Liu, C.-C. (2000). Local and national cultural industries: Is there life after globalization? In G. Wang, J. Servaes, & A. Goonasekera (Eds.), *The new communications landscape: Demystifying media globalization* (pp. 52–73). New York: Routledge.

Wang, G., & Servaes, J. (2000). Introduction. In G. Wang, J. Servaes, & A. Goonasekera (Eds.), *The new communications landscape: Demystifying media globalization* (pp. 1–18). New York: Routledge.

Ward, S., Wackman, D. B., & Wartella, E. (1977). *How children learn to buy.* Beverly Hills, CA: Sage.

Wartella, E., Heintz, K., Aidman, A., & Mazzarella, S. (1990). Television and beyond: Children's video in one community. *Communication Research, 17*(1), 45–64.

Wartella, E., & Reeves, B. (1985). Historical trends in research on children and the media: 1900–1960. *Journal of Communication, 35*(2), 118–133.

Waters, M. (2001). *Globalization* (2nd ed.). New York: Routledge.

Weaver, D. (1980). Audience need for orientation and media effects. *Communication Research, 7,* 361–380.

Wellman, B., & Haythornthwaite, C. (Eds.). (2002). *The Internet in everyday life.* Malden, MA: Blackwell.

White, M. (1992). Ideological analysis and television. In R. Allen (Ed.), *Channels of discourse, reassembled: Television and contemporary criticism* (2nd ed., pp. 161–202). Chapel Hill: University of North Carolina Press.

Whitney, D. C. (1987). *The media and the people: Americans' experience with the news media, a fifty-year review.* New York: Columbia University, Gannett Center for Media Studies Working Paper Series.

Whitney, D. C., & Becker, L. B. (1982). Keeping the gates for gatekeepers: The effects of wire news. *Journalism Quarterly, 59,* 60–65.

Whitney, D. C., Fritzler, M., Jones, S., Mazzarella, S., & Rakow, L. (1989). Geographic and source biases in network television news. *Journal of Broadcasting & Electronic Media, 33*(2), 159–174.

Whitney, D. C., & Goldman, S. B. (1985). Media use and time of vote decision: A study of the 1980 Presidential election. *Communication Research, 12*, 511–529.

Whitney, D. C., & Wartella, E. (1988). The public as dummies. *Knowledge: Creation, Diffusion, Utilization, 10*, 99–110.

Whitney, D. C., & Wartella, E. (2001). Violence and media. In N. J. Smelser & P. B. Baltes (Eds.), *International encyclopedia of the social and behavioral sciences* (Vol. 24, pp. 16187–16192). Oxford, UK: Elsevier Science.

Whorf, B. (1956). *Language, thought and reality.* Cambridge, MA: MIT Press.

Wilhoit, G. C., & deBock, H. (1976). *All in the Family* in Holland. *Journal of Communication, 26*(4), 75–84.

Wilk, R. (1995). Learning to be local in Belize: Global systems of common difference. In D. Miller (Ed.), *Worlds apart: Modernity through the prism of the local* (pp. 110–133). New York: Routledge.

Williams, L. (1989). *Hard core: Power, pleasure, and the "frenzy of the visible."* Berkeley: University of California Press.

Williams, R. (1958). *Culture and society 1780–1950.* New York: Harper & Row.

Williams, R. (1965). *The long revolution.* Middlesex, UK: Penguin.

Williams, R. (1989). Culture is ordinary. In R. Gable (Ed.), *Resources of hope: Culture, democracy, socialism* (pp. 3–18). New York: Verso.

Williams, R. (1992). *Television: Technology and cultural form.* Hanover, CT: Wesleyan University Press. (Original work published 1975.)

Wright, C. R. (1960). Functional analysis and mass communication. *Public Opinion Quarterly, 24*, 606–620.

Wright, J. C., & Huston, A. C. (1995). *Effects of educational TV viewing of lower income preschoolers on reading skills, school readiness, and social adjustment.* Lawrence: University of Kansas, Center for Research on the Influences of Television on Children.

Wright, W. (1975). *Six guns and society: A structural study of the Western.* Berkeley: University of California Press.

Wyatt, R. O. (1991). *Free expression and the American public.* Washington, DC: American Society of Newspaper Editors.

Zillman, D. (1982). Television viewing and arousal. In D. Pearl, L. Bouthilet, & J. Lazar (Eds.), *Television and behavior* (Vol. 2, pp. 53–67). Washington, DC: U.S. Government Printing Office.

Zwingle, E. (1999, August). Goods move. People move. Ideas move. And cultures change. *National Geographic, 196*, 12–33.

# Index

# About the Authors

**Lawrence Grossberg** is the Morris Davis Distinguished Professor of Communication Studies and Cultural Studies and the Director of the University Program in Cultural Studies at the University of North Carolina at Chapel Hill. He is an internationally renowned scholar of cultural studies and popular culture and the coeditor of the international journal *Cultural Studies*. Alone or with others, he has authored or edited 20 books and published close to 200 essays. His work has been translated into 10 languages, and he has lectured all over the world. He has won the highest awards for both scholarship and mentorship from the National Communication Association and the International Communication Association. Grossberg's latest books include *Bringing It All Back Home: Essays on Cultural Studies* and *Dancing in Spite of Myself: Essays on Popular Culture* (both 1997), *New Keywords: A Revised Vocabulary of Culture and Society* (with Tony Bennett and Meaghan Morris, 2005), and *Caught in the Crossfire: Kids, Politics and America's Future* (2005).

**Ellen A. Wartella** was appointed Executive Vice Chancellor and Provost at University of California at Riverside (UCR) in 2004 after serving as Dean of the College of Communication at the University of Texas at Austin, the largest and most comprehensive communication college in the country. She also is a Distinguished Professor of Psychology at UCR. Wartella earned her Ph.D. in Mass Communication from the University of Minnesota in 1977 and completed her postdoctoral research in development psychology in 1981 at the University of Kansas. As an active scholar whose research focuses on the effects of media on child development, she has written and edited several books and has published numerous book chapters and journal articles on mass media and communications. Wartella is coprincipal investigator on a five-year, multisite research project funded by the National Science Foundation on the impact of digital media on children's development. She serves on several national boards, including the Decade of Behavior National Advisory Committee; the National Academies of Sciences Board on Children, Youth, and Families; The Sesame Workshop; Kraft Foods Global Health & Wellness Advisory Council; and the National Educational Advisory Board for the Council of Better Business Bureaus.

**D. Charles Whitney** became Associate Chair and Professor in the Department of Creative Writing and Professor of Sociology at the University of California at Riverside in 2004. He was Professor in the School of Journalism at the University of Texas at Austin from 1993 to 2004, where he also held an appointment as Professor of Radio-TV-Film. In 1985–1986, he was research director of the Gannett Center for Media Studies (later the Freedom Forum Media Studies Center) at Columbia University. Currently, Whitney is Associate Principal Investigator for Time-Sharing Experiments for the Social Sciences (TESS), a national research consortium for large-scale Internet- and telephone-based social science experiment funded by the National Science Foundation. Whitney also was senior researcher on a U.S. Department of Defense Threat Reduction Agency contract to examine communications responses to biological terrorist attacks 1999–2001, and senior researcher and University of Texas site manager of the three-year National Television Violence Study of violence on cable and network television. He is former editor of the research journal *Critical Studies in Mass Communication* and author of more than 75 book chapters, journal articles, reports, and papers, including *AudienceMaking: How the Media Create the Audience* (1994), the *Mass Communication Review Yearbook* Vols. 3 (1982) and 4 (1983), and *Individuals in Mass Media Organizations: Creativity and Constraint* (1982).

**J. Macgregor Wise** is Associate Professor and Chair of the Department of Communication Studies at Arizona State University. After completing his Ph.D. in Speech Communication at the University of Illinois at Urbana-Champaign, he taught at Clemson University before moving out West. He is author of *Exploring Technology and Social Space* (1997) and coauthor with Jennifer Daryl Slack of *Culture and Technology: A Primer* (2005). He has been Chair of the Philosophy of Communication Division of the International Communication Association and currently sits on the editorial boards of *Communication Review, Communication Theory, Cultural Studies,* and the *Journal of Communication.* His research concerns communication, culture, and technology with emphases on new media, globalization, and surveillance.